Beyond Communal and Individual Ownership

Over the last decade, Australian governments have introduced a series of land reforms in communities on Indigenous land. This book is the first in-depth study of these significant and far reaching reforms. It explains how the reforms came about, what they do and their consequences for Indigenous landowners and community residents. It also revisits the rationale for their introduction and discusses the significant gap between public debate about the reforms and their actual impact.

Drawing on international research, the book describes how it is necessary to move beyond the concepts of communal and individual ownership in order to understand the true significance of the reforms. The book's fresh perspective on land reform and careful assessment of key land reform theories will be of interest to scholars of indigenous land rights, land law, indigenous studies and aboriginal culture not only in Australia but also in any other country with an interest in indigenous land rights.

Leon Terrill is a Research Director at the Indigenous Law Centre and a Lecturer at the University of New South Wales, Sydney, Australia. He has previously worked as a senior lawyer with the Central Land Council, coordinator of the University of the South Pacific Community Legal Centre and as a lawyer with Victoria Legal Aid.

Routledge Complex Real Property Rights Series
Series editor: Professor Spike Boydell
University of Technology, Sydney, Australia

Real Property Rights are central to the global economy and provide a legal framework for how society (be it developed or customary) relates to land and buildings. We need to better understand property rights to ensure sustainable societies, careful use of limited resources and sound ecological stewardship of our land and water. Contemporary property rights theory is dynamic and needs to engage thinkers who are prepared to think outside their disciplinary limitations.

The Routledge Complex Real Property Rights Series strives to take a transdisciplinary approach to understanding property rights and specifically encourages heterodox thinking. Through rich international case studies our goal is to build models to connect theory to observed reality, allowing us to inform potential policy outcomes. This series is both an ideal forum and reference for students and scholars of property rights and land issues.

Land, Indigenous Peoples and Conflict
Edited by Alan Tidwell and Barry Zellen

Beyond Communal and Individual Ownership
Indigenous land reform in Australia
Leon Terrill

Beyond Communal and Individual Ownership

Indigenous land reform in Australia

Leon Terrill

LONDON AND NEW YORK

First published 2016
by Routledge
2 Park Square, Milton Park, Abingdon, Oxon OX14 4RN

and by Routledge
711 Third Avenue, New York, NY 10017

First issued in paperback 2018

Routledge is an imprint of the Taylor & Francis Group, an informa business

© 2016 Leon Terrill

The right of Leon Terrill to be identified as author of this work has been asserted by him in accordance with sections 77 and 78 of the Copyright, Designs and Patents Act 1988.

All rights reserved. No part of this book may be reprinted or reproduced or utilised in any form or by any electronic, mechanical, or other means, now known or hereafter invented, including photocopying and recording, or in any information storage or retrieval system, without permission in writing from the publishers.

Trademark notice: Product or corporate names may be trademarks or registered trademarks, and are used only for identification and explanation without intent to infringe.

British Library Cataloguing-in-Publication Data
A catalogue record for this book is available from the British Library

Library of Congress Cataloging-in-Publication Data
Terrill, Leon, author.
Beyond communal and individual ownership : indigenous land reform in Australia / Leon Terrill.
    pages cm. – (Routledge complex real property rights series)
    1. Aboriginal Australians–Land tenure. 2. Land tenure–Law and legislation–Australia. I. Title.
    KU2562.T49 2016
    331.3'194089–dc23   2015016283

ISBN 13: 978-1-138-62601-0 (pbk)
ISBN 13: 978-1-138-85391-1 (hbk)

Typeset in Sabon
by Wearset Ltd, Boldon, Tyne and Wear

Contents

List of figures	vii
Series editor introduction	viii
Acknowledgements	x
Addendum	xi
List of abbreviations	xii

1   Introduction: from land rights to land reform   1

1.1 *The shifting consensus 1*
1.2 *Background to the reforms 4*
1.3 *The reforms and their consequences 12*
1.4 *Overview of the book 16*

2   Land reform: theory, terminology and concepts   24

2.1 *Introduction 24*
2.2 *Key terminology and concepts 26*
2.3 *Two influential ideas 35*
2.4 *Types of property rights 39*
2.5 *Types of land tenure reform 45*
2.6 *Concluding comments 50*

3   Aboriginal land in the Northern Territory   66

3.1 *Aboriginal land ownership 66*
3.2 *Ownership of land under Aboriginal law 67*
3.3 *Formal ownership of Aboriginal land 72*
3.4 *Conclusion 81*

4   Communities on Aboriginal land   94

4.1 *Identifying the starting point for reform 94*
4.2 *Communities on Aboriginal land in the Northern Territory 95*
4.3 *Characteristics of the informal tenure arrangements 99*
4.4 *Summary and discussion 110*

vi *Contents*

5   **Australian debate about land reform and the new political consensus**   128

5.1 Introduction 128
5.2 The first period of debate: communal and individual ownership 129
5.3 Between 2007 and 2013: a need for 'secure tenure' 149
5.4 Since 2013: a renewed focus on land reform 151
5.5 Conclusion: the new political consensus 153

6   **The reforms**   172

6.1 Introduction 172
6.2 Township leasing 173
6.3 The Northern Territory Emergency Response 186
6.4 Housing reforms and 'secure tenure' policies 193
6.5 Allotment of Indigenous land in Queensland 200
6.6 Summarising the reforms 204

7   **Making sense of the reforms**   222

7.1 Introduction 222
7.2 Residential housing 223
7.3 Infrastructure occupied by enterprises and service providers 235
7.4 Conclusion: was it necessary to be so interventionist? 245

8   **Alternative approaches?**   258

8.1 Introduction 258
8.2 Framework for developing a land reform model 259
8.3 Defining the parameters of an ideal model 267
8.4 Conclusion: the need for a detailed, realistic and integrated land reform policy 280

9   **Conclusion**   290

9.1 A striking contrast 290
9.2 Major conclusions of this book 291
9.3 The need for better policy 295

Index   297

Figures

1.1	Indigenous land ownership over time	7
1.2	Map of town camps in the Northern Territory	10
1.3	The 73 larger remote Aboriginal communities in the Northern Territory	11
6.1	The pre-existing tenure arrangements	175
6.2	Outcome under a township lease	175
6.3	Table of Wurrumiyanga subleases	183
6.4	Outcome under 'secure tenure' policies	198

Series editor introduction

Real property rights are central to the economy and provide a legal framework for how society (be it developed or customary) relates to land and buildings. Property rights are both institutional arrangements and social relations. We need to better understand property rights to ensure sustainable societies, careful use of limited resources and sound ecological stewardship of our land and water.

Land conflict is all around us – from corporate and political corruption over land dealings in the developed world, to land grab in developing countries, to compromised indigenous property rights, to resource exploitation. At a time where global food security, water security and shelter are paramount, an understanding of property rights is key to sustainability.

Contemporary property rights theory is dynamic and this series strives to engage thinkers who are prepared to step beyond their disciplinary limitations. 'Property rights' is a broad term that is fundamentally about social relations. Real property rights, obligations and restrictions can be found in and change across the full range of human societies, both in time and space. Property rights research has emerged from a broad range of disciplines including (but not limited to) archaeology, anthropology, ethics, sociology, psychology, law, geography, history, philosophy, economics, planning and business studies. What makes this series special is that it facilitates a transdisciplinary approach to understanding property rights and specifically promotes heterodox thinking.

Beyond Communal and Individual Ownership: Indigenous Land Reform in Australia is the second volume in this Routledge series on Complex Real Property Rights. In this first book-length study of the contemporary reforms introduced by Australian governments in the post-*Mabo* era, Dr Leon Terrill provides a meticulous, significant and timely analysis of how these reforms have engineered property rights over Indigenous land and residential communities in a way that increases state property and government control.

Leon is uniquely well placed to craft this volume having previously worked for several years as a senior lawyer with an Aboriginal Land

Council in the Northern Territory, working with Aboriginal landowners on a variety of land rights issues. He was working in this role when the reforms were introduced, and his familiarity with Land Council processes and the circumstances of Aboriginal communities adds considerably to the level of analysis he is able to provide. He subsequently moved into academe, and his doctoral studies explored the reforms as they were being implemented in the Northern Territory of Australia.

Three main arguments are central in *Beyond Communal and Individual Ownership: Indigenous Land Reform in Australia*. Leon first highlights the way in which debate and discussion about land reform in Australia has been compromised by flawed rhetoric, inappropriate language and misguided emphasis. The second argument centres on how the expensive and intrusive reforms have harmed the relationship between governments and Indigenous communities. This harm manifested through a lack of clear policy vision. The third argument is that while alternative approaches to land reform are available, it is first necessary to make a clear and transparent judgement about three matters: market conditions, the desired model of governance and understandings of benefit provision. Prior failings in strategy and implementation on these very complex matters of social engineering impact significantly on the lives and well-being of Aboriginal and Torres Strait Islanders people, and their aspirations in contemporary Australia.

Skilfully drawing on a diversity of perspectives on property rights, *Beyond Communal and Individual Ownership: Indigenous Land Reform in Australia* engages a transdisciplinary approach to articulate the necessity of moving beyond the contested concepts of communal and individual ownership in order to understand the true significance of land reform and property rights over Indigenous land, not just in Australia but internationally. The contrast between the significant research Australian governments have undertaken in promoting pro-poor land reform in the wider Pacific and the dearth of both research and consultation on its land reform policies at home could not be more stark. The book's fresh perspective on land reform and careful assessment of key land reform theories will be of interest to scholars of indigenous land rights, land law, indigenous studies and aboriginal culture not only in Australia but also in any other country with an interest in indigenous land rights and contested real property rights.

Spike Boydell, *General Editor*
Sydney, June 2015

Acknowledgements

I'd first like to thank Sean Brennan, who has been a remarkable supervisor, colleague and friend, and to whom this book owes a great deal. I am also very grateful for the terrific support and feedback I have received from Megan Davis. There are many other colleagues from the UNSW Law School – too many to list – who have helped at different times with feedback, suggestions, comments and encouragement. Thanks to you all.

I learned a great deal about the subject matter of this book during the five years I spent working at the Central Land Council. A lot of people contributed to my education there, particularly the people I met in communities and worked with out bush. I have also learnt a great deal from conversations with Land Council staff in the period since I left, including Virginia Newell, Jayne Weepers, Julian Cleary, Danielle Campbell, Jeremy Dore, Brian Connelly, Siobhan McDonnell, James Nugent and David Avery.

I thank the Lionel Murphy Foundation for their financial support.

I am grateful for the excellent feedback and suggestions I received at an earlier stage from Tim Rowse and Daniel Fitzpatrick. I have also enjoyed fruitful conversations about the topic of this book with a number of informed people over the years, including Nicolas Peterson, Jon Altman, Jonathon Kneebone, Kirsty Howey, Shannon Burns, Trang Dang and Charlie Ward.

Chapter 1 of the book contains one of Jon Altman and Francis Markham's excellent maps on Indigenous land ownership, which is reproduced here with their permission and the permission of the Federation Press (with thanks to Jason Monaghan). That chapter also contains two very useful maps belonging to the Australian Government, which are again reproduced with permission. Special thanks to Annette Berry, Matthew James and Christian Beitzel for their help with this.

My final thanks go to Gerald and Mary, to whom the book is dedicated.

Addendum

In the period between the manuscript being finalised and the book going to print, there was a development of note with respect to township leasing in the Northern Territory. On 31 July 2015, the Australian Government announced that it had entered into a preliminary agreement for a township lease over the community of Gunyangara in Arnhem Land.[1] Reports indicate that the township lease will be held by a body representing the Gumatj clan.[2] This is the first time the Australian Government has agreed to a township lease to an Aboriginal organisation rather than the Executive Director of Township Leasing. Full details of the proposed lease for Gunyangara are yet to be made public and it is not clear, for example, how rent will be calculated, how the relationship between traditional owners and residents will be accommodated or what approach will be taken to the grant of subleases. The agreement does nevertheless appear to signal a shift in the Australian Governmentís land reform policy, as part of its ongoing efforts to secure township leases over all major communities on Aboriginal land in the Northern Territory.

Leon Terrill
Sydney, 18 August 2015

Notes

1 Nigel Scullion, ëGunyangara a Step Closer to Township Leaseí (Media Release, 31 July 2015) http://minister.indigenous.gov.au/media/2015-07-31/gunyangara-step-closer-township-lease.
2 Neda Vanovac, ëArnhem Land Agreement ìAn Important Stepîí, NT News (online), 1 August 2015 http://www.ntnews.com.au/news/national/indigenous-people-want-role-in-nt-plans/story-fnjbnvyj-1227465892599.

Abbreviations

ABA	Aboriginal Benefits Account
ABC	Australian Broadcasting Corporation
ACT	Australian Capital Territory
ALRA	*Aboriginal Land Rights (Northern Territory) Act 1976* (Cth)
ALRA land	Land held under the *Aboriginal Land Rights (Northern Territory) Act 1976* (Cth)
ANAO	Australian National Audit Office
ATSIC	Aboriginal Torres Strait Islander Commission
AusAID	Australian Agency for International Development
CLA	community living area
CLA land	community living area land
CLC	Central Land Council
COAG	Council of Australian Governments
CYI	Cape York Institute
DOGIT	Deed of Grant in Trust
EDTL	Executive Director of Township Leasing
HOIL Program	Home Ownership on Indigenous Land Program
ICHO	Indigenous Community Housing Organisation
NGO	non-government organisation
NIC	National Indigenous Council
NLC	Northern Land Council
NT	Northern Territory
NTER	Northern Territory Emergency Response
UN-Habitat	United Nations Human Settlements Programme

1 Introduction

From land rights to land reform

We will legislate to give aborigines land rights – not just because their case is beyond argument, but because all of us as Australians are diminished while the aborigines are denied their rightful place in this nation.

Gough Whitlam, 1972[1]

In the Northern Territory 45 percent of land is Aboriginal land [however] being land rich but dirt poor is not good enough. There is no romance in communal poverty. It crushes individual motivation and condemns all to passive acceptance of more of the same. Something has to change and it will.

Amanda Vanstone, 2005[2]

1.1 The shifting consensus

From land rights to land reform

Behind the reforms that this book describes is the story of two shifts in the Australian political consensus with respect to Indigenous people and their rights to land. The first was the shift that led to the belated introduction of land rights, through schemes such as the iconic *Aboriginal Land Rights (Northern Territory) Act 1976* (Cth). One of the remarkable things about that Act is that it was enacted with the support of both major political parties. This would not have been possible just a few years earlier. On Australia Day 1972, Prime Minister William McMahon announced that his conservative Liberal–Country Party had approved a plan to make it easier for Aboriginal people to acquire leases over reserve land but opposed any transfer of ownership.[3] This was an improvement on existing practice but fell short of what a growing number of people thought necessary. *The Australian* newspaper, for example, described the measures outlined by McMahon as a 'set of fringe proposals' and lamented the fact that Australia could be pointed to 'as the only country which offers no land rights to its native people'.[4]

It was the Opposition Labor Party under the leadership of Gough Whitlam that first promised a more comprehensive land rights scheme.

2 Introduction

Whitlam's stated reason for doing so, as set out in the quotation above, reflected a growing desire among non-Aboriginal Australians to right a historical wrong. Elections held in December 1972 saw the Labor Party form government, and one of Whitlam's first acts as prime minister was to appoint Edward Woodward to conduct a royal commission into the recognition of Aboriginal land rights in the Northern Territory.[5] In the course of reporting, Woodward took the opportunity to set down what he understood to be 'the aims underlying such recognition'. First and foremost, he saw it as 'the doing of a simple justice to a people who have been deprived of their land without their consent and without compensation'.[6]

In late 1975, Whitlam was controversially dismissed by the Governor-General and in the ensuing elections his party were voted out of office. It was one of the most acrimonious periods in Australian political history. Despite this, the new conservative prime minister, Malcolm Fraser, agreed to support legislation to enable Aboriginal land rights in the Northern Territory. The Fraser Government made some changes to the model that the Whitlam Government had developed but they also left a great deal more intact. The parties then voted together to pass the *Aboriginal Land Rights (Northern Territory) Act 1976* (Cth) (the ALRA),[7] reflecting a shift in the political consensus towards a shared belief that the grant of Aboriginal land rights was the 'doing of a simple justice'.

Of course, this shift was neither universal nor complete. Aboriginal land rights, and later native title, remained contentious. In the ensuing years very different approaches were taken to weighing up the interests of Indigenous and non-Indigenous Australians with respect to land, resulting in the patchwork of schemes that exist across the country today. The key point of tension was the extent of land rights, the amount required to do justice. For example, in 1997, Prime Minister John Howard argued that a recent High Court decision on native title had 'pushed the pendulum too far in the Aboriginal direction'.[8] Within the framework of the new consensus, contestation about the proper ambit of land rights was ongoing.

In 2004, a new and very different type of debate about Aboriginal land rights emerged. This time the terms of debate were set by the conservative Liberal–National Coalition. This was a debate about the *way* Aboriginal land was owned. By then, the ALRA had resulted in around 45 per cent of the Northern Territory becoming Aboriginal land. It was argued that ownership of that land had not delivered sufficient economic benefits to Aboriginal people because it was owned communally. Stating that 'being land rich but dirt poor is not good enough', the Minister for Indigenous Affairs, Amanda Vanstone, directed her department to develop reforms that would enable Aboriginal people to 'draw economic benefits from their land'.[9] Her successor as minister, Mal Brough, was even more emphatic about the need for reform. He argued that together with 'sit down money', the land rights legislation introduced by the Fraser Government had done

Introduction   3

'more to harm indigenous culture … than any two other legislative instruments ever put into the Parliament'.[10]

When this debate first emerged, the Opposition Labor Party disagreed with the Coalition's arguments and opposed reform.[11] This began to shift during 2007, and when Labor took office in November of that year they agreed to retain all of the reforms that the Coalition had introduced. As Fraser had done in 1976, the Labor Party made some changes but did not alter the fundamentals. The symmetry is striking. Three decades after the introduction of land rights there had once again been a shift in the political consensus, this time towards a shared belief that Indigenous land ownership in Australia was in need of reform.[12]

About this book

This book considers the reforms that arose out of this second shift in the political consensus. It describes how the reforms came about, what they do, what they mean for Indigenous communities and how they compare to other options. It is also the first book-length monograph on the Australian reforms.[13] While land tenure reform is a new development in Australia, it has a longer history in many other countries and there is by now a well-developed body of international literature about reform and its consequences. In some respects, this book can be seen as an attempt to apply the lessons from that 'international literature' to Australia and the Australian reforms. Chapter 2, which deals with land reform theory and terminology, is drawn almost exclusively from that international literature.

However, the book aims to do more than this. It also clarifies some of the issues that are particular to the reform of Indigenous land in a country such as Australia. The Australian reforms raise different issues to, for example, titling programmes for urban squatters in Peru or even customary land reform in the Pacific. The book describes how Australia fits in and exactly how it differs. It also draws out the nature of certain issues arising out of the Australian reforms that are not addressed in the international literature. One of those issues is the relationship between land reform and welfare reform, which has impacted significantly on the way that land reform has been debated and implemented in this country.

There are three main arguments that unite the chapters of this book. The first is that the way in which Indigenous land reform has been debated and discussed in Australia has been flawed. In particular, the frequent use of a communal–individual ownership dualism has resulted in the wrong issues being debated and pertinent issues receiving too little attention. As the title of the book suggests, it is necessary to go beyond communal and individual ownership to properly understand Indigenous land reform in Australia, particularly as it relates to residential communities. This book moves beyond that binary approach by separating out property systems (state property, communal property, private property, open access) from

4 *Introduction*

property features or characteristics (such as tenure security, alienability, individual and collective ownership). This provides a more useful framework for talking about the array of tenure possibilities, which better captures both the nature of earlier arrangements and the variety of potential reform outcomes.

The second main argument is that there are significant problems with the way in which Australian governments have implemented land tenure reforms over the last decade. This is largely because those reforms were introduced without a clear or coherent understanding of what it was they should do. This has resulted in mistakes being made and has meant that options have been foreclosed without due regard to the consequences of doing so. The reforms have also been expensive and intrusive and have harmed the relationship between governments and Indigenous communities. The third main argument is that alternative approaches to reform are available, but that in order to determine which approach should be taken it is first necessary to make a clear and transparent judgement about three 'cardinal issues': the nature of the market conditions in which the reforms will operate, the desired model of governance to be implemented and the approach being taken to the question of what it is that can make the provision of welfare harmful. These are clearly very complex matters, not easily decided upon. However, as the book makes clear, any land reform model will implement a particular approach to them. It is better to be clear about the decisions that are being made than to allow them to remain unexamined.

The book also has a number of subsidiary objectives. It clarifies the nature of land-use arrangements in residential communities on Indigenous land in Australia and the role of traditional law in those arrangements. In doing so, it explains why it is so misleading to simply describe those communities as places of communal ownership. It provides some basic tools for understanding the relationship between land tenure arrangements and economic development. It sets out clear and workable definitions for key terminology and concepts, such as communal ownership, tenure security and formalisation. It introduces new terminology to better clarify the nature of the recent Australia reforms, such as 'exogenous formalisation'. And it considers what the recent reforms to Indigenous land tenure reflect about the current direction of Indigenous policy in Australia.

1.2 Background to the reforms

The debate

The public debate that led to the introduction of Indigenous land tenure reform in Australia began in late 2004. As the Central Land Council (one of Australia's largest Aboriginal land councils) noted at the time, the debate centred on 'the merits of individual ownership versus communal ownership of land', particularly with respect to enabling home ownership and economic development in Aboriginal communities.[14] It was, however, about more than just home ownership and economic development. From the beginning, the debate about land reform was also a debate about culture. The introduction of 'individual ownership' was presented as a means of enabling a shift away from a separate or traditional culture, towards a more economically integrated or 'entrepreneurial culture'.[15] Debate about land reform was also understood as forming part of a broader dialogue about the direction of Indigenous policy. The Australian Government said that it was changing the emphasis from engaging with 'the collective Aboriginal community' to engaging directly with 'individuals and families'.[16]

This debate – particularly in the period between 2004 and 2007 – was widespread, intense, significant, divisive and deeply flawed. Describing the pre-existing arrangements in Aboriginal communities as 'communal ownership' is misleading to the point of confusion. Presenting the outcome of reforms as the introduction of 'individual ownership' or 'private property' is in most cases simply wrong. The use of these terms – which were usually left undefined – resulted in several distinct issues being conflated and, to an extent that is in hindsight remarkable, meant that the likely impact of reform was misunderstood. This book describes how one of the more common outcomes of reform has been an increase in government control over land use, the very opposite of what terms such as 'individual ownership' suggest.

This was also a debate with a very concrete outcome. It led to a bipartisan consensus that there is a pressing need for widespread reform to land tenure arrangements in Indigenous communities. To be clear, it is not simply that concerns emerged about the nature of the earlier arrangements, the arrangements that governments and Indigenous residents had relied upon for decades. The shift was more significant. Those earlier arrangements have come to be characterised as fundamentally flawed, and governments – particularly the Australian Government – have spent tens of millions of dollars on permanently overhauling them.

Indigenous land ownership in Australia

When colonisation of Australia began, no formal recognition was given to prior ownership of the land by Indigenous peoples. This remained the approach for the best part of two centuries. Governments did create a large number of missions and reserves, areas of land that were set aside for the use of Indigenous people; however, this arrangement did not convey any ownership rights. This was the situation that prevailed until the mid-1960s, since which time there has been what Altman and Markham describe as an 'Indigenous land titling revolution'. As a result, today Indigenous groups have exclusive legal rights to around 22.4 per cent of the

6 Introduction

country.[17] This remarkable shift does require some context. The overwhelming majority of this land – around 98.6 per cent – is located in areas classified as 'very remote'.[18] The impact in areas of higher population, and on land of greater economic value, has been far more contained.

It is nevertheless a significant transformation, and it has come about in two ways. The first is through the grant of statutory land rights schemes such as the ALRA. Australia has a federal legal system, under which power is shared between the Australian/Commonwealth Government and the various state and territory governments. The introduction of statutory schemes has been uneven, with some jurisdictions introducing relatively generous schemes and others none at all.[19] In some jurisdictions, including the Northern Territory, there are multiple schemes aimed at different groups. Altman and Markham identify a total of 34 separate legislative regimes across the country.[20] The result is a patchwork of ownership, with the different schemes varying significantly in terms of their coverage, the strength of the rights that they afford, their ownership structures, the restrictions that they impose upon the use and alienation of land and their funding arrangements.

The second component of this transformation has been native title. In 1992, in *Mabo v Queensland No 2 (Mabo)*,[21] six out of seven judges of the Australian High Court found that the common law of Australia did in fact recognise prior ownership of land by Indigenous peoples, and that this prior ownership gave rise to ongoing rights where those rights had not been extinguished. A key difference between statutory land rights schemes and native title is that while the former are created by parliaments the latter came about as the result of judicial recognition. It quickly became apparent, however, that the recognition of native title required a legislative response. This led to the *Native Title Act 1993* (Cth), which to a considerable extent regulates the actual impact of native title.

Often a declaration of native title results in an exclusive set of rights to the land – which in some respects is then treated as equivalent to, although not the same as, ownership of a fee simple. In other places native title coexists with other property interests, most commonly with a pastoral lease. Where that occurs, the native title holders have a more limited set of rights. More broadly, native title only survives where it has not been extinguished by inconsistent government action and consequently it no longer exists over most of Australia. Extinguishment has been more common in highly populated areas. Conversely, in those areas where strong land rights schemes already existed prior to *Mabo*, such as in the Northern Territory and parts of South Australia, the need for native title was less. Schemes such as the ALRA already gave Aboriginal people a high level of ownership and control, higher in some respects than a declaration of native title could deliver. It is consequently in Western Australia and Queensland, with their relatively weak land rights schemes, that the impact of native title has been greatest. The combined outcome of statutory land rights schemes and native title is shown in Figure 1.1, with its four maps depicting the Indigenous dispossession and partial repossession of Australia.[22]

Aboriginal and Torres Strait Islander Australians

When the colonisation of Australia began in 1788 there were hundreds of separate nations occupying mainland Australia and the offshore islands. There was no single, area-wide government. Today, the term 'Aboriginal' is used to describe people from the mainland nations (including Tasmania), and 'Torres Strait Islander' to describe people from the nations occupying the islands of the Torres Strait. The term 'Indigenous' refers to Aboriginal and Torres Strait Islander people collectively, though many Indigenous people identify first as belonging to a particular area, clan or language group. It is estimated that there are currently around 670,000 Indigenous Australians, which represents 3 per cent of the total Australian population.[23] This group remains very diverse, not least with respect to the

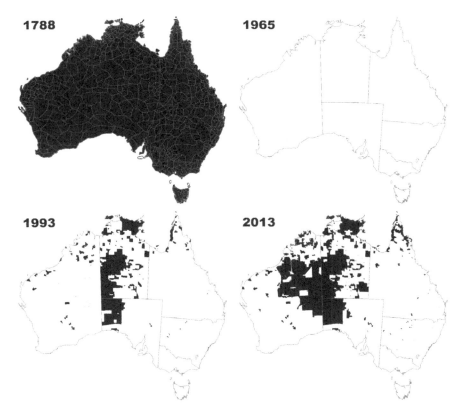

Figure 1.1 Indigenous land ownership over time (courtesy of Altman and Markham).

8 Introduction

different ways in which people engage with the non-Indigenous population. The majority of Indigenous people – more than three-quarters – live in either major cities or regional areas.[24] Only 21.4 per cent – or around 142,900 – live in the remote and very remote regions where most Indigenous land is found.[25] It is this group that is most affected by the recent reforms that are the subject of this book.

Scope of the reforms

Not all Indigenous land in Australia has been affected by the recent introduction of land reform. Perhaps the single most important point for understanding the scope of the reforms is that they target the land in and immediately around residential communities, particularly in remote areas. With some minor exceptions, they do not affect the much larger areas of Indigenous land outside those communities. This means that only a small fraction of Indigenous land has been affected, albeit the fraction on which most people live.

This is consequently a book about urban and peri-urban land reform. If the reforms were instead directed at those large areas of land outside communities, it would be a different book. The issues with respect to residential communities are both more contained and more complex. The book describes how until recently almost all land and infrastructure in communities on Indigenous land was allocated under *informal tenure arrangements* that developed at a local level. Those informal arrangements have been to some extent distinct from the land ownership system. This means that in order to understand the recent reforms, their impact and consequences, it is necessary to begin with an understanding of both the underlying land ownership system *and* the informal tenure arrangements that evolved in communities. Both have been affected by the reforms.

As a further comment on the scope of the reforms, it is noted that they target Indigenous land held under statutory schemes. Native title has not been directly targeted. In some places it is affected, in that certain of the reforms will result in its extinguishment, but the focus of reform has been on communities situated on statutory land.

Case study: the Northern Territory

The communities most affected by the reforms are those located on Aboriginal land in the Northern Territory. One reason for this is that the reforms have largely been driven by the Australian Government, which, for historical reasons, plays a more direct role in Aboriginal affairs in the Northern Territory. The ALRA itself is Commonwealth legislation applying only to the Northern Territory and, to date, communities on ALRA land have been the primary focus of reform.

Certain of the reforms also affect communities on Indigenous land in Western Australia, South Australia, Queensland and to a lesser extent New

South Wales. The reforms in those states are less well developed. With the exception of one recent development in Queensland, which is discussed below, they are also similar in nature to the reforms being implemented in the Northern Territory. Consequently, the book takes the Northern Territory reforms as its primary case study. There are several advantages to this. The narrower focus enables a more detailed description of both the reforms and the circumstances in which they operate, while avoiding repetition. And those details matter. One significant problem with debate about land reform in Australia is that too often it has been abstracted from the actual circumstances of communities.

The focus on the Northern Territory begins in Chapter 3, which describes how Aboriginal land in the Northern Territory is owned under both Aboriginal law and under the formal or mainstream legal system.[26] Three types of Aboriginal land are described. The first is land held under the ALRA, or 'ALRA land', which is by far the most widespread. The second is Aboriginal community living area land, or 'CLA land'. Areas of CLA land tend to be smaller and have often been excised from pastoral leases. The third is 'town camp land', which is explained below.

By 2006 – the year the first set of reforms were introduced – there were 41,681 people[27] living in 641 discrete Aboriginal communities across the Northern Territory.[28] All but a handful of these were situated on one of these three types of Aboriginal land. These 641 discrete communities can be usefully divided into two groups. The first are *town camps*, which are housing areas situated on the fringes of towns and cities such as Darwin, Alice Springs and Tennant Creek. There are around 47 town camps across the Territory, at the locations depicted in Figure 1.2.[29]

In the second group are *remote settlements*, which are located further away from the major urban centres. The size of these remote settlements varies considerably, and they can be further subdivided into two groups: larger settlements called 'communities' and smaller settlements called 'outstations' or 'homelands'. In the course of the recent reforms, the Australian Government has identified 73 remote settlements as generally having a population of more than 100. Together with town camps, it is these larger remote communities (rather than outstations or homelands) that have been the focus of recent land reforms. These 73 larger remote communities are illustrated in Figure 1.3.[30]

Chapter 4 describes the nature of the informal tenure arrangements that have evolved in remote communities over the past few decades. This description reveals something that is often overlooked. There are many places around the world where people living on indigenous land have relatively exclusive rights with respect to their houses *under customary law*. That has not been the case on mainland Australia, where traditional laws with respect to land ownership were developed in the context of hunter-gather societies and not permanent residential communities. Individuals did not have exclusive rights to particular areas. And yet today people

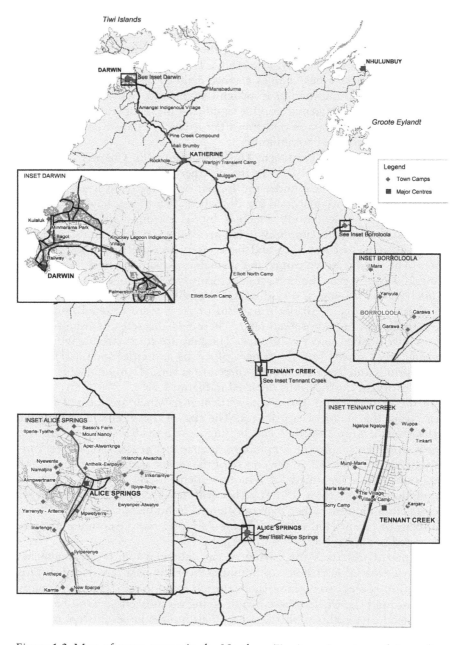

Figure 1.2 Map of town camps in the Northern Territory (courtesy of Australian Government, Department of Prime Minister and Cabinet).

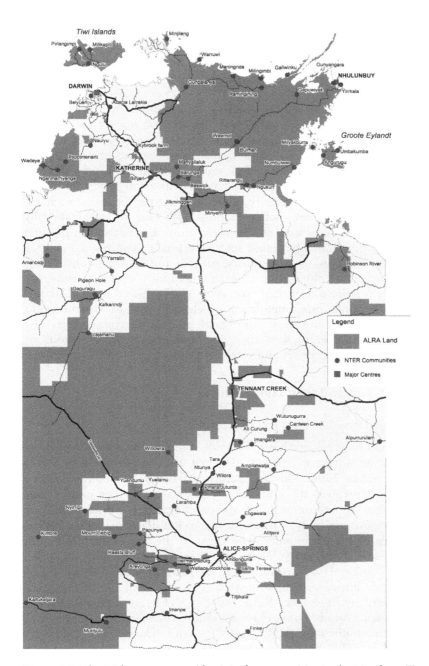

Figure 1.3 The 73 larger remote Aboriginal communities in the Northern Territory (courtesy of Australian Government, Department of Prime Minister and Cabinet).

12 *Introduction*

living on Aboriginal land do reside in permanent communities and often have exclusive rights to their houses. This book explains how this occurs, and what role traditional law plays in that process. It is a mistake to think of the informal tenure arrangements as simply an expression of traditional law, but it is also a mistake to think that traditional law is irrelevant.[31]

Before introducing the reforms themselves, it is useful to have a clearer picture of what these communities look like. In this respect town camps are different from remote communities. Town camps are basically housing areas. Some have additional facilities such as a learning centre,[32] but in most cases the residents shop and seek out services in the nearby town or city. Remote communities necessarily have a wider range of facilities. In addition to housing for community residents, there can be found such services as childcare centres, police stations, schools, recreational halls, churches, land council offices, media associations and outstation resource centres. There might also be found such enterprises as stores, art centres, visitor accommodation, tour operators, garages and contract construction workers. The actual composition of each community varies considerably. This is partly a reflection of their size: even within this group of 73 larger communities, populations range from a little over 100 to around 2,600. While most residents are local Aboriginal people, all communities also have a smaller number of non-Aboriginal residents, most of whom are employees of local enterprises and service providers.

1.3 The reforms and their consequences

The Northern Territory: three sets of reforms

The Australian Government has now made three sets of reforms to Aboriginal land in the Northern Territory. The first was township leasing, which was introduced in 2006. This is a reform particular to communities on ALRA land. It involves the grant of a head lease over community land (that is, the land in and immediately surrounding a larger residential community) to a statutory body, whose role it is to grant and manage subleases over portions of the community. The grant of the head lease itself – the township lease – is voluntary. There are 52 larger communities on ALRA land, and to date only six are subject to a township lease. The second set of reforms was introduced the following year as part of the controversial Northern Territory Emergency Response (the NTER), or Intervention. The NTER included a number of land reforms and affected town camps as well as remote communities on ALRA and CLA land. The majority (although not all) of the NTER measures expired in 2012, and were replaced by a new set of measures called Stronger Futures. The Stronger Futures package included one additional land reform, which is particular to CLA and town camp land.

The third set of reforms was also introduced in 2007, and while it has attracted much less publicity it has become the most wide-ranging. In September of that year the Australian and Northern Territory governments entered into a memorandum of understanding with respect to housing in Aboriginal communities. This agreement embedded the core elements of what have since come to be known as 'secure tenure' policies. Under those policies, funding for certain infrastructure – initially housing, and then a wider range of infrastructure – has come to be contingent on tenure arrangements being formalised through the grant of a lease. Most of those leases are granted to government agencies. For example, before it will provide funding for new houses, the Australian Government requires that all community housing in the subject community be leased to Territory Housing, the Northern Territory Government public housing body. This is a very different reform to the introduction of home ownership (to the limited extent that the latter has occurred). The housing leases have primarily been used to implement a change in housing management, a shift from community housing to mainstream public housing.

The book is primarily concerned with the reforms as they affect remote communities. The more limited reforms to town camps are an important part of the reform context and understanding them provides a fuller picture of the Australian Government's reform policy. For this reason, the book includes a description of town camp land and of the town camp reforms. It is, however, remote communities that are the focus of book.

Beyond the Northern Territory

The Australian Government's reforms to housing are also being rolled out in certain larger communities on Indigenous land in Western Australia, South Australia, Queensland and New South Wales. Some of those states – particularly South Australia and Queensland – have also introduced reforms that make it easier to grant leases over Indigenous land. Such reforms raise similar issues to the Northern Territory reforms. There is, however, a more recent development in Queensland which is different. In 2014, the Queensland Government legislated to allow certain areas of Indigenous land in 34 communities to be divided up and converted to ordinary freehold. All other reforms – including the Northern Territory reforms – have involved the grant of leases and subleases over Indigenous land. While some of those leases and subleases are lengthy, they do not change underlying ownership by Indigenous groups. The Queensland amendments are the first to do so. This raises a broader set of issues, and so a detailed description of the Queensland reforms and their consequences is provided in later chapters.

14 *Introduction*

Consequences of the reforms

Impact on governance

The Northern Territory reforms do not – as it was suggested they would – replace communal ownership of land with individual ownership. Nor do they necessarily enable more secure tenure, as the Australian Government has also argued. For the most part, they are more accurately described as a type of *mandatory formalisation*. However, even this description only partly captures the significance of the reforms. Their short-term effect has been to disrupt, disempower and to some extent antagonise Indigenous landowners and community residents in a manner that was unhelpful and unnecessary. In the long term they have two main consequences. The first is the impact that they have on governance. The meaning of the term 'governance' in this context can be elusive, partly because there are two, interrelated elements. It refers first to the 'formal and informal structures and processes through which a group' – in this case a residential community – 'conducts and regulates its internal affairs as well as its relations with others'.[33] It also describes the way 'government engages with – and governs – its citizens and institutions' in those communities.[34] To put it another way, governance in the context of Indigenous communities refers to both the way communities govern themselves and the way that governments exercise their authority in those communities. These two aspects of governance intersect and diverge at different points. Both have been affected by the recent reforms. Those reforms result in governments playing a more embedded and controlling role in the management of remote communities. Concomitantly, they reduce the scope for communities to govern themselves. In many places, the reforms also result in one group of Aboriginal people – the traditional owners – having an increased say in certain decision-making at the expense of another group of Aboriginal people, being non-traditional owner residents. The exact meaning of this distinction is described in some detail in Chapter 3.

Rent

The second major consequence of the reforms, which emerged later in the reform process and has a more convoluted history, is that a far greater proportion of land users in Aboriginal communities are now paying rent. The rent referred to here is different from that paid by Aboriginal residents of community housing. That rent has always been paid to the organisation responsible for housing management, rather than the landowners, and this has not changed. It is other occupiers – service providers such as the childcare centre, enterprises such as the art centre – who are now far more likely to pay rent, and that rent is paid to landowners.

The impact of this development is complicated. From the perspective of occupiers, rent adds to the cost of doing business in communities on

Indigenous land. As the amount of rent is small relative to other costs, however, the impact of this should not be overstated. From the perspective of landowners, rent is a new form of income, and there are some very different perspectives on how this income should be characterised. Those perspectives are explored in Chapters 7 and 8.

Home ownership and economic development

The aims most often referred to during debate about land reform have been home ownership and economic development. Here, the impact of the reforms has been modest. To accompany its reforms, in 2006 the Australian Government set up a programme to encourage the uptake of home ownership in communities on Indigenous land. As of October 2014, that programme had achieved a total of 25 grants of home ownership across the country.[35] This is despite the expenditure of considerable effort and tens of millions of dollars. Further, the approach to the pricing of housing in some communities may be putting purchasers at risk.[36] The book argues that a focus on the tenure aspects of home ownership has actually impeded the development of more nuanced and effective home-ownership policies.

The book also describes how, in the course of implementing the reforms, the Australian Government's approach to enabling economic development has effectively been inverted. Originally, it argued that land reform would lead to economic development by providing *occupiers* with more economically useful forms of tenure, or by making it easier for enterprises to acquire access to land cheaply. In the course of implementing the reforms it took a different tack. While the reforms have in fact made access to land more expensive, through more occupiers paying rent, the government argues that this enables economic development by assisting *landowners* to better exploit their asset.

Allotment: a different type of reform

Legislation to enable the allotment of Indigenous land in Queensland only commenced on 1 January 2015, and as the process is both expensive and involved it is likely to be some time before the amendments are utilised. When they are utilised it will be an Australian first, as allotment involves a slightly different set of issues to formalisation through leasing and subleasing. There are two elements to this. The first is the impact on underlying Indigenous ownership and the consequences this has for relationships around land use. Allotment puts an end to underlying ownership by the Indigenous group and extinguishes native title. Effectively, this resolves the tension between *traditional ownership* and *residence* in the opposite manner to the Northern Territory reforms. The Northern Territory reforms have resulted in the empowerment of traditional owners at the expense of non-traditional owner residents. Allotment involves a transfer

16 *Introduction*

of ownership to select residents with no ongoing role for the traditional owners.

Second, where tenure arrangements are formalised through leasing and subleasing it is possible for a centralised body to retain some level of control over the ongoing reallocation of land. For example, the terms of a lease can provide that it can only be transferred to certain persons or with landowner consent. This makes it possible to create closed or regulated markets. Allotment leads to ordinary freehold, which can then be transferred to anyone. This raises questions about when or in what circumstances freely transferable forms of property are likely to be more helpful than harmful in the context of remote Indigenous communities. Chapter 8 introduces a framework for considering this issue, and argues that it would be naive to assume that freely transferable forms of ownership are always preferable.

1.4 Overview of the book

Book structure

The book is composed of nine chapters. Drawing heavily from the international literature on land reform, Chapter 2 provides explanations for key land reform terms and concepts, with a focus on those terms and concepts that are most relevant to a discussion of land tenure reform in a country such as Australia. It also identifies the potential benefits and risks of engaging in land tenure reform and describes two theories that have had a big impact on debate about land reform in Australia and more broadly, being evolutionary theory and Hernando de Soto's theory of capital.

Chapter 3 contains two related sections. The first describes ownership of land under Aboriginal law, while the second describes the way Aboriginal land ownership is provided for under Northern Territory law. The first section is drawn primarily from the published research of anthropologists, much of which has been written in the context of land claims. The second section is instead an analysis of the legislation behind ALRA land, CLA land and town camp land, combined with some commentary on how the legislation works in practice. So as to keep the distinction clear, the book uses the term *Aboriginal land tenure* when referring to (understandings of) rights and responsibilities to land under Aboriginal law; and *Aboriginal land* when referring to any form of Aboriginal-specific land ownership under mainstream law.

In Chapter 4, the book departs from existing research by providing a detailed description of the *informal tenure arrangements* that operated in remote communities prior to the recent reforms. During public debate about land reform, those tenure arrangements have often been treated as being synonymous with the land ownership system or as being a type of laissez-faire collectivism. Chapter 4 instead describes how those informal arrangements were a developed, relatively structured, stable, inexpensive, sometimes effective and sometimes flawed system for allocating land and infrastructure in communities to particular occupiers. It was not the case that everyone simply owned everything, nor did everything belong to the 'traditional owners'. Rather, in response to their changed circumstances and in the course of their interaction with governments, Aboriginal residents had developed a new set of arrangements that better met their modern-day needs.

Chapter 5 considers the public debate about land reform and how it led to the development of a new political consensus. It is described how there have been different periods of debate. The first and most important was between 2004 and 2007. This was the period during which the political consensus shifted and when the use of a communal–individual ownership dualism was at its most prevalent. In 2008, the Labor Government introduced a new and slightly different set of terminology to explain the purpose of land reform, in the form of frequent references to a need for 'secure tenure'. This did not entirely displace the earlier language, but terms such as communal and individual ownership came to be used less often. It also coincided with a broadening of the rationale for land reform. The government argued that land reform was required not just to enable home ownership and economic development, but also to clarify responsibility for the maintenance and upkeep of infrastructure in communities. Since 2013, a re-elected Coalition Government has dropped the use of 'secure tenure' terminology and re-emphasised home ownership and economic development as the rationale for reform.

The reforms and their consequences are described in Chapters 6 and 7. During debate, proponents argued that the reforms would enable new types of relationships in Aboriginal communities. In particular they suggested that the reforms would make it easier for Aboriginal community residents to engage economically with mainstream Australia. There is no evidence of this occurring. More significant has been the impact of the reforms on existing relationships, such as those between governments, community residents and traditional owners. As described above, certain reforms have altered the governance arrangements in communities in a way that has institutionalised a greater role for government and changed the relationship between traditional owners and non-traditional owner residents. The reforms also result in a larger proportion of occupiers paying rent. While these are the two most significant consequences of the reforms, they are not the only ones. These two chapters also detail the impact of the reforms on home ownership and economic development and consider the consequences of housing precinct leases and the shift to public housing.

Chapter 8 then sets out a framework for developing an alternative approach to land reform in remote communities. The framework is presented in two steps. The first step is to identify the main variables, or *what*

18   *Introduction*

needs to be decided upon. The second step is to identify the key issues, or what it is that determines *how* these variables should be decided upon. The book argues that there are 'three cardinal issues' that, above all others, determine the approach that should be taken to land reform. They are an assessment of market conditions, the intended model of governance and understandings of benefit provision. The first two are fairly self-explanatory. The last – understandings of benefit provision – refers to understandings about how and why government benefits might sometimes be regarded as harmful. In recognition of the dominant role that governments play in the economy of remote communities, it is argued that this is one of the key issues for developing a land reform model. This relates to a broader argument that Chapter 8 presents, which is that expectations as to the transformative impact of land reform need to be moderated. New forms of tenure will not transcend the broader economic environment, nor will formalising tenure and centralising decision-making result in the type of order and clarity that governments have suggested. Chapter 9 provides some concluding statements and summarises the book's arguments.

Some important terminology

This book uses a number of terms that are defined as they are introduced, such as 'formalisation', 'tenure security' and 'benefit provision'. In addition to this, there are some words that are used throughout and for which a definition is given here. The first of these is 'culture', a word whose meaning is so notoriously difficult to pin down that Johada argues that 'it is quite practicable and defensible simply to use the term without seeking to define it'.[37] He goes on to suggest that, if clarification is required, it is better to explain the manner in which the term is being used rather than attempt a universal definition. That is the intention here. In this book, the word culture is used to refer to what Trigger summarises as the 'key assumptions (not always articulated consciously) and practices which inform everyday-life'.[38] It is in this sense something dynamic rather than static and relational as well as internal. As Trigger notes, sometimes the word culture is used in a narrower sense to mean 'art and/or associated spiritual beliefs and ceremonies'.[39] That is not the sense in which the word is being used here. Further, when applied to Aboriginal people, the word culture can sometimes take on a more essentialised meaning. Chapter 5 describes how, during debate about land reform, Aboriginal culture was sometimes characterised as something 'traditional' that people can and should discard so as to successfully take their place in the broader Australian community. Indeed, the debate about land reform perpetuated this construction of culture, which was one of the problems with the debate. When this book refers to the distinct cultural circumstances of Aboriginal communities, it refers to the distinct set of assumptions and practices that inform everyday-life as it occurs today.

Introduction 19

The term 'Aboriginal community' can be used to describe a variety of groupings of Aboriginal people. In this book it is used to describe larger residential settlements, which in context can be either remote settlements or remote settlements and town camps. Where smaller settlements are intended, the term 'outstation' is used. Accordingly 'community land' refers to the land in and immediately around a residential community, comprising at most a few square kilometres, as opposed to the much larger areas of Aboriginal land that surround many communities.

The term 'secure tenure' has a clear meaning in the research literature on land reform. Used correctly, it is a foundational land reform concept. The term has also been used by the Australian Government in a non-technical manner, both to describe a concept (upon examination several different concepts) and a set of policies. To avoid confusion, when the term secure tenure is used here in its technical sense, it is not in inverted commas. When referring to the term as it is used by the government, inverted commas are employed. Thus the government's policies are referred to as 'secure tenure' policies, and its terminology referred to as 'secure tenure' terminology.

The terms 'Aboriginal land' and 'Aboriginal land tenure' have already been defined above: the former to describe Aboriginal-specific forms of land ownership under mainstream law, and the latter to describe the allocation of rights and responsibilities to land under Aboriginal law. When referring to communities on Aboriginal land, the term 'informal tenure arrangements' is used to describe the arrangements that developed for the allocation of land and infrastructure to particular occupiers. Finally, a distinction is made between two forms of housing in communities. 'Residential housing' describes the housing occupied by Aboriginal community residents and 'staff housing' occupied by the staff of organisations operating in communities, who are often non-Aboriginal. The reason for the distinction is that different arrangements have been, and continue to be, used with respect to each.

Notes

1 Gough Whitlam, 'It's Time for Leadership' (Speech delivered at Blacktown Civic Centre, Sydney, 13 November 1972).
2 Amanda Vanstone, 'Beyond Conspicuous Compassion: Indigenous Australians Deserve More than Good Intentions' (Speech delivered to the Australia and New Zealand School of Government, Australian National University, Canberra, 7 December 2005).
3 William McMahon, 'Australian Aborigines: Commonwealth Policy and Achievement' (Statement by the Prime Minister, 26 January 1972). McMahon also announced $13 million over five years to fund the acquisition of further reserves. See also Peter H. Russell, *Recognizing Aboriginal Title: The Mabo Case and Indigenous Resistance to English-Settler Colonialism* (University of Toronto Press, 2005) 159–63.
4 Editorial, 'A Price on Our Guilt', *The Australian*, 26 January 1972, 8.

20 Introduction

5 Russell, above n 3, 163.
6 Edward Woodward, 'Aboriginal Land Rights Commission: Second Report' (Australian Government, 1974) 2.
7 Sean Brennan, 'Economic Development and Land Council Power: Modernising the *Land Rights Act* or Same Old Same Old?' (2006) 10(4) *Australian Indigenous Law Reporter* 1, 2.
8 See Heather McRae *et al.*, *Indigenous Legal Issues, Commentary and Materials* (Thomson Reuters, 2009) 311.
9 Vanstone, above n 2.
10 Mal Brough, 'On the Federal Government's Intervention into Northern Territory Indigenous Communities' (Speech delivered at the Alfred Deakin Lecture, University of Melbourne, 2 October 2007).
11 Chapter 3 describes how there were exceptions to this within the party.
12 Perche characterises this shift in terms of a changing approach to problem definition; Diana Perche, 'Indigenous Land Reform and the Market: Changing Social Constructions in Indigenous Land Policy during the Howard era' (Paper presented at Australian Political Studies Association Annual Conference, Macquarie University, Sydney, 30 September 2009).
13 There is an earlier edited collection with several chapters on the Australian reforms; see Lee Godden and Maureen Tehan (eds), *Comparative Perspectives on Communal Land and Individual Ownership: Sustainable Futures* (Routledge, 2010).
14 Central Land Council, 'Communal Title and Economic Development' (Policy Paper, 2005) 2.
15 Prime Minister John Howard, quoted in Mark Metherell, 'PM Backs Indigenous Enterprise', *The Sydney Morning Herald*, 10 December 2004, 7.
16 Mal Brough, 'Blueprint for Action in Indigenous Affairs' (Speech delivered at the National Institute of Governance, Canberra, 5 December 2006).
17 Jon Altman and Francis Markham, 'Burgeoning Indigenous Land Ownership: Diverse Values and Strategic Potentialities' in Sean Brennan *et al.* (eds), *Native Title from Mabo to Akiba: A Vehicle for Change and Empowerment?* (Federation Press, 2015) 126, 135.
18 Jon Altman, Geoff Buchanan and Libby Larsen, 'The Environmental Significance of the Indigenous Estate: Natural Resource Management as Economic Development in Remote Australia' (Discussion Paper No 286/2007, Centre for Aboriginal Economic Policy Research, 2007) 7.
19 For a detailed overview, see Chapter 11 ('Australian Land Rights Legislation') of Garth Nettheim, Gary Meyers and Donna Craig, *Indigenous Peoples and Governance Structures: A Comparative Analysis of Land and Resource Management Rights* (Aboriginal Studies Press, 2002).
20 Altman and Markham, above n 17, 133.
21 (1992) 175 CLR 1.
22 Source: Altman and Markham, above n 17, insert following page 132. Reproduced with the permission of the authors and Federation Press. © Altman and Markham.
23 Australian Bureau of Statistics, *Estimates of Aboriginal and Torres Strait Islander Australians June 2011* (30 August 2013) www.abs.gov.au/ausstats/abs@.nsf/mf/3238.0.55.001.
24 34.8 per cent in major cities, 22.0 per cent in inner regional areas and 21.8 per cent in outer regional areas; ibid.
25 Ibid.
26 For reasons described in Chapter 2, this book follows the practice of describing mainstream Australian law as 'formal law'. This is not intended to suggest that Aboriginal law is lesser or is lacking in structure.

27 See Australian Bureau of Statistics, *4710.0: Housing and Infrastructure in Aboriginal and Torres Strait Islander Communities, Australia, 2006* (17 April 2007) www.abs.gov.au/AUSSTATS/abs@.nsf/Latestproducts/4710.0Main%20Features42006?opendocument&tabname=Summary&prodno=4710.0&issue=2006&num=&view=.
28 Jon Altman, 'The "National Emergency" and Land Rights Reform: Separating Fact from Fiction' (Briefing paper for Oxfam Australia prepared by the Centre for Aboriginal Economic Policy Research, 7 August 2007) 4.
29 This is an edited version of 'Map B: Prescribed areas – town camps', which can be found at Australian Government, Department of Families, Housing, Community Services and Indigenous Affairs, 'Evaluation of Income Management in the Northern Territory' (Occasional Paper No 34, Australian Institute of Health and Welfare) 71. Some text has been removed. Map is for illustrative purposes only. Reproduced with permission. © Commonwealth of Australia.
30 This is an edited version of 'Map A: Prescribed areas – Aboriginal (Alra) land', which can be found at ibid, 70. Some text has been removed. Map is for illustrative purposes only. Reproduced with permission. © Commonwealth of Australia.
31 This is an argument that is particular to larger residential communities. If the reforms were instead directed at land outside communities, including outstations, different considerations would arise.
32 See, eg, Tangentyere Council, *Hidden Valley Community Centre* (2008) www.tangentyere.org.au/services/family_youth/towncamp_learning.
33 The quotation is from David Martin, 'Rethinking Aboriginal Community Governance' in Paul Smyth, Tim Reddel and Andrew Jones (eds), *Community and Local Governance in Australia* (University of New South Wales Press, 2005) 108, 114; however, a number of other authors use a similar definition.
34 Bruce Walker, Douglas Porter and Ian Marsh, 'Fixing the Hole in Australia's Heartland: How Government Needs to Work in Remote Australia' (Desert Knowledge Australia, 2012) 5.
35 Indigenous Business Australia, 'Home Ownership on Indigenous Land Now a Reality in Yarrabah' (Media Release, 22 October 2014).
36 See Chapter 7.
37 Gustav Jahoda, 'Critical Reflections on Some Recent Definitions of "Culture"' (2012) 18(3) *Culture & Psychology* 289, 300.
38 David Trigger, 'Mining Projects in Remote Aboriginal Australia: Sites for the Articulation and Contestation of Economic and Cultural Features' in Diane Austin-Broos and Gaynor Macdonald (eds), *Culture, Economy and Governance in Aboriginal Australia* (Sydney University Press, 2005) 41, 42.
39 Ibid.

Bibliography

Books/articles/reports/web pages

Altman, Jon, 'The "National Emergency" and Land Rights Reform: Separating Fact from Fiction' (Briefing paper for Oxfam Australia prepared by the Centre for Aboriginal Economic Policy Research, 7 August 2007).

Altman, Jon and Francis Markham, 'Burgeoning Indigenous Land Ownership: Diverse Values and Strategic Potentialities' in Sean Brennan *et al.* (eds), *Native Title from Mabo to Akiba: A Vehicle for Change and Empowerment?* (Federation Press, 2015) 126.

22 Introduction

Altman, Jon, Geoff Buchanan and Libby Larsen, 'The Environmental Significance of the Indigenous Estate: Natural Resource Management as Economic Development in Remote Australia' (Discussion Paper No 286/2007, Centre for Aboriginal Economic Policy Research, 2007).

Australian Bureau of Statistics, *4710.0: Housing and Infrastructure in Aboriginal and Torres Strait Islander Communities, Australia, 2006* (17 April 2007) www.abs.gov.au/AUSSTATS/abs@.nsf/Latestproducts/4710.0Main%20Features42006?opendocument&tabname=Summary&prodno=4710.0&issue=2006&num=&view=.

Australian Bureau of Statistics, *Estimates of Aboriginal and Torres Strait Islander Australians June 2011* (30 August 2013) www.abs.gov.au/ausstats/abs@.nsf/mf/3238.0.55.001.

Australian Government, Department of Families, Housing, Community Services and Indigenous Affairs, 'Evaluation of Income Management in the Northern Territory' (Occasional Paper No 34, Australian Institute of Health and Welfare).

Brennan, Sean, 'Economic Development and Land Council Power: Modernising the *Land Rights Act* or Same Old Same Old?' (2006) 10(4) *Australian Indigenous Law Reporter* 1.

Brough, Mal, 'Blueprint for Action in Indigenous Affairs' (Speech delivered at the National Institute of Governance, Canberra, 5 December 2006).

Brough, Mal, 'On the Federal Government's Intervention into Northern Territory Indigenous Communities' (Speech delivered at the Alfred Deakin Lecture, University of Melbourne, 2 October 2007).

Central Land Council, 'Communal Title and Economic Development' (Policy Paper, 2005).

Editorial, 'A Price on Our Guilt', *The Australian*, 26 January 1972, 8.

Godden, Lee and Maureen Tehan (eds), *Comparative Perspectives on Communal Land and Individual Ownership: Sustainable Futures* (Routledge, 2010).

Indigenous Business Australia, 'Home Ownership on Indigenous Land Now a Reality in Yarrabah' (Media Release, 22 October 2014).

Jahoda, Gustav, 'Critical Reflections on Some Recent Definitions of "Culture"' (2012) 18(3) *Culture & Psychology* 289.

McMahon, William, 'Australian Aborigines: Commonwealth Policy and Achievement' (Statement by the Prime Minister, 26 January 1972).

McRae, Heather *et al.*, *Indigenous Legal Issues, Commentary and Materials* (Thomson Reuters, 2009).

Martin, David, 'Rethinking Aboriginal Community Governance' in Paul Smyth, Tim Reddel and Andrew Jones (eds), *Community and Local Governance in Australia* (University of New South Wales Press, 2005) 108.

Metherell, Mark, 'PM Backs Indigenous Enterprise', *The Sydney Morning Herald* (Sydney), 10 December 2004, 7.

Nettheim, Garth, Gary Meyers and Donna Craig, *Indigenous Peoples and Governance Structures: A Comparative Analysis of Land and Resource Management Rights* (Aboriginal Studies Press, 2002).

Perche, Diana, 'Indigenous Land Reform and the Market: Changing Social Constructions in Indigenous Land Policy during the Howard era' (Paper presented at Australian Political Studies Association Annual Conference, Macquarie University, Sydney, 30 September 2009).

Russell, Peter H., *Recognizing Aboriginal Title: the Mabo Case and Indigenous Resistance to English-Settler Colonialism* (University of Toronto Press, 2005).

Tangentyere Council, *Hidden Valley Community Centre* (2008) www.tangentyere. org.au/services/family_youth/towncamp_learning.

Trigger, David, 'Mining Projects in Remote Aboriginal Australia: Sites for the Articulation and Contestation of Economic and Cultural Features' in Diane Austin-Broos and Gaynor Macdonald (eds), *Culture, Economy and Governance in Aboriginal Australia* (Sydney University Press, 2005) 41.

Vanstone, Amanda, 'Beyond Conspicuous Compassion: Indigenous Australians Deserve More than Good Intentions' (Speech delivered to the Australia and New Zealand School of Government, Australian National University, Canberra, 7 December 2005).

Walker, Bruce, Douglas Porter and Ian Marsh, 'Fixing the Hole in Australia's Heartland: How Government Needs to Work in Remote Australia' (Desert Knowledge Australia, 2012).

Whitlam, Gough, 'It's Time for Leadership' (Speech delivered at Blacktown Civic Centre, Sydney, 13 November 1972).

Woodward, Edward, 'Aboriginal Land Rights Commission: Second Report' (Australian Government, 1974).

Legislation

Aboriginal Land Rights (Northern Territory) Act 1976 (Cth).
Native Title Act 1993 (Cth).

Cases

Mabo v Queensland (No. 2) (1992) 175 CLR 1.

2 Land reform
Theory, terminology and concepts

2.1 Introduction

In the last decade, a lot has been said about land reform and its potential to help or harm Aboriginal and Torres Strait Islander communities. It has often been argued that communal ownership of land and businesses has prevented economic development. Together with communal ownership of housing, it has been said, this has compounded the problem of welfare dependence in Indigenous communities. Often these statements have been made as if they were self-evident. But are they? Is it true that communal ownership is an impediment to economic development? More fundamentally, what do we mean when we describe something as communal ownership?

It turns out that this is not a straightforward question. It is clear that communal ownership – or more correctly, communal property – involves ownership by a group of people. But then so does ownership by a corporation, and corporate ownership is not seen an impediment to economic development. To the contrary, corporations are key enablers of growth and prosperity. So how is it that one form of collective ownership is seen as essential to economic development and another as inimical to it? Relatedly, it has been popular to characterise communal ownership of Indigenous land as a 'socialist experiment' and compare it to the failure of communism. But is communal property really the same thing as, or similar to, communism?

Then there is the concept of a commons. Many of us are familiar with the saying 'tragedy of the commons', a term made famous by Garrett Hardin. Where does this concept fit in? It might at first seem reasonable to associate a commons tragedy with communal property, but it turns out that this also is more involved. Yet another term that has appeared frequently in Australian Government publications is 'secure tenure'. Chapter 5 describes how for several years this came to be presented as a key aim of land reform, to some extent displacing the earlier aims of enabling individual ownership or private property. But what exactly is secure tenure? And how is it related to private property?

This chapter provides answers to these and related questions by setting out the meaning of key terminology and introducing some of the fundamentals of land reform theory. Somewhat surprisingly, it is the first time this has been done in the Australian context. Even though debate has been running – sometimes quietly, sometimes prominently – for more than 10 years, little attention has been paid to these questions. This has resulted in considerable confusion. Indeed, it has at times meant that the issues being contested in public forums are completely detached from the actual circumstances of Indigenous communities.

While the debate about Indigenous land reform in Australia is young, and has been relatively shallow, there has been a far longer discussion about land reform in international forums and in other countries, particularly developing countries. This has led to the creation of a large body of research on land reform, what I refer to here as the 'international literature' (in fact some contributors have been Australian, but writing about other countries). That international literature forms the basis for this chapter. Section 2.2 provides definitions for key land reform terminology, such as communal property, formalisation and tenure security. While the international literature is the source of these definitions, they are at times modified or developed so as to make them more applicable to a country such as Australia. Section 2.3 sets out two influential ideas or theories, partly to illustrate how the terminology from Section 2.2 is used. For example, the discussion of evolutionary theory makes clearer the relationship between property systems and particular forms of tenure.

Section 2.4 provides a more detailed analysis of the potential benefits and drawbacks of tenure systems providing for property rights with certain characteristics, particularly tenure security and alienability. Section 2.5 then combines the earlier sections to describe the potential consequences of particular types of land reform, and introduces further ways of distinguishing between reform types. This proves useful for clarifying how recent Australian reforms differ, for example, from historic reforms to indigenous land in the United States and New Zealand. Some concluding comments are made in Section 2.6.

One of the aims of this chapter is to provide a framework for talking about Indigenous land reform that goes beyond binaries. It separates out property systems (state property, communal property, private property and open access) from property features or characteristics (such as tenure security, alienability, individual and collective ownership). It also explains why, contrary to common perceptions, Indigenous land reform is not a simple choice between retaining distinct Indigenous forms of ownership and introducing mainstream forms of ownership. There are in fact several different starting points and a variety of reform options. The chapter sets out some of the theories that help in understanding the consequences of those different options.

26 *Theory, terminology and concepts*

2.2 Key terminology and concepts

Land reform

Like tax reform or welfare reform, the term land reform is very broad. It can include many different types of reform. At a general level it can be divided into two categories, land redistribution and land tenure reform. Land redistribution refers to a large-scale transfer of land ownership from one group of people to another. The introduction of Indigenous land rights in Australia might be thought of as an example of land redistribution, as it led to the return of areas of land to Indigenous people. Land tenure reform instead describes changes to the way in which land is owned (although, as will become apparent, this too can have redistributive consequences).[1] This book is concerned with land tenure reform, as the recent reforms to Indigenous land in Australia fall into this category. Land redistribution was historically the more common reform, and for some authors the term 'land reform' retains that more specific meaning.[2] For convenience, this book follows the common practice of using the term 'land reform' inclusively, to refer to either category.

Land tenure reform effects an alteration to 'property', that notoriously complex 'institution by means of which all societies regulate access to material resources'.[3] Narrowly defined, property can be understood as a system of rules that govern resource use. In another sense it is also broader than this. It is a social institution whose features are embedded in practice, such that people constantly 'make assumptions and claims, and defer to the claims of others, against a background in which the institution of property is taken for granted'.[4] Land reform, even where it is successful, does not directly alter property in this broader sense. It operates only at the level of rules, and changes to those rules will occur in a cultural context, certain elements of which are beyond the control of reformers.

In a modern property system, such as the Australian system, the most important feature of property is *property rights*: the rights of owners, and the corresponding duty of non-owners to respect those rights. This is not all there is to property. Even within the Australian system, the concept of property also includes elements of property as a responsibility, property as a reflection of the facts,[5] and property as jurisdiction.[6] As the description of Aboriginal land tenure in Chapter 3 illustrates, other property regimes provide for different forms of obligation, such as the responsibility to maintain sacred sites. It is, however, property rights that are the main focus of the literature on land reform in the context of development.

For a property right to be meaningfully described as a 'right' there must be a corresponding duty on others to observe it. This need not necessarily be a duty that arises under state law. It can also be a duty that arises under customary law, and even under 'informal social practices which enjoy social legitimacy at a given time and place'.[7] The element of legitimacy is important: it distinguishes what may be regarded as a property right, even an insecure or incomplete property right, from a mere privilege or claim.[8] This does not mean that all property rights are equal, or equally secure, as is discussed below.

Property regimes

State property, communal property, private property and open access

When the Australian Government first began implementing its recent reforms to Indigenous land ownership, it argued those reforms were required to support a shift from 'communal ownership' to 'individual ownership' or 'private property'. It was through the use of these and related terms that the reforms were debated; however, for the most part the terms themselves were left undefined.[9] This resulted in considerable confusion and harmed the conduct of debate. This section considers the meaning of these terms in some detail, and describes how they are more complex than they first appear.

The starting point for this discussion is the concept of 'property regimes'[10] or 'tenure systems'.[11] In modern typology, property regimes fall into four categories: state property, communal property, private property and non-property or open access.[12] Sometimes only three are referred to, particularly where communal property and non-property are conflated, a common mistake in some earlier literature.[13]

There is in fact some divergence in the way these terms are used. The meaning of state property and open access is relatively clear. State property describes circumstances where land is vested in a national, regional or local government, and where rules in relation to access and use are determined by a government agency.[14] Examples of state property include parks and reserves, as well as buildings such as Parliament House. Open access describes circumstances where no individual or group has the right to exclude others.[15] As Bromley notes, this is less a property regime than the absence of a regime.[16] Open access is often used to described the situation where property rights have not developed, the 'initial state of the world';[17] however, it is also remains the situation with respect to certain resources such as the atmosphere and the open sea. It also describes the circumstances that develop when all other property systems break down.[18]

It is the distinction between private property and communal property that causes the most confusion. During debate about land reform in Australia, the terms 'private property' and 'individual ownership' have often been used interchangeably. This is in effect one way of approaching the distinction: ownership of land by individuals or families might be regarded as private property, while ownership of land by a group can be treated as communal property. This approach has been used in some international

28 Theory, terminology and concepts

literature,[19] but proves limiting.[20] Other literature instead takes a systemic approach to the distinction, which is the approach preferred here.

This systemic approach is usefully summarised by van den Brink *et al.*, who state that under communal property 'individual rights are regulated by the community', while under private property 'individual rights are regulated by the state'.[21] This means that it is possible for private property to be owned collectively, provided that it is state law which regulates the rights of individual owners, and conversely it is possible to have individual ownership on communal property, provided that it is the community which regulates the rights of individual owners. This systemic approach is more useful as it allows the role of the state to be more clearly distinguished from the characteristics of a particular set of property rights. The significance of this is clarified below.

The allocation of rights to individuals is not just possible on communal property, it is also common. There are many places around the world where individuals and families are allocated relatively exclusive rights to use customary land for housing and agriculture. Adams *et al.* use the term 'the holding' to describe such allocations.[22] Holdings on customary land are not the equivalent of individual ownership on private property, as their content and boundaries are determined by customary law rather than the state. Below it is described how they also tend to be more contingent, overlapping and negotiated.

Conversely, collective ownership of private property is also widespread. A common example of this is referred to above, being where land is owned by, or through, a corporation. This raises an interesting issue. Chapter 3 describes how 'Aboriginal community living area land' in the Northern Territory is owned by incorporated associations, a corporate structure under which members have fluid rather than fixed rights. This is widely regarded as an example of communal property. Yet no one suggests that ownership of land by a corporation such as Rio Tinto is communal property. It is clearly private property. But why is that? This is not an esoteric question. There is something significant about the difference between these two forms of ownership. But what exactly is that difference? Extrapolating from the approach described by van den Brink *et al.*, the distinction might be characterised as follows: on collective private property, the rights of individual owners are fixed on acquisition and may be altered only by a transfer in accordance with state law; whereas on communal property, the rights of individual owners may be altered by the group.

Applying this approach to collective ownership in Australia results in land (or a business, etc) owned by a company or fixed trust being described as private property, with land owned by an incorporated association, Indigenous corporation, discretionary trust or a statutory land trust being described as communal property. This tends to accord with general understandings and also captures something useful. If individual rights can be altered by the group, they are an inherently different sort of right.

Theory, terminology and concepts 29

Property regimes may overlap

Having set out this approach to the definition of property regimes, it is necessary to problematise it a little. This is because, however well-defined, the four categories of property regime will always be 'ideal, analytic types'.[23] In practice, land may be subject to overlapping regimes, which may even be in competition. This might occur in two ways. First, in a legal system that provides for the layering of tenure through the grant of exclusive rights that are enforceable against the owner, such as a lease, one property regime may sit on top of another. Where, for example, Crown land is leased to a corporation or individual, for the duration of that lease there is a shift from state property towards private property. This is a common arrangement in some parts of Australia. It would clearly mislead to simply describe land subject to a 99-year or perpetual pastoral lease as 'state property'. Conversely, when a government agency takes a lease over private or communal land there is a shift towards state property. The *extent* of the shift will depend on the terms of the lease and whether the landowner retains some control over the allocation of rights and duties. The shorter and more restrictive the lease, the smaller the shift.

The second way in which property regimes overlap is where elements of two systems are combined. Strata title (as it is called in New South Wales) provides an example of this. Here, there are two slightly different regimes: the first with respect to apartments and the second for common areas. Apartments are mostly private property, although not entirely. The 'owners' corporation' can regulate some activities of individual owners even with respect to their own apartments, which introduces an element of communal property. In common areas the features of communal property are more pronounced.[24]

It is the first type of overlap that is most relevant to Indigenous land reform in Australia. The most common outcome of the reforms has been the grant of leases over Indigenous land to governments. This represents a shift towards state property rather than the introduction of individual ownership or private property, as was suggested during debate.

Private property rights

It is apparent from the above discussion that different types of rights might be found on both communal and private property: not just individual and collective rights, but also alienable and inalienable rights, exclusive and overlapping rights, etc. It is nevertheless common for the terms 'private property' and 'private property rights' to be used to refer to property with particular characteristics. A difficulty with this approach is that it is not clear exactly what constitutes 'private property'. Is it any land that is occupied relatively exclusively by an individual or family? Is it still private property where some access rights are shared? Or does private

30 *Theory, terminology and concepts*

property require something even more, such as a set of rights that are alienable?[25]

A further problem with this approach is that it conveys the impression that all private property has similar characteristics. In particular, it contributes to an impression that introducing private property means that everyone gets a fee simple or full ownership. This seems implicit in the frequent assertion during Australian debate about land reform that individual ownership or private property would enable businesses to obtain mortgages. However, many Australian businesses situated on private property do not own the land on which they operate. Leasing is widespread, and not all leases are in a form that can be mortgaged. As it turns out, the recent reforms to Aboriginal land in the Northern Territory also usually result in a form of leasehold that cannot be mortgaged.

In other words, it is better to identify the type of property rights on a case by case basis, rather than simply assume them from the property regime or tenure system.[26] Having said that, there is a significant difference in the types of property rights that different property regimes *tend* to enable. This is considered in the following section.

Customary and traditional ownership

In overseas literature the term 'customary ownership' is generally used in the same way that 'traditional ownership' is used in Australia: to describe ownership of land in accordance with customary laws. Customary ownership is treated as an example or subcategory of communal property, rather than a distinct category of property regime. Conversely, not all communal property is customary. Fitzpatrick draws a useful distinction between communal systems that are 'norm-based' and those that are based on a 'purely contractual coalition'.[27] Customary systems are often based on deep-seated norms, practices and beliefs, but as Fitzpatrick points out communal property can also arise on a more pragmatic or situational basis, such as in a squatter settlement. Below it is described how in some places there is in effect a combination of both.

Several authors note that terms such as 'customary tenure' are potentially misleading in that they imply the existence of a discrete, autonomous and perhaps unchanging indigenous system, whereas the nature and content of customary systems reflect their dynamic engagement with the state and with colonial processes.[28] References to customary tenure are nevertheless common, and it is frequently noted that issues with respect to customary tenure arise differently. One reason for this is that customary approaches to tenure can survive changes in the formal ownership system. Another is that forms of property tend to be different. On customary tenure, rights to land are often overlapping, and as such the interests of secondary or ancillary rights holders also need to be considered.[29] Perhaps more significantly, under customary tenure the rights of owners tend to be more contingent, negotiated and connected to ongoing compliance with social obligations. Fourie argues that their negotiated nature is one of the defining characteristics of customary tenure.[30] As described in Chapter 3, similar observations have been made of Aboriginal land tenure in Australia, although the context for those observations takes some understanding.

Commons and anticommons

A useful place to finish this discussion of property regimes is with Hardin's oft-quoted 'tragedy of the commons', which predicts that resources used in common will inevitably be overexploited in the long term.[31] The presence of a commons is sometimes conflated with communal property. It has alternatively been argued that the tragedy of the commons is better described as the 'tragedy of open access'.[32] This is more accurate, in that open access land is a commons, but it is not the only situation in which a commons can occur. A commons is an access arrangement rather than a property regime, and commons can and frequently do occur on state property and private property, as well as on communal property and open access land. Parks and reserves are very much a commons, which in Australia are mostly situated on state land. Not all commons are beset by tragedy, and since Hardin wrote his seminal essay on the topic our understanding of when a 'commons tragedy' can occur has improved considerably.[33]

While it was mentioned by several authors during public debate,[34] and may have been thought of by others, Hardin's 'tragedy of the commons' is of little relevance to the recent Australian reforms to Indigenous land. That is because those reforms have focused on the land inside residential communities, which for the most part is not a commons. Nearly all land and infrastructure has been allocated to particular individuals, families and organisations, albeit that, as Chapter 4 describes, this previously occurred under informal arrangements. So while it is an interesting topic in itself, this book has nothing more to say about commons tragedies.

More relevant to Indigenous land reform in Australia is what is known as an 'anticommons', where too many people have the ability to prevent a development or activity.[35] Where an anticommons exists, the potential tragedy is underinvestment rather than overexploitation. To prevent this form of tragedy, it is important to ensure that certain decision-making with respect to the use of community land is not fragmented. This is discussed further in Chapter 8.

Land tenure, secure tenure and insecure tenure

An interesting feature of public discussion about Indigenous land reform in Australia is that there was a shift in the language used by the Australian

32 *Theory, terminology and concepts*

Government once implementation of the reforms themselves commenced. Rather than the introduction of 'individual ownership', the reforms instead came to be characterised as the creation of 'secure tenure'. While this term has been used widely, with various positive features ascribed to it, it has again been left undefined. Consequently, in Australia the term 'secure tenure' has been used in a manner that is both internally inconsistent and at odds with its use in the international literature.[36]

When properly defined, tenure security is a foundational land reform concept. A succinct definition was provided by AusAID – the Australian Government aid agency – in a 2008 publication about customary land in the Pacific. They described tenure security as 'the certainty that a person's rights to land will be protected'.[37] There are several other definitions used in the literature, including some that more narrowly focus on state protection of rights.[38] This latter approach, however, can elide the important distinction between formality of a tenure system and security of tenure and give the impression that only formal rights can be secure. This is not the case: well-functioning informal tenure systems often provide a high level of tenure security, despite a lack of government involvement. This has tended to be true of Aboriginal communities in the Northern Territory.[39] Conversely, property rights might be legally protected but contested at a local level in a way that makes references to security illusory.

The broader definition is better because it is more consistent with the understanding that tenure security is something that is experienced, 'a matter of perception based on past experiences and world views' rather than some objectively determined status.[40] This is inherent in the way the concept is used. Several of the benefits that are predicted to flow from more secure tenure relate to the property holder's incentives, which means that in order to be effective tenure security must be felt and believed.[41] For example, if you do not believe your rights are secure you will be reluctant to make improvements.

Tenure formality

Formal tenure, informal tenure and formalisation

The next concept of significance to the book is that of tenure formality. Chapter 4 describes how communities on Aboriginal land in the Northern Territory are better described as *informal settlements*, or examples of *informal tenure*, rather than of communal property. To understand why this is the case, it is first necessary to understand what is meant by terms such as formal tenure, informal tenure and formalisation.

Tenure formality describes the extent to which tenure arrangements are defined by or come under the regulation of state law. There is overlap, and indeed alignment, between this and the definition of property regimes described above, a matter returned to below. While this focus on state legal integration is shared by several authors,[42] it is not universal. For example, van den Brink *et al.* argue that the term informality 'carries with it a vision of squatters on state lands outside Lima'. However, 'Unlike a squatter in Lima or Dar Es Salaam, the African landholder in most rural areas does not hold land informally, but according to an *alternative formality*, a community-based formality.'[43] Here, the authors take a broader approach to the concept of formality. They do so for the purpose of emphasising the existence of alternative systems of property. Their point is well made: the word 'informal' can convey a sense of inferiority or absence, which is unfortunate. However, the problem with including 'alternative formalities' within the definition of 'formal tenure' is that it would be at odds with the way in which the term 'formalisation' is used. Generally 'formalisation' is used to describe an increase in the involvement of state law, rather than, for example, an increase in the ambit of a customary system.

Informal tenure systems and informal settlements

The above quotation from van den Brink *et al.* has also been included to demonstrate a second practice with respect to the concept of formality. The term 'informality' can be used with respect to both land ownership ('African landholders') and a set of occupancy arrangements ('squatters in Lima'). Because informality is defined negatively, as an absence of formality, the same word is generally used without distinction with respect to both informal systems of ownership (*informal tenure systems*) and to circumstances where the relationship between landowners and occupiers is informal (*informal settlements*). While there is a relationship between these two types of informality, they are not synonymous, and the distinction is important. To understand this distinction, it is necessary to return to the four categories of property regime that are set out above.

Both private property and state property are of their nature *formal tenure systems*, as they are created and regulated by state law. Conversely open access is of its nature informal, as it is not subject to any form of regulation, state or otherwise. Communal property, on the other hand, can occur at different levels of formality.[44] It might be entirely informal, or recognised by the state only to the extent that the law establishes a 'tenurial shell' beyond which it plays no role.[45] Alternatively the ownership system might be regulated to some extent through the appointment of agents, incorporation or the establishment of land boards.[46] Chapter 3 describes how Aboriginal land in the Northern Territory tends to be relatively formalised, although different land has been formalised in very different ways.

An *informal settlement* instead describes those circumstances where the relationship between the landowner(s) and occupier(s) has not been formally defined. An informal settlement can occur on any type of property regime, including private or state property. There are millions of people living in different types of informal settlements all over the world, and

34 *Theory, terminology and concepts*

those settlements can be grouped and categorised in several different ways.[47] A description of those categories is not essential to this book; what is more important is to understand the variety of potential relationships between landowners and occupiers in informal settlements.

The relationship between landowners and occupiers in an informal settlement

The sometimes complex relationship between occupiers and landowners in informal settlements is best illustrated through the use of examples. The first is of a village on customary land in sub-Saharan Africa, where housing areas are allocated to particular families. Here, it is the customary land ownership system itself that determines the rights and duties of occupiers. As such there is no need to differentiate between land ownership and tenure arrangements in the village. The two are effectively one and the same, and the village itself can be described as 'customary tenure' or 'communal property'.

However, this is something of a special case rather than the norm. A second example of an informal settlement is a squatter settlement on state land in Peru. Here the situation is very different. The rights and duties of individual occupiers are determined not by the land ownership system, but by the arrangements that occupiers develop between themselves. The land ownership system is not irrelevant; to the contrary, the fact that squatters do not own the land can be of enormous consequence. However, describing such a settlement as 'state property' would mislead. In the informal settlement itself, the property regime is better described as a type of communal property, of the type that Fitzpatrick categorises as a 'purely contractual coalition' rather than a 'norm-based system'.[48]

In other places the situation is more complex yet. Between these two examples, there are situations where different elements are combined. For example, there are urban settlements in South Africa where elements of 'customary tenure' have emerged among squatters on state or private land, not because the land traditionally belonged to them, rather because certain customary norms have informed their approach to property. Thus, for example, Barry describes how an 'indigenous social land ethic' contributes to the tenure arrangements developed by the immigrant Xhosa-speaking residents of the Marconi Beam squatter settlement.[49]

Conversely, there are places where customary land has come under the occupation of outsiders. The resulting informal settlement may in part reflect the terms on which the land has been acquired from customary owners (to the extent that this had been voluntary or negotiated) as well as the arrangements that settlers have developed between themselves. This is technically a form of communal property, but simply describing it as such occludes the fact that there are two groups or 'communities', whose interests may be in conflict.

Theory, terminology and concepts 35

There are three points that emerge from this discussion. The first is that it is important in some circumstances to distinguish between the land ownership system and the tenure arrangements in an informal settlement. The two are not always one and the same. Second, the nature of the informal tenure arrangements in a particular settlement need to be investigated, they cannot be assumed. And third, it is not the case that land ownership is either determinative or irrelevant. There are circumstances between, where land ownership can be one part of a complex tenure environment.

Chapter 4 describes how this has been the case in communities on Aboriginal land in the Northern Territory. Those communities are unlike the example of a village on customary land, in that they are not simply a manifestation of the underlying land ownership system. They are also unlike the squatter settlement on state land, in that underlying ownership is one element of the way in which tenure arrangements have been developed at a community level. And it is those tenure arrangements, rather than 'communal ownership', that are the real starting point for the recent reforms.

2.3 Two influential ideas

This section describes two influential ideas in relation to land reform. The description is necessarily brief, and not all of their complexity is captured. It is nevertheless useful, partly because both ideas have been referred to during debate about the Australian reforms (particularly de Soto's theories), but also because this discussion illustrates how the terminology set out in Section 2.2 is used in practice and sheds some light on certain of the major themes and divisions in the international literature on land reform.

Evolutionary theory

The first idea is that of the evolution of property rights.[50] As originally formulated, evolutionary theory was used to explain the emergence of property in circumstances where it purportedly did not exist.[51] In more recent literature, it instead tends to be used to explain two separate developments: first, the shift towards certain types of property rights within a system, usually on communal property; and second, the shift towards greater formality, and potentially the transition from communal property to private property.[52]

The shift towards certain types of property rights

Evolutionary theory predicts that changes in certain conditions, such as an increase in population density, changes in the technology of production, or an increase in demand for outputs, will create pressure for the emergence

36 Theory, terminology and concepts

of more clearly demarcated, secure, individualised and alienable property rights.[53] As these developments are common, the evolutionary approach is generally used to explain the move *towards* property rights with these characteristics. However, the evolutionary approach has also been used to explain the retention of more collective or flexible forms of ownership in some circumstances,[54] and even their reintroduction in others.[55]

There are two preconceptions underlying the idea of evolving property rights: that for each set of circumstances there is a corresponding set of economically optimal tenure arrangements,[56] and that under the right conditions a property system will evolve towards those arrangements. However, the development of property rights is 'not just a matter of relative prices and transactions costs', it is also 'the result of political or social processes'.[57] For some authors, the impact of political and social processes is used to explain why economically optimal arrangements do not evolve more often.[58] More fundamental is the question of whether it is possible to disentangle an ideal form of property from the 'warp and woof of social and economic struggle'.[59] Development entails decisions about entitlement allocation, growth direction, the balancing of rights, and even 'what is considered to be valuable to protect'.[60] References to ideal models can be used to disguise the impact of decision-making, or skew it in favour of certain groups.[61]

Further, a change in circumstances can lead to communal property systems breaking down rather than evolving.[62] This might simply be the result of invasion,[63] or the external imposition of self-serving arrangements such as was common during colonisation.[64] Even where there is no invasion, an increase in dealings with outsiders can undermine the normative system on which customary regimes depend. It has been noted that more than the development of secure or individualised rights, the form of property rights that customary systems most resist is rights that are alienable beyond the group.[65] To some extent this is constitutional, in that underlying group ownership is a 'defining characteristic of customary tenure', and 'allowing the permanent transfer of land to outsiders formally and definitively ends the customary tenure regime'.[66] Yet even dealings short of permanent alienation will have an impact on customary tenure. An increase in demand for access to land can lead to higher levels of disputation, straining the capacity of customary governance mechanisms,[67] while at the same time the group's ability to impose sanctions might be weakened.[68]

An increase in dealings with outsiders may change not only land-use practices but also the way that *transactions* are conceived of. This has been explained by reference to what Demsetz calls 'compactness'.[69] Within a sufficiently small group, personal benefit is highly dependent on social relations, including societal esteem, reciprocal kinship obligations, neighbourly goodwill and the well-being of the community. This is reflected in the way that transactions occur. In dealings with strangers, personal benefit has a narrower meaning, and there is greater emphasis on price.[70] An increase in price-based dealings with strangers can also alter the balance of self-interest within the group.[71] It can lead to rights in relation to land becoming commoditised, and those who stand to gain from asserting exclusionary rights might attempt to 'defect' from the communal system.[72]

There is a converse side to 'compactness' that Demsetz does not specifically address: in some cases, local norms such as kinship obligations will survive the introduction of new property forms, although it may be in an altered form. For example, Platteau observes that the retention of kinship norms has in some places prevented land from becoming commoditised in the sense that reformers intended.[73] The relevance of this to the Australian reforms will be made clear. There are kinship and sharing norms in Aboriginal communities that will survive the introduction of reforms and interact with any new forms of property that are created, such as home ownership.

Increased formalisation and the role of governments

At its most optimistic, evolutionary theory predicts that demand for formal property rights will grow as new forms of property emerge that are better suited to state-based law than community-based norms.[74] For example, where there is an increase in property dealings with strangers, people may request the assistance of legal institutions to enforce agreements.[75] Or as land becomes more valuable, there may be an increase in demand for a more systematic demarcation of boundaries.[76] Less optimistic accounts suggest the potential for a deterioration in norms and an increase in inequality and conflict.[77] In either case, where there is demand from the group for more formal property rights, it is more likely to be uneven and contested than universal.[78]

Even where there is demand for formal property rights from within the group, the state will not necessarily be willing and able to supply them. Only under naive or ideal models can governments be portrayed as capable, responsive and coherent decision-makers who simply carry out the 'will of the people'.[79] In practice, the motivations of governments are more complex.[80] Particularly in developing countries, the supply of formal property rights will also be limited by the financial and institutional capacity of government bodies.[81] In Australia, while government bodies tend to be relatively capable, the development of policies for Aboriginal people takes place in a highly politicised sphere. This is reflected in the way land reform has been introduced.

Relevantly to Australia, while changes in economic conditions may lead to pressure for new forms of property, 'the causality does not automatically run the other way: introducing formal and individualized property rights in situations where economic conditions do not make such rights efficient can be a waste of resources'.[82] Platteau goes further, arguing that

38   *Theory, terminology and concepts*

'premature' intervention can itself be a cause of failure.[83] Where property institutions are instead able to act responsively, then causality can flow both ways,[84] creating a 'virtuous cycle' of economic growth and further development.[85]

Hernando de Soto: The Mystery of Capital

Hernando de Soto's book *The Mystery of Capital* is the most well-known work on land reform of recent times.[86] As well as attracting the attention of several world leaders,[87] de Soto's ideas have influenced key international organisations,[88] and have been the subject of considerable academic debate.[89] De Soto has also been referred to on several occasions in relation to Aboriginal land reform in Australia,[90] although it is not always clear from those references that his theories are well understood.[91]

De Soto argues that informal tenure arrangements keep people poor because they prevent property from being used as 'capital'. He acknowledges that some informal systems deliver very secure forms of tenure, and can do so efficiently, but says that this alone is insufficient.[92] Where land ownership takes place through a formal and integrated system that allows its value to be represented abstractly in a reliable manner, it can be transformed into something more than just a physical asset. It is able to take on a parallel life as 'capital', in which it can be used as collateral for a loan, security for business dealings or a reliable basis on which to deliver services. In short, where land can be used as capital it is more useful to its owner and society. Conversely, those people whose land is held informally are at a competitive disadvantage.

One of de Soto's contributions has been to expand on earlier arguments as to why a formal and integrated property system might support wealth creation.[93] For example, he has emphasised the role of property as a means for making people accountable to strangers.[94] This can enable transactions that were previously considered too risky, or enable other transactions to take place at a lower cost. This requires that property rights are transferable or alienable. At a time when there had been a shift away from a singular focus on 'market-based tenures',[95] de Soto has provided additional arguments as to why they should play a central role in land reform policy.[96]

There are, however, some 'quite obvious but puzzling blank spots' in de Soto's work.[97] He fails to acknowledge that his version of formalising squatter settlements on other people's land involves not just legal recognition but a transfer of ownership.[98] He appears to attribute landlessness among the poor solely to government inaction, ignoring the role of land markets in disenfranchisement.[99] And as described in Section 2.4, the empirical evidence in relation to the benefits of collateralisation is weaker than he reports, and the risks are greater than he suggests.

De Soto also has a tendency to present all informal tenure in straightforward terms, including customary tenures. He frequently references an anecdote from a trip to Bali, where he was walking through some rice fields and was able to tell when he crossed from one person's land to the next because a different dog would bark.[100] As Rose notes, this story neatly captures the sort of tenure arrangements that de Soto has in mind when presenting his theories: rights based on exclusive possession, similar to and compatible with Western-style property rights.[101] It is this representation that allows de Soto to characterise formalisation as an integration of 'the people's law',[102] rather than the creation of new tenure arrangements.[103] This is significant, as one of de Soto's key messages is that, in order to be effective, formalisation must reflect the existing 'social contract' and reforms that introduce new arrangements from the top down will continue to fail.[104] This suggests that, by his own logic, de Soto's theories are less applicable to complex tenures.[105]

What is perhaps more problematic than the gaps in his arguments is the grandness of the vision that de Soto presents. There is a quiet, pedestrian logic to much land reform theory, often based on the impact of property rights on abilities and incentives – such as the common observation that tenure insecurity is a disincentive to investment. De Soto goes further than this, arguing that enabling land to be used as capital will unlock a dormant potential, with ongoing benefits that fall outside a standard cost–benefit analysis.[106] His invocation of the 'mystery' of capital appears to explain some of his work's broad appeal, as well as the extent to which he has been singled out for criticism.

2.4 Types of property rights

This section considers the consequences of tenure systems providing for, or failing to provide for, property rights with certain features or characteristics. The first of these is tenure security, which, as described above, refers to 'the certainty that a person's rights to land will be protected'.[107] The second is alienability, or the ability of rights holders to transfer their property to others. Tenure security and alienability are the characteristics most relevant to a discussion of Indigenous land reform in Australia and so are given the most attention here. There is a briefer discussion of the benefits and drawbacks of individual and collective ownership, and the trade-off between consistency and flexibility.

The discussion provided here is relevant not just to the question of whether there were problems with the tenure arrangements in communities on Aboriginal land prior to the recent reforms, but also to the question of what the reforms should be trying to do. Particularly important is the question of whether the reforms should attempt to introduce alienable forms of tenure. Due to the way land reform has been debated in Australia, this issue has received very little research attention.

40 *Theory, terminology and concepts*

Tenure security

The benefits of an increase in tenure security are several, manifold and relatively uncontroversial. There is no downside to an increase in tenure security for the person or persons who experience it, only the potential for benefit. However, that potential depends on the extent to which tenure insecurity was previously an issue. This can be difficult to assess. There is no simple test for tenure security, and it includes subjective elements that are not easily ascertained.[108] For example, there might be several factors at play that make it difficult to isolate the role of tenure insecurity in contributing to underinvestment. Tenure insecurity may also stem from different causes. A squatter might experience insecurity because the informal system for the allocation of rights is unstable, or instead because of the prospect of eviction by the landowner. Addressing the wrong cause will be ineffective.[109]

The most commonly noted problem with tenure insecurity is its impact on investment: if a land user is not confident of reaping the benefits of an investment, they may refrain from making it.[110] Different types of investment require different *levels* of security. Clear and reliable landowner permission may be sufficient to repair or improve a house or plant a crop, but the installation of expensive technology will require a greater level of assurance.[111] Different investments also require different *forms* of tenure. It is useful here to distinguish between tenure security and the length and breadth of a property right.[112] A property right might be secure but for too short a period, or be too narrow in scope for a particular form of investment. In addition to being sufficiently secure, the form of tenure must be 'incentive compatible'.[113]

Somewhat counter-intuitively, in some circumstances tenure insecurity can be an incentive to invest. Several authors describe occupiers making improvements to land as a means of demonstrating their claim or shoring up their position.[114] This can be inefficient, in that it results in limited resources being diverted from more productive investments to the protection of tenure. However, the use of tenure insecurity to promote investment is not always seen negatively. A common practice of governments around the world has been to require landowners to make or maintain certain improvements in order to retain or convert their rights to land.[115] This is an example of tenure insecurity being used as an additional investment incentive, on the understanding that this is beneficial rather than inefficient.[116] In the same way, customary tenure systems may be structured to reward individual endeavour.[117]

Insecure tenure can also impede people's ability to leave land unattended. This might restrict their movement, making it more difficult to obtain employment.[118] More generally, where tenure arrangements are insecure it can result in ongoing contestation, causing conflict, social disruption and predatory behaviour.[119] Even where there is no overt conflict, tenure insecurity can lead to individuals being required to expend energy and resources on maintaining their rights.[120] A reduction in conflict and contestation is an end in itself, but it can also result in resources being used more productively.[121]

It is relevant to the Australian context to note that certain of these benefits relate specifically to housing, while others could apply equally to the occupation of land and infrastructure by organisations and enterprises. For example, the improvements in workforce participation in Peru that Field identifies are based on her study of housing arrangements.[122] Where reforms do not lead to more secure housing, those particular benefits will not be available. This is relevant because in most cases the Australia reforms have led to less, rather than more, secure housing, for reasons described in later chapters.

This leads to a final and important issue with respect to tenure security. While there is no downside to an increase in tenure security for those who experience it, an increase for one person or group may result in a reduction in tenure security or access to land for others.[123] It is consequently important to consider not just whether tenure needs to be more secure, but also *for whom*.[124] So for Indigenous communities in Australia, the question is not just whether tenure is secure, but for whom it should be more secure. This is closely related to the allocation of rights under formalisation, which is considered below.

Alienability and land markets

Well-developed *informal* land markets have been observed in many places around the world, including in some places on customary land.[125] They have, however, not previously been observed in communities on Indigenous land in Australia. Nor for the most part have the recent reforms led to the creation of land markets, primarily because they have not resulted in the creation of marketable forms of tenure.[126] The discussion in this section provides the tools for considering whether and when the Australian reforms *should* provide for alienable tenure. It has been argued, for example, that the 'main goal' of Indigenous land reform should be the 'creation of a long-term property market'.[127] This section helps understand why that is not always the case.

The realisability effect

Where land can be bought and sold, improvements to the land may be reflected in an increase in its market value. Depending on the size of the increase, owners may recoup the costs of making the improvement, or a meaningful proportion of those costs. This can lead to an increase in investment pursuant to what has been called the 'realisability effect'.[128] Whether the realisability effect will be observed depends on both the type

42 *Theory, terminology and concepts*

of improvement and the nature of the market, the latter being particularly relevant to reforms in remote Indigenous communities. A more contained version of the realisability effect might occur when owners have the right to devise their property to family, even where there is no broader land market.

Collateralisation

Where land can be traded in a manner that allows for it to be used as collateral for a loan, it can provide landowners with additional access to credit. For theorists such as de Soto, this is an issue of considerable importance.[129] A useful critique of this aspect of de Soto's work is provided by Woodruff. He points out that for the benefits predicted by de Soto to be realised, not only does land need to be transformed into collateral, collateral must be transformed into credit, and credit transformed into income.[130] He argues that each of these transformations is subject to 'leakage'.[131] With respect to the transformation from collateral into credit, there might be both 'demand' and 'supply' reasons why credit does not increase. On the supply side, credit markets might still be underdeveloped,[132] and credit-providing institutions might remain reluctant to lend, particularly to applicants on a low income.[133] On the demand side, poor landowners might be reluctant to put their land at risk,[134] might be distrustful of the security process,[135] or there may be a lack of information about the available options.[136] As a result, several authors describe the empirical impact of land reform on credit supply as either modest or disappointing.[137]

There have been varied outcomes with respect to the transformation of credit into income. This transformation itself has two parts: it first requires that credit is used to fund investments, and, second, requires that those investments result in an increase in productivity. Some authors have noted that there is a high possibility of credit being used to fund consumption rather than investment.[138] Where credit is used to fund consumption, there will be no increase in productivity, only an increased risk that land will be forfeited.[139] However, the use of credit to fund consumption is not necessarily or always a bad thing: the credit supply may also provide a buffer that enables the landowner to survive a shock, thereby avoiding a permanent loss of land through distressed sale. Where credit is used to fund investment, its effectiveness will depend on the availability of suitable investments that actually increase productivity. Woodruff himself concludes that there will in some circumstances be better ways of increasing access to credit than collateralisation programmes.[140]

As well as being risky, reforms to enable collateralisation can be among the most expensive. Deininger concludes that 'where effective demand for credit exists' then reforms that enable collateralisation can have several benefits, but that 'in situations where the credit effect associated with title

Theory, terminology and concepts 43

is unlikely to materialize in the near future' there should be a 'more gradual and lower-cost approach to securing land rights and improving tenure security'.[141]

The framework provided by Woodruff proves particularly helpful for considering the real benefits of collateralisation in the context of Indigenous communities. It has been frequently argued that Indigenous land ownership restricts economic development because it cannot be mortgaged. This argument, which is intuitively appealing, is only partly accurate. While most Indigenous land cannot be mortgaged, it is usually possible to grant long-term leases that can be mortgaged. More important is the question of whether collateralisation will actually be useful. This is given much closer consideration in Chapter 8.

Market allocation

Where property rights are freely alienable, they can be bought and sold in a market place, which means that instead of property being allocated centrally, by a local authority or by group norms and processes, it is allocated through the outcome of individual transactions. This can have several consequences. Market theory predicts that over time land will be transferred to those persons who are able to make the most efficient use out of it.[142] However, this theory is based on certain market assumptions that are not always borne out in practice. Markets are subject to various forms of failure that can prevent shifts towards efficiency, such as land banking, information asymmetry and credit market imperfections.[143] The existing allocation of property will also have an impact.[144] Where pre-existing arrangements give authority or privilege to particular groups, they may use this to further consolidate their position.[145] As such, Kennedy argues that there is a 'premium on getting it as close to right as possible whenever the opportunity for reallocation arises'.[146] This too is relevant to the allocation of rights under formalisation, discussed below.

In some cases land markets, particularly rental markets, can enable those with little or no land to gain greater access.[147] On the other hand, land markets can instead lead to more concentrated ownership and a reduction in equity.[148] This may in fact reflect a more efficient overall allocation, particularly where there have been changes in the technology of production.[149] Where land is allocated more efficiently, overall production increases and the benefits of this can flow through to non-owners who may find, for example, that their labour is more valued.[150] However, overall efficiency is only one part of the complex role played by land ownership. Inequitable ownership can result in disharmony and conflict, particularly in communities where egalitarianism has previously been valued.[151] It has also been argued that a certain level of equality is required for the development of effective democratic government.[152] Further, the move towards market allocation may disenfranchise women, as markets are not

44 *Theory, terminology and concepts*

necessarily gender-neutral.[153] On the other hand, neither is centralised allocation necessarily gender-neutral. One of the arguments for market allocation is that it can reduce an avenue for corruption and maladministration.[154]

As this discussion indicates, one of the more contentious issues in the land reform literature is the question of whether or in what circumstances land markets are considered more helpful than harmful.[155] This is of some relevance to Australian reforms. It would be naive, and ultimately harmful, to simply introduce land markets and rely on them to best meet the tenure needs of Indigenous communities. The introduction of marketable tenure needs to be more considered and more targeted.

Individual and collective ownership

It is described above how the issue of individual and collective ownership is separate to that of communal and private property or formal and informal tenure. There can be individual ownership on communal property or under informal tenure arrangements, just as there can be collective ownership on private property and under formal tenure arrangements. As will become increasingly clear, this is a point of some significance to the Australian reforms. While they were debated on the basis that they would enable 'individual ownership', and in particular individual ownership of enterprises, this has not been their outcome. Instead, formal rights have been granted to the same collectively owned enterprises that have always operated in Aboriginal communities.

The question of whether the reforms *should* favour the introduction of individual ownership is complex. This is one area where only limited assistance is available from the international literature, beyond clarifying the concepts. Individual ownership is frequently described as being more efficient because there is better alignment between incentives and control over resources and because decisions can be made more quickly.[156] Expressed in these terms, the argument is somewhat misleading. In developed economies, the use of collective ownership (through corporate bodies) is widespread.[157] Conversely several authors note that there are circumstances where collective ownership can be more efficient, provided that the ownership structure is well-functioning.[158] However, arguments for the introduction of individual ownership in Australia are based on a broader set of concerns, not just efficiency. This is to do with the complex issue of avoiding harmful welfare, which is explored in later chapters.

Consistency and flexibility

Where property rights are consistent, they are easier to predict and more easily understood, particularly for those unfamiliar with local circumstances. This makes it easier for a property dealing to occur with a wider

Theory, terminology and concepts   45

range of people at a lower cost.[159] There can, however, be a trade-off between consistency and flexibility. In some places, flexible practices developed under customary law can be the most efficient and best adapted to local conditions.[160] For example, on arid country where rainfall is irregular, herders may be better served by a tenure system that allows them to negotiate variable movement over large areas rather than each having clearer rights over a small area.[161] The flexibility exhibited by customary tenure can also have an insurance function, by ensuring some access to land for those who are in need.[162] However, that same flexibility can also be used to exclude or marginalise those who are socially or politically weak, such as widows or outsiders.[163] As Fourie puts it, customary systems can be 'anti-poor' in some places but 'pro-poor' in others.[164]

Flexibility does not necessarily equate to uncertainty, particularly for participants. In a stable set of informal arrangements, outcomes can be negotiated in a manner that participants experience as reliable. However, too much variability is likely to lead to uncertainty, which undermines the security and usefulness of people's property rights and increases the risk of conflict or predatory behaviour. The most relevant point for the Australian reforms is that the functionality of informal tenure arrangements, and their suitability for the circumstances in which they operate, needs to be investigated. It should not be assumed that informal arrangements equate to uncertainty.

2.5 Types of land tenure reform

There is of course no single type of land reform. There is a variety of potential reforms, each with their own purpose and their own set of risks and benefits. This has not always been made clear during debate about land reform in Australia, with the consequence that both the risks and benefits of reform have been articulated with a variety of quite different reforms in mind. This section describes some of the different types of land tenure reform – in particular formalisation, and its varieties – as well as some of their potential consequences.

Formalisation

Types of formalisation

Formalisation refers to any process that results in a shift from informal to more formal tenure; that is, towards greater regulation of tenure by the state legal system. This captures a broad array of reforms. To take just a few examples: in some areas of Mozambique and Tanzania, formalisation has involved the state giving legal protection to the usufruct rights of customary land users, but retaining underlying ownership of the land.[165] The *Land Act 1998* (Uganda) provides for the issuing of single titles to villages,

46 *Theory, terminology and concepts*

leaving the allocation of internal rights to the village.[166] In Dakar, Senegal, informal occupants of urban slums are given 'superficies rights', a kind of registered leasehold.[167] In Peru, the occupiers of informal settlements on the fringes of cities such as Lima have been granted freehold titles.[168] In Botswana, authority over traditional land has been transferred from tribal chiefs to district and subdistrict Land Boards.[169]

These are all examples of formalisation, but they each involve very different processes with very different consequences. Part of the purpose of this section is to clarify how different types of formalisation can be distinguished, so that the exact nature of the Australian reforms can be better understood. While they have been, for the most part, a type of formalisation, they are very different from the issuing of titles to villages in Uganda or freehold to settlers in Peru. The discussion below makes clear how they are different and where they fit in.

Formalisation of an informal tenure system

Above it is described how informal tenure can refer to an *informal tenure system* or an *informal settlement*. One consequence of this distinction is that formalisation can mean something different in each case. Formalisation of a land tenure system describes increased legal regulation of the ownership system itself, such as the introduction of Land Boards in Botswana. Formalisation of a tenure system usually occurs at the point of recognition or grant. Chapter 3 describes how different approaches have been taken to the formalisation of Aboriginal land ownership in the Northern Territory, and some of the consequences of this. However, the focal point for recent reforms has been communities on Aboriginal land. These communities themselves are a type of informal settlement, and so the discussion here concentrates on the formalisation of informal settlements.

Formalisation of an informal settlement: endogenous and exogenous formalisation

The formalisation of an informal settlement results in greater regulation or definition of the relationship between landowners and occupiers, through the grant of a lease or other legal interest. There is still a variety of programmes within this category. They can be distinguished from each other by such matters as the type of rights that are granted (alienable or inalienable, short- or long-term, etc) and the basis on which they are granted (group membership, length of occupation, conformity with planning norms, etc).[170] One particularly important ground for distinguishing between programmes is the nature and extent of government involvement in the formalisation process. Particularly on communal property, the formalisation process might occur in two quite distinct ways. The state can either enable landowners to formalise the rights of occupiers or it can undertake the role itself. In the former instance, landowners are provided with the legal machinery to determine how formal rights will be allocated. The most obvious example is where landowners are given the ability to grant leases over their land. Where the landowners themselves control the formalisation process, it might be described as 'endogenous formalisation'.

Alternatively, the government might intervene by itself determining the eligibility criteria for the grant of formal rights, or deciding how those rights should be allocated to occupiers. The level of government intervention might vary from supervision through collaboration to exclusive control. To the extent that the state does control the formalisation process, it might be described as 'exogenous formalisation'. These are ideal types; in practice a formalisation programme is likely to have both endogenous and exogenous elements.

This is useful for clarifying one of the distinguishing features of the recent Australian reforms, particularly reforms in the Northern Territory. In most residential communities, endogenous formalisation was always possible but rarely occurred. The effect of recent reforms has been to create greater pressure for formalisation to occur, to the point where in some cases the Australian Government has effectively made formalisation mandatory. This makes the Northern Territory reforms very different, in their purpose and consequence, from reforms that instead simply enable formalisation to occur.

Formalisation and the allocation of legal rights

At its most basic, the outcome of formalisation is the creation and allocation of formal property rights. Some of the benefits and risks of formal rights – as compared to informal rights – are discussed further below. This section first considers issues that can arise out of the formalisation process itself, particularly with respect to allocation.

A good starting point is to acknowledge that formalisation is never just a change of form.[171] Whether it is deliberate or unintentional, minor or significant, formalisation will always result in an alteration of the existing arrangements. In some cases, formalisation results in a fundamental shift. For example, the formalisation of a squatter settlement on state land involves the reallocation of property rights from the landowner to settlers. Where such a programme includes the grant of freehold titles there is a complete transfer of ownership, which, as Peñalver notes, effectively makes it a redistributive reform.[172]

Particularly on a tenure system that includes customary elements, formal property rights will usually be more exclusive and defined than the informal rights they replace. This simplification will result in the creation of winners and losers, and secondary or ancillary rights holders are particularly vulnerable to loss.[173] Formalisation can also exacerbate or entrench existing inequalities.[174] Several authors note that poorly

48 *Theory, terminology and concepts*

implemented programmes have institutionalised the marginalised position of women, although more targeted and responsive programmes may instead improve their position.[175]

The formalisation process can also give rise to conflict, or bring latent conflicts to the surface.[176] Further, whether endogenous or exogenous the formalisation process may be open to manipulation by local elites or influential outsiders.[177] And where formalisation results in a significant shift or reallocation of rights, it can lead to normative pluralism with the consequent risk of confusion and conflict.[178] Several of these issues are less significant where the existing informal tenure arrangements are already more akin to the 'Western-style' property rights that de Soto predicts.

This discussion indicates the importance of clearly identifying the nature of existing arrangements prior to undertaking formalisation, and of catering for the needs of vulnerable groups during the formalisation process. The next section deals with the situation where the process has been completed and formal rights allocated. In particular, it considers the relationship between formal property rights, tenure security and alienability.

Formalisation and types of property rights

Formalisation and tenure security

In various publications over recent years, the Australian Government has effectively equated formalisation with the introduction of secure tenure. However, the relationship between formalisation and tenure security is not so simple. It first depends on whether tenure was secure or insecure under the pre-existing informal arrangements.[179] This varies considerably between different informal settlements, and is something that needs to be investigated in each case.[180] Further, formalisation can only improve tenure security if the institutions responsible for administering formal property rights are effective. This is one of the key issues affecting formalisation in developing countries,[181] but is likely to be much less of an issue in Australia.

Where the process is poor or allocation outcomes are problematic, formalisation can have a negative impact on tenure security regardless of institutional capacity. Where, for example, there is an increase in conflict or resentment,[182] or where the reforms lead to normative pluralism or undermine cooperative norms,[183] even those land users who acquire formal property may not be secure in exercising their rights. Particularly in small or isolated communities, tenure security relies also on social acceptance. Legal security may be an incomplete guard against social insecurity.[184] Finally, whether formalisation increases tenure security will depend on the terms of the formal grant. Where, for example, formalisation occurs by way of a short-term lease or a lease with terms that might be readily breached it can instead result in a decrease in tenure security, as has occurred under certain of the recent Australian reforms.

Theory, terminology and concepts   49

Formalisation and alienability

As indicated above, informal land markets are common in many parts of the world. When formalisation programmes provide for the grant of alienable rights (which they do not always do) this can have a significant impact on existing land markets, with consequences both positive and negative.[185] This is an issue of some significance in many developing countries. However, informal land markets have not been a feature of communities on Indigenous land in Australia, where the issues are different. More relevant is Quan's observation that 'where markets are not well developed, formalisation of tenure will not produce land sales'.[186] In other words, while formalisation might result in the creation of alienable property rights, this does not mean that a land market, or at least a functional land market, will necessarily emerge.

Another way of thinking about this is to make a distinction between *land markets* and *market conditions*. It is one thing to create a land market – or a market for a particular subset of land use, such as home ownership – but another for the right market conditions to emerge such that the hoped-for benefits will result. The latter cannot be assumed. The issue of market conditions needs separate and explicit attention. For example, it has been suggested during debate about Indigenous land reform in Australia that the creation of land markets will enable home owners to access additional forms of credit through mortgaging. This is less likely where house prices are low. It is less likely still where people initially take on a mortgage that is greater than the resale value of their house, which appears to have been the outcome for some purchasers under recent Australian reforms.

Allotment

The majority of this section has been devoted to a discussion of formalisation and its consequences. For a different reason, it is useful to conclude with a brief discussion of a different type of reform, referred to here as 'allotment' but also known as 'individuation' or 'individualisation'. Allotment describes circumstances where ownership of communal property is divided up and individual portions are allocated to individuals and families. This division of ownership can occur through the land being broken up into smaller parcels, such as occurred with the allotment of Indian reserves under the *Dawes Act* in the United States.[187] Alternatively, it might occur through the conversion of ownership rights into fixed shares, which was one element of reforms to Māori land in New Zealand, where Māori became collective owners of a freehold title as tenants in common.[188]

These allotment programmes in the United States and New Zealand in the late 19th and early 20th centuries had a devastating impact on indigenous land ownership in both countries. They resulted in massive land

50 Theory, terminology and concepts

losses, often combined with highly complicated or 'fractionated' ownership of the remaining indigenous land. Consequently they have often been referred to in Australia as a cautionary tale, an example of the risks involved in indigenous land reform.[189]

These disastrous histories should not be ignored, however, two comments can be made on their relevance to land reform in Australia. First, the majority of the recent reforms to Indigenous land in Australia do not involve allotment. They are instead the formalisation of an informal settlement, which is a different type of reform giving rise to a slightly different set of issues. There is, however, an exception: in 2014, the Queensland Government enacted legislation that enables Indigenous land in 34 communities to be divided up and sold as ordinary freehold. If and when this legislation is utilised, which is likely to take some time,[190] it will be the first example of allotment in the Australian context, for which the lessons from New Zealand and the United States will be more directly relevant.

The second point to be made is that there is considerable historical evidence that in both the United States and New Zealand a key aim behind the reforms was to give settlers greater access to indigenous land. This is perhaps most apparent in the United States, where land that was deemed 'surplus' after allotment had occurred was then sold to settlers, in most cases without tribal consent.[191] It would, in my view, be unwarranted to attribute a similar intention to current Australian governments. Whatever their flaws, and as this book reveals there are many flaws, the recent Australian reforms are not a brazen attempt at divesting Indigenous people of their land.

2.6 Concluding comments

The main purpose of this chapter is to fill the need for a clear definition of land reform terminology as it applies to the Australian context. It sets out the meaning of terms such as communal property, private property and tenure security, terms that have been used often during debate about Indigenous land reform in Australia. It also introduces new terminology that has not been used much previously but proves useful, such as formalisation and allotment. Beyond this, the chapter provides a framework for distinguishing between different types of land reform: between formalisation and allotment, between endogenous and exogenous formalisation. This allows debate to move beyond a dialogue about land reform in general terms to a more targeted discussion of the benefits and drawbacks of particular types of reform.

As will be made clear, Australian governments have been far less careful about terminology and concepts. This is not without consequence. Later chapters describe the impact of poorly defined terminology on debate about Indigenous land reform. This has resulted in debate being far more divisive and ideological than was necessary or helpful. Indeed, it resulted

Theory, terminology and concepts 51

in ideological issues crowding out a more considered discussion of the way these reforms actually impact on the lives of Indigenous community residents. It also contributed to the wrong approach being taken to the implementation of reform. Rather than investigating the existing arrangements, to determine what was working and not working, there emerged a political consensus that the need for reform was clear and urgent. The potential for more targeted approaches was ignored in favour of widespread, expensive and highly interventionist reforms with an uncertain purpose.

This chapter also provides an overview of certain land reform theory. It describes two influential theoretical frameworks – the evolutionary theory of land rights and de Soto's theory of capital – as well as a number theoretical devices that help clarify the impact of particular reforms, such as the way alienable property rights can lead to an increase in investment through the 'realisability effect'. The discussion here helps clarify the relevance of these theories to Indigenous land reform in Australia. For example, the discussion of de Soto, who has previously been referred to often in the Australian context, makes clearer the steps required for capitalisation to have the positive benefits that de Soto predicts. More generally, the section on the risks and benefits of alienability helps clarify why land markets should not be treated as a panacea, as they so frequently are. The benefits, and risks, of alienable property rights are highly dependent on the context in which they operate. And as following chapters make clear, communities on Indigenous land are a very particular context for reasons that extend well beyond their underlying land tenure.

Notes

1 Rogier van den Brink *et al.*, 'Consensus, Confusion, and Controversy: Selected Land Reform Issues in Sub-Saharan Africa' (Working Paper No 71, World Bank, 2006) v.
2 This needs to be kept in mind when reading some publications, most notably Klaus Deininger, 'Land Policies for Growth and Poverty Reduction' (Policy Research Report, World Bank, 2003).
3 Brendan Edgeworth *et al.*, *Sackville & Neave Australian Property Law* (Butterworths, 8th ed, 2008) 1.
4 J.W. Harris, 'Private and Non-Private Property: What Is the Difference?' (1995) 111(Jul) *Law Quarterly Review* 421, 422, and see also Edgeworth *et al.*, above n 3, 1–2.
5 Edgeworth *et al.*, above n 3, 5.
6 For example, Sherry describes how master-planned estates operate as a 'fourth level of government'; Cathy Sherry, 'The Legal Fundamentals of High Rise Buildings and Master Planned Estates: Ownership, Governance and Living in Multi-owned Housing with a Case Study on Children's Play' (2008) 16(1) *Australian Property Law Journal* 1, 8, 11.
7 United Nations Human Settlements Programme (UN-Habitat), 'Secure Land Rights for All' (2008) 5.
8 Daniel W. Bromley, 'Property Relations and Economic Development: The Other Land Reform' (1989) 17(6) *World Development* 867, 871.

52 *Theory, terminology and concepts*

9 It was not until 2010 that these terms were fully defined in the context of Australian debate; see Jude Wallace, 'Managing Social Tenure' in Lee Godden and Maureen Tehan (eds), *Comparative Perspectives on Communal Land and Individual Ownership: Sustainable Futures* (Routledge, 2010) 25, 34.

10 Bromley, above n 8, 872; van den Brink *et al.*, above n 1, 4–7. David Feeny *et al.*, 'The Tragedy of the Commons: Twenty-Two Years Later' (1990) 18(1) *Human Ecology* 1, 4 use the related term 'property-rights regimes'.

11 Klaus Deininger and Hans Binswanger, 'The Evolution of the World Bank's Land Policy' in Alain de Janvry *et al.* (eds), *Access to Land, Rural Poverty and Public Action* (Oxford University Press, 2001) 406, 408. Wallace, above n 9, 34, uses the term 'tenure type'. Harold Demsetz, 'Toward a Theory of Property Rights' (1967) 57(2) *American Economic Review* 347, 354, uses the term 'forms of ownership'. The FAO refer to categories of land tenure; Food and Agriculture Organization of the United Nations (FAO), 'Land Tenure and Rural Development' (2002) 8.

12 This is the most common typology, although Harris describes an alternative approach; see Harris, above n 4.

13 See, eg, Demsetz, above n 11, 354. Ostrom attributes the clarification of this distinction to an article by Ciriacy-Wantrup and Bishop in 1975; see Elinor Ostrom, 'The Puzzle of Counterproductive Property Rights Reforms: A Conceptual Analysis' in Alain de Janvry *et al.* (eds), *Access to Land, Rural Poverty and Public Action* (Oxford University Press, 2001) 129, 131.

14 Bromley, above n 8, 872. Similar definitions are used by several others, including Feeny *et al.*, above n 10, 5; Wallace, above n 9, 34; FAO, above n 11, 8.

15 Bromley, above n 8, 872.

16 Ibid.

17 Louis De Alessi, quoted in Daniel Fitzpatrick, 'Evolution and Chaos in Property Rights Systems: The Third World Tragedy of Contested Access' (2006) 115 *Yale Law Journal* 996, 1001.

18 Fitzpatrick suggests this situation might instead be described as 'contested access'; see ibid, 1047.

19 See, eg, FAO, above n 11, 8.

20 See discussion below on 'private property rights'.

21 Van den Brink *et al.*, above n 1, 6.

22 Martin Adams, Sipho Sibanda and Stephen Turner, 'Land Tenure Reform and Rural Livelihoods in Southern Africa' in Camilla Toulmin and Julian Quan (eds), *Evolving Land Rights, Policy and Tenure in Africa* (International Institute for Environment and Development, 2000) 135, 139.

23 Feeny *et al.*, above n 10, 4.

24 See generally Sherry, above n 6, 8–15.

25 Elinor Ostrom, 'How Types of Goods and Property Rights Jointly Affect Collective Action' (2003) 15(3) *Journal of Theoretical Politics* 239, 250 notes that 'in much of the economics literature, private property is defined as equivalent to the right of alienation'. This is similar to the economic/market-based approach to formality that Assies critiques; see Willem Assies, 'Land Tenure, Land Law and Development: Some Thoughts on Recent Debates' (2009) 36(3) *Journal of Peasant Studies* 573, 576.

26 A similar point is made by Feeny *et al.*, above n 10, 5.

27 Fitzpatrick, above n 17, 1029. Baxter and Trebilcock also make a distinction between 'non-formal tenures' and 'Indigenous tenures'; Jamie Baxter and Michael Trebilcock, ' "Formalizing" Land Tenure in First Nations: Evaluating the Case for Reserve Tenure Reform' (2009) 7(2) *Indigenous Law Journal* 45, 75.

28 See Daniel Fitzpatrick, ' "Best Practice" Options for the Legal Recognition of

Customary Tenure' (2005) 36(3) *Development and Change* 449, 454; Camilla Toulmin and Julian Quan, 'Evolving Land Rights, Tenure and Policy in Sub-Saharan Africa' in Camilla Toulmin and Julian Quan (eds), *Evolving Land Rights, Policy and Tenure in Africa* (International Institute for Environment and Development, 2000) 1, 10; Patrick McAuslan, 'Only the Name of the Country Changes: The Diaspora of "European" Land Law in Commonwealth Africa' in Camilla Toulmin and Julian Quan (eds), *Evolving Land Rights, Policy and Tenure in Africa* (International Institute for Environment and Development, 2000) 75, 84; Leigh Toomey, 'A Delicate Balance: Building Complementary Customary and State Legal Systems' (2010) 3(1) *Law and Development Review* 155, 161.

29 Van den Brink *et al.*, above n 1, 5; Toulmin and Quan, above n 28, 24–5; Ben Cousins, 'Tenure and Common Property Resources in Africa' in Camilla Toulmin and Julian Quan (eds), *Evolving Land Rights, Policy and Tenure in Africa* (International Institute for Environment and Development, 2000) 151, 158; Geoffrey Payne, Alain Durand-Lasserve and Carole Rakodi, 'Social and Economic Impacts of Land Titling Programmes in Urban and Peri-Urban Areas: A Review of the Literature' (Paper presented at World Bank Urban Research Symposium, Washington DC, 14–16 May 2007) 1, 37.

30 Clarissa Fourie, 'Land Readjustment for Peri-Urban Customary Tenure: The Example of Botswana' in Robert Hume and Hilary Lim (eds), *Demystifying the Mystery of Capital: Land Tenure and Poverty in Africa and the Caribbean* (Routledge Cavendish, 2004) 31, 31, an approach that is followed by Michael Barry, 'Formalising Informal Land Rights: The Case of Marconi Beam to Jo Slovo Park' (2006) 30 *Habitat International* 628, 630–1.

31 Garrett Hardin, 'The Tragedy of the Commons' (13 December 1968) 162 *Science* 1243.

32 Van den Brink *et al.*, above n 1, 7.

33 The term 'commons tragedy' is preferable to 'tragedy of the commons' as it makes it clearer that tragedy does not always occur. The term is used by Gregory S. Alexander and Eduardo M. Peñalver, *An Introduction to Property Theory* (Cambridge University Press, 2012) 25, who point to the contribution of Ostrom in clarifying when commons tragedies are more likely to occur: see, eg, Elinor Ostrom, *Governing the Commons: The Evolution of Institutions for Collective Action* (Cambridge University Press, 1990); Elinor Ostrom, Marco Jansen and John Anderies, 'Going Beyond Panaceas' (2007) 104(39) *Proceedings of the National Academy of Sciences* 15176.

34 Tom Calma, 'Native Title Report 2005' (Australian Human Rights Commission, 2005) 118; Samantha Hepburn, 'Transforming Customary Title to Individual Title: Revisiting the Cathedral' (2006) 11(1) *Deakin Law Review* 63, 78; Jon Altman, Craig Linkhorn and Jennifer Clarke, 'Land Rights and Development Reform in Remote Australia' (Discussion Paper No 276/2005, Centre for Aboriginal Economic Policy Research, 2005) 18; Ed Wensing and Jonathon Taylor, 'Secure Tenure for Home Ownership and Economic Development on Land Subject to Native Title' (Research Discussion Paper No 31, AIATSIS Research Publications, August 2012) 16.

35 See Michael Heller, 'The Tragedy of the Anticommons: Property in the Transition from Marx to Markets' (1998) 111(3) *Harvard Law Review* 622; Michael Heller, *The Gridlock Economy: How Too Much Ownership Wrecks Markets, Stops Innovation and Costs Lives* (Basic Books, 2008); Larissa Katz, 'Red Tape and Gridlock' in D. Benjamin Barros (ed), *Hernando de Soto and Property in a Market Economy* (Ashgate, 2010) 109, 110, 122; Carol M. Rose, 'Invasions, Innovation, Environment' in D. Benjamin Barros (ed), *Hernando de Soto and Property in a Market Economy* (Ashgate, 2010) 21, 33.

54 *Theory, terminology and concepts*

36 This is described in Chapter 5.
37 Australian Agency for International Development (AusAID), 'Making Land Work, Volume One, Reconciling Customary Land and Development in the Pacific' (Commonwealth of Australia, 2008) 129.
38 See, eg, United Nations Human Settlements Programme (UN-Habitat), 'Urban Land for All' (2004) 6, relying on a definition also used by Assies, above n 25, 575; Payne, Durand-Lasserve and Rakodi, above n 29, 1 n 1; Anisha Sharma, Shayak Barman and Paramita Datta Dey, 'Land Tenure Security: Is Titling Enough?' (National Institute of Urban Affairs, December 2006) 1.
39 This is described in Chapter 4.
40 Baxter and Trebilcock, above n 27, 62. See also UN-Habitat, 'Urban Land for All', above n 38, 7; Payne, Durand-Lasserve and Rakodi, above n 29, 6.
41 See especially Rikke J. Broegaard, 'Land Tenure Insecurity and Inequality in Nicaragua' (2005) 36(5) *Development and Change* 845, 851.
42 See, eg, Alain Durand-Lasserve and Harris Selod, 'The Formalisation of Urban Land Tenure in Developing Countries' (Paper prepared for World Bank Urban Research Symposium, Washington DC, 14–16 May 2007) 7; Baxter and Trebilcock, above n 27, 62; Deininger, above n 2, xxiii; Sharma, Barman and Dey, above n 38, 1; Wallace, above n 9, 35–6; AusAID, above n 37.
43 Van den Brink *et al.*, above n 1, 12 (emphasis in original).
44 Wallace, above n 9, 36 notes that social tenures may be 'formally or informally constructed'. See also Michael Barry, 'Land Restitution and Communal Property Associations: The Elandskloof Case' (2011) 28 *Land Use Policy* 139, 141.
45 Fitzpatrick, 'Best Practice', above n 28, 457–9.
46 Fitzpatrick, 'Best Practice', above n 28, 459–65; UN-Habitat, 'Secure Land Rights for All', above n 7, 23.
47 See, eg, Alain Durand-Lasserve and Lauren Royston, 'International Trends and Country Contexts: From Tenure Regularization to Tenure Security' in Alain Durand-Lasserve and Lauren Royston (eds), *Holding Their Ground: Secure Land Tenure for the Urban Poor in Developing Countries* (Earthscan Publications, 2002) 1, 4–5; Sharma, Barman and Dey, above n 38, 4; Banashree Banerjee, 'Security of Tenure in Indian Cities' in Alain Durand-Lasserve and Lauren Royston (eds), *Holding Their Ground: Secure Land Tenure for the Urban Poor in Developing Countries* (Earthscan Publications, 2002) 37, 45–6.
48 Fitzpatrick, 'Evolution and Chaos', above n 17, 1029.
49 Barry, 'Marconi Beam', above n 30, 630.
50 Wallace, above n 9, 37, argues that although not referred to specifically by name, a simplified evolutionary approach was used to justify the recent Australian reforms to Aboriginal land.
51 The classical formulation is enunciated by Demsetz, above n 11.
52 Demsetz's original formulation did not directly address this second issue of state involvement; Fitzpatrick, 'Evolution and Chaos', above n 17, 1007.
53 Jean-Philippe Platteau, 'The Evolutionary Theory of Land Rights as Applied to Sub-Saharan Africa: A Critical Assessment' (1996) 27 *Development and Change* 29, 31–4; Michael Trebilcock and Paul-Erik Veel, 'Property Rights and Development: The Contingent Case for Formalization' (Legal Studies Research Series No 08–10, University of Toronto Faculty of Law, 2008) 69; Deininger, above n 2, xviii; Wallace, above n 9, 36; Fitzpatrick, 'Evolution and Chaos', above n 17, 998; Fitzpatrick, 'Best Practice', above n 28, 451–2; Demsetz, above n 11, 352; van den Brink *et al.*, above n 1, 8.
54 Deininger, above n 2, 29–30; Platteau, above n 53, 31–5; van den Brink *et al.*, above n 1, 10–12. See also Trebilcock and Veel, above n 53, 10.

Theory, terminology and concepts 55

55 Fitzpatrick, 'Best Practice', above n 28, 452.
56 Understandings of optimality have become more nuanced; see, eg, Deininger, above n 2, 34–5.
57 Van den Brink *et al.*, above n 1, 16.
58 See, eg, Deininger, above n 2, xviii. Several authors also refer to the role of 'path dependence' in this regard; see Mariana Prado and Michael Trebilcock, 'Path Dependence, Development and the Dynamics of Institutional Reform' (Legal Studies Research Series, No 09–04, University of Toronto Faculty of Law, 30 April 2009) 11–12, 29–30; Fitzpatrick, 'Best Practice', above n 28, 452; Baxter and Trebilcock, above n 27, 67.
59 David Kennedy, 'Some Caution about Property Rights as a Recipe for Economic Development' (2011) 1(1) *Accounting, Economics and Law* 1, 8–9.
60 Elizabeth Fortin, 'Reforming Land Rights: The World Bank and the Globalization of Agriculture' (2005) 14(2) *Social & Legal Studies* 154, 157.
61 Kennedy, above n 59, 8–12, 16–20. See also Fortin, above n 60, 158, who is critical of Deininger's approach to optimal property rights (see above n 56).
62 See especially Fitzpatrick, 'Evolution and Chaos', above n 17, generally.
63 Ibid, 1003, 1031–3.
64 Deininger, above n 2, xviii.
65 Platteau, above n 53, 33.
66 Deininger, above n 2, 52.
67 Platteau, above n 53, 34–6; Fitzpatrick, 'Evolution and Chaos', above n 17, 1036.
68 Fitzpatrick, 'Evolution and Chaos', above n 17, 1036. See also Trebilcock and Veel, above n 53, 55–6.
69 Harold Demsetz, 'Toward a Theory of Property Rights II: The Competition between Private and Collective Ownership' (2002) 31 *Journal of Legal Studies* S653, S658.
70 Ibid, S659–62; Trebilcock and Veel, above n 53, 55–6; Laura Rivall, 'Response to Marilyn Strathern' in Timothy Chesters (ed), *Land Rights: Oxford Amnesty Lectures* (Oxford University Press, 2009) 39, 44.
71 Platteau, above n 53, 52.
72 Fitzpatrick, 'Evolution and Chaos', above n 17, 1035.
73 Platteau, above n 53, 50–2, 67–8. For an example of the retention of customary norms, see Barry, 'Marconi Beam', above n 30, 640.
74 Platteau quotes Bruce as an exemplar of this approach, which he then critiques; see Platteau, above n 53, 38.
75 Demsetz, 'Toward a Theory of Property Rights II', above n 69, S664–5.
76 Platteau, above n 53, 37. See also Trebilcock and Veel, above n 53, 56; van den Brink *et al.*, above n 1, 15.
77 See, eg, Platteau, above n 53, 41, 44–5.
78 Ibid, 67–8.
79 Ibid, 69–70.
80 Toulmin and Quan, above n 28, 9; Durand-Lasserve and Selod, above n 42, 15.
81 Platteau, above n 53, 69–72; Fitzpatrick, 'Evolution and Chaos', above n 17, 1038–46; Trebilcock and Veel, above n 53, 56.
82 Van den Brink *et al.*, above n 1, 15–16.
83 Platteau, above n 53, 38.
84 Van den Brink *et al.*, above n 1, 15–16.
85 Deininger, above n 2, xviii.
86 Hernando de Soto, *The Mystery of Capital: Why Capitalism Triumphs in the West and Fails Everywhere Else* (Black Swan, 2001).
87 See Ronald Coase, *About Hernando de Soto and the Institute for Liberty and*

56 Theory, terminology and concepts

Democracy, Free to Choose Media (2009) www.freetochoosemedia.org/broadcasts/power_poor/docs/hernando_de_soto_bio.pdf.

88 Including the United Nations, see Assies, above n 25, 573, and the World Bank; see Rashmi Dyal-Chand, 'Leaving the Body of Property Law? Meltdowns, Land Rushes, and Failed Economic Development' in D. Benjamin Barros (ed), *Hernando de Soto and Property in a Market Economy* (Ashgate, 2010) 83, 87 including n 21.

89 See below.

90 Michael Warby, 'What Makes a Third World Country?' (1 January 2001) *Institute of Public Affairs* www.ipa.org.au/news/520/what-makes-a-third-world-country-/pg/10; Noel Pearson, 'Review: *The Mystery of Capital: Why Capitalism Triumphs in the West and Fails Everywhere Else* by Hernando de Soto' (September 2001) *Australian Public Intellectual Network*; Noel Pearson and Lara Kostakidis-Lianos, 'Building Indigenous Capital: Removing Obstacles to Participation in the Real Economy' (Cape York Institute, 2004); Noel Pearson, 'Properties of Integration', *The Weekend Australian*, 14 October 2006, 28; Commonwealth, *Parliamentary Debates*, House of Representatives, 19 June 2006, 90 (David Tollner); Penny Lee, 'Individual Titling of Aboriginal Land in the Northern Territory: What Australia Can Learn from the International Community' (2006) 29(2) *University of New South Wales Law Journal* 22, 26–8; Helen Hughes and Jenness Warin, 'A New Deal for Aborigines and Torres Strait Islanders in Remote Communities' (Issues Analysis No 54, Centre for Independent Studies, 1 March 2005) 4 including n 9; Ron Duncan, 'Agricultural and Resource Economics and Economic Development in Aboriginal Communities' (2003) 47(3) *Australian Journal of Agricultural and Resource Economics* 307, 314–15; Calma, above n 34, 112, 132; Wensing and Taylor, above n 34, 16.

91 This varies between authors. It is clear, for example, that Pearson had read de Soto as he summarises the book accurately. Other authors such as Hughes and Warin refer to de Soto as authority for a more general proposition that 'communal ownership' impedes productive land use and prevents economic development.

92 De Soto, above n 86, 58. See also Nestor M. Davidson, 'The Bell Jar and the Bullhorn: Hernando de Soto and Communication through Title' in D. Benjamin Barros (ed), *Hernando de Soto and Property in a Market Economy* (Ashgate, 2010) 97, 97; Christopher Woodruff, 'Review of de Soto's *The Mystery of Capital*' (2001) 39(4) *Journal of Economic Literature* 1215, 1216.

93 Espen Sjaastad and Ben Cousins, 'Formalisation of Land Rights in the South: An Overview' (2008) 26 *Land Use Policy* 1, 2.

94 De Soto, above n 86, 53.

95 Wallace, above n 9, 26; and see also Assies, above n 25, 585; Robert Home, 'Outside de Soto's Bell Jar: Colonial/Postcolonial Land Law and the Exclusion of the Peri-Urban Poor' in Robert Home and Hilary Lim (eds), *Demystifying the Mystery of Capital: Land Tenure and Poverty in Africa and the Caribbean* (Glasshouse Press, 2004) 11, 22; Fitzpatrick, 'Best Practice', above n 28, 453; van den Brink *et al.*, above n 1, 12; Julian Quan, 'Land Tenure, Economic Growth and Poverty in Sub-Saharan Africa' in Camilla Toulmin and Julian Quan (eds), *Evolving Land Rights, Policy and Tenure in Africa* (International Institute for Environment and Development, 2000) 31, 38 (although see also 36); Fortin, above n 60, 159.

96 Sjaastad and Cousins, above n 93, 2.

97 Rose, above n 35, 38.

98 Woodruff, above n 92, 1218; Eduardo M. Peñalver, 'The Costs of Regulation or the Consequences of Poverty? Progressive Lessons from de Soto' in

D. Benjamin Barros (ed), *Hernando de Soto and Property in a Market Economy* (Ashgate, 2010) 8; Rose, above n 35, 25.

99 Peñalver, above n 98, 10.

100 De Soto, above n 86, 170–1, and see also 178, 189–93.

101 Rose, above n 35, 31–2, and see, eg, de Soto, above n 86, 190, 200.

102 De Soto, above n 86, 171, 190, 194 and 197. See also Assies, above n 25, 584; Davidson, above n 92, 104.

103 Rose, above n 35, 24.

104 De Soto, above n 86, 174–81 ('The Failure of Mandatory Law'), 181–4 ('Rooting Law in the Social Contract'), 184–9 ('The Solidity of Pre-capitalist Social Contracts') and 189–92 ('Listening to the Barking Dogs').

105 Assies, above n 25, 584–5, 579; Rose, above n 35, 23; and see generally Peñalver, above n 98, 7–8.

106 Woodruff, above n 92, 1217.

107 AusAID, above n 37, 129.

108 Durand-Lasserve and Selod, above n 42, 23.

109 Fitzpatrick, 'Best Practice', above n 28, 454.

110 Deininger, above n 2, xxv; Payne, Durand-Lasserve and Rakodi, above n 29, 13; van den Brink *et al.*, above n 1, 4; Klaus Deininger, Daniel Ayelew Ali and Tekie Alemu, 'Impacts of Land Certification on Tenure Security, Investment and Land Markets: Evidence from Ethiopia' (Policy Research Working Paper No 4764, World Bank Development Research Group, October 2008) 3; Trebilcock and Veel, above n 53, 9–10.

111 Trebilcock and Veel, above n 53, 56, who also argue that this may result in increased pressure for property rights to be formalised.

112 Van den Brink *et al.*, above n 1, 4. See also UN-Habitat, 'Secure Land Rights for All', above n 7, 6.

113 Van den Brink *et al.*, above n 1, 4.

114 Payne, Durand-Lasserve and Rakodi, above n 29, 14; Deininger, above n 2, xxv; Platteau, above n 53, 36; Banerjee, above n 47, 53.

115 An example of this is 'delayed freehold', described at UN-Habitat, 'Urban Land for All', above n 38, 8.

116 There may also be other reasons for this practice, such as preventing land banking or discouraging further land invasions; see Bernadette Atuahene, 'Land Titling: A Mode of Privatization with the Potential to Deepen Democracy' (2006) 50 *Saint Louis University Law Journal* 761, 769–70.

117 Van den Brink, above n 1, 9; Deininger, above n 2, 40, and see also 47.

118 See especially Erica Field, 'Entitled to Work: Urban Property Rights and Labor Supply in Peru' (2007) *Quarterly Journal of Economics* 1561, 1567. See also Trebilcock and Veel, above n 53, 13; Payne, Durand-Lasserve and Rakodi, above n 29, 21.

119 Trebilcock and Veel, above n 53, 13.

120 Deininger, above n 2, xxvi; Trebilcock and Veel, above n 53, 13.

121 Field, above n 118, 1563. See also Trebilcock and Veel, above n 53, 13; Payne, Durand-Lasserve and Rakodi, above n 29, 22; Deininger, above n 2, xxvi.

122 Field, above n 118, 1563.

123 Toulmin and Quan, above n 28, 21.

124 Deininger, above n 2, xxvi–xxvii; UN-Habitat, 'Urban Land for All', above n 38, 9; Banerjee, above n 47, 50, 54.

125 See van den Brink *et al.*, above n 1, 5; Trebilcock and Veel, above n 53, 25; Quan, above n 95, 47.

126 The exceptions are home ownership, of which there have been very few grants, and recent Queensland reforms to enable ordinary freehold, which are yet to be utilised. This is described in Chapters 6 and 7.

58 Theory, terminology and concepts

127 Bob Beadman, 'Northern Territory Coordinator General for Remote Services: Report No 2 December 2009 to May 2010' (Northern Territory Government, 2010) 75.

128 Jean-Philippe Platteau, 'Does Africa Need Land Reform?' in Camilla Toulmin and Julian Quan (eds), *Evolving Land Rights, Policy and Tenure in Africa* (International Institute for Environment and Development, 2000) 51, 55. While the term is from Platteau, the concept is used more broadly, see, eg, Trebilcock and Veel, above n 53, 12.

129 De Soto states that in the United States, 'up to 70% of the credit that new business receive come from using formal titles as collateral for mortgages'; de Soto, above n 86, 86.

130 Woodruff, above n 92, 1219.

131 Ibid.

132 Ibid, 1220.

133 Chadzimula Molebatsi, Charisse Griffith-Charles and John Kangwa, 'Conclusions' in Robert Hume and Hilary Lim (eds), *Demystifying the Mystery of Capital: Land Tenure and Poverty in Africa and the Caribbean* (Routledge Cavendish, 2004) 145, 148; Payne, Durand-Lasserve and Rakodi, above n 29, 17–21; Fortin, above n 60, 161.

134 Payne, Durand-Lasserve and Rakodi, above n 29, 20; Assies, above n 25, 583; Molebatsi, Griffith-Charles and Kangwa, above n 133, 147; Chadzimula Molebatsi, 'Botswana: "Self-Allocation", "Accommodation" and "Zero Tolerance" in Mogoditshane and Old Naledi' in Robert Home and Hilary Lim (eds), *Demystifying the Mystery of Capital: Land Tenure and Poverty in Africa and the Caribbean* (Glasshouse Press, 2004) 73, 83–5.

135 Molebatsi, above n 133, 85.

136 Ibid, 82–5.

137 Four separate studies of titling programmes in Peru found that there was no effect on business credit: Field, above n 118, 1596, 1598; Quan, above n 95, 46, states that '[t]he importance of land markets as a means to provide better access to credit has been seriously overstated'; Woodruff, above n 92, 1219, finds that '[m]ost evidence suggests that access to credit is increased, though in limited proportions'; Deininger, Ali and Alemu, above n 110, 4, conclude that collateralisation benefits 'may be less readily realized than sometimes suggested by their protagonists'.

138 For example, Dyal-Chand argues that in the United States, credit obtained through subprime mortgages was often used to fund short-term consumption rather than the long-term investment in productivity; Dyal-Chand, above n 88, 88 and generally. See also Fortin, above n 60, 161–2.

139 Fortin, above n 60, 162.

140 Woodruff, above n 92, 1220. See also Quan, above n 95, 46.

141 Deininger, above n 2, xxvi. See also Trebilcock and Veel, above n 53, 56.

142 Van den Brink *et al.*, above n 1, 7; Platteau, 'Does Africa Need Reform', above n 128, 55; Trebilcock and Veel, above n 53, 10–11; Quan, above n 95, 34, 44, 47; Deininger, above n 2, xxx–xxxii, 113.

143 Van den Brink *et al.*, above n 1, 7; Quan, above n 95, 46–7; Platteau, 'Evolutionary Theory', above n 53, 53–4, 59.

144 Fortin, above n 60, 170.

145 Kennedy, above n 60, 12.

146 Ibid.

147 Deininger, above n 2, xxix.

148 Platteau, 'Evolutionary Theory', above n 53, 37; Fortin, above n 60, 160–3; Platteau, 'Does Africa Need Reform', above n 128, 68.

Theory, terminology and concepts 59

149 Platteau, 'Evolutionary Theory', above n 53, 37; Platteau, 'Does Africa Need Reform', above n 128, 55.
150 Rose, above n 35, 29.
151 Platteau, 'Evolutionary Theory', above n 53, 56–8.
152 See Peñalver, above n 98, 15–18; Gregory S. Alexander, 'Culture and Capitalism: A Comment on de Soto' in D. Benjamin Barros (ed), *Hernando de Soto and Property in a Market Economy* (Ashgate, 2010) 41, 59; De Soto, above n 86, 206–9. See also Atuahene, above n 116, 761, 775 and 781.
153 Trebilcock and Veel, above n 53, 52.
154 Deininger, above n 2, xxxviii.
155 See especially Assies, above n 25.
156 See especially Demsetz, 'Toward a Theory of Property Rights', above n 11, 347–50. See also Deininger, above n 2, 28; Tom Flanagan, Christopher Alcantara and André Le Dressay, *Beyond the Indian Act: Restoring Aboriginal Property Rights* (McGill-Queen's University Press, 2010) 19; Trebilcock and Veel, above n 53, 9.
157 Kennedy, above n 60, 14–15.
158 Deininger, above n 2, 28–30; Trebilcock and Veel, above n 53, 10; Flanagan, Alcantara and Le Dressay, above n 156, 20; van den Brink *et al.*, above n 1, 8.
159 De Soto, above n 86, 51–3.
160 Deininger, above n 2, 52–3; Feeny *et al.*, above n 10, 13.
161 Van den Brink *et al.*, above n 1, 10–11; Ruth Meinzen-Dick and Esther Mwangi, 'Cutting the Web of Interests: Pitfalls of Formalizing Property Rights' (2008) 26 *Land Use Policy* 36, 40; Toulmin and Quan, above n 28, 21.
162 Home, above n 95, 22; Assies, above n 25, 580; Deininger, above n 2, 29; Quan, above n 95, 32; Trebilcock and Veel, above n 53, 56; van den Brink *et al.*, above n 1, 8.
163 Fortin, above n 60, 156; and see van den Brink *et al.*, above n 1, 7–8, who also note that in some cases negotiating authority is distributed in a manner that actually protects certain vulnerable groups, such as the elderly.
164 Fourie, above n 30, 46.
165 Van den Brink *et al.*, above n 1, 14.
166 Ibid, 15.
167 Durand-Lasserve and Selod, above n 42, 43.
168 Ibid, 44.
169 Fitzpatrick, 'Best Practice', above n 28, 463.
170 Durand-Lasserve and Selod, above n 42, 15.
171 Platteau, 'Evolutionary Theory', above n 53, 72.
172 Peñalver, above n 98, 13–14, commenting on de Soto.
173 Payne, Durand-Lasserve and Rakodi, above n 29, 8; Durand-Lasserve and Selod, above n 42, 10; Platteau, 'Evolutionary Theory', above n 53, 40; Fortin, above n 60, 159–60; van den Brink *et al.*, above n 1, 5; Trebilcock and Veel, above n 53, 50–1.
174 Durand-Lasserve and Selod, above n 42, 10. For a Canadian example, see Tom Flanagan and Christopher Alcantara, 'Individual Property Rights on Canadian Indian Reserves' (2004) 29 *Queen's Law Journal* 489, 512.
175 Fortin, above n 60, 160; Payne, Durand-Lasserve and Rakodi, above n 29, 10, 30; Home, above n 95, 22; UN-Habitat, 'Secure Land Rights for All', above n 7, 26 (see discussion of titling programmes in Laos); Trebilcock and Veel, above n 53, 52–4.
176 Durand-Lasserve and Selod, above n 42, 10; Trebilcock and Veel, above n 53, 51.
177 Payne, Durand-Lasserve and Rakodi, above n 29, 30; Trebilcock and Veel, above n 53, 54; van den Brink *et al.*, above n 1, 12.

60 Theory, terminology and concepts

178 Assies, above n 25, 586; Trebilcock and Veel, above n 53, 49–50; and see the example provided by Barry, 'Marconi Beam', above n 30, 641.
179 Payne, Durand-Lasserve and Rakodi, above n 29, 8, 13.
180 Ibid, and see also Durand-Lasserve and Selod, above n 42, 7; van den Brink *et al.*, above n 1, 5; Platteau, 'Evolutionary Theory', above n 53, 33 including n 6; Trebilcock and Veel, above n 53, 58.
181 Payne, Durand-Lasserve and Rakodi, above n 29, 13, 30; Trebilcock and Veel, above n 53, 50, 64–8; Daniel W. Bromley, 'Formalising Property Relations in the Developing World: The Wrong Prescription for the Wrong Malady' (2008) 26 *Land Use Policy* 20, 21, 26; Lani Roux and Michael Barry, 'A Historical Post-Formalisation Comparison of Two Settlements in South Africa' (Paper presented at XXIVth FIG (International Federation of Surveyors) International Congress 2010, 'Facing the Challenges: Building the Capacity', Sydney, 11–16 April 2010) 2, 6–7.
182 Platteau, 'Evolutionary Theory', above n 53, 56.
183 Trebilcock and Veel, above n 53, 48–9.
184 Broegaard, above n 41, 850–1.
185 See especially Quan, above n 95, 44–7. See also Woodruff, above n 92, 1221; Payne, Durand-Lasserve and Rakodi, above n 29, 9, 15–16; Fortin, above n 60, 160, 163–6; Durand-Lasserve and Selod, above n 42, 10, 13; Trebilcock and Veel, above n 53, 10, 16; Deininger, Ali and Alemu, above n 110, 4; Platteau, 'Does Africa Need Reform', above n 128, 55.
186 Quan, above n 95, 45. See also Platteau, who states that 'in ordinary circumstances the land market does not appear to be activated by the provision of greater tenure security through titling'; Platteau, 'Does Africa Need Reform', above n 128, 62.
187 See Jessica A. Shoemaker, 'Like Snow in the Spring Time: Allotment, Fractionation, and the Indian Land Tenure Problem' (2003) *Wisconsin Law Review* 729; Ezra Rosser, 'Anticipating de Soto: Allotment of Indian Reservations and the Dangers of Land-Titling' in D. Benjamin Barros (ed), *Hernando de Soto and Property in a Market Economy* (Ashgate, 2010) 61; Judith V. Royster, 'The Legacy of Allotment' (1995) 27 *Arizona State Law Journal* 2.
188 See Richard Boast, 'Individualization: An Idea Whose Time Came and Went' in Lee Godden and Maureen Tehan (eds), *Comparative Perspectives on Communal Lands and Individual Ownership: Sustainable Futures* (Routledge, 2010) 145; Craig Linkhorn, 'Māori Land and Development Finance' (Discussion Paper No 284/2006, Centre for Aboriginal Economic Policy Research, 2006).
189 See Margaret Stephenson, 'You Can't Always Get What You Want: Economic Development on Indigenous Individual and Collective Titles in North America – Which Land Tenure Models Are Relevant to Australia?' in Lee Godden and Maureen Tehan (eds), *Comparative Perspectives on Communal Lands and Individual Ownership: Sustainable Futures* (Routledge, 2010) 100, 107–9; Tom Calma, 'Native Title Report 2007' (Australian Human Rights Commission, 2007) 55, 91; Hepburn, above n 34, 70, 82–4; Nicole Watson, 'Howard's End: The Real Agenda behind the Proposed Review of Indigenous Land Titles' (2005) 9(4) *Australian Indigenous Law Reporter* 1, 3; Altman, Linkhorn and Clarke, above n 34, 23–4; Lee, above n 90, 34.
190 Chapter 6 describes how there are several steps required before allotment can occur.
191 Rosser, above n 187, 70; Royster, above n 187, 13–16; Flanagan, Alcantara and Le Dressay, above n 156, 45, 48–9.

Bibliography

Books/articles/reports/web pages

Adams, Martin, Sipho Sibanda and Stephen Turner, 'Land Tenure Reform and Rural Livelihoods in Southern Africa' in Camilla Toulmin and Julian Quan (eds), *Evolving Land Rights, Policy and Tenure in Africa* (International Institute for Environment and Development, 2000) 135.

Alexander, Gregory S., 'Culture and Capitalism: A Comment on de Soto' in D. Benjamin Barros (ed), *Hernando de Soto and Property in a Market Economy* (Ashgate, 2010) 41.

Alexander, Gregory S. and Eduardo M. Peñalver, *An Introduction to Property Theory* (Cambridge University Press, 2012).

Altman, Jon, Craig Linkhorn and Jennifer Clarke, 'Land Rights and Development Reform in Remote Australia' (Discussion Paper No 276/2005, Centre for Aboriginal Economic Policy Research, 2005).

Assies, Willem, 'Land Tenure, Land Law and Development: Some Thoughts on Recent Debates' (2009) 36(3) *Journal of Peasant Studies* 573.

Atuahene, Bernadette, 'Land Titling: A Mode of Privatization with the Potential to Deepen Democracy' (2006) 50 *Saint Louis University Law Journal* 761.

Australian Agency for International Development (AusAID), 'Making Land Work, Volume One, Reconciling Customary Land and Development in the Pacific' (Commonwealth of Australia, 2008).

Banerjee, Banashree, 'Security of Tenure in Indian Cities' in Alain Durand-Lasserve and Lauren Royston (eds), *Holding Their Ground: Secure Land Tenure for the Urban Poor in Developing Countries* (Earthscan Publications, 2002) 37.

Barry, Michael, 'Formalising Informal Land Rights: The Case of Marconi Beam to Jo Slovo Park' (2006) 30 *Habitat International* 628.

Barry, Michael, 'Land Restitution and Communal Property Associations: The Elandskloof Case' (2011) 28 *Land Use Policy* 139.

Baxter, Jamie and Michael Trebilcock, ' "Formalizing" Land Tenure in First Nations: Evaluating the Case for Reserve Tenure Reform' (2009) 7(2) *Indigenous Law Journal* 45.

Beadman, Bob, 'Northern Territory Coordinator General for Remote Services: Report No 2 December 2009 to May 2010' (Northern Territory Government, 2010).

Boast, Richard, 'Individualization: An Idea Whose Time Came and Went' in Lee Godden and Maureen Tehan (eds), *Comparative Perspectives on Communal Lands and Individual Ownership: Sustainable Futures* (Routledge, 2010) 145.

Broegaard, Rikke J., 'Land Tenure Insecurity and Inequality in Nicaragua' (2005) 36(5) *Development and Change* 845.

Bromley, Daniel W., 'Property Relations and Economic Development: The Other Land Reform' (1989) 17(6) *World Development* 867.

Bromley, Daniel W., 'Formalising Property Relations in the Developing World: The Wrong Prescription for the Wrong Malady' (2008) 26 *Land Use Policy* 20.

Calma, Tom, 'Native Title Report 2005' (Australian Human Rights Commission, 2005).

Calma, Tom, 'Native Title Report 2007' (Australian Human Rights Commission, 2007).

62 Theory, terminology and concepts

Coase, Ronald, *About Hernando de Soto and the Institute for Liberty and Democracy*, Free to Choose Media (2009) www.freetochoosemedia.org/broadcasts/power_poor/docs/hernando_de_soto_bio.pdf.

Cousins, Ben, 'Tenure and Common Property Resources in Africa' in Camilla Toulmin and Julian Quan (eds), *Evolving Land Rights, Policy and Tenure in Africa* (International Institute for Environment and Development, 2000) 151.

Davidson, Nestor M., 'The Bell Jar and the Bullhorn: Hernando de Soto and Communication through Title' in D. Benjamin Barros (ed), *Hernando de Soto and Property in a Market Economy* (Ashgate, 2010) 97.

Deininger, Klaus, 'Land Policies for Growth and Poverty Reduction' (Policy Research Report, World Bank, 2003).

Deininger, Klaus and Hans Binswanger, 'The Evolution of the World Bank's Land Policy' in Alain de Janvry *et al.* (eds), *Access to Land, Rural Poverty and Public Action* (Oxford University Press, 2001) 406.

Deininger, Klaus, Daniel Ayelew Ali and Tekie Alemu, 'Impacts of Land Certification on Tenure Security, Investment and Land Markets: Evidence from Ethiopia' (Policy Research Working Paper No 4764, The World Bank Development Research Group, October 2008).

Demsetz, Harold, 'Toward a Theory of Property Rights' (1967) 57(2) *American Economic Review* 347.

Demsetz, Harold, 'Toward a Theory of Property Rights II: The Competition between Private and Collective Ownership' (2002) 31 *Journal of Legal Studies* S653.

de Soto, Hernando, *The Mystery of Capital: Why Capitalism Triumphs in the West and Fails Everywhere Else* (Black Swan, 2001).

Duncan, Ron, 'Agricultural and Resource Economics and Economic Development in Aboriginal Communities' (2003) 47(3) *Australian Journal of Agricultural and Resource Economics* 307.

Durand-Lasserve, Alain and Lauren Royston, 'International Trends and Country Contexts: From Tenure Regularization to Tenure Security' in Alain Durand-Lasserve and Lauren Royston (eds), *Holding Their Ground: Secure Land Tenure for the Urban Poor in Developing Countries* (Earthscan Publications, 2002) 1.

Durand-Lasserve, Alain and Harris Selod, 'The Formalisation of Urban Land Tenure in Developing Countries' (Paper prepared for World Bank Urban Research Symposium, Washington DC, 14–16 May 2007).

Dyal-Chand, Rashmi, 'Leaving the Body of Property Law? Meltdowns, Land Rushes, and Failed Economic Development' in D. Benjamin Barros (ed), *Hernando de Soto and Property in a Market Economy* (Ashgate, 2010) 83.

Edgeworth, Brendan *et al.*, *Sackville & Neave Australian Property Law* (Butterworths, 8th ed, 2008).

Feeny, David *et al.*, 'The Tragedy of the Commons: Twenty-Two Years Later' (1990) 18(1) *Human Ecology* 1.

Field, Erica, 'Entitled to Work: Urban Property Rights and Labor Supply in Peru' (2007) *The Quarterly Journal of Economics* 1561.

Fitzpatrick, Daniel, ' "Best Practice" Options for the Legal Recognition of Customary Tenure' (2005) 36(3) *Development and Change* 449.

Fitzpatrick, Daniel, 'Evolution and Chaos in Property Rights Systems: The Third World Tragedy of Contested Access' (2006) 115 *Yale Law Journal* 996.

Flanagan, Tom and Christopher Alcantara, 'Individual Property Rights on Canadian Indian Reserves' (2004) 29 *Queen's Law Journal* 489.

Flanagan, Tom, Christopher Alcantara and André Le Dressay, *Beyond the Indian Act: Restoring Aboriginal Property Rights* (McGill-Queen's University Press, 2010).

Food and Agriculture Organization of the United Nations (FAO), 'Land Tenure and Rural Development' (2002).

Fortin, Elizabeth, 'Reforming Land Rights: The World Bank and the Globalization of Agriculture' (2005) 14(2) *Social & Legal Studies* 154.

Fourie, Clarissa, 'Land Readjustment for Peri-Urban Customary Tenure: The Example of Botswana' in Robert Hume and Hilary Lim (eds), *Demystifying the Mystery of Capital: Land Tenure and Poverty in Africa and the Caribbean* (Routledge Cavendish, 2004) 31.

Hardin, Garrett, 'The Tragedy of the Commons' (13 December 1968) 162 *Science* 1243.

Harris, J.W., 'Private and Non-Private Property: What Is the Difference?' (1995) 111(Jul) *Law Quarterly Review* 421.

Heller, Michael, 'The Tragedy of the Anticommons: Property in the Transition from Marx to Markets' (1998) 111(3) *Harvard Law Review* 622.

Heller, Michael, *The Gridlock Economy: How Too Much Ownership Wrecks Markets, Stops Innovation and Costs Lives* (Basic Books, 2008).

Hepburn, Samantha, 'Transforming Customary Title to Individual Title: Revisiting the Cathedral' (2006) 11(1) *Deakin Law Review* 63.

Home, Robert, 'Outside de Soto's Bell Jar: Colonial/Postcolonial Land Law and the Exclusion of the Peri-Urban Poor' in Robert Home and Hilary Lim (eds), *Demystifying the Mystery of Capital: Land Tenure and Poverty in Africa and the Caribbean* (Glasshouse Press, 2004) 11.

Hughes, Helen and Jenness Warin, 'A New Deal for Aborigines and Torres Strait Islanders in Remote Communities' (Issues Analysis No 54, Centre for Independent Studies, 1 March 2005).

Katz, Larissa, 'Red Tape and Gridlock' in D. Benjamin Barros (ed), *Hernando de Soto and Property in a Market Economy* (Ashgate, 2010).

Kennedy, David, 'Some Caution about Property Rights as a Recipe for Economic Development' (2011) 1(1) *Accounting, Economics and Law* 1.

Lee, Penny, 'Individual Titling of Aboriginal Land in the Northern Territory: What Australia Can Learn from the International Community' (2006) 29(2) *University of New South Wales Law Journal* 22.

Linkhorn, Craig, 'Māori Land and Development Finance' (Discussion Paper No 284/2006, Centre for Aboriginal Economic Policy Research, 2006).

McAuslan, Patrick, 'Only the Name of the Country Changes: The Diaspora of "European" Land Law in Commonwealth Africa' in Camilla Toulmin and Julian Quan (eds), *Evolving Land Rights, Policy and Tenure in Africa* (International Institute for Environment and Development, 2000) 75.

Meinzen-Dick, Ruth and Esther Mwangi, 'Cutting the Web of Interests: Pitfalls of Formalizing Property Rights' (2008) 26 *Land Use Policy* 36.

Molebatsi, Chadzimula, 'Botswana: "Self-Allocation", "Accommodation" and "Zero Tolerance" in Mogoditshane and Old Naledi' in Robert Home and Hilary Lim (eds), *Demystifying the Mystery of Capital: Land Tenure and Poverty in Africa and the Caribbean* (Glasshouse Press, 2004) 73.

Molebatsi, Chadzimula, Charisse Griffith-Charles and John Kangwa, 'Conclusions' in Robert Hume and Hilary Lim (eds), *Demystifying the Mystery of Capital:*

64   *Theory, terminology and concepts*

Land Tenure and Poverty in Africa and the Caribbean (Routledge Cavendish, 2004) 145.

Ostrom, Elinor, *Governing the Commons: The Evolution of Institutions for Collective Action* (Cambridge University Press, 1990).

Ostrom, Elinor, 'The Puzzle of Counterproductive Property Rights Reforms: A Conceptual Analysis' in Alain de Janvry *et al.* (eds), *Access to Land, Rural Poverty and Public Action* (Oxford University Press, 2001) 129.

Ostrom, Elinor, 'How Types of Goods and Property Rights Jointly Affect Collective Action' (2003) 15(3) *Journal of Theoretical Politics* 239.

Ostrom, Elinor, Marco Jansen and John Anderies, 'Going Beyond Panaceas' (2007) 104(39) *Proceedings of the National Academy of Sciences* 15176.

Payne, Geoffrey, Alain Durand-Lasserve and Carole Rakodi, 'Social and Economic Impacts of Land Titling Programmes in Urban and Peri-Urban Areas: A Review of the Literature' (Paper presented at World Bank Urban Research Symposium, Washington DC, 14–16 May 2007).

Pearson, Noel, 'Review: *The Mystery of Capital: Why Capitalism Triumphs in the West and Fails Everywhere Else* by Hernando de Soto' (September 2001) *Australian Public Intellectual Network*.

Pearson, Noel, 'Properties of Integration', *The Weekend Australian*, 14 October 2006, 28.

Pearson, Noel and Lara Kostakidis-Lianos, 'Building Indigenous Capital: Removing Obstacles to Participation in the Real Economy' (Cape York Institute, 2004).

Peñalver, Eduardo M., 'The Costs of Regulation or the Consequences of Poverty? Progressive Lessons from de Soto' in D. Benjamin Barros (ed), *Hernando de Soto and Property in a Market Economy* (Ashgate, 2010) 8.

Platteau, Jean-Philippe, 'The Evolutionary Theory of Land Rights as Applied to Sub-Saharan Africa: A Critical Assessment' (1996) 27 *Development and Change* 29.

Platteau, Jean-Philippe, 'Does Africa Need Land Reform?' in Camilla Toulmin and Julian Quan (eds), *Evolving Land Rights, Policy and Tenure in Africa* (International Institute for Environment and Development, 2000) 51.

Prado, Mariana and Michael Trebilcock, 'Path Dependence, Development and the Dynamics of Institutional Reform' (Legal Studies Research Series, No 09–04, University of Toronto Faculty of Law, 30 April 2009).

Quan, Julian, 'Land Tenure, Economic Growth and Poverty in Sub-Saharan Africa' in Camilla Toulmin and Julian Quan (eds), *Evolving Land Rights, Policy and Tenure in Africa* (International Institute for Environment and Development, 2000) 31.

Rivall, Laura, 'Response to Marilyn Strathern' in Timothy Chesters (ed), *Land Rights: Oxford Amnesty Lectures* (Oxford University Press, 2009) 39.

Rose, Carol M., 'Invasions, Innovation, Environment' in D. Benjamin Barros (ed), *Hernando de Soto and Property in a Market Economy* (Ashgate, 2010) 21.

Rosser, Ezra, 'Anticipating de Soto: Allotment of Indian Reservations and the Dangers of Land-Titling' in D. Benjamin Barros (ed), *Hernando de Soto and Property in a Market Economy* (Ashgate, 2010) 61.

Roux, Lani and Michael Barry, 'A Historical Post-Formalisation Comparison of Two Settlements in South Africa' (Paper presented at XXIVth FIG (International Federation of Surveyors) International Congress 2010, 'Facing the Challenges – Building the Capacity', Sydney, 11–16 April 2010).

Royster, Judith V., 'The Legacy of Allotment' (1995) 27 *Arizona State Law Journal* 2.

Sharma, Anisha, Shayak Barman and Paramita Datta Dey, 'Land Tenure Security: Is Titling Enough?' (National Institute of Urban Affairs, December 2006).

Sherry, Cathy, 'The Legal Fundamentals of High Rise Buildings and Master Planned Estates: Ownership, Governance and Living in Multi-owned Housing with a Case Study on Children's Play' (2008) 16(1) *Australian Property Law Journal* 1.

Shoemaker, Jessica A., 'Like Snow in the Spring Time: Allotment, Fractionation, and the Indian Land Tenure Problem' (2003) *Wisconsin Law Review* 729.

Sjaastad, Espen and Ben Cousins, 'Formalisation of Land Rights in the South: An Overview' (2008) 26 *Land Use Policy* 1.

Stephenson, Margaret, 'You Can't Always Get What You Want: Economic Development on Indigenous Individual and Collective Titles in North America – Which Land Tenure Models Are Relevant to Australia?' in Lee Godden and Maureen Tehan (eds), *Comparative Perspectives on Communal Lands and Individual Ownership: Sustainable Futures* (Routledge, 2010) 100.

Tollner, David, Commonwealth, *Parliamentary Debates*, House of Representatives, 19 June 2006, 90 (David Tollner).

Toomey, Leigh, 'A Delicate Balance: Building Complementary Customary and State Legal Systems' (2010) 3(1) *Law and Development Review* 155.

Toulmin, Camilla and Julian Quan, 'Evolving Land Rights, Tenure and Policy in Sub-Saharan Africa' in Camilla Toulmin and Julian Quan (eds), *Evolving Land Rights, Policy and Tenure in Africa* (International Institute for Environment and Development, 2000) 1.

Trebilcock, Michael and Paul-Erik Veel, 'Property Rights and Development: The Contingent Case for Formalization' (Legal Studies Research Series No 08–10, University of Toronto Faculty of Law, 2008).

United Nations Human Settlements Programme (UN-Habitat), 'Urban Land for All' (2004).

United Nations Human Settlements Programme (UN-Habitat), 'Secure Land Rights for All' (2008).

van den Brink, Rogier *et al.*, 'Consensus, Confusion, and Controversy: Selected Land Reform Issues in Sub-Saharan Africa' (Working Paper No 71, World Bank, 2006).

Wallace, Jude 'Managing Social Tenure' in Lee Godden and Maureen Tehan (eds), *Comparative Perspectives on Communal Land and Individual Ownership: Sustainable Futures* (Routledge, 2010) 25.

Warby, Michael, 'What Makes a Third World Country?' (1 January 2001) *Institute of Public Affairs* www.ipa.org.au/news/520/what-makes-a-third-world-country-/pg/10.

Watson, Nicole, 'Howard's End: The Real Agenda behind the Proposed Review of Indigenous Land Titles' (2005) 9(4) *Australian Indigenous Law Reporter* 1.

Wensing, Ed and Jonathon Taylor, 'Secure Tenure for Home Ownership and Economic Development on Land Subject to Native Title' (Research Discussion Paper No 31, AIATSIS Research Publications, August 2012).

Woodruff, Christopher, 'Review of de Soto's *The Mystery of Capital*' (2001) 39(4) *Journal of Economic Literature* 1215.

3 Aboriginal land in the Northern Territory

3.1 Aboriginal land ownership

In some respects, the history of Indigenous land ownership in Australia is unique. In comparable countries such as the United States, Canada and New Zealand, colonial laws gave at least some recognition to prior ownership of land by indigenous peoples. That recognition was both limited and problematic and, in the United States and New Zealand, it was accompanied by disastrous programmes for the allotment of land. It did nevertheless result in some indigenous groups retaining ownership of land after colonisation, which in North America was accompanied by a contained form of jurisdictional recognition. None of this happened in Australia. Until fairly recently, Australian law did not recognise prior Indigenous ownership of land at all. There were missions and reserves, areas of land that had been set aside for the use of Indigenous people, but this arrangement did not convey ownership rights of any kind, let alone jurisdiction. This was the situation that prevailed until the mid-1960s, since which time there has been a remarkable shift. Through statutory land rights schemes, and later through native title, Indigenous groups have regained exclusive rights to around 22.4 per cent of Australia.[1] The scope of this achievement requires some context, in that nearly all of this land is located in remote and very remote areas, but it remains a significant restructuring of the Australian property landscape.

This chapter does two things. It first summarises key elements of the way in which land is owned under *Aboriginal law*, according to current understandings. This is provided in Section 3.2, primarily by reference to published anthropological materials. Second, it describes how Aboriginal-specific forms of land ownership are provided for under *the formal legal system*.[2] This is provided in Section 3.3. In order to make it clear which is intended, the term 'Aboriginal land tenure' is used when referring to the system under which rights and obligations to land are allocated under Aboriginal law, and the term 'Aboriginal land' is used when referring to land owned by Aboriginal groups under the formal legal system.

This book takes as its primary case study the recent reforms to Aboriginal land in the Northern Territory, and this chapter is the first to take that narrower focus. The reason for this will be readily apparent – there are 34 distinct statutory regimes and land acquisition mechanisms in operation across the country, in addition to native title.[3] Describing them all would require pages of repetitious detail. At the same time, those details matter. Without them it is not possible to get a proper sense of who is, and who is not, an Aboriginal landowner, and what the recent land reforms actually mean for Aboriginal land.

The Northern Territory is the jurisdiction in which the recent reforms are most widespread and advanced. It is also the jurisdiction with the largest proportion of Aboriginal land ownership. There are three statutory land rights schemes that together account for around half of the Territory. The first is land held under the *Aboriginal Land Rights (Northern Territory) Act 1976* (Cth), or 'ALRA land'. The second is called Aboriginal community living area land, or 'CLA land', which is usually much smaller in area. The third is the land on which town camps are situated, or 'town camp land'. Town camps are found in or on the fringes of larger urban centres such as Alice Springs, Tennant Creek and Darwin.

Each of these schemes has a distinct history and land ownership structure. This chapter provides a picture of how they operate in practice, and in particular the relationship between these formal ownership systems and Aboriginal law. It is described how, of these three forms of Aboriginal land, it is only ALRA land that attempts to provide for formal ownership in accordance with Aboriginal law. The other two usually instead provide for ownership by the residential group. The important, and at times complex, distinction between *traditional ownership* and *residence* is fundamental to understanding how Aboriginal communities operate and how they have been impacted by the recent land reforms. This chapter makes clear how Aboriginal land tenure in the Northern Territory – in common with other parts of mainland Australia – was designed to support the activities of hunter-gatherer societies. Historically, there were no permanent settlements and no arrangements under Aboriginal law for 'holdings', or the allocation of exclusive rights over small areas to particular individuals and families. Instead, groups of people held collective rights to larger areas of land. Today, permanent settlements are the norm. Who, then, owns the land on which those settlements are situated, as well as the larger areas of land surrounding them? And what does it mean to talk about the 'traditional owners' for a community? This chapter answers these questions.

3.2 Ownership of land under Aboriginal law

Aboriginal land tenure

Providing a brief description of Aboriginal land tenure is not easy. As Sutton states, 'neat and simple models for Aboriginal land tenure have very limited usefulness' in either the academic or legal context.[4] This is not because there is some impenetrable aura surrounding Aboriginal law, but that like any property system it is complex. A particular statement might be at the same time accurate and misleading, in the same way that it would mislead to say only of English law that all rights to land are ultimately derived from the Crown.

The description of Aboriginal land tenure below is provided by reference to the classical model enunciated by Justice Edward Woodward in his two reports into Aboriginal land rights in the Northern Territory, which formed the basis for the introduction of the ALRA. Woodward was well positioned to comment on Aboriginal land tenure: he had previously acted for the Aboriginal claimants in the Gove land rights case (see below),[5] and received assistance from some of Australia's most respected anthropologists.[6] He was, however, writing at a time when anthropological understandings were still developing. Some of the changes in those understandings are also referred to here. For ease of understanding, the description is framed around the five key elements of the model that Woodward identified (although he himself did not explicitly use this structure).[7] Those five elements are: estates; levels of connection; clans; family groups; and the interplay between economy and religion.

The five key elements

Estates

Woodward found the primary unit of Aboriginal land tenure was an area of land called an 'estate'.[8] An estate is a reasonably large area of country, the boundaries of which are determined by reference to key locations called 'sites', although the way in which sites are used to determine estate boundaries varies from region to region.[9] There is some dispute about the extent to which estates were a Territory-wide phenomena. Some anthropologists have instead identified a larger area of land called 'countries', particularly (but not exclusively[10]) when describing Aboriginal land tenure in what is known as the 'Western Desert' area. The term 'Western Desert' describes a large area that crosses Western Australia, South Australia and the Northern Territory and which is commonly treated as culturally distinct. In particular, Western Desert land tenure is often described as more flexible and less regimented than land tenure in other regions.[11] It has been argued that this includes the use of a larger basic unit of tenure. This became a point of dispute in the recent *Yulara* native title case,[12] and anthropological debate about that case suggests that it remains contentious.[13] Sutton has also recorded the emergence of larger units of land holding among those Aboriginal people whose systems have been most disrupted by colonisation, a development discussed further below in relation to the identity of land holding groups.

Aboriginal land in the Northern Territory 69

Levels of connection and rights

The second 'element of Woodward's model is the existence of different levels of rights, which as described in Chapter 2 is a common feature of customary tenure systems around the world. Woodward found that there was a central, fairly well-defined group with primary rights and responsibilities,[14] and then a broader and less-defined group with lesser rights and responsibilities.[15] In his view, the most important distinguishing feature was that the first group had not only a right to use the land but also the primary spiritual responsibility for sites. As described below, this understanding is reflected in the definition of 'traditional Aboriginal owner' under the ALRA.

Over the years there have been different approaches to differentiating levels of rights to land under Aboriginal tenure, with a trend towards increased complexity.[16] Sutton argues that it is useful to draw a distinction between *forms of connection or affiliation*, which might be 'primary' and 'non-primary',[17] and *types of rights*, which he instead describes as 'core' and 'contingent'.[18] While there is a strong correlation between primary connection and core rights, this is by no means complete. Sutton argues that this differentiation allows for a better articulation of how rights are derived, in that context and negotiation remain a part of that process.[19]

Clans

Woodward found that for each estate there was a group of people called the 'land-owning clan' who were the primary owners, and that the membership of this group was determined by patrilineal descent.[20] This finding is now generally considered too narrow in several respects, and over time there has been a 'progressive expansion' of understandings about how people establish a primary connection.[21] For example, a common feature of Aboriginal land tenure is the sharing of responsibilities between 'owners' and 'managers'.[22] Woodward found that managers did not fit within the definition of 'traditional Aboriginal owner',[23] but since the 1980s it has been recognised that they do.[24] This is just one of several ways in which understandings of ownership have expanded.

The role and significance of the clan varies both regionally and as a result of adaptive processes following colonisation. Several authors argue that in more sparsely populated areas, such as the Western Desert region, land-based identity has always been more negotiable, to the point where Myers found that among Pintubi ownership 'is not a given, but an accomplishment'.[25] Where there is less emphasis on membership of the clan group, individual factors such as knowledge of ritual and country become more important.[26] Sutton observes that one consequence of colonisation has been the rise in the importance of regional identities such as the

70 Aboriginal land in the Northern Territory

language group, which has often corresponded with a partial or complete decline in the importance of the clan.[27] Merlan recorded this phenomenon when preparing a land claim for the Katherine Gorge region, where she found that 'for even many of the oldest Jawoyn ... [clans] no longer had great salience as territory groups' at any level.[28]

Family groups and bands

Woodward also found that while the land-owning clan were 'a group of people who share the same links with the same land', they were not the group around which daily life was organised.[29] Daily life was instead organised around the 'family group', a collection of extended family members who travelled, hunted and harvested food together, at times on their own, at times as part of a larger 'band'.[30] A family group might contain people from several clans and the movements of family groups were not contained to any particular estate.[31] That is, family groups and bands meet their need for food and other resources through hunting and gathering on the lands of more than one clan.

A religious and economic institution

A final element of Aboriginal land tenure is that it shares both religious and economic features.[32] As Langton and Peterson note, there has been a tendency among non-Aboriginal Australians to focus on the religious or spiritual elements of the Aboriginal relationship to land, at times at the expense of recognising its economic features.[33] There are many examples of this: one is the practice of characterising Aboriginal land tenure as 'ownership of people by the land' rather than 'ownership of land by people'.[34] It appears that a similar practice has sometimes occurred with respect North American Indians.[35] It is clear, however, that spiritual responsibility for sites has not prevented Aboriginal landowners from also seeing their land as an economic asset.[36] It is very common for Aboriginal landowners to engage in or authorise development on their land provided that certain areas are protected.

Residential communities

Historically, Aboriginal land tenure in the Northern Territory was structured around the spiritual and economic activities of mobile groups of hunter-gatherers. One of the more significant changes in the period since colonisation has been the shift to permanent residential settlements. When those settlements were formed, they invariably fell within the boundaries of one particular estate or country but included people from a broader area. This has resulted in a new dynamic, being the relationship between *traditional owners* and permanent or long-term *residents*.

Aboriginal land in the Northern Territory 71

A good entry point to discussing this relationship is a document known as the Reeves Report,[37] and the debate that surrounded it. In 1998, the Australian Government appointed Northern Territory barrister John Reeves QC to conduct a review of the operation of the ALRA. In his report, Reeves surveyed the anthropological literature and concluded that it is not possible to 'identify a corporate group within Aboriginal tradition as the "owners" of traditional lands'.[38] Drawing on a distinction that Justice Blackburn had used in the Gove land rights case,[39] he argued that while clans had spiritual responsibility for land this did not equate to economic ownership.[40] In fact, a number of anthropologists had previously argued that Justice Blackburn had been wrong on this point.[41] Williams states that it is religion which gives land ownership its normative base, and that spiritual responsibility is central to the mediated political process pursuant to which ownership rights are exercised, including the way in which permission must be sought.[42] Reeves took a different view. He concluded that Woodward's focus on the clan paid too little attention to the dynamics of Aboriginal tradition within wider regional populations.[43] On this basis, he recommended removing the distinction between traditional ownership and residence for the purpose of decision-making under the ALRA.[44] He argued that this would better support self-determination by allowing Aboriginal people to create their own leadership structures on a regional basis.[45]

It is certainly the case that aspects of Woodward's model have since been found to be too narrow or simplistic. In particular, it is common for anthropologists to emphasise the extent to which ownership rights are contextual, such that it is misleading to try to locate them in all circumstances at 'any single "level" of grouping'.[46] However, the volume of criticism directed at the Reeves Report suggests that its findings went too far.[47] Sutton, who was appointed by the Australian Anthropological Society to respond to the report, said that in practice attempts to merge the categories of residence and ownership were rare, and they were typically met with fierce opposition.[48] Merlan, on whose work Reeves relied, described his conclusions as 'incoherent in certain respects', and 'quite different' from the ones she would draw.[49] A parliamentary inquiry into the report rejected all its major recommendations, including his recommendation that the distinction between traditional ownership and residence be collapsed.[50]

At the same time, that distinction is not always clear-cut. Some events that can give rise to a recognised connection to country (conception, birth, burial) are incidents of residence; moreover, through growing up or working on country a person may acquire access to ritual knowledge that enhances authority.[51] It appears that the level of connection that flows from activities associated with residence will vary from region to region. In the Western Desert, it may give rise to a high level of connection, but this may be less so in other regions.[52] There are also areas of land where ownership has been acquired through succession, a now well-recognised process

72 *Aboriginal land in the Northern Territory*

under which groups acquire rights to neighbouring land.[53] In that context, occupation plays a greater role in the acquisition of rights,[54] and as such the distinction between traditional ownership and residence will be less clear.[55] And as this above discussion has illustrated, Aboriginal land tenure has evolved and will continue to evolve in response to the new circumstances in which Aboriginal people find themselves. Sutton notes that the 'rising importance of residential community identities, among younger generations' is one of the several factors that 'impact on land relationships'.[56]

Summary of Aboriginal land tenure

To recap, Aboriginal land tenure provides for ownership of areas of land by groups of people. The exact nature of the landholding unit (estates, countries) varies between regions, as does the composition of the landholding group. This is partly due to differences in cultural and economic practices and partly due to differences in the way colonisation has impacted. One of the key points to emerge from the description above is that there is no single level or form of ownership under Aboriginal land tenure. There are clear systems, but negotiation and contestation are also part of the process by which connection to country is converted into the exercise of ownership rights. It is against this backdrop that the relationship between traditional ownership and residence is best understood. While there remains a clear distinction between the two concepts, there is also scope – more so in some places than others – for particular individuals to elevate their ownership claims as a result of events that arise out of their residence. Both the distinction between traditional ownership and residence *and* the potential for contestation are important when considering such land reform issues as the payment of rent for leases in communities on Aboriginal land.

3.3 Formal ownership of Aboriginal land

This section now turns to the question of how the *formal legal system* provides for Aboriginal-specific forms of land ownership. There are of course Aboriginal people and organisations who own land under standard forms of ownership, such as where an Aboriginal couple own the fee simple to a house in Darwin. That is not the concern here. Rather, this section describes the three distinctive forms of land ownership that have been created for Aboriginal people in the Northern Territory.[57]

ALRA land

The first, and by far the most widespread, type of Aboriginal land in the Northern Territory is land held under the ALRA. Today almost half of all land in the Territory is ALRA land.[58] And as Chapter 6 makes clear, this is the land that has been most affected by recent land reforms. Of the 73 remote settlements targeted by those reforms, 52 are situated on ALRA land.

History of the ALRA

Above, reference was made to the decision of Justice Blackburn in the Gove land rights case, or *Milirrpum v Nabalco*.[59] That decision relates to an area of Arnhem Land, which is at the top end of the Northern Territory. Since the 1930s, Arnhem Land had been set aside as a reserve for the benefit of Aboriginal residents. The creation of a reserve did not give Aboriginal people any form of ownership rights, the consequences of which became apparent in the early 1960s when the Australian Government unilaterally excised an area from the reserve for the purpose of granting a mining lease. Under Aboriginal land tenure, that land belonged to a group of Yolngu people who – with the assistance of Edward Woodward, then a barrister – took proceedings in the Supreme Court of the Northern Territory to have their traditional rights to land recognised.[60] They were unsuccessful, with Justice Blackburn handing down a decision in 1971 in which he found that while there was a coherent system of traditional laws in relation to land, that system could not be recognised by Australian law.[61]

Justice Blackburn's conclusions about the recognition of native title were later overturned by the High Court in *Mabo*;[62] however, that was not for another two decades. In the meantime, one outcome of the Gove land rights was increased pressure on the Australian Government to introduce land rights via legislation. Initially it refused to do so. On Australia Day 1972, Liberal Prime Minister McMahon made a speech in which he agreed to the acquisition of select properties for Aboriginal people and the grant of leases over reserve land, but ruled out any more widespread form of land rights. Rather than placating land rights advocates, this led to increased protests including the establishment of the Aboriginal Tent Embassy.[63] The opposition Labor party took a different approach. Under the leadership of Gough Whitlam, they agreed to support the introduction of land rights. The Labor Party won the general elections in December of that year, and one of Whitlam's first acts as Prime Minister was to appoint Woodward to conduct a judicial inquiry into the process for the grant of Aboriginal land rights in the Northern Territory, which, as a territory, was an area for which the Commonwealth Government had greater responsibility.[64] As part of his brief, Woodward produced a set of drafting instructions, which formed the basis for a Bill presented to Parliament in October 1975.[65] The following month, however, Whitlam was dismissed by the Governor-General and in the ensuing elections the Labor Party was voted out of government. The Bill presented in October had not been passed and subsequently lapsed.[66]

74   Aboriginal land in the Northern Territory

Despite its earlier opposition, during the 1975 election campaign the Liberal–Country Party Coalition, led by Malcolm Fraser, agreed to support a similar form of land rights to that proposed by Whitlam.[67] In June 1976 the Fraser Government introduced a new Bill,[68] which differed in several respects from the version that Whitlam had earlier presented.[69] After further negotiation, the Bill was passed in December 1976,[70] and commenced on Australia Day 1977,[71] exactly five years after McMahon's speech.

This description makes two things clear. First, as with much legislation the final shape of the ALRA was the outcome of a situation in which the expertise of select individuals intersected with political processes. In different circumstances, that outcome would have been different. As discussed below, it is conceivable that the ALRA might have ended up with a very different ownership structure to the one it does today. Second, the ALRA's enactment by a conservative government reflected a shift in the political consensus of the time. This could not have occurred five years earlier. It would, however, mislead to overstate the level of bipartisan support the legislation enjoyed. Woodward credits Malcolm Fraser and Ian Viner with ensuring the passage of the ALRA in the face of strong opposition from within the Coalition.[72] Further, the final version of the Act differed from the model suggested by Woodward in two important respects. Provisions to enable land to be acquired for Aboriginal people for commercial purposes and on the basis of need had been removed,[73] and certain issues, such as the protection of sacred sites and the enactment of a permit system, were left to be legislated upon by the Northern Territory (NT) Government, which was less supportive of land rights.[74]

The ALRA provided for existing Aboriginal reserves to be immediately transferred into Aboriginal ownership. It also included a land claims mechanism, whereby unalienated Crown land might be returned to those people who could demonstrate that they were the traditional Aboriginal owners of the land.[75] Together, these have resulted in nearly half of the Territory becoming ALRA land.

Land ownership under the ALRA

(A) AIM OF THE OWNERSHIP STRUCTURE

Woodward was required to make recommendations about how Aboriginal land should be owned under formal law. He saw it as his role to give 'effect, as closely as possible, to what [he] believed to be the Aboriginal law on the subject'.[76] Interestingly, his beliefs about Aboriginal law changed over time. Initially he formed the view that land should be owned by residential communities, as they had become 'the basic social grouping for Aborigines in modern society'.[77] To be clear: Woodward was not making a distinction here between land in communities and other land.

He was suggesting that *all* land should be divided up and allocated to the nearest residential community.[78] However, in his second report Woodward reached a different conclusion. He found that his 'statement of the significance of the community in modern Aboriginal society undervalued the continuing importance of the clan structure'.[79] He was instead persuaded that the ownership system should give 'maximum possible authority to the older men of importance in the clan structure',[80] relying 'on them in their turn to recognise and respect the lesser rights of others in that land'.[81]

In fact Woodward recommended not one ownership structure, but two. He suggested that land granted through needs-based claims should be owned by 'approved corporations' on behalf of Aboriginal residents,[82] while former reserves and successful land claims should be owned in accordance with tradition.[83] Needs-based claims were not included in the final version of the Act, and Maddock argues that their removal 'accentuated ... the firmness with which the Act comes down on the side of Aborigines who are traditionally connected'.[84]

(B) TRIPARTITE OWNERSHIP STRUCTURE

Brennan describes the ownership system for ALRA land as a 'tripartite structure',[85] as it involves three parties: Aboriginal Land Trusts, Aboriginal Land Councils and the Aboriginal owners. It is Aboriginal Land Trusts who hold formal title to land; however, their role is largely passive.[86] Their only function is to deal with the land as directed by an Aboriginal Land Council.[87] They have no powers outside of this. They are not able to accept money,[88] nor take an action in relation to the land otherwise than as directed by a Land Council.[89]

Aboriginal Land Councils provide a single point of contact for outsiders and the governance machinery for land dealings.[90] It is their role to consult, negotiate with third parties, collect and distribute land-use payments and (provided that they have consulted, etc) direct the Land Trusts to take actions such as the granting of a lease. However, it is not the Aboriginal Land Councils that are the ultimate decision-makers: this role belongs to the Aboriginal groups with whom they are required to consult, and in particular the traditional Aboriginal owners.

The Act defines 'traditional Aboriginal owners' as:

> a local descent group of Aboriginals who:
>
> (a) have common spiritual affiliations to a site on the land, being affiliations that place the group under a primary spiritual responsibility for that site and for the land; and
>
> (b) are entitled by Aboriginal tradition to forage as of right over that land.[91]

76   *Aboriginal land in the Northern Territory*

This definition is based on the anthropological conclusions of Woodward described earlier. The same definition is used to determine eligibility during the land claims process, and in that context its meaning has broadened over time. As Layton notes, it is paragraph (a) that is the more limiting, in that the right to forage tends to encompass a wider area than primary spiritual responsibility.[92]

It is the traditional Aboriginal owners who exercise the highest degree of control over land-use decision-making. For example, a Land Council cannot direct a Land Trust to grant a lease unless: '(a) the traditional Aboriginal owners (if any) of that land understand the nature and purpose of the proposed grant ... and, as a group, consent to it.'[93] The traditional Aboriginal owners have similar authority with respect to land-use payments, such as rent on a lease. Land Councils must within six months pay such monies 'to or for the benefit of the traditional Aboriginal owners of the land'.[94] Relevantly, this means that where rent is paid for a lease in a community on ALRA land, the Land Council must distribute it 'to or for the benefit of traditional Aboriginal owners', rather than to or for the benefit of Aboriginal community residents.

The ALRA also recognises a wider set of lesser rights to land. This is achieved in two slightly different ways. It first provides that Aboriginal Land Trusts hold title not just for the benefit of the traditional Aboriginal owners, but for the benefit of all 'Aboriginals entitled by Aboriginal tradition to the use or occupation of the land concerned, *whether or not the traditional entitlement is qualified as to place, time, circumstance, purpose or permission*'.[95] This encompasses a broader group, who do not have primary spiritual responsibility and might hold only qualified rights under Aboriginal law.[96]

While Land Trusts hold title for the benefit of this broader group, however, the only section of the Act that specifically grants them rights to that land is s 71(1), which protects their entitlement to enter, use and occupy land 'to the extent that that entry, occupation or use is in accordance with Aboriginal tradition'.[97] This means that where there is no lease, the rights of Aboriginal people to occupy ALRA land are those given by Aboriginal law, which include people with secondary rights. Of course, where there is a lease those rights might be curtailed.

The second way in which a wider set of rights is recognised is through the consultation process. The Act requires a Land Council to consult with a broader group than just the traditional Aboriginal owners. For example, a Land Council cannot direct a Land Trust to grant a lease unless: '(b) any Aboriginal community or group that may be affected by the proposed grant, transfer or surrender has been consulted and has had adequate opportunity to express its view to the Land Council.'[98] To be clear, it is only the traditional Aboriginal owners who can withhold consent. This broader group has only a right to be consulted, not a right to decide the outcome. However, through the consultation process they may make their views known to the traditional owners and call upon them to respect their wishes, invoking any obligation they may have under Aboriginal law or in accordance with local politics. To return to the example of granting a lease in a community on ALRA land, the Land Council is clearly required to consult with Aboriginal community residents, who have the opportunity to present arguments, make their views known and perhaps even to assert some authority with respect to decision-making. It then falls to the group recognised as the traditional Aboriginal owners for that land to grant or withhold consent.

(C) CHECKS ON THE EXERCISE OF AUTHORITY

There are several checks and balances on decision-making under the ALRA. The first is the tripartite structure itself. Woodward concluded that it would be impractical to simply vest individual clans with ownership of particular areas of land,[99] and so recommended a structure that he believed was more workable yet achieved substantially the same result.[100] The outcome was a system that effectively splits ownership (by Land Trusts) from management (by Land Councils) and decision-making (primarily by traditional Aboriginal owners), which creates a check on the exercise of authority by any particular party. For example, Woodward envisaged that if a Land Trust did not approve of a direction from a Land Council it would have to be 'further debated or resolved by court proceedings'.[101]

The role of Land Councils goes slightly beyond merely consulting and providing directions. They are also required to exercise some independent judgement. For example, a Land Council cannot direct a Land Trust to enter into a lease unless it is satisfied that 'the terms and conditions on which the grant is to be made are reasonable'.[102] This is the case even where the traditional Aboriginal owners have provided consent. Land Councils are also the point of contact for people wanting a lease over Aboriginal land, and they determine how consultations are undertaken. As Toohey notes, this too involves a 'subjective element'.[103] In some circumstances, the Minister for Indigenous Affairs provides a further check on decision-making. For example, any lease for more than 40 years requires ministerial consent.[104]

(D) LAND ACCESS AND THE PERMIT SYSTEM

Woodward recommended that access to ALRA land be regulated by a permit system. He saw this as something of a balancing act – while the ability to control access was 'one of the most important proofs of genuine Aboriginal ownership of land',[105] it also needed to be managed expediently and it was unrealistic to always obtain each landowner's permission. Woodward suggested that the permit system be included in the ALRA itself, which was reflected in the Bill that Whitlam presented.[106] The Fraser

78 *Aboriginal land in the Northern Territory*

Government instead wanted this to fall under the control of the NT Government.[107] This is achieved through the ALRA containing a general prohibition on access,[108] supplemented by a provision enabling the NT Government to make laws authorising entry.[109] Pursuant to this, the NT Government introduced a permit system under the *Aboriginal Land Act 1979* (NT).[110]

The Territory Act provides that either a Land Council or the traditional Aboriginal owners may issue a permit for a person to enter and remain on ALRA land, which may be granted subject to conditions.[111] Permits are not required for Aboriginal people who are entitled to enter land under Aboriginal tradition,[112] or for certain other persons, such as members of parliament when acting in the course of their duties.[113] In addition, the responsible NT Minister may issue a permit to a person who is 'employed under or by virtue of an Act', or is a member of the staff of a Minister, the Leader of the Opposition or the Deputy Leader of the Opposition.[114] The Land Council or traditional Aboriginal owners may also waive the need for permits for a particular area.[115]

For practical reasons, a Land Council is not required to obtain the consent of traditional Aboriginal owners for each and every permit. Rather, before commencing to issue permits they must consult and 'come to an agreement with the traditional Aboriginal owners' of the relevant area 'as to the terms and conditions upon which the Land Council may issue permits'.[116] Each Land Council has developed forms and procedures for persons wanting to apply for a permit.

CLA land

Of the 73 remote Aboriginal settlements in the Northern Territory that have been targeted by recent land reforms, 16 are situated on land owned as an 'Aboriginal community living area'. This land – described here as 'CLA land' – differs from ALRA land in several respects. While the ALRA is Commonwealth legislation, CLA land is created entirely under NT law. Areas of CLA land tend to be smaller. Rather than a tripartite ownership structure, CLA land is simply owned by a body corporate. There are greater statutory restrictions on the transfer and use of CLA land, and they tend to provide for ownership by residents rather than traditional owners. These features are a reflection of the distinct historical origins of CLA land.

History of CLA land

By 1970 there were around 4,305 Aboriginal people living on pastoral properties around the Northern Territory.[117] This number had been gradually reducing as a result of the declining role of Aboriginal people in the pastoral industry, but still represented around 20 per cent of Aboriginal people in the Territory.[118] In addition, a number of Aboriginal people

Aboriginal land in the Northern Territory 79

living on the fringes of towns had expressed an interest in returning to the pastoral leases on which they had previously lived and worked.[119] This was consequently an issue that came before Woodward during his inquiry into land rights in 1973–4.

The Central Land Council (CLC) and Northern Land Council (NLC)[120] submitted to Woodward that traditional owners should be able to claim underlying ownership of land that was subject to a pastoral lease.[121] This was one area where Woodward felt unable to accede to their claims.[122] He instead recommended that Aboriginal people currently living on pastoral leases be granted small areas of land called 'community areas'.[123] These would be excised from the pastoral lease and granted to an Aboriginal corporation pursuant to a special purpose lease.[124] As the areas in question were small relative to the size of pastoral leases, he hoped that the process might occur by agreement, but in the event of no agreement he recommended a claims process under the ALRA.[125]

This recommendation was not reflected in the final version of the ALRA, with the issue instead left to the NT Government. Some grants were made by agreement, but it was not until 1989 that a formal claims process was finally established under NT law.[126] This was as part of an agreement between the NT and Commonwealth governments settling land claims over stock routes.[127] As it was concerned to prevent 'a flood of claims which may [result from] a land rights approach',[128] the NT Government imposed strict rules on eligibility. The claims process excludes any consideration of traditional connection, and is instead limited to those Aborigines who can demonstrate a sufficiently extensive historical connection and a 'present need for a community living area'.[129] Despite these restrictions, a large number of Aboriginal people have obtained CLAs through either claim or negotiation. The CLC reports that there are 65 CLAs in its region alone.[130]

Ownership structure

Many CLA grants were initially made by way of special purpose lease, but most have since been converted to freehold.[131] That freehold is owned by a body corporate, which can be either an incorporated association[132] or an Aboriginal corporation.[133] Until recently, the landholding association needed ministerial permission to deal with CLA land other than by way of disposal or grant to the NT Government or by way of a short-term lease (up to 12 months). More importantly, the Minister could only grant permission in a limited range of circumstances.[134] The result was that ownership of CLA land was far more restrictive than ownership of ALRA land, where a lease can be granted 'to any person for any purpose'.[135] It meant, for example, that the grant of a lease to an art centre or a store was not permitted on CLA land. This has changed as a result of certain of the recent reforms.

80 *Aboriginal land in the Northern Territory*

There is no permit system regulating access to CLA land. Instead, access is controlled by the landholding association in accordance with general law.

CLA land also tends to be owned by residents rather than traditional owners, although this is not always the case. It depends on the wording of the membership clause for the landholding association. For example, at Lake Nash membership of the landholding association is open to Aboriginal people who are 'normally a [permanent] resident at Alpurrurulum (Lake Nash) ... or at such other location or locations as the directors shall from time to time determine'.[136] This appears to be the most common approach;[137] however, there are exceptions: in the Yupanalla community, only residents who are also 'traditional Aboriginal owners' are eligible for membership of the landholding association.[138]

Town camp land

History of town camps

Historically Aboriginal people were prevented from living in urban centres by a range of discriminatory laws and practices such as curfews. They were instead required to live in 'fringe camps'[139] of their own creation – some of which were in authorised camping areas, others of which were illegal – or in government or mission-controlled compounds.[140] None of these arrangements provided Aboriginal residents with any form of legal ownership.[141] Woodward reported that by 1971 there were around 4,000 Aboriginal people living in and around the four major urban centres (Darwin, Katherine, Tennant Creek and Alice Springs).[142] It was part of his role to consider how their land needs might be met.

Woodward found some diversity within this group. He was persuaded by the NLC that a variety of housing options should be made available from a 'white community style of accommodation', through 'village'-style living to more traditional bush-style camping.[143] On this basis he made a range of recommendations, including the accommodation of Aboriginal groups in planning processes, the grant of specific areas to existing groups, and for the Aboriginal Land Commissioner to hear claims on the basis of need.[144] The Whitlam Government accepted these recommendations and in 1975 appointed Justice Ward as interim Aboriginal Land Commissioner, even though legislation had not yet been enacted. The CLC immediately submitted needs-based claims over 12 areas of land in the Alice Springs area and, after preliminary hearings, Justice Ward indicated that he was likely to recommend their grant. Shortly thereafter Whitlam was dismissed and caretaker Prime Minister Malcolm Fraser ordered that Justice Ward cease hearing claims.[145] The needs-based claims provisions were then removed from the final version of the ALRA.[146]

Instead, and after considerable negotiation,[147] the Department of the Northern Territory (and later the NT Government) began to administratively

Aboriginal land in the Northern Territory 81

grant leases over particular areas of land. Twenty-six leases had already been granted by 1983,[148] and today there are around 47 town camps across the Northern Territory: 19 in Alice Springs, nine in Tennant Creek, six in Darwin, four in Borroloola, three in Katherine, two in Elliott and one each in Adelaide River, Mataranka, Pine Creek and Jabiru.[149] In all cases they are relatively small areas, consisting mainly of housing for residents.

Ownership structure

Unlike ALRA land and CLA land, most town camp land is held as lease-hold rather than freehold, although many leases are now held in perpetuity. Only four town camps are freehold, while a further five have not been granted any form of tenure.[150] Beyond this, the ownership structure for town camp land is similar to that for CLA land. Legal title is held by incorporated bodies – commonly referred to as 'town camp housing associations' – on behalf of members. In Alice Springs and Tennant Creek, housing associations have grouped together to form collective representative bodies, called Tangentyere Council and Julalikari Council; however, unlike Aboriginal Land Councils these bodies do not play a legal role in land ownership. There are also strict legislative restrictions on the grant of subleases over town camp land,[151] and the general law rather than a statutory permit system regulates access.

3.4 Conclusion

Chapter 2 describes how there are four different categories of property regime: state property, communal property, private property and non-property or open access. Both ALRA and CLA land are examples of communal property. They are also quite different from each other. The ALRA reflects an attempt to embody or formalise ownership of land in accordance with Aboriginal land tenure, or ownership of land under Aboriginal law. It does so through a tripartite structure under which ownership, management and decision-making authority are to some extent separated. Those people who are recognised as being traditional owners have the greatest decision-making authority. A wider group of Aboriginal people have the right to be consulted in relation to developments, such as the grant of a lease, but it is the traditional owners who have the right to grant or withhold consent. The ALRA is a classic example of an attempt to formalise customary ownership of land.

The ownership structure on CLA land is much simpler; land is both owned and managed by the landholding association. However, there have been several statutory restrictions on the grant of interests over CLA land that have made leasing far more difficult, to the extent that it is difficult to find any historical record of such leases. Chapter 6 describes how this

82 *Aboriginal land in the Northern Territory*

became a significant problem when the Australian Government introduced its 'secure tenure' policies, which required leases to be granted before government funding would be made available.

A significant difference between ALRA and CLA land is the ownership group. On most – but not all – CLAs, membership of the landholding association is open to all community residents. In some places, such as the community of Yupanalla, membership of the landholding association is only open to those residents who are also traditional owners. This creates a similar dynamic with respect to the relationship between ownership and residence as occurs in communities on ALRA land.

Strictly, most town camp land remains state property as underlying ownership belongs to the Crown. Clearly the leases reflect a significant shift towards communal property, and in many cases those leases have been made perpetual. It is nevertheless a slightly more vulnerable, less secure, form of ownership. In other respects, town camp land is very similar to CLA land.

One of the things that Section 3.2 of this chapter makes clear is that holdings, or the allocation of exclusive rights over smaller areas of land to particular individuals and families, have not traditionally been a feature of Aboriginal land tenure. Today, however, there are a number of residential communities situated on Aboriginal land in which individuals and families – as well as governments and organisations – enjoy exclusive rights to infrastructure such as houses, offices, workshops and stores. The following chapter now turns to the question of how this has come about, and its relationship to land ownership under both Aboriginal law and the formal legal system.

Notes

1 Jon Altman and Francis Markham, 'Burgeoning Indigenous Land Ownership: Diverse Values and Strategic Potentialities' in Sean Brennan *et al.*, *Native Title from Mabo to Akiba: A Vehicle for Change and Empowerment?* (Federation Press, 2015) 126, 135.

2 For reasons described in Chapter 2, this book follows the practice of describing the mainstream Australian legal system as formal law. This is not intended to suggest that Aboriginal law lacks either structure or legitimacy.

3 Altman and Markham, above n 1, 133.

4 Peter Sutton, *Country: Aboriginal Boundaries and Land Ownership in Australia* (Aboriginal History Inc, Monograph 3, 1995) 49.

5 *Milirrpum v Nabalco Pty Ltd* (1971) 17 FLR 141.

6 Woodward was advised by Professors W.E.H. Stanner and R.M. Berndt and assisted by Dr Nicolas Peterson; see Sir Edward Woodward, *One Brief Interval* (Miegunyah Press, 2005) 100, 134; Edward Woodward, Submission No 47 to the House of Representatives Standing Committee on Aboriginal and Torres Strait Islander Affairs, *Inquiry into the Recommendations of the Reeves Report Review of the Aboriginal Land Rights (Northern Territory) Act 1976* (1999), 3.

Aboriginal land in the Northern Territory 83

7 Woodward set out his main findings in relation to Aboriginal land ownership in his first report, Edward Woodward, 'Aboriginal Land Rights Commission: First Report' (Australian Government, 1973) 4–10. Those same provisions were then replicated in his second report, Edward Woodward, 'Aboriginal Land Rights Commission: Second Report' (Australian Government, 1974) Appendix A.

8 Sutton argues that the 'basic notion of the estate as a primary unit of tenure has endured', not in all areas of the Western Desert but virtually everywhere else; see Peter Sutton, *Native Title in Australia: An Ethnographic Perspective* (Cambridge University Press, 2003) 69.

9 Ibid; and see Woodward, 'First Report', above n 7, 19 [112].

10 See, eg, Ian Keen, 'The Western Desert vs the Rest: Rethinking the Contrast' in Francesca Merlan, John Morton and Alan Rumsey (eds), *Scholar and Sceptic: Australian Aboriginal Studies in Honour of LR Hiatt* (Aboriginal Studies Press, 1997) 65, 69.

11 Dousset and Glaskin trace the notion of a distinct Western Desert cultural bloc to Berndt; see Laurent Dousset and Katie Glaskin, 'Western Desert and Native Title: How Models Become Myths' (2007) 17(2) *Anthropological Forum* 127, 128–30 including n 2. The authors also refer to an extensive list of scholars who have noted the flexibility of the Western Desert systems with respect to land tenure, see 131–2. Keen has argued that the distinction between 'The West' and 'The Rest' has been overstated, Keen, above n 10, a position that has drawn criticism from Sansom; Basil Sansom, '*Yulara* and Further Expert Reports in Native Title Cases' (2007) 17(1) *Anthropological Forum* 71, 79.

12 *Jango v Northern Territory of Australia* [2006] FCA 318.

13 See, eg, Sansom, above n 11, who was a witness for the Northern Territory, and the various responses to Sansom's article in the following edition of *Anthropological Forum* (17(2), pp. 163–92). See also Dousset and Glaskin, above n 11, 135. For an earlier perspective, see Robert Layton, 'Ambilineal Descent and Traditional Pitjantjatjara Rights to Land' in Nicolas Peterson and Marcia Langton (eds), *Aborigines, Land and Land Rights* (Australian Institute of Aboriginal Studies, 1983) 15.

14 Woodward, 'First Report', above n 7, 19 [111].

15 Woodward, 'First Report', above n 7, 8 [53], 9 [56], 19 [113]–[114]. For a discussion of those who fit within this broader group, see also Woodward, Submission No 47, above n 6, 16; John Toohey, 'Seven Years On: Report by Mr Justice Toohey to the Minister for Aboriginal Affairs on the *Aboriginal Land Rights (Northern Territory) Act 1976* and Related Matters' (Australian Government, 1983) 38 [261]; Nicolas Peterson, 'Rights, Residence and Process in Australian Territorial Organisation' in Nicolas Peterson and Marcia Langton (eds), *Aborigines, Land and Land Rights* (Australian Institute of Aboriginal Studies, 1983) 134, 137–8.

16 For an overview, see Sutton, *Native Title in Australia*, above n 8, 1–14. See also Justice John Toohey, 'Uluru (Ayers Rock) National Park and Lake Amadeus/Luritja Land Claim' (Report by the Aboriginal Land Commissioner, 1979) 5 [27]; Layton, above n 13, 25; Nancy Williams, 'Yolngu Concepts of Land Ownership' in Nicolas Peterson and Marcia Langton (eds), *Aborigines, Land and Land Rights* (Australian Institute of Aboriginal Studies, 1983) 94, 103, 105–6.

17 Sutton, *Native Title in Australia*, above n 8, 10.

18 Ibid, 11–12. Sutton presents this as one of the ways rights might be differentiated.

19 Ibid, 13.

84 Aboriginal land in the Northern Territory

20 Woodward, 'First Report', above n 7, 6–9.
21 Graeme Neate, *Aboriginal Land Rights Law in the Northern Territory* (Alternative Publishing Co-operative Ltd, 1989) 42, and see also 49–60.
22 See, eg, Kenneth Maddock, ' "Owners", "Managers" and the Choice of Statutory Traditional Owners by Anthropologists and Lawyers' in Nicolas Peterson and Marcia Langton (eds), *Aborigines, Land and Land Rights* (Australian Institute of Aboriginal Studies, 1983) 211, 213. Prior to the 1960s it was common for anthropologists to concentrate on owners to the exclusion of managers; Peterson, above n 15, 137. Layton states that the owner/manager relationship is not a feature of land tenure among Pitjantjatjara; see Layton, above n 13, 30.
23 See Woodward, 'First Report', above n 7, 19 [114].
24 Marc Gumbert, 'Paradigm Lost: Anthropological Models and Their Effect on Aboriginal Land Rights' (1981) 52(2) *Oceania* 103, 119; Neate, above n 21, 49; Toohey, 'Seven Years On', above n 15, 37; Heather McRae *et al.*, *Indigenous Legal Issues, Commentary and Materials* (Thomson Reuters, 2009) 232–3.
25 Fred Myers, *Pintupi Country, Pintupi Self: Sentiment, Place, and Politics among Western Desert Aborigines* (University of California Press, 1991) 129. See also Sutton, *Country: Aboriginal Boundaries and Land Ownership in Australia*, above n 4, 50, although cf Sansom, above n 11, 73.
26 For an example in the context of a land claim see Justice Michael Maurice, 'Lake Amadeus Land Claim No 28' (Report by the Aboriginal Land Commissioner, 1988) 12 [88] and 80.
27 Sutton, *Country: Aboriginal Boundaries and Land Ownership in Australia*, above n 4, 47; Peter Sutton, *Native Title and the Descent of Rights* (National Native Title Tribunal, 1998) 55.
28 Francesca Merlan, 'The Regimentation of Customary Practice: From Northern Territory Land Claims to Mabo' (1995) 6(1/2) *Australian Journal of Anthropology* 64, 76. Merlan noted that the area had been subject to 'unremitting social and cultural impacts' and found that instead of clans there was a 'higher-level, socio-territorial Jawoyn identity'.
29 Woodward, 'First Report', above n 7, 7 [41].
30 Ibid, 8 [52].
31 Peterson, above n 15, 134; Woodward, Submission No 47, above n 6, 5 [17]–[18]; Sutton, *Native Title in Australia*, above n 8, 44–53.
32 Woodward acknowledged this but dealt with it only briefly; see, eg, Woodward, 'Second Report', above n 7, 34 [196].
33 Marcia Langton and Nicolas Peterson, 'Introduction' in Nicolas Peterson and Marcia Langton (eds), *Aborigines, Land and Land Rights* (Australian Institute of Aboriginal Studies, 1983) 3, 5.
34 Langton and Peterson describe it as a 'frequently quoted axiom', and one that is 'superficial and inaccurate'; ibid, 5. Neate reports that this originated with A.P. Elkin but has been repeated widely; Neate, above n 21, 30. Notably, Justice Blackburn adopted this characterisation in the Gove land rights case (see below), *Milirrpum v Nabalco Pty Ltd* (1971) 17 FLR 141, 270–1.
35 See Tom Flanagan, Christopher Alcantara and André Le Dressay, *Beyond the Indian Act: Restoring Aboriginal Property Rights* (McGill-Queen's University Press, 2010) 30.
36 David Dalrymple, 'Land Rights and Property Rights' (2007) 51(1) *Quadrant* 61. For a more detailed analysis of this relationship, see Peter Sutton, 'Suggestions for a Bicameral System' (1984) 5(3) *Anthropological Forum* 395.
37 John Reeves, 'Building on Land Rights for the Next Generation: The Review of the *Aboriginal Land Rights (Northern Territory) Act 1976*' (Australian Government, 1998). The Reeves Report is also discussed in Chapter 5.

38 Ibid, 202.
39 *Milirrpum v Nabalco Pty Ltd* (1971) 17 FLR 141, 181–2, 272.
40 Reeves, above n 37, 203–4.
41 Williams, above n 16, 94. See also Peter Sutton, 'Anthropological Submission on the Reeves Review' (1999) 9(2) *Anthropological Forum* 189, 203, 207 n 8.
42 Williams, above n 16, 99, 107.
43 Reeves, above n 37, 119, 140, 146–8.
44 See Sutton, 'Anthropological Submission on the Reeves Review', above n 41, 190.
45 Reeves, above n 37, ii, 200–1, 213.
46 Sutton, 'Anthropological Submission on the Reeves Review', above n 41, 204.
47 Brennan describes 'a chorus of anthropological disapproval for the way in which [Reeves] collapsed the distinction between traditional owners and residents of Aboriginal land'; Sean Brennan, 'Economic Development and Land Council Power: Modernising the *Land Rights Act* or Same Old Same Old?' (2006) 10(4) *Australian Indigenous Law Reporter* 1, 7.
48 Sutton, 'Anthropological Submission on the Reeves Review', above n 41, 191.
49 Francesca Merlan, Submission No 29 to the House of Representatives Standing Committee on Aboriginal and Torres Strait Islander Affairs, *Inquiry into the Recommendations of the Reeves Report Review of the Aboriginal Land Rights (Northern Territory) Act 1976* 28 March 1999, 1.
50 House of Representatives Standing Committee on Aboriginal and Torres Strait Islander Affairs, *The Report of the Inquiry into the Reeves Review of the Aboriginal Land Rights (Northern Territory) Act 1976* (1999). See also Brennan, above n 47, 3–6.
51 For an example of this in the land claim context, see Justice Peter Gray, 'Tempe Downs and Middleton Ponds/Luritja Land Claim No 147' (Report by the Aboriginal Land Commissioner, 1998) 18 [3.6]; Justice Maurice, above n 26, 28–9 [210].
52 Peterson, above n 15, 137; Sutton, 'Anthropological Submission on the Reeves Review', above n 41, 193.
53 For a discussion of succession, see Woodward, 'First Report', above n 7, 7 [46]; Peterson, above n 15, 138; Williams, above n 16, 104; John Stanton, 'Old Business, New Owners: Succession and "The Law" on the Fringe of the Western Desert' in Nicolas Peterson and Marcia Langton (eds), *Aborigines, Land and Land Rights* (Australian Institute of Aboriginal Studies, 1983) 160; Sutton, *Native Title in Australia*, above n 8, 5–8, 121–2; Ron Levy, 'Twenty Year of Land Rights: Lessons for the Native Title Act' (1996) 3(85) *Aboriginal Law Bulletin* 22, 25.
54 Langton and Peterson, above n 33, 6.
55 Sarah Holcombe, 'Traditional Owners and "Community-Country" Anangu: Distinctions and Dilemmas' (2004) 2 *Australian Aboriginal Studies* 64, 68–9.
56 Peter Sutton, 'Stanner and Aboriginal Land Use: Ecology, Economic Change, and Enclosing the Commons' in Melinda Hinkson and Jeremy Beckett (eds), *An Appreciate of Difference: WEH Stanner and Aboriginal Australia* (Aboriginal Studies Press, 2008) 169, 173.
57 There is in fact a fourth type of Aboriginal land in the Northern Territory called 'Park Land Trusts', which are used to support the joint management of certain national parks. These have not been affected by the recent reforms and are not described further here.
58 Northern Land Council, *What we do*, www.nlc.org.au/articles/info/what-does-the-northern-land-council-do.
59 (1971) 17 FLR 141.
60 McRae *et al.*, above n 24, 283–5.

86 Aboriginal land in the Northern Territory

61 Ibid and see also Woodward, *One Brief Interval*, above n 6, 105–6.
62 *Mabo v Queensland (No 2)* (1992) 175 CLR 1.
63 David Pollack, 'Indigenous Land in Australia: A Quantitative Assessment of Indigenous Landholdings in 2000' (Discussion Paper No 221/2001, Centre for Aboriginal Economic Policy Research, 2001) 6, 11; Gary Foley and Tim Anderson, 'Land Rights and Aboriginal Voices' (2006) 12(1) *Australian Journal of Human Rights* 83, 90; Kenneth Maddock, *Your Land Is Our Land* (Penguin, 1983) 29.
64 The inquiry was announced on 15 December 1972, less than two weeks after the election; Gregory Jones, *Aboriginal Land Rights Legislation: An Examination of the Publications Associated with the Commonwealth Legislation* (Canberra College of Advanced Education, 1983) 1. See also Woodward, *One Brief Interval*, above n 6, 133.
65 The *Aboriginal Land Rights (Northern Territory) Bill 1975* was presented to the House of Representatives on 16 October 1975; Jones 1983, above n 64, 10.
66 Ibid, 11–13.
67 Central Land Council (CLC), *The Land Is Always Alive: The Story of the Central Land Council* (1994) 10.
68 The *Aboriginal Land Rights (Northern Territory) Bill 1976*.
69 CLC, above n 67, 10.
70 Ibid.
71 Jones, above n 64, 17.
72 Woodward, *One Brief Interval*, above n 6, 143; and see also Brennan, above n 47, 2.
73 Woodward, *One Brief Interval*, above n 6, 143.
74 Neate, above n 21, 5. This occurred in the context of the Northern Territory being provided with a form of self-government in 1978.
75 A sunset clause in the ALRA prevents the bringing of new claims after 5 June 1997.
76 Woodward, Submission No 47, above n 6, 3 [9]; and see also Woodward, 'Second Report', above n 7, 14 [84].
77 Woodward, 'Second Report', above n 7, 13 [78]. Woodward nevertheless expected that the community landowning bodies 'would talk to the clan owners and managers of a particular piece of land before making any decision affecting it'; see Woodward, 'First Report', above n 7, 51 [16].
78 Woodward recognised that this would involve the creation of a new set of boundaries between communities that might require a dispute resolution procedure; Woodward, 'First Report', above n 7, 46 [286]–[288].
79 Woodward, 'Second Report', above n 7, 14 [82]. Woodward was persuaded on this point by the NLC. The NLC was represented by then Gerard Brennan QC, who 'did an outstanding job'; Woodward, *One Brief Interval*, above n 6, 135. Brennan was later Chief Justice of the High Court and author of the primary judgment in *Mabo*.
80 Woodward, 'Second Report', above n 7, 14 [82].
81 Woodward, Submission No 47, above n 6, 4 [15]. Woodward anticipated that over time traditional links would weaken in favour of more regional community identity; however, he was concerned that 'such a process should not be forced along by the imposition of such arrangements where they are not wanted and would not willingly be accepted and observed'; Woodward, 'Second Report', above n 7, 14 [86]–[87].
82 Woodward, 'Second Report', above n 7, 170 [26] and 169 [25].
83 Ibid, 165 [13].
84 Maddock, above n 63, 80; and see also Neate, above n 21, 41.

85 Sean Brennan, '*Wurridjal v Commonwealth*: The Northern Territory Intervention and Just Terms for the Acquisition of Property' (2009) 33 *Melbourne University Law Review* 957, 960.

86 See generally *Aboriginal Land Rights (Northern Territory) Act 1976* (Cth) ss 4–9.

87 Ibid, s 5(1).

88 Ibid, s 6.

89 Ibid, s 5(2).

90 Land Councils are bodies corporate whose membership is drawn from Aboriginal people in their region; see ibid, ss 22(1) and 29(1). There are four Land Councils: the Central Land Council, Northern Land Council, Tiwi Land Council and Anindilyakwa Land Council, each with discrete regions.

91 Ibid, s 3(1).

92 Layton, above n 13, 15; and see also Holcombe, above n 55, 69.

93 *Aboriginal Land Rights (Northern Territory) Act 1976* (Cth) s 19(5). For a description of the role of traditional Aboriginal owner under the Act, see also Toohey, 'Seven Years On', above n 15, 37 [258]; Neate, above n 21, 356.

94 *Aboriginal Land Rights (Northern Territory) Act 1976* (Cth) s 35(4). For a discussion, see Neate, above n 21, 356–7. Note that different provisions operate with respect to exploration and mining payments, in which case Aboriginal communities that are affected by the exploration or mining are also entitled to a portion of the payments.

95 *Aboriginal Land Rights (Northern Territory) Act 1976* (Cth) s 4(1) (emphasis added).

96 See also Toohey, 'Seven Years On', above n 15, 38 [262]–[264].

97 Ibid, s 71(1). For a discussion of s 71(1), see McRae *et al.* 2009, above n 24, 238; Neate, above n 21, 357.

98 Ibid, s 19(5). The same provision applies to the grant of a township lease (s 19A(2)), the exercise of Land Council functions generally (s 23(3)), consent to exploration and mining (ss 42(2), 48A(4)), the grant of an interest over land subject to claim (s 67B(3)) and for consent to a road over Aboriginal land (s 68(2)).

99 Albrecht is critical of the decision not to vest title directly in owners and managers, saying it ' "white-anted" the whole traditional authority structure'; Paul Albrecht, *Relhiperra: About Aborigines* (Bennelong Society, 2008) 46. See also Paul Albrecht, 'Comments on the Reeves Report' (Paper presented at the Quadrant seminar: Rousseau v Reality – Aborigines and Australian Civilisation, Sydney, 21 August 1999) 4.

100 Woodward, 'Second Report', above n 7, 14 [83]. Woodward recommended a slightly different structure than that contained in the Act: he suggested that Land Trusts hold land on trust for the Land Councils (page 166 [16]), and receive and distribute money (page 164 [10(c)]).

101 Ibid, 71 [362].

102 *Aboriginal Land Rights (Northern Territory) Act 1976* (Cth) s 19(5). Substantially the same provision applies to the grant of an interest in land under claim (s 11(3) and s 67B(3)), the grant of a township lease (s 19A(2)) and for consent to exploration and mining agreements (s 42(6), s 43(2) and s 46(4)).

103 Toohey, 'Seven Years On', above n 15, 37 [259]. The process by which Land Councils have consulted upon a proposal has been the subject of dispute and litigation – see, eg, *Alderson v Northern Land Council* (1983) 67 FLR 353, which is discussed by Toohey at pages 56–7 and Neate, above n 21, 361–7. Maddock also discussed the important interpretive role that Land Councils play; Maddock, above n 63, 78.

104 *Aboriginal Land Rights (Northern Territory) Act 1976* (Cth) s 19(7). Prior to

88   *Aboriginal land in the Northern Territory*

2006 this applied to leases of more than 10 years; Brennan, above n 47, 11 including n 106. Ministerial consent is also required under s 19A(1)(b) (grant of a township lease), s 27(3) (any agreement that provides for payment or receipt of an amount exceeding $1,000,000), s 36 (certain payments) and s 42(8) (exploration and mining).

105 Woodward, 'Second Report', above n 7, 18 [109].

106 Ibid, 174 [41]; and see Maddock, above n 63, 79.

107 CLC, *The Land Is Always Alive*, above n 67, 10–11.

108 *Aboriginal Land Rights (Northern Territory) Act 1976* (Cth) s 70.

109 Ibid, s 73(1)(b).

110 Formerly the *Aboriginal Land Ordinance 1978* (NT), which commenced on 26 January 1979. While the majority of the ALRA (including s 73(1)(b)) commenced on 26 January 1977. The prohibition in s 70 did not commence until 1 February 1979, to give time for the Territory Act to come into operation.

111 *Aboriginal Land Act 1979* (NT) s 5.

112 Ibid, ss 4(2), (3). This makes the *Aboriginal Land Act* consistent with s 73(1)(b) of the ALRA, which requires that 'any such laws shall provide for the right of Aboriginals to enter such land in accordance with Aboriginal tradition'.

113 *Aboriginal Land Act 1979* (NT) s 7.

114 Where it is required for that person to perform his or her duties; see ibid, s 6(1).

115 Ibid, s 5(8) and see also 11(1).

116 Ibid, s 5(7).

117 Woodward, 'First Report', above n 7, 13 [81].

118 Ibid.

119 See Toohey, 'Seven Years On', above n 15, 12 [82]–[83].

120 On the recommendation of Woodward, the CLC and NLC were created in an informal capacity prior to the enactment of the ALRA so as to help Aboriginal people in their regions put their views to the inquiry.

121 Woodward, 'Second Report', above n 7, 33 [191].

122 Ibid, 3 [11].

123 Ibid, 39 [228].

124 Ibid.

125 Ibid, 40 [232]–[232], 48 [273].

126 *Miscellaneous Acts Amendment (Aboriginal Community Living Areas) Act 1989* (NT), now Part 8 of the *Pastoral Land Act 1992* (NT).

127 The terms of that agreement are reproduced in the Schedule to the *Miscellaneous Acts Amendment (Aboriginal Community Living Areas) Act 1989* (NT). See also Central Land Council (CLC), Submission No 347 to Senate Standing Committees on Community Affairs, Parliament of Australia, *Inquiry into Stronger Futures in the Northern Territory Bill 2011 and Two Related Bills*, 1 February 2012, 6–7.

128 Wording from the Schedule to the *Miscellaneous Acts Amendment (Aboriginal Community Living Areas) Act 1989* (NT).

129 See definition of 'applicant' in s 91(1) of the *Pastoral Land Act 1992* (NT) and see also Paul Burke, 'Who Needs a Community Living Area? The "Need" Requirement in N.T. Excisions Legislation' (1991) *Aboriginal Law Bulletin* 49.

130 Central Land Council (CLC), *Community Living Areas* www.clc.org.au/articles/cat/community-living-areas.

131 CLC, Submission No 347, above n 127, 6.

132 Under the *Associations Act 2003* (NT).

133 Under the *Corporations (Aboriginal and Torres Strait Islander) Act 2006* (Cth).

Aboriginal land in the Northern Territory 89

134 *Associations Act 2003* (NT) s 110. See also the additional restrictions described at CLC, Submission No 347, above n 127, 6.

135 *Aboriginal Land Rights (Northern Territory) Act 1976* (Cth) s 19(4A).

136 Extract from the rules of the Alpurrurulam Land Aboriginal Corporation, available from the website of the Office of the Registrar of Indigenous Corporations (www.oric.gov.au).

137 See also the rules of the Atitjere Land Aboriginal Corporation (Atitjere community), Binjari Community Aboriginal Corporation (Binjari community) and Imangara Aboriginal Corporation (Imangara community), all of which are among the 16 communities on CLA land targeted by recent reforms.

138 See rules of the Yupanalla Aboriginal Corporation. See also Northern Land Council (NLC), Submission No 361 to Senate Standing Committees on Community Affairs, Parliament of Australia, *Inquiry into Stronger Futures in the Northern Territory Bill 2011 and Two Related Bills*, 10 February 2012, 2, who state that residents of some CLAs in their region may be ineligible for membership of the landholding association.

139 Ross states that the term 'town camps' was established by a 1982 report of the House of Representatives Standing Committee on Aboriginal Affairs, prior to which they were described as 'fringe camps', Helen Ross, 'Lifescape and Lived Experience' in Peter Read (ed), *Settlement: A History of Australian Indigenous Housing* (Aboriginal Studies Press, 2000) 3, 12.

140 Frances Coughlan, *Aboriginal Town Camps and Tangentyere Council: The Battle for Self-Determination in Alice Springs* (MA Dissertation, La Trobe University, 1991) xxii–xxiii, xxvi–xxxvi; Samantha Wells, 'Labour, Control and Protection: The Kahlin Aboriginal Compound, Darwin, 1911–38' in Peter Read (ed), *Settlement: A History of Australian Indigenous Housing* (Aboriginal Studies Press, 2000) 64–74; Tim Rowse, 'Housing and Colonial Patronage, Alice Springs, 1920–1965' in Peter Read (ed), *Settlements: A History of Australian Indigenous Housing* (Aboriginal Studies Press, 2000) 85–98.

141 In 1954 the Finke River Mission 'sold' huts on the Mission Block to families, but this was an informal arrangement and did not pass any legal rights to the land. A few years later those families moved or were moved on; see Rowse, above n 140, 96–7.

142 Out of a total Aboriginal population of 23,253, see Woodward, 'First Report', above n 7, 15 [94]–[95]. This appears to include Aboriginal people living in town. Rowse describes how particularly after the Second World War some Aboriginal people, predominantly of mixed descent, lived in government-supplied housing in town; Rowse, above n 140, 91–2.

143 Woodward, 'Second Report', above n 7, 51 [277].

144 Ibid, 63 [328]. See also item 26 of Appendix D (the suggested drafting instructions) on page 170.

145 CLC, *The Land Is Always Alive*, above n 67, 9; Wenten Rubuntja and Jenny Green, *The Town Grew up Dancing: The Life and Art of Wenten Rubuntja* (Jukurrpa Books, 2002) 111–13; Coughlan, above n 140, lxx–lxxiii.

146 The Act also prohibited any claim over land in towns; see definition of 'unalienated Crown land' in *Aboriginal Land Rights (Northern Territory) Act 1976* (Cth) s 3(1).

147 Rubuntja and Green, above n 145, 130; Coughlan, above n 140, lxxvi–lxxvii.

148 Toohey, 'Seven Years On', above n 15, 12 [89].

149 See *Northern Territory National Emergency Response (Town Camps) Declaration 2007 (No. 1)* (Cth), *Northern Territory National Emergency Response (Town Camps) Declaration 2007 (No. 2)* (Cth).

150 Ibid.

151 See *Associations Act 2003* (NT) s 110(2).

90 *Aboriginal land in the Northern Territory*

Bibliography

Books/articles/reports/web pages

Albrecht, Paul, 'Comments on the Reeves Report' (Paper presented at the Quadrant seminar: Rousseau v Reality – Aborigines and Australian Civilisation, Sydney, 21 August 1999).

Albrecht, Paul, *Relhiperra: About Aborigines* (Bennelong Society, 2008).

Altman, Jon and Francis Markham, 'Burgeoning Indigenous Land Ownership: Diverse Values and Strategic Potentialities' in Sean Brennan *et al.*, *Native Title from Mabo to Akiba: A Vehicle for Change and Empowerment?* (Federation Press, 2015) 126.

Australian Government, Office of the Registrar of Indigenous Corporations, *Home Page*, www.oric.gov.au.

Brennan, Sean, 'Economic Development and Land Council Power: Modernising the *Land Rights Act* or Same Old Same Old?' (2006) 10(4) *Australian Indigenous Law Reporter* 1.

Brennan, Sean, '*Wurridjal v Commonwealth*: The Northern Territory Intervention and Just Terms for the Acquisition of Property' (2009) 33 *Melbourne University Law Review* 957.

Burke, Paul, 'Who Needs a Community Living Area? The "Need" Requirement in N.T. Excisions Legislation' (1991) *Aboriginal Law Bulletin* 49.

Central Land Council, *The Land Is Always Alive: The Story of the Central Land Council* (1994).

Central Land Council, Submission No 347 to Senate Standing Committees on Community Affairs, Parliament of Australia, *Inquiry into Stronger Futures in the Northern Territory Bill 2011 and Two Related Bills*, 1 February 2012.

Central Land Council, *Community Living Areas* www.clc.org.au/articles/cat/community-living-areas.

Coughlan, Frances, *Aboriginal Town Camps and Tangentyere Council: The Battle for Self-Determination in Alice Springs* (MA Dissertation, La Trobe University, 1991).

Dalrymple, David, 'Land Rights and Property Rights' (2007) 51(1) *Quadrant* 61.

Dousset, Laurent and Katie Glaskin, 'Western Desert and Native Title: How Models Become Myths' (2007) 17(2) *Anthropological Forum* 127.

Flanagan, Tom, Christopher Alcantara and André Le Dressay, *Beyond the Indian Act: Restoring Aboriginal Property Rights* (McGill-Queen's University Press, 2010).

Foley, Gary and Tim Anderson, 'Land Rights and Aboriginal Voices' (2006) 12(1) *Australian Journal of Human Rights* 83.

Gray, Justice Peter, 'Tempe Downs and Middleton Ponds/Luritja Land Claim No 147' (Report by the Aboriginal Land Commissioner, 1998).

Gumbert, Marc, 'Paradigm Lost: Anthropological Models and Their Effect on Aboriginal Land Rights' (1981) 52(2) *Oceania* 103.

Holcombe, Sarah, 'Traditional Owners and "Community-Country" Anangu: Distinctions and Dilemmas' (2004) 2 *Australian Aboriginal Studies* 64.

House of Representatives Standing Committee on Aboriginal and Torres Strait Islander Affairs, *The Report of the Inquiry into the Reeves Review of the Aboriginal Land Rights (Northern Territory) Act 1976* (1999).

Aboriginal land in the Northern Territory   91

Jones, Gregory, *Aboriginal Land Rights Legislation: An Examination of the Publications Associated with the Commonwealth Legislation* (Canberra College of Advanced Education, 1983).

Keen, Ian, 'The Western Desert vs the Rest: Rethinking the Contrast' in Francesca Merlan, John Morton and Alan Rumsey (eds), *Scholar and Sceptic: Australian Aboriginal Studies in Honour of LR Hiatt* (Aboriginal Studies Press, 1997) 65.

Langton, Marcia and Nicolas Peterson, 'Introduction' in Nicolas Peterson and Marcia Langton (eds), *Aborigines, Land and Land Rights* (Australian Institute of Aboriginal Studies, 1983) 3.

Layton, Robert, 'Ambilineal Descent and Traditional Pitjantjatjara Rights to Land' in Nicolas Peterson and Marcia Langton (eds), *Aborigines, Land and Land Rights* (Australian Institute of Aboriginal Studies, 1983) 15.

Levy, Ron, 'Twenty Year of Land Rights: Lessons for the Native Title Act' (1996) 3(85) *Aboriginal Law Bulletin* 22.

McRae, Heather *et al.*, *Indigenous Legal Issues, Commentary and Materials* (Thomson Reuters, 2009).

Maddock, Kenneth, ' "Owners", "Managers" and the Choice of Statutory Traditional Owners by Anthropologists and Lawyers' in Nicolas Peterson and Marcia Langton (eds), *Aborigines, Land and Land Rights* (Australian Institute of Aboriginal Studies, 1983) 211.

Maddock, Kenneth, *Your Land Is Our Land* (Penguin, 1983).

Maurice, Justice Michael, 'Lake Amadeus Land Claim No 28' (Report by the Aboriginal Land Commissioner, 1988).

Merlan, Francesca, 'The Regimentation of Customary Practice: From Northern Territory Land Claims to Mabo' (1995) 6(1/2) *Australian Journal of Anthropology* 64.

Merlan, Francesca, Submission No 29 to the House of Representatives Standing Committee on Aboriginal and Torres Strait Islander Affairs, *Inquiry into the Recommendations of the Reeves Report Review of the Aboriginal Land Rights (Northern Territory) Act 1976*, 28 March 1999.

Myers, Fred, *Pintupi Country, Pintupi Self: Sentiment, Place, and Politics among Western Desert Aborigines* (University of California Press, 1991).

Neate, Graeme, *Aboriginal Land Rights Law in the Northern Territory* (Alternative Publishing Co-operative Ltd, 1989).

Northern Land Council, Submission No 361 to Senate Standing Committees on Community Affairs, Parliament of Australia, *Inquiry into Stronger Futures in the Northern Territory Bill 2011 and Two Related Bills*, 10 February 2012.

Northern Land Council, *What We Do*, www.nlc.org.au/articles/info/what-does-the-northern-land-council-do.

Peterson, Nicolas, 'Rights, Residence and Process in Australian Territorial Organisation' in Nicolas Peterson and Marcia Langton (eds), *Aborigines, Land and Land Rights* (Australian Institute of Aboriginal Studies, 1983) 134.

Pollack, David, 'Indigenous Land in Australia: A Quantitative Assessment of Indigenous Landholdings in 2000' (Discussion Paper No 221/2001, Centre for Aboriginal Economic Policy Research, 2001).

Reeves, John, 'Building on Land Rights for the Next Generation: The Review of the *Aboriginal Land Rights (Northern Territory) Act 1976*' (Australian Government, 1998).

Ross, Helen, 'Lifescape and Lived Experience' in Peter Read (ed), *Settlement: A History of Australian Indigenous Housing* (Aboriginal Studies Press, 2000) 3.

92 Aboriginal land in the Northern Territory

Rowse, Tim, 'Housing and Colonial Patronage, Alice Springs, 1920–1965' in Peter Read (ed), *Settlements: A History of Australian Indigenous Housing* (Aboriginal Studies Press, 2000) 85.

Rubuntja, Wenten and Jenny Green, *The Town Grew up Dancing: The Life and Art of Wenten Rubuntja* (Jukurrpa Books, 2002).

Sansom, Basil, '*Yulara* and Futher Expert Reports in Native Title Cases' (2007) 17(1) *Anthropological Forum* 71.

Stanton, John, 'Old Business, New Owners: Succession and "The Law" on the Fringe of the Western Desert' in Nicolas Peterson and Marcia Langton (eds), *Aborigines, Land and Land Rights* (Australian Institute of Aboriginal Studies, 1983) 160.

Sutton, Peter, 'Suggestions for a Bicameral System' (1984) 5(3) *Anthropological Forum* 395.

Sutton, Peter, *Country: Aboriginal Boundaries and Land Ownership in Australia* (Aboriginal History Inc, Monograph 3, 1995).

Sutton, Peter, *Native Title and the Descent of Rights* (National Native Title Tribunal, 1998).

Sutton, Peter, 'Anthropological Submission on the Reeves Review' (1999) 9(2) *Anthropological Forum* 189.

Sutton, Peter, *Native Title in Australia: An Ethnographic Perspective* (Cambridge University Press, 2003).

Sutton, Peter, 'Stanner and Aboriginal Land Use: Ecology, Economic Change, and Enclosing the Commons' in Melinda Hinkson and Jeremy Beckett (eds), *An Appreciate of Difference: WEH Stanner and Aboriginal Australia* (Aboriginal Studies Press, 2008) 169.

Toohey, Justice John, 'Uluru (Ayers Rock) National Park and Lake Amadeus/Luritja Land Claim' (Report by the Aboriginal Land Commissioner, 1979).

Toohey, John, 'Seven Years On: Report by Mr Justice Toohey to the Minister for Aboriginal Affairs on the *Aboriginal Land Rights (Northern Territory) Act 1976* and Related Matters' (Australian Government, 1983).

Wells, Samantha, 'Labour, Control and Protection: The Kahlin Aboriginal Compound, Darwin, 1911–38' in Peter Read (ed), *Settlement: A History of Australian Indigenous Housing* (Aboriginal Studies press, 2000) 64.

Williams, Nancy, 'Yolngu Concepts of Land Ownership' in Nicolas Peterson and Marcia Langton (eds), *Aborigines, Land and Land Rights* (Australian Institute of Aboriginal Studies, 1983) 94.

Woodward, Edward, 'Aboriginal Land Rights Commission: First Report' (Australian Government, 1973).

Woodward, Edward, 'Aboriginal Land Rights Commission: Second Report' (Australian Government, 1974).

Woodward, Edward, Submission No 47 to the House of Representatives Standing Committee on Aboriginal and Torres Strait Islander Affairs, *Inquiry into the Recommendations of the Reeves Report Review of the Aboriginal Land Rights (Northern Territory) Act 1976*, 1999.

Woodward, Sir Edward, *One Brief Interval* (Miegunyah Press, 2005).

Legislation and subordinate legislation

Aboriginal Land Act 1979 (NT).
Aboriginal Land Ordinance 1978 (NT).
Aboriginal Land Rights (Northern Territory) Act 1976 (Cth).
Associations Act 2003 (NT).
Corporations (Aboriginal and Torres Strait Islander) Act 2006 (Cth).
Miscellaneous Acts Amendment (Aboriginal Community Living Areas) Act 1989 (NT).
Northern Territory National Emergency Response (Town Camps) Declaration 2007 (No 1) (Cth).
Northern Territory National Emergency Response (Town Camps) Declaration 2007 (No 2) (Cth).
Pastoral Land Act 1992 (NT).

Cases

Alderson v Northern Land Council (1983) 67 FLR 353.
Jango v Northern Territory of Australia [2006] FCA 318.
Mabo v Queensland (No 2) (1992) 175 CLR 1.
Milirrpum v Nabalco Pty Ltd (1971) 17 FLR 141.

4 Communities on Aboriginal land

4.1 Identifying the starting point for reform

This chapter describes the tenure arrangements in communities on Aboriginal land in the Northern Territory prior to the recent reforms. It considers the way that housing and infrastructure were allocated to particular individuals, families and organisations and the nature of the rights that those occupiers held. Somewhat surprisingly, this has never been done before. While the reforms have been under way for nearly a decade, and were debated for several years prior to their introduction, this is the first time that the pre-existing arrangements in communities have been described in any detail. There is a lot of excellent scholarship on Aboriginal land ownership, including the complex intersection between the formal legal system and traditional law. However, in larger residential communities on Aboriginal land – the target of recent reforms – the land ownership system is only part of the story. There, a set of *informal tenure arrangements* have developed that are to some extent distinct from land ownership under either formal or Aboriginal law.

It is those informal tenure arrangements that are the real starting point for the reforms. It is useful here to revisit one of Hernando de Soto's key arguments, one that is often overlooked in discussion of his work. De Soto states that, in order to be effective, any land reform programme must begin by identifying and engaging with the existing arrangements, what he refers to as the 'social contract'. He argues that 'property law and titles imposed without reference to existing social contracts continually fail'.[1] As is often the case, de Soto presents this argument in the strongest of terms. His point about identifying the existing social contract is nevertheless well made. Even if the aim is to alter the existing arrangements, it is clear that identifying those arrangements is the most appropriate starting point for reform.

One reason this was not done in Australia is because the language we have used to debate land reform made it seem unnecessary. Communities on Aboriginal land have often been described as places of 'communal ownership'. This chapter makes it clear why this is such a misleading characterisation, and why referring only to the land ownership system provides

Communities on Aboriginal land 95

an incomplete picture. The description provided here also enables the actual impact of the recent reforms to be better understood. In certain important ways, the reforms alter rather than reference the existing social contract. They have been used to introduce new governance arrangements and alter the balance of power in communities: not just between community residents and governments, but also between traditional owners and non-traditional owner residents.

The chapter is presented in three parts. Section 4.2 describes the emergence of residential settlements and provides a framework for understanding the relationship between land ownership and tenure arrangements in those settlements. Section 4.3 describes the characteristics of the pre-existing informal tenure arrangements, by reference to different categories of infrastructure. It also clarifies the relationship between forms of property and sharing norms. Section 4.4 considers the best way of describing the tenure arrangements in communities on Aboriginal land and provides some more general discussion.

4.2 Communities on Aboriginal land in the Northern Territory

Background information about communities

The emergence of residential communities

One of the more dramatic changes for Aboriginal people in the post-contact era has been the shift from dynamic and highly mobile hunter-gatherer societies to fixed, sedentary residential communities. Austin-Broos uses the term 'ontological shift' to capture the significance of this transition. She argues that it was not just a change in circumstances, but a change in the 'very materiality of life', in the order and fabric of meaning.[2] This was not a uniform transition; it occurred very differently and at different times across Australia: on the fringes of white settlements, in towns and town camps, on pastoral leases and in missions, reserves and government ration depots. In all cases it meant the beginning of a very different life for those Aboriginal people who survived the transition.

Starting in the 1960s and 1970s, there was another significant transformation. The advent of land rights was one component of this, combined with the extension of the welfare system to Aboriginal people, the decline of missions, a gradual increase in the penetration of the market economy and 'an emerging policy of self determination'.[3] It was during this period that a number of Aboriginal people moved away from existing communities and set up homelands or outstations on Aboriginal land. In some cases these grew into new, fully fledged communities. In the Northern Territory the result was that, by 2006 (the year the first reforms were introduced), there were around 41,681 people[4] living in 641 discrete Aboriginal

96 Communities on Aboriginal land

communities.[5] The majority are 'homelands' or 'outstations', small settlements comprising just one or two families and often located within range of a larger community. There are also 73 communities that were identified by the Australian Government as having a population of more than 100,[6] and which have been the focus of recent reforms.

There is considerable variation within this group of 73 communities. Populations range from a little over 100 to around 2,700.[7] The majority are very remote, but some are located close to towns or major highways.[8] Fifty-two are situated on land held under the *Aboriginal Land Rights (Northern Territory) Act 1976* (Cth) (the ALRA)[9] and 16 on community living area (CLA) land,[10] while five are on land subject to distinct forms of title.[11] Most sit within larger areas of Aboriginal land, though some are instead surrounded by pastoral lease. Many have a number of smaller outstations nearby. The majority were created before the land on which they were situated became Aboriginal land, while others arose out of the land rights movement itself.[12]

What do these communities look like?

This chapter is concerned with the tenure arrangements under which the use of land and infrastructure in communities was regulated. It is useful to start with a picture of the sort of infrastructure that can be found. In all communities, the most common form of infrastructure is housing, both for Aboriginal residents and for outside staff working in the community. In a small community, such as Imanpa with a population of between 140 and 217, there might also be a recreational hall, health clinic, community centre, school, council office, council workshop, store, cemetery, sports oval, rubbish tip, and power, water and sewerage facilities.[13] Some of these facilities will be in the community, some on land just outside it. A medium-sized community such as Yuendumu, with a population of between 500 and 900 Aboriginal residents and around 100 non-Aboriginal residents, might additionally have media and videoconferencing facilities, an adult education centre, youth centre, substance misuse programme, church, art centre, garage, a second store, Land Council office, women's centre, old people's respite centre, childcare centre and police station.[14] A larger community, such as Maningrida with a population of between 2,068 and 2,700,[15] might also contain basic tertiary education facilities, an airstrip, a small hotel, chartered fishing company, credit union and an outstation resource centre.[16] There is of course no set pattern. Some communities are relatively well resourced, others less so, and the range of facilities will vary.

The composition and identity of communities

Residential communities are a relatively new social grouping for Aboriginal people in the Northern Territory. They bring together Aboriginal people from different clan and family groups, and often from different language areas. Even in a small community such as Imanpa, five language groups are represented.[17] It is consequently a mistake to think of communities as a single or unified group.[18] On the other hand, it would also be a mistake to treat the now long-standing existence of communities as irrelevant. They have become 'places that are more than a jumble of housing and infrastructure'.[19] They are now part of the way in which people relate and identify, even if it is only one part.[20] A striking example of this is the emergence of Pintubi-Luritja language and identity out of shared settlement life at Haasts Bluff during a period of relative insularity between the 1930s and 1960s.[21]

In this context, there are different views on the best way of describing these residential centres. Musharbash prefers the term 'settlement', as 'community' can misleadingly suggest the existence of a singular identity.[22] In the course of recent reforms, the Australian Government introduced the term 'township', and the Northern Territory (NT) Government the term 'growth towns', with respect to certain larger communities. This was for the purposes of emphasising that Aboriginal communities are, or should be, treated in a similar way to non-Aboriginal towns. The term 'community' is used here not as a comment on those debates but because, as Musharbash herself notes, it remains the term most commonly used in practice.[23]

Chapter 3 describes how communities are inevitably situated on the 'estate' or 'country' of one particular landholding group under Aboriginal land tenure, and not the traditional land of each and every resident. Recently, in the course of granting township leases, the Tiwi Land Council took the unusual step of listing traditional owners for the subject communities.[24] They list 250 traditional owners for Wurrumiyanga (formerly Nguiu), a community of between 1,265 and 1,582,[25] and 225 traditional owners for Milikapiti, a community of around 559.[26] Conversely they list 320 traditional owners for the community of Wurankuwu, with its population of just 50.[27] This gives some indication of the range of possibilities, and supports the observation that in many larger communities the majority of Aboriginal residents will not be regarded as traditional owners,[28] while some, possibly many, traditional owners will live elsewhere. In some cases, communities are situated on the land of an entirely different language group, such as Areyonga, a predominantly Pitjantjatjara community on Western Arrernte land.[29]

Tenure arrangements in communities prior to the reforms

The absence of leases

The ALRA has always provided a mechanism for leasing ALRA land, which at its broadest allows for land to be leased to any person for any

98 *Communities on Aboriginal land*

purpose.[30] It appears that Woodward anticipated that leases would be commonplace, primarily to Aboriginal individuals and organisations.[31] He suggested that initially those leases should be short as 'there is a danger that mistakes might be made in early years, due to inexperience'.[32] He also anticipated some leases to government entities, which he recommended be rent-free and for an indefinite term where 'for the benefit of Aborigines', and for a commercial rent otherwise. Woodward also suggested there be leases to existing missions, which he said should be at a nominal rent and renewable from year to year.[33] He anticipated that leases to other non-Aboriginal interests would initially be rare.[34]

Despite this, prior to the reforms described by this book, there were very few leases in communities on ALRA land. For example, in the community of Wurrumiyanga, out of approximately 473 administrative lots,[35] only 15 were the subject of a lease in 2007.[36] This appears to be typical.[37] There has, however, been some regional variation in leasing practices, at least with respect to certain types of infrastructure: the Northern Land Council (NLC) reports that almost all stores in its region were subject to leases,[38] while the Central Land Council (CLC) reports only two store leases.[39] Neither report widespread leasing in communities for any other purpose.

In the absence of a lease, the ALRA provides some organisations with a statutory right of occupancy. Where the Crown[40] was occupying land at the time that land came under the ALRA, then it remains entitled to occupy that land for as long as it wants,[41] during which period any buildings or improvements are deemed to be the property of the Crown.[42] Rent is only required where the land is used 'for a purpose that is not a community purpose'.[43] There is a similar provision for missions, although their rights are more curtailed in that they can effectively be given 12 months' notice.[44] Curiously, while the NLC has argued that this explains why governments have so rarely applied for leases,[45] there are no reports of governments attempting to rely on their section 14 rights, including during recent debates. This is presumably because where those rights still exist they would cover only a portion of the infrastructure occupied by the Australian and NT governments. Most communities have grown considerably in the decades since the land was made ALRA land, and some communities were only started in the period following grant.[46] And while these statutory rights apply to the Crown and 'Authorities',[47] they do not cover infrastructure occupied by local councils or NGOs other than missions.

There is no equivalent to these provisions on CLA land, which is also subject to greater restrictions on the grant of leases. While it is still possible in some circumstances, I could find no reports of leases being granted over CLA land.[48]

In summary, aside from the small number of lots on ALRA land that were subject to a lease, and an unknown number of lots subject to statutory occupancy rights, prior to the recent reforms the relationship between landowners and the occupiers of a particular lot in communities on Aboriginal land had not been formally defined. Communities on Aboriginal land were predominantly a type of *informal settlement*.

The relationship between the land ownership system and informal tenure arrangements

Informal settlements take a number of forms and vary considerably, particularly with respect to the relationship between the *land ownership system* and the *informal tenure arrangements* in the settlement. This is explained in Chapter 2 by reference to examples. One example given is that of a village on customary land in some parts of Africa, where the land ownership system itself determines the (informal) rights of occupiers. In other words, people occupy under the customary tenure system. This is different from a squatter settlement on state land in Peru, where it is the arrangements between occupiers that regulate their informal rights, rather than the underlying state property system. Between these two examples, there are situations where the two elements combine. That is, it is not simply the case that underlying land ownership is either determinative or irrelevant. There are also circumstances where land ownership is one part of a complex informal tenure environment.

Below, I argue that this has been the case in communities on Aboriginal land in the Northern Territory. The description provided here suggests that tenure arrangements in communities have been the negotiated outcome of three spheres of authority: community authority, traditional authority and government authority. Importantly, this has varied between the different types of infrastructure or land use in communities, and so the discussion below is divided into three land-use categories. It has also varied over time and between communities. I argue that all three spheres of authority have tended to be relevant, including in communities on CLA land, although it is likely that traditional authority has played less of a role on CLA land than on ALRA land.

4.3 Characteristics of the informal tenure arrangements

As background to the description of the pre-existing tenure arrangements, this section commences with an overview of the organisations and governance arrangements that have operated in communities and a discussion of how sharing norms interact with, but are separate from, forms of property.

Overview of organisations and governance arrangements

The frequent use of terms such as 'elder', 'community leader' and 'traditional owner' with respect to leadership in Aboriginal communities can

100 *Communities on Aboriginal land*

convey an impression that authority structures are clear, stable and widely agreed-upon, and perhaps that they are, or at least should be, derived from 'culture' or 'tradition'. The reality is far more complicated, and often authority is dynamic and contested. The relevance of this to tenure arrangements is that there has been no single site of authority for determining those arrangements. They have instead been negotiated, the outcome of *consensus* and *contestation*. The parties to this negotiation are described below, followed by a discussion of 'dispersed governance' as a useful framework for understanding authority and decision-making in Aboriginal communities, including with respect to tenure.

Local councils

Until 2008 there were a large number of small local councils servicing remote Aboriginal communities across the Northern Territory, with most servicing a single community.[49] Local councils were responsible for core municipal services such as garbage collection and the upkeep of parks, but they also played a number of other roles. They were usually the body responsible for the management of residential housing, which is discussed in greater detail below. There are several other services that, where they were provided, were in some communities delivered by the local council and in other communities delivered by a local or regional NGO.[50] This includes childcare, health services, aged care, night patrol, employment programmes and the resourcing of outstations.

There has also been a similar dynamic with respect to enterprises. In some communities the local council was directly responsible for enterprises such as the community store, takeaway shop, garage, visitor accommodation or campground.[51] In other communities these enterprises were owned separately.[52] Finally, and in conjunction with the NT Government, local councils also played an important role in community planning. Consequently, local councils in Aboriginal communities have played something of a hybrid role. On the one hand, they were local government bodies, the 'de facto third tier of government',[53] and agents of the state.[54] On the other hand, they were an Aboriginal community forum, sometimes one of several, but often the most important site for decision-making and the expression of Aboriginal authority at the community level.

One of the points to emerge from the description provided below is that local councils played a key role in the operation of the pre-existing tenure arrangements in communities on Aboriginal land. Importantly, those local councils no longer exist in the same form. From 1 July 2008, the majority of small local councils were amalgamated into 11 regional shire councils. This has significantly altered their character at a community level.[55] Initially, the impact of these changes on community tenure arrangements was masked by the Australian Government's compulsory acquisition of 'five-year leases' over the majority of affected communities in late 2007.[56] In the

Communities on Aboriginal land   101

longer term, the local government reforms have altered the range of land reform options that are available.

Non-government organisations

The make-up of NGOs providing services in Aboriginal communities varies. There are several churches and former missions operating in some communities. There are a larger number of Aboriginal-owned and -managed NGOs, part of what some authors refer to as the 'Indigenous sector'.[57] In addition, there are several non-Aboriginal NGOs, such as Mission Australia, providing particular services.[58] Smith argues that over the last few decades the number of NGOs has increased to such an extent that by 2004 local councils were 'simply one amongst many Indigenous organisations operating in communities'.[59] Sanders, on the other hand, observes that in more recent times the number of separate organisations has been decreasing, as governments have instead preferred to fund larger, more sustainable organisations (the same trend that has resulted in the amalgamation of local councils themselves).[60] Despite this more recent trend, there are still a large number of different NGOs providing a variety of services in remote Aboriginal communities.[61]

The Australian and Northern Territory governments

The Australian and NT governments have also been involved in tenure arrangements in several ways. Both have been directly involved in the delivery of some services (such as education, health care, Centrelink, law enforcement) to Aboriginal communities, and as such have themselves been occupiers. Both are also indirectly involved in service delivery through the funding of local councils and NGOs. The NT Government has been further involved through its supervision of local councils, the provision of essential service infrastructure (power, water and sewerage) and through its role in informal community planning processes.

Land Councils

On ALRA land, the functions of Land Councils and local councils potentially overlapped.[62] This was particularly the case inside communities, where both might potentially play a role in the allocation of land. It could also occur on land outside communities, where both might be involved in such activities as controlling feral animals or supporting enterprise development. Historically this has been a source of tension not just between Land Councils and local councils, but also between Land Councils and the NT Government.[63] This tension formed part of a broader 'adversarial political culture' that persisted throughout the 1980s and 1990s,[64] and which is reflected in the politics surrounding the Reeves Report.[65] Land

102 *Communities on Aboriginal land*

Councils were concerned not just that local councils might encroach on the rights of landowners, but also that the NT Government might use local councils as an 'organisational base for the promotion of breakaway land councils'.[66] For its part, the NT Government was opposed to the way the (Commonwealth) ALRA represented a limit on its own jurisdictional authority and tended to promote an expanded role for local councils, over which it had more control.[67] Whether or not as a result of this tension, Land Councils have tended not to play an active role in land allocation within communities even on ALRA land.[68] On CLA land, Land Councils do not have a formal role in land-use decision-making.

The traditional owners

It appears, however, that traditional owners have often exercised their authority in the community directly through their involvement in community politics and organisations such as local councils, rather than indirectly through Land Councils and the land ownership system. One result is that the importance given to traditional ownership has varied. Sanders describes some communities giving voting rights on council to non-residential traditional owners.[69] Holcombe observes that control over religious knowledge, local and regional, is one of the factors that contributes to a person's ability to assert authority within a community.[70] However, she also observes that it is not just people who meet the definition of 'traditional owner' who are able to make use of their knowledge and traditional status.[71]

Traditional authority with respect to country, even in a broad sense, does not always translate into authority within community structures.[72] Martin and Finlayson state that local councils usually comprised 'a wider range of younger, less (traditionally) authoritative people'.[73] Altman has argued that 'in most townships traditional owners do not actually have a huge amount of authority in relation to what happens to houses – or, for that matter, to other forms of infrastructure'.[74] In some communities, the make-up of the local council formally reflected the diversity of groups in the community, not just the traditional owners.[75] This reflects the fact that, as Smith notes, councils were responsible to all community residents, not just those with a traditional connection to community land.[76] However, as local councils effectively exercised some authority over land, even on ALRA land, some commentators have criticised council processes for failing to appropriately recognise the interests of traditional owners.[77] As described in Chapter 6, one outcome of township leasing has been a significant increase in the authority of traditional owners vis-à-vis non-traditional owner residents.

To some extent, it appears that claims to traditional ownership may have been relevant in an informal sense on CLA land as well as ALRA land. Orr describes the president of the local council at Laramba, a community on CLA land, as 'the traditional owner'.[78] It is also possible that traditional ownership tended to be less important in communities on CLA land. There is no research that specifically addresses this issue. Moreover, it appears that even in communities on ALRA land the authority of traditional owners has varied between communities.

Dispersed governance

The lack of a single or unified authority structure in Aboriginal communities has led to them being described as an example of 'dispersed governance'.[79] There are three aspects to the way in which this dispersal of governance authority has occurred. First, authority is to some extent shared between different community organisations: for example, different areas of responsibility might be shared between a local council, a women's council, a health council and a store association.[80] Second, authority is shared between organisations and their funding bodies, primarily the Australian and NT governments.[81] Third, authority is also exercised outside of formal organisations, between community members at a social level.

This relationship between formal organisations and social authority is complex. The societies that Aboriginal people lived in prior to contact were non-stratified, with a 'diffuse authority structure'.[82] While senior knowledge holders commanded respect, it has been argued that this was not the equivalent of political authority, as the society itself was the locus of power.[83] However, in the social order created by residential communities new types of leaders have emerged.[84] The authority of such leaders does not simply stem from their holding of a formal position, such as the chairperson of the local council.[85] It is instead sustained through relationship and action. One of the ways it is sustained is through influence over the allocation of resources and in particular through acts of generosity.[86] In this context, formal organisations become both sites for exercising authority and contested forums for the acquisition and maintenance of authority. Authority is also determined by a wider range of factors, including kinship networks, access to or control over religious knowledge, a person's ability to engage with administrative and other secular issues that affect the community,[87] and their ability to gain the effective support of key non-Aboriginal staff.[88]

It is against this background of dispersed authority that the observations below on the informal tenure arrangements in communities on Aboriginal land need to be considered, particularly with respect to the central role played by local councils. However, there is also a further piece of background that requires consideration, which is the relationship between property and sharing norms.

104 *Communities on Aboriginal land*

Property and sharing norms

In any society, property owners are under several obligations to share their property with certain others. A person may, for example, be under social, or even legal, obligations to apply what they own to the support of their children or spouse. In Aboriginal communities, the obligation to share is often both broader and deeper: broader in the sense that it applies to a wider group of people, and deeper in that the ramifications of failing to share can be more significant. Anthropologist Nicolas Peterson (who was earlier an adviser to Woodward) introduced the term 'demand sharing' to describe the fact that much sharing in Aboriginal communities occurs as the result of culturally sanctioned demands rather than unsolicited giving.[89] While the act of sharing can increase status and social capital, and indeed authority, these sharing obligations are also a 'social burden'.[90] Property owners do not necessarily like them, they may even go to some lengths to avoid them, but they nevertheless remain compelling in many urban and remote Aboriginal communities because the consequences of rejecting a demand can be high.[91] Schwab observes that in the post-contact era the kinship (including putative kinship) networks pursuant to which these obligations are exercised have become more extensive.[92]

While there are connections between sharing practices and traditional forms of land tenure, these obligations are not limited to traditional or communal property. They can, and often do, apply to objects owned by individuals as private property, such as vehicles and cash. Martin describes how the introduction of cash has been incorporated into existing cultural practices, imbuing it with a distinct and particular meaning in Aboriginal communities, but at the same time it has altered those cultural practices, significantly and at times detrimentally.[93]

These sharing practices and obligations are relevant to land reform in several ways. As described below, they affect how individuals and families exercise their housing rights. Indeed, Neutze argues that sharing obligations operate with considerable force with respect to housing.[94] As they can affect resources that a person has an influence over, not just resources that a person owns, they can impact on the management of enterprises and service-providing NGOs.[95] These obligations are also relevant to the way in which collective property is managed, including communal property that is owned by the entire community, or a section of the community such as women.[96] Sharing obligations with respect to that property tend to be interpreted through kinship networks – an 'extended and flexible' grouping,[97] but nevertheless only a subset of the community – and not the entire community.[98] The result can be a disjuncture between the ownership system and the obligations experienced by participants.[99]

More generally, the existence of these sharing obligations had a significant impact on debate about land reform. The retention of 'communal ownership' was frequently associated with the retention of a communal ethic, and conversely the introduction of 'individual ownership' was associated with the introduction of a more individualistic ethic. Chapter 5 describes how this attributes too great a determinative role to property. Communal property – to the extent it exists – is not the *source* of sharing norms, nor will land reform simply result in their reformation or dissolution. Rather, new forms of property will *interact* with existing sharing norms in potentially complex ways.

For example, several authors note that the introduction of cash, particularly in the form of transfer payments, has had a profound and problematic impact on sharing norms. One consequence of this is that 'ineffectual demanders', such as older women whose social power has waned, are now 'at constant risk' of exploitation.[100] Overseas experience points to the need to protect vulnerable groups during land reform processes. In the context of Aboriginal communities, this will include those people who find themselves at a disadvantage under modified sharing norms.

Housing for Aboriginal residents

With this background in mind, this section now considers the nature of the informal tenure arrangements in communities on Aboriginal land. Those tenure arrangements are not uniform, and in particular have been slightly different with respect to the three main categories of land use: housing for Aboriginal residents, service infrastructure and infrastructure occupied by enterprises.[101] These three categories are each described below, followed by a brief description of vacant land and planning practices. The first category is housing for Aboriginal residents, referred to here as 'residential housing'. Residential housing is distinguished from 'staff housing' – housing for outside staff of organisations operating in communities – because they were treated differently. Staff housing was treated in the same way as other service and enterprise infrastructure, while residential housing was managed in accordance with the system set out below.

Overcrowding, mobility and demographic shifts

The Productivity Commission estimated that in 2006, 65.9 per cent of Aboriginal people in the Northern Territory lived in overcrowded housing.[102] While there are issues around the definition of 'overcrowded',[103] it is clear that in Aboriginal communities the number of house occupants is often substantially higher than the Australian norm.[104] A 2004 study of the community of Wadeye found that the average number of people per house was 16.[105] A more recent study of Maningrida found that the average household size was 15 persons during the dry season, but this often swelled to 20–30 during the wet season.[106] These numbers are not uniform:[107] for example, a survey in Alpurrurulam found an average of around 6 people per house, with some houses having up to 13 people.[108]

106 *Communities on Aboriginal land*

The existence of long waiting lists suggests that overcrowding is primarily due to a shortage of housing.[109] However, it also takes place in the context of the sharing norms referred to above, which not only oblige people to share housing space but also mean that 'a crowded house [can be] a source of cultural and social security'.[110] Also relevant are high levels of mobility, which can result in significant fluctuations in population levels.[111] In some places people move seasonally, but they may also move for a variety of other reasons including events such as sports carnivals and sorry business,[112] to access services (including housing), to visit family, or to avoid family conflict.[113] Due to demographic factors, overcrowding is also a problem that is increasing over time. In 2008, Dillon and Westbury estimated there was a total shortfall of around 8,000 houses in Indigenous communities across Australia, which without additional housing would increase to 13,500 by the year 2020.[114]

The problem with defining household

The combination of high occupancy and mobility levels mean that the composition of a 'household' can be fluid and complex to the point where some argue the term itself is misleading.[115] This is well illustrated in several studies of housing practices in the predominantly Warlpiri community of Yuendumu.[116] Three types of domiciliary groups are observed, each having their origin in the historical composition of camps. In addition to the more familiar married people's camp, or *yupukarra*, there are men's camps called *jangkayi* and women's camps called *jilimi*.[117] In a detailed study of one modern *jilimi* over 221 non-consecutive days, Musharbash observed more than 160 different people stay overnight, at an average of 17 people per night.[118] She identified a core group of 11 residents who spent more than 100 nights, as well as a regular group of 12 who spent more than 44 nights, with others falling into categories of less frequent occupancy.[119]

The particular house that Musharbash describes was highly complex and fluid; however, this is partly due to the type of household (a women's camp) she was researching. Not all households are this dynamic;[120] there is rather a spectrum between households of the type described by Musharbash and households that more closely align with the standard nuclear family, albeit in a more crowded context. It is not clear from the existing research where the majority of households are on this spectrum.

The size, complexity and dynamism of households have implications for the application of land reform theory. It is far more difficult to establish unity of interest or intention in such circumstances, as a consequence of which terms such as 'tenure security' take on a more complicated meaning. The potential for land reform to create winners and losers is exacerbated by the fact that more rigid rules around household composition might leave some people without housing.

Communities on Aboriginal land   107

Housing in Aboriginal communities: informal community housing

In Australia, social (or non-private) housing can broadly be divided into two groups: public housing, which is delivered by mainstream housing departments, and community housing, which is delivered by community organisations, with or without government funding. Prior to the recent reforms, housing in communities on Aboriginal land has been an example of government-funded community housing. Houses were managed by local or regional bodies called Indigenous Community Housing Organisations, or ICHOs, which in many communities were the local council.[121] The role of ICHOs included repairs and maintenance, tenancy management and the allocation of housing. In many places, including all communities on ALRA land, ICHOs were not the landowner and did not have a lease but were regarded as the effective owners and managers of the housing under their control.[122]

ICHOs have generally allocated houses under their management to particular individuals or families. It is not entirely clear on what basis allocation decisions have been made. The use of waiting lists has already been referred to, but there also appears to have been an element of negotiation. Musharbash describes how meetings to discuss housing allocation in Yuendumu were 'by far the most heated as well as the best attended'.[123] Dillon and Westbury refer to allocation being 'determined very much by the exigencies of community social life and politics and the need to relieve the most serious overcrowding'.[124] Fien *et al.* report that in Maningrida housing has historically been clustered into regions reflecting family groupings.[125] There are some reports of housing allocation being affected by favouritism or nepotism,[126] which may in some communities have favoured traditional owners.[127] Memmott *et al.* report that in Wurrumiyanga (then Nguiu) residents were able to devise or pass their house on to their children and grandchildren.[128] This is not usually a feature of community housing in Australia, and it is not clear how widespread it has been. Others instead argue that mourning rituals requiring families to vacate houses for a period of time can mean that people place less importance on houses being inheritable, at least in some areas.[129] This is not necessarily an immutable barrier: housing might pass to family members following the necessary period of mourning.[130]

In many communities, rent has historically been collected on a per-individual rather than per-household basis.[131] Sanders argues that this was more effective because in large and complex households it is unrealistic to think of incomes as being fully shared and available for a household-level expense.[132]

108   *Communities on Aboriginal land*

Service infrastructure

The second category of land use in communities is the infrastructure occupied by service providers: local councils, NGOs and the Australian and NT governments. This includes infrastructure that has been created for a particular purpose, such as council workshops, classrooms, police stations, recreational halls and power stations, as well as infrastructure that is more transferable, such as office space and staff housing. A slightly broader set of issues arise in relation to the latter, as infrastructure created for a particular purpose is less likely to be the subject of contestation. It is unlikely, for example, that the occupation of a police station or sewage pond would become a matter of dispute. If there were a dispute, it would be with respect to whether a particular service provider should be removed and replaced with another, to the extent that there were others available. With respect to transferable infrastructure such as staff housing, there is the potential for competition over access between organisations. For example, if a particular service provider were to leave their staff housing vacant for a period of time, they might find it occupied by someone else when they wished to return.[133] There is unfortunately no research that describes how often this has occurred, or how and by whom disputes have been resolved.[134] If it were widespread, it would be surprising that it were not referred to more often in submissions and reports, such as the Reeves Report or submissions from governments and NGOs in relation to the recent land reforms. The fact that for several decades governments funded and occupied infrastructure without obtaining or requiring leases suggests that it was not widespread.[135]

To the extent it has occurred, there will have been a downside and upside to organisations having 'their' houses reallocated to others during a period of absence. On the upside, it may have resulted in a more efficient allocation of housing, which was in short supply. On the downside it may have led some occupiers to experience insecure tenure. In this context, the Australian and NT governments had several non-tenure means open to them to protect their occupancy rights. As well as being service providers, they were also the main providers of funding for a variety of services. With respect to some services, such as police and education, they were either the monopoly provider or monopoly funder. This gave them some leverage in negotiations around infrastructure use. The NT Government was also involved in community planning and the provision of essential service infrastructure (power, water and sewerage), and both governments were repeat players in community life. NGOs on the other hand may have been more vulnerable, particularly if they commanded little support in the community forums in which reallocation decisions were contested. It is more likely that they were at risk of tenure insecurity; but as stated above, the exact extent of this is not known.

Enterprises

The most common form of enterprise in Aboriginal communities is the community store, which commonly includes a takeaway food service.[136] In some smaller communities the community store may be the only enterprise.[137] In other communities there are also businesses such as art centres, garages, visitor accommodation and tourism enterprises.[138] As with service providers, enterprises have occupied infrastructure created for a particular purpose, such as art studios and store buildings, as well as transferable infrastructure such as staff housing.

The majority of community stores have been owned by the community in some way, through either the local council or a separately incorporated community store association, although a significant number have also been owned 'privately'.[139] There has frequently been a distinction between ownership and management, with stores being run by non-Aboriginal staff.[140] Particularly in larger communities, stores can be quite profitable, and profits are sometimes returned to the community through either payments to individuals or contributions to community projects.[141] This can result in competition between families for control over the store and the distribution process.[142]

As described above, while the NLC reports that almost all shops in its region are subject to leases, the CLC reports very few store leases.[143] It appears that the reason for store leases has been to secure rent for traditional owners, which is sometimes considerable.[144]

Vacant land and informal planning processes

While until recently there have been no formal planning schemes in Aboriginal communities, there has long been an informal planning process conducted by the NT Government in conjunction with local councils.[145] Informal planning information is recorded on a series of maps called Serviced Land Availability Program (SLAP) maps.[146] The layout of infrastructure in some communities will reflect particular local practices and preferences. For example, Fien *et al.* describe five housing districts in Maningrida corresponding to distinct family groups.[147] They also report that a shortage of housing has led to greater intermingling in recent years.[148] Musharbash observes that in Yuendumu the distinction between different housing zones has lessened over time due to changes in the way people identify.[149]

Most new developments – whether for housing, an enterprise or service provision – will require power, water and sewerage, and in some cases even a new road. The provision of this infrastructure is an integral part of the planning and allocation process. It is not simply a matter of communities or community organisations deciding where they want things to be, with or without the assistance of government planners. It is also

110   *Communities on Aboriginal land*

necessary to find an existing serviced lot, or construct new essential service infrastructure.[150] This deepens the role of governments, particularly the NT Government, in the allocation process.

4.4 Summary and discussion

Housing for residents

Informal and community housing

Housing for residents in communities on Aboriginal land has been a type of *informal community housing*. There are two distinct elements to this. There is, first, the fact that the arrangements were *informal*;[151] and second, that it has been a type of *community housing*, rather than public housing, occupier-ownership or commercial rental. That is, if an attempt were made to formalise these arrangements in a way that most closely reflected current circumstances, the outcome would be formal community housing. As described in Chapter 6, this is not what the recent reforms have done. In addition to formalisation, there has been a large-scale shift from community housing (a form of communal property, although see below) to public housing (state property). Indeed, formalisation has been integral to implementing this shift.

What type of tenure system?

The description of community housing as a form of communal property needs to be modified where it relies on government funding. On communal property, the rights and duties of members are determined by the group, through the outcome of group processes or the application of group norms.[152] Government funding complicates this. Through controls over funding, the government can influence the way in which rights and duties are allocated and exercised within the group. This effects a practical shift towards state property. This is not simply a technical or definitional issue: describing government-funded community housing as communal property conveys a misleading impression of autonomy. The limited and dependent nature of that autonomy is itself an important feature of community housing. Further, government funding can alter perceptions about where *responsibilities* lie. For example, the responsibility to repair a broken septic system might be thought of as a government responsibility, rather than an individual or group responsibility. This can have implications for the way in which houses are cared for.[153]

Communities on Aboriginal land   111

Traditional authority, community authority and government authority

The description provided above demonstrates that the pre-existing informal tenure arrangements in communities on Aboriginal land were not simply a manifestation of land ownership. They were instead the negotiated outcome of three spheres of authority: traditional authority, community authority and government authority. *Traditional authority* could derive from a traditional connection to the country on which the community is situated. In some places, traditional owners were allocated a formal role on local councils. In other places they were not. Holcombe observes how in some cases a wider group of people can also make claims to authority under Aboriginal law and tradition.

The factors that determine *community authority* are far broader than this. They include kinship networks within the community, relationships with key non-Aboriginal staff, the ability to engage well with administrative issues and external organisations, and the capacity to handle the competing demands that come with holding formal positions. *Government authority* is exercised by the Australian and NT governments in a wide variety of ways, particularly through control over funding and participation in planning processes.

It is important to note that this is not a general comment on Aboriginal land ownership, rather a statement about informal tenure arrangements in communities, which are a special case. It is likely that on other areas of Aboriginal land, including outstations, Aboriginal land tenure plays a greater and more direct role in the allocation of rights. However, the great majority of the recent land reforms have affected only land in and immediately around larger residential communities.

An intercultural context

In her 1998 book *Caging the Rainbow*, Francesca Merlan used the adjective 'intercultural' to describe the situation of Aboriginal people living in the town of Katherine. In doing so, her aim was to find a better way of describing the way in which Aboriginal and non-Aboriginal people and institutions engage and influence each other.[154] The term has since been applied and developed by several other authors.[155] In a more recent article, Merlan argued that intercultural should be understood not as a space between discrete, bounded and self-reproducing cultures, but as an 'inter-relationship'. This better reflects the existence of shared ground and common influences, and the relational and dynamic nature of identity and its reproduction.[156] Relevantly, one of Merlan's concerns in introducing this concept was to subvert the dichotomisation of 'culture' as the term is applied to Aboriginal people, whereby it becomes something 'traditional' that they are required to rigidly adhere to, or are found to have lost.[157]

112   *Communities on Aboriginal land*

One author to use this concept is Martin, who has argued that Aboriginal corporations are best described as intercultural institutions rather than 'manifestations of a supposedly autonomous Aboriginal domain'. Indeed, as they are created under state law, and serve governmental as well as Aboriginal ends, he argues that Aboriginal corporations are 'quintessentially intercultural'.[158] I argue that the same can be said of the informal tenure arrangements in communities on Aboriginal land. They reflect a high level of government involvement through planning processes, infrastructure provision and control over funding. Many organisations involved in the negotiation of tenure are managed by non-Aboriginal staff. Structures such as local councils and the community-housing model are derived from their non-Aboriginal counterparts. On the other hand, the tenure arrangements are also influenced by, and even accommodating of, distinct approaches to relationship, authority, responsibility, household formation and house occupation. It can also be argued that their negotiated nature itself reflects Fourie's characterisation of the 'customary way of doing business', which 'includes the manipulation of land tenure rules, flexibility, uncertainty, ambiguity and coalition forming linked to entrepreneurship'.[159]

That is, tenure arrangements in communities on Aboriginal land are at the same time modern-Aboriginal and part of something broader, relational and deeply engaged with governments. They represent an Aboriginal response to sedentarisation, to the conglomeration of formerly separate groups, and to the policies, planning practices and funding rules of governments (which have changed over time). They also represent an ongoing government response to the existence of particular Aboriginal values and practices.

Several authors have made a similar point in relation to modern-customary tenure arrangements in other countries.[160] However, this is not the approach that has previously been taken in Australia. Through the use of terms such as 'communal property', tenure arrangements in communities on Aboriginal land have often been characterised as forming part of, even an integral part of, a distinct Aboriginal domain. This has resulted in an unfortunate dichotomisation of debate. Under 'secure tenure' policies, those same arrangements have instead been presented as akin to informal state property, ignoring, perhaps strategically, the existence of something more complex and more valued at a local Aboriginal level. Both stages of debate are described in greater detail in Chapter 5.

Informal tenure arrangements or communal ownership?

I argue here that it is better to describe the pre-existing tenure arrangements in communities on Aboriginal land as 'informal tenure arrangements' rather than 'communal property', even where the term 'communal property' has been properly defined. There are several reasons for this. The first is that 'communal property' can imply the existence of one single

Communities on Aboriginal land 113

overarching property regime in communities. The description provided here demonstrates that there were in fact several different regimes. The regime with respect to residential housing was slightly different to that with respect to service and enterprise infrastructure. The term 'informal tenure' does not convey the same sense of uniformity. The term 'communal property' might also suggest that those informal arrangements are determined by or a manifestation of the land ownership system. To be clear, both ALRA and CLA land can rightly be described as examples of communal property. What this chapter demonstrates is that the informal tenure arrangements in communities on Aboriginal land have been to some extent distinct from the land ownership system. This distinction is much clearer if land ownership is described as 'communal property' while the tenure arrangements in communities are described as 'informal tenure arrangements'. Further, while the term 'communal property' is suitable to some aspects of those informal tenure arrangements, it is only accurate up to a point. This is described above with respect to residential housing. As a type of (informal) community housing, it might be described as communal property; however, this is complicated by the impact of government funding.

There is also a final reason that is arguably more important still. Writing in relation to Aboriginal organisations, Martin uses the term 'strategic engagement' to describe an alternative approach to organisational governance. Martin explains how he introduced this term as a deliberate attempt to 'circumvent what is often a rather sterile public debate conducted in Australia using such loaded terminology as "assimilation", "cultural maintenance", "tradition", "economic independence", "self-determination" and so forth'.[161] I have similar concerns here. For reasons that will become clearer in Chapter 5, I argue that the term 'communal property' has long since stopped being helpful in this context. It has become so caught up in a highly divisive and ideological debate that the true consequences of a set of reforms that have a real impact on the lives of Aboriginal people have been lost. While it is less evocative, the term 'informal tenure' forms part of a more useful set of terminology for analysing and debating the reforms.

Concluding comments

In the absence of leases, most infrastructure in communities on Aboriginal land has, as a fixture, belonged legally to the Land Trust (on ALRA land) or the land-holding association (on CLA land). That is, however, only one part of the story. On top of this, a well-developed set of non-legal (informal) tenure arrangements have evolved. The use of, and responsibility for, infrastructure has been allocated pursuant to those informal arrangements. Those arrangements were *distinct* from, but not entirely *separate* from, land ownership. In some cases those people with a traditional connection to country, or other forms of traditional authority, could assert priority in the

114 *Communities on Aboriginal land*

community forums in which decisions were made. However, those claims would compete with other claims to authority both formal and informal. In addition to this, different government agencies contributed to decision-making as occupiers and funding bodies and through their role in planning processes and the provision of infrastructure.

The informal regime also varied between different categories of infra-structure. Housing for residents was a type of informal community housing. It could be distinguished from other examples of community housing by its informality, but also by the fact that certain distinct prac-tices developed in some communities in response to local conditions, such as collecting rent on a per-person basis. Service infrastructure and the infrastructure used by enterprises were instead allocated to particular organisations, pursuant to arrangements under which the extent of their rights to that infrastructure were negotiated rather than fixed.

The description provided here can now be compared with the way in which the starting point for reform was characterised by politicians, scholars and other participants during the debate about land reform that is described in the next chapter.

Notes

1 Hernando de Soto, *The Mystery of Capital: Why Capitalism Triumphs in the West and Fails Everywhere Else* (Black Swan, 2001) 182. See also Chapter 2.
2 Diane Austin-Broos, *Arrernte Present, Arrernte Past: Invasion, Violence, and Imagination in Indigenous Central Australia* (University of Chicago Press, 2009) 5 and see generally.
3 Ibid, 17.
4 Australian Bureau of Statistics, *4710.0 – Housing and Infrastructure in Abori-ginal and Torres Strait Islander Communities, Australia, 2006* (17 April 2007) www.abs.gov.au/AUSSTATS/abs@.nsf/Latestproducts/4710.0Main%20Featur es42006?opendocument&tabname=Summary&prodno=4710.0&issue=2006 &num=&view=.
5 Jon Altman, 'The "National Emergency" and Land Rights Reform: Separating Fact from Fiction' (Briefing paper for Oxfam Australia prepared by the Centre for Aboriginal Economic Policy Research, 7 August 2007) 4.
6 Ibid.
7 The NT Government provides population data on the Bushtel website: North-ern Territory Government, *Northern Territory Government Bushtel* (2007) www.bushtel.nt.gov.au. The two smallest communities are Milyakburra and Nturiya, the two largest are Wadeye and Maningrida.
8 Of the 41,681 people living in discrete Aboriginal communities in the North-ern Territory, 741 were classified as living in outer regional areas, 4,350 in remote area and 36,590 in very remote areas; Australian Bureau of Statistics, above n 4.
9 A list of these communities is provided at Schedule 7 of the *Aboriginal Land Rights (Northern Territory) Act 1976* (Cth). This list includes Mutitjulu, which is on Aboriginal land although inside Uluru-Kata Tjuta National Park and leased to the Director of National Parks.
10 A list of these communities is provided at *Northern Territory National Emer-gency Response Act 2007* (Cth) sch 1 pt 2.

Communities on Aboriginal land   115

11 Those five communitites are: Finke/Aputula (declared town composed predominantly of fee simple), Canteen Creek (vacant Crown land subject to a land claim), Daly River/Nauiyu (leased to a Catholic Church property trust), Kalkarindji (mixture of leasehold and freehold) and Kybrook Farm (held in fee simple by Pine Creek Aboriginal Advancement Association Inc); see Australian Government, 'Report on the Northern Territory Emergency Response Redesign Consultations' (2009) 64–6.
12 For a list of the communities in existence prior to the advent of land rights see Edward Woodward, 'Aboriginal Land Rights Commission: Second Report' (Australian Government, 1974) 67–8 [347]–[348].
13 See Imanpa Community Council, 'The Intervention and Beyond' (December 2007). Due to fluctuating populations and uncertainties about population data, estimates vary and it is sometimes the practice to provide a range rather than a single figure. The figure of 140 comes from page 5 of the council's report while the figure of 217 comes from the Bushtel website at above n 7.
14 Yasmine Musharbash, *Yuendumu Everyday: Contemporary Life in Remote Aboriginal Australia* (Aboriginal Studies Press, 2008) 17–25, 158–62. Musharbash's observations date from around 2000.
15 Brian Gleeson, 'Coordinator General for Remote Indigenous Services Six Monthly Report July–November 2009' (Australian Government, 2009) 28.
16 See Northern Territory Government, 'Maningrida Study' (Department of Regional Development, Primary Industry, Fisheries and Resources, 2008).
17 Imanpa Community Council, above n 13, 5.
18 Paul Albrecht, *Relhiperra: About Aborigines* (Bennelong Society, 2008) 4–5; Sarah Holcombe, 'Luritja Management of the State' (2005) 75 *Oceania* 222, 223; Nicolas Peterson, 'Community Development, Civil Society and Local Government in the Future of Remote Northern Territory Growth Towns' (2013) 14(4) *Asia Pacific Journal of Anthropology* 339, 342–4.
19 Sarah Holcombe, 'Socio-Political Perspectives on Localism and Regionalism in the Pintubi Luritja Region of Central Australia: Implications for Service Delivery and Governance' (Working Paper No 25/2004, Centre for Aboriginal Economic Policy Research, 2004) 10.
20 Writing of the Arrernte, Austin-Broos describes 'a kin-based society half in and half out of a very different order'; Austin-Broos, above n 2, 155.
21 Holcombe, 'Socio-Political Perspectives', above n 19, 8, 11. The various families who came to settle at Haasts Bluff and amalgamated into the 'Luritja' were Pintubi, Ngaliya Warlpiri, Kukatja, Pitantjatjara, Ngaatjatjarra and Anmatyerre. This story reflects not only the way in which new identities evolve but also the way in which identities are layered.
22 Musharbash, above n 14, 3 n 1.
23 Ibid.
24 Lists were annexed to each township lease. The township leases are registered, and the author obtained copies through the Northern Territory Land Titles Office.
25 Gleeson, above n 15, 30.
26 See the Bushtel website at above n 7.
27 Ibid.
28 Jon Altman, Craig Linkhorn and Jennifer Clarke, 'Land Rights and Development Reform in Remote Australia' (Discussion Paper No 276/2005, Centre for Aboriginal Economic Policy Research, 2005) 9.
29 John Reeves, 'Building on Land Rights for the Next Generation: The Review of the *Aboriginal Land Rights (Northern Territory) Act 1976*' (Australian Government, 1998) 499.
30 *Aboriginal Land Rights (Northern Territory) Act 1976* (Cth) ss 19(2), (3), (4A).

116 *Communities on Aboriginal land*

31 Edward Woodward, 'Aboriginal Land Rights Commission: First Report' (Australian Government, 1973) 20 [119]; Woodward, 'Second Report', above n 12, 16 [96]–[97].

32 Woodward, 'First Report', above n 31, 47 [299].

33 Woodward, 'Second Report', above n 12, 24 [144 (xxii), (xxiii)].

34 Ibid, 16 [99].

35 See Evidence to Senate Standing Committee on Community Affairs (Budget Estimates), Parliament of Australia, Canberra, 28 May 2007, 66 (John Hicks). Administrative lots are areas of land allocated pursuant to formal and informal planning processes; see discussion below on planning.

36 This information is contained in Annexure 5 of the Wurrumiyanga township lease.

37 Michael Dillon and Neil Westbury, *Beyond Humbug: Transforming Government Engagement with Indigenous Australia* (Seaview Press, 2007) 131–2; Evidence to Senate Community Affairs Legislation Committee, Parliament of Australia, Darwin, 21 July 2006, 78 (Dennis Bree); Reeves, above n 29, 499–500.

38 Northern Land Council (NLC), Submission No 13 to the Senate Community Affairs Committee, Parliament of Australia, *Inquiry into Aboriginal Land Rights (Northern Territory) Amendment Bill 2006*, 21 July 2006, 14, 21. See also Evidence to Senate Community Affairs Legislation Committee, Parliament of Australia, Darwin, 21 July 2006, 12 (Ron Levy).

39 Central Land Council (CLC), 'Communal Title and Economic Development' (Policy Paper, 2005) 6. See also Evidence to Senate Community Affairs Legislation Committee, Parliament of Australia, Darwin, 21 July 2006, 26 (David Ross).

40 A reference in the Act to the Crown means the either the Crown in right of the Commonwealth or the Northern Territory or both, as the case requires; see *Aboriginal Land Rights (Northern Territory) Act 1976* (Cth) s 3(6).

41 Ibid, s 14(1). This provision applies to both the Crown and an Authority 'with the licence or permission of the Crown', where 'Authority' means an authority established by or under a law of the Commonwealth or a law of the Northern Territory; see s 3(1).

42 Ibid, s 14(2).

43 Ibid, s 15(1). Section 3 provides that 'community purpose means a purpose that is calculated to benefit primarily the members of a particular community or group'.

44 Ibid, s 18.

45 NLC, above n 38, 14. See also Michael Dodson and Diana McCarthy, 'Communal Land and the Amendments to the *Aboriginal Land Rights (Northern Territory) Act*' (Research Discussion Paper No 19, Australian Institute of Aboriginal and Torres Strait Islander Studies, 2006) 7. Dillon and Westbury instead state that this was only one of the reasons why the NT Government has not applied for leases; Dillon and Westbury, above n 37, 131.

46 Cf Evidence to Senate Community Affairs Legislation Committee, Parliament of Australia, Darwin, 21 July 2006, 12 (Ron Levy).

47 See above n 41.

48 See, eg, Central Land Council, Submission No 347 to Senate Standing Committees on Community Affairs, Parliament of Australia, *Inquiry into Stronger Futures in the Northern Territory Bill 2011 and Two Related Bills*, 1 February 2012; Northern Land Council, Submission No 361 to Senate Standing Committees on Community Affairs, Parliament of Australia, *Inquiry into Stronger Futures in the Northern Territory Bill 2011 and Two Related Bills*, 10 February 2012, who make no reference to existing leases.

49 In 2006, there were 57 local councils outside of the six main urban areas; Will Sanders, 'Local Governments and Indigenous Interests in Australia's Northern Territory' (Discussion Paper No 285/2006, Centre for Aboriginal Economic Policy Research, 2006) 3. This number has changed over time.

50 Ibid, 12; John Fien *et al.*, 'Towards a Design Framework for Remote Indigenous Housing' (Final Report No 114, Australian Housing and Urban Research Institute, March 2008) 23.

51 See, eg, Sanders, above n 49, 12.

52 See, eg, Thamarrurr Development Corporation, *About Us*, http://thamarrurr. org.au/index.php/about-us. See also discussion below on enterprises.

53 Patrick Sullivan, 'The Aboriginal Community Sector and the Effective Delivery of Services: Acknowledging the Role of Indigenous Sector Organisations' (Working Paper No 73, Desert Knowledge CRC, 2010) 3.

54 For a more complete analysis of this point see Philip Batty, 'Private Politics, Public Strategies: White Advisers and Their Aboriginal Subjects' (2005) 75(3) *Oceania* 209; David Martin, 'Rethinking the Design of Indigenous Organisations: The Need for Strategic Engagement' (Discussion Paper No 248/2003, Centre for Aboriginal Economic Policy Research, 2003) 5.

55 The extent of this shift is documented in Central Land Council, 'The Governance Role of Local Boards: A Scoping Study from Six Communities' (2010).

56 Five-year leases are described in Chapter 6.

57 See, eg, Tim Rowse, 'The Indigenous Sector' in Diane Austin-Broos and Gaynor Macdonald (eds), *Culture, Economy and Governance in Aboriginal Australia* (Sydney University Press, 2005) 213 (and earlier work by Rowse); Sullivan, above n 53.

58 David Martin, 'Why the "New Direction" in Federal Indigenous Affairs Policy Is as Likely to "Fail" as the Old Directions' (Topical Issue No 05/2006, Centre for Aboriginal Economic Policy Research, 2006) 9.

59 Diane Smith, 'From Gove to Governance: Reshaping Indigenous Governance in the Northern Territory' (Discussion Paper No 265/2004, Centre for Aboriginal Economic Policy Research, 2004) 7.

60 Sanders, above n 49, 4. See also Rowse's discussion of fission and aggregation; Rowse, above n 57, 222–23.

61 Sullivan, above n 53, 2. See also Musharbash, above n 14, 24, 158–62.

62 Will Sanders, 'Dispersal, Autonomy and Scale in Indigenous Community Governance: Some Reflections on Recent Northern Territory Experience' (Paper presented at the North Australian Research Unit, Darwin, 30 October 2003) 3.

63 Martin Mowbray, 'Municipalising Land Councils: Land Rights and Local Governance' in Jon Altman, Tim Rowse and Frances Morphy (eds), *Land Rights at Risk? Evaluations of the Reeves Report* (Centre for Aboriginal Economic Policy Research, 1999) 167; Will Sanders, 'Local Governments and Indigenous Australians: Developments and Dilemmas in Contrasting Circumstances' (Discussion Paper No 84/1995, Centre for Aboriginal Economic Policy Research, 1995) 20–1; Neil Westbury and Will Sanders, 'Governance and Service Delivery for Remote Aboriginal Communities in the Northern Territory: Challenges and Opportunities' (Working Paper No 6/2000, Centre for Aboriginal Economic Policy Research, 2000) 3–5; Smith, above n 59, 5.

64 Westbury and Sanders, above n 63, 2–3.

65 See, eg, Mowbray, above n 63. Aspects of the Reeves Report are described in Chapters 3 and 5.

66 Ibid, 171, and see also 168, 174–5. Mowbray reports the NT Government actively providing support to breakaway groups. Sanders on the other hand states that Land Council fears were not always well founded; Sanders, 'Local

118 *Communities on Aboriginal land*

Governments and Indigenous Australians', above n 63, 21. See also Westbury and Sanders, above n 63, 3.

67 Mowbray, above n 63, 171; Smith, above n 59, 29. See also Reeves, above n 29, Appendix R, 410, although note also Reeves' comments on 397–8.

68 This is remarked upon critically by Dillon and Westbury, above n 37, 133–5.

69 Sanders, 'Dispersal, Autonomy and Scale', above n 62, 4.

70 Holcombe, 'Socio-Political Perspectives', above n 19, 9.

71 Sarah Holcombe, 'Traditional Owners and "Community-Country" Anangu: Distinctions and Dilemmas' (2004) 2 *Australian Aboriginal Studies* 64, 64.

72 Austin-Broos observes that '[r]itual knowledge per se does not bring material power', it needs to be made use of in a political context; Austin-Broos, above n 2, 143.

73 David Martin and Julie Finlayson, 'Linking Accountability and Self-Determination in Aboriginal Organisations' (Discussion Paper No 116/1996, Centre for Aboriginal Economic Policy Research, 1996) 14.

74 Evidence to Senate Community Affairs Legislation Committee, Parliament of Australia, Darwin, 21 July 2006, 70 (Jon Altman). Cf Peterson, above n 18, 344, who refers to communities being 'dominated by the local traditional owners'.

75 A still-existing website of the former local council for Wadeye describes how two councillors are elected from each language group; see Wadeye Aboriginal Community, *Wadeye Council* (1998) www.indiginet.com.au/wadeye/index. htm.

76 Smith, above n 59, 6.

77 Mowbray, above n 63, 172–3; Dodson and McCarthy, above n 45, 7. See also Reeves, above n 29, 499.

78 Andrea Orr, *Remote Indigenous Housing System: A Systems Social Assessment* (PhD Thesis, Murdoch University, 2005) 110. Orr studies two communities, Papunya and Laramba, and finds no need to distinguish between them despite the fact that Papunya is on ALRA land while Laramba is on CLA land.

79 The term was developed by Jackie Wolfe in 1989, and expanded upon by Tim Rowse in 1992; see Will Sanders, 'Thinking about Indigenous Community Governance' (Discussion Paper No 262/2004, Centre for Aboriginal Economic Policy Research, 2004) 7. See also Will Sanders, 'Good Governance for Indigenous Communities and Regions: More Diverse Than Unified, as Much Process as Structure' (Paper presented at the Indigenous Governance Conference, Canberra, 3–5 April 2002); Sanders, 'Dispersal, Autonomy and Scale', above n 62; Westbury and Sanders, above n 63, 3, 6–8; David Martin, 'Rethinking Aboriginal Community Governance' in Paul Smyth, Tim Reddel and Andrew Jones (eds), *Community and Local Governance in Australia* (University of New South Wales Press, 2005) 108, 108. Rowse himself appears to be more circumspect about use of the term in a later publication; see Rowse, 'The Indigenous Sector', above n 57, 223.

80 Sanders, 'Good Governance for Indigenous Communities and Regions', above n 79, 2; Smith, above n 59, 7; Fien *et al.*, above n 50, 23.

81 See, eg, Sanders, 'Dispersal, Autonomy and Scale', above n 62, 8.

82 Albrecht, above n 18, 4. See also Patrick Sullivan, 'From Land Rights to the Rights of the People' (1996) 3(85) *Aboriginal Law Bulletin* 16; Holcombe, 'Socio-Political Perspectives', above n 19, 5–6; Marcia Langton, 'Anthropology, Politics and the Changing World of Aboriginal Australians' (March 2011) 21(1) *Anthropological Forum* 1, 6.

83 Holcombe, 'Socio-Political Perspectives', above n 19, 5–6, 9. See also David Martin, 'Money, Business and Culture: Issues for Aboriginal Economic Policy'

Communities on Aboriginal land 119

(Discussion Paper No 101/1995, Centre for Aboriginal Economic Policy Research, 1995) 5.

84 Austin-Broos, above n 2, 148–51; Holcombe, 'Socio-Political Perspectives', above n 19, 9–11.

85 Fred Myers, *Pintupi Country, Pintupi Self: Sentiment, Place, and Politics among Western Desert Aborigines* (University of California Press, 1991) 265 and ch 9 generally. See also Holcombe, 'Socio-Political Perspectives', above n 19, 9.

86 Will Sanders, 'Being a Good Senior Manager in Indigenous Community Governance: Working with Public Purpose and Private Benefit' (Discussion Paper No 280/2006, Centre for Aboriginal Economic Policy Research, 2006) 2; Holcombe, 'Socio-Political Perspectives', above n 19, 9.

87 Holcombe, 'Socio-Political Perspectives', above n 19, 9.

88 In this context see Mark Moran, 'What Job, Which House?: Simple Solutions to Complex Problems in Indigenous Affairs' (March 2009) *Australian Review of Public Affairs* www.australianreview.net/digest/2009/03/moran.html; Sanders, 'Being a Good Senior Manager', above n 86; Batty, above n 54.

89 Nicolas Peterson, 'Demand Sharing: Reciprocity and the Pressure for Generosity among Foragers' *American Anthropologist* (1993) 95(4) 860. See generally Robert G. Schwab, 'The Calculus of Reciprocity: Principles and Implications of Aboriginal Sharing' (Discussion Paper No 100/1995, Centre for Aboriginal Economic Policy Research, 1995); Austin-Broos, above n 2, 143–51; Martin, 'Money, Business and Culture', above n 83.

90 Schwab, above n 89, 9.

91 Schwab, above n 89, 9–12; Max Neutze, 'Housing for Indigenous Australians' (2000) 15(4) *Housing Studies* 485, 493–4.

92 Schwab, above n 89, 7–8.

93 Martin, 'Money, Business and Culture', above n 83. See also Austin-Broos, above n 2, 143.

94 Neutze, above n 91, 493–4. See also Schwab, above n 89, 15.

95 See, eg, Neutze, above n 91, 497; Martin, 'Money, Business and Culture', above n 83, 19; Austin-Broos, above n 2, 144, 148–51; but see also Musharbash's discussion of CDEP firewood, Musharbash, above n 14, 132–5.

96 See story about vehicle given to the 'women of Walungurru'; Sanders, 'Being a Good Senior Manager', above n 86, 3–4.

97 Schwab, above n 89, 12. See also Smith, who (quoting Sutton) refers to 'families of polity'; Diane Smith, 'Indigenous Families, Households and Governance' in Diane Austin-Broos and Gaynor Macdonald (eds), *Culture, Economy and Governance in Aboriginal Australia* (Sydney University Press, 2005) 175, 182.

98 Sanders, 'Being a Good Senior Manager', above n 86, 3–4; Martin, 'Rethinking Aboriginal Community Governance', above n 79, 111; Albrecht, above n 18, 3–5, 20–36.

99 See especially Peterson's discussion about the development of an idea of civil society; Peterson, 'Community Development, Civil Society and Local Government', above n 18.

100 Austin-Broos, above n 2, 147. See also Martin, 'Money, Business and Culture', above n 83, 3, 7, 14–15; Schwab, above n 89, 13.

101 A similar schema is used by CLC, 'Communal Title and Economic Development', above n 39, 19–22.

102 Steering Committee for the Review of Government Service Provision, 'Overcoming Indigenous Disadvantage: Key Indicators 2009' (Productivity Commission, 2009) 9.9. The criteria for 'overcrowded' are described at 9.5.

120 *Communities on Aboriginal land*

103 See especially Paul Memmott *et al.*, 'Modelling Crowding in Aboriginal Australia' (Positing Paper No 141, Australian Housing and Research Institute, August 2011).

104 Nicholas Biddle, 'The Scale and Composition of Indigenous Housing Need, 2001–06' (Working Paper No 47/2008, Centre for Aboriginal Economic Policy Research, 2008) 5–6.

105 Steering Committee for the Review of Government Service Provision, above n 102, 9.4.

106 Fien *et al.*, above n 50, 25.

107 See also Dillon and Westbury, above n 37, 160; Imanpa Community Council, above n 13, 14.

108 Paul Memmott, Stephen Long and Linda Thomson, 'Indigenous Mobility in Rural and Remote Australia' (Final Report No 90, Australian Housing and Urban Research Institute, 2006) 44.

109 Ibid; Dillon and Westbury, above n 37, 162; Fien *et al.*, above n 50, 25.

110 Schwab, above n 89, 15.

111 Dillon and Westbury, above n 37, 168.

112 Sorry business refers to the rituals and activities that follow from someone's death, which can include travelling to participate in a funeral and 'sorry camp'.

113 Daphne Habibis *et al.*, 'Improving Housing Responses to Indigenous Patterns of Temporary Mobility' (Final Report No 162, Australian Housing and Urban Research Unit, 2011) 121–7; Memmott, Long and Thomson, above n 108, 55.

114 Figures based on standard occupancy levels of 3.5 persons per house; see Dillon and Westbury, above n 37, 160.

115 Musharbash, above n 14, 60. See also Neutze, above n 91, 492; Smith, 'Indigenous Families, Households and Governance', above n 97, 175–80.

116 Musharbash, above n 14; Catherine Keys, 'The House and the *Yupukarra*, Yuendumu 1946–96' in Peter Read (ed), *Settlement: A History of Australian Indigenous Housing* (Aboriginal Studies Press, 2000) 118; Catherine Keys, 'Housing Design Principles from a Study of Warlpiri Women's *Jilmi*' in Paul Memmott (ed), *Take 2: Housing Design in Indigenous Australia* (Royal Australian Institute of Architects, 2003) 64.

117 Musharbash, above n 14, 32–3; Keys, 'The House and the *Yupukarra*', above n 116, 118–19.

118 Musharbash, above n 14, 61–2.

119 Ibid, 63.

120 Musharbash notes that the level of throughput in other types of housing was lower; ibid, 59. See also Memmott, Long and Thomson, above n 108, 52–3.

121 Nadia Rosenman and Alex Clunies-Ross, 'The New Tenancy Framework for Remote Aboriginal Communities in the Northern Territory' (2011) 7(24) *Indigenous Law Bulletin* 11, 11. See also Fien *et al.*, above n 50, 25; Musharbash, above n 14, 13, 151.

122 Dillon and Westbury, above n 37, 159, 166.

123 Musharbash, above n 14, 151, and see also 70, 91, 152–3.

124 Dillon and Westbury, above n 37, 162.

125 Fien *et al.*, above n 50, 25.

126 PricewaterhouseCoopers, 'Living in the Sunburnt Country: Indigenous Housing – Findings of the Review of the Community Housing and Infrastructure Programme' (Report to the Department of Families, Community Services and Indigenous Affairs, 2007) 20.

127 PricewaterhouseCoopers refer to nepotism in general but make no reference to traditional owners; ibid. Dillon and Westbury state that in 'broad terms,

traditional owners are treated equally with non-traditional owners (except perhaps in terms of housing allocations)'; Dillon and Westbury, above n 37, 134, and see also 159. McDonnell and Martin instead refer to traditional owners in Maningrida receiving more favourable treatment with rent; Siobhan McDonnell and David Martin, 'Indigenous Community Stores in the "Frontier Economy": Some Competition and Consumer Issues' (Discussion Paper No 234/2002, Centre for Aboriginal Economic Policy Research, 2002) 27, although cf Northern Territory Government, above n 16, 6. See also Evidence to Senate Community Affairs Legislation Committee, Parliament of Australia, Darwin, 21 July 2006, 70 (Jon Altman).

128 Paul Memmott *et al.*, 'Indigenous Home-Ownership on Communal Title Lands' (Final Report No 139, Australian Housing and Urban Research Institute, November 2009) 77.

129 Evidence to Senate Community Affairs Legislation Committee, Parliament of Australia, Darwin, 21 July 2006, 26–7 (David Avery). See also Keys, 'The House and the *Yupukarra*', above n 116, 126; Musharbash, above n 14, 70.

130 See, eg, Austin-Broos, above n 2, 22 n 25 (on page 282), 225.

131 Rosenman and Clunies-Ross, above n 121, 11; Musharbash, above n 14, 152 n 2; Northern Territory Government, above n 16, 6.

132 Will Sanders, 'Housing Tenure and Indigenous Australians in Remote and Settled Areas' (Discussion Paper No 275/2005, Centre for Aboriginal Economic Policy Research, 2005) 16.

133 Dillon and Westbury, above n 37, 135.

134 Dillon and Westbury refer only to houses 'returning to community control'; ibid.

135 Land Councils report that very few occupiers have applied for leases over staff housing; see Evidence to Senate Community Affairs Legislation Committee, Parliament of Australia, Darwin, 21 July 2006, 27 (David Avery) and CLC, 'Communal Title and Economic Development', above n 39, 21.

136 House of Representatives Standing Committee on Aboriginal and Torres Strait Islander Affairs, Parliament of Australia, *Everybody's Business: Remote Aboriginal and Torres Strait Community Stores* (2009) 7 [2.10].

137 Evidence to Senate Community Affairs Legislation Committee, Parliament of Australia, Darwin, 21 July 2006, 32 (Siobhan McDonnell). Imanpa appears to be such a community, although the community owns a tourism business nearby; Imanpa Community Council, above n 13, 5.

138 See, eg, Thamarrurr Development Corporation, above n 52; Northern Territory Government, above n 16, 5–6.

139 In 2008, the NT Government surveyed 66 community stores and found that 35 were community owned, 16 privately owned, 11 were owned by an Aboriginal corporation, 2 were 'leased from the community' and a further 2 were owned jointly; Northern Territory Government, 'Market Basket Survey 2008' (Department of Health and Families, 2008) 4. The terms are not defined, so it is not clear what 'private ownership' means.

140 McDonnell and Martin, above n 127, 20. See also Arnhem Land Progress Aboriginal Corporation, Submission No 61 to House of Representatives Standing Committee on Aboriginal and Torres Strait Islander Affairs, Parliament of Australia, *Inquiry into Community Stores in Remote Aboriginal and Torres Strait Islander Communities*, 17 February 2009, 1.

141 Ranse describes households in Docker River each receiving a $1,000 purchase order, with residual profits accumulated for community projects; Greg Ranse, Submission No 50 to House of Representatives Standing Committee on Aboriginal and Torres Strait Islander Affairs, Parliament of Australia, *Inquiry into Community Stores in Remote Aboriginal and Torres Strait Islander*

122 *Communities on Aboriginal land*

Communities, 20 February 2009, 1. See also McDonnell and Martin, above n 127, 21.

142 McDonnell and Martin, above n 127, 21. The authors argue that traditional owners may be able to assert priority in this context, at 26–8.

143 See above n 38 and 39.

144 NLC, Submission No 13, above n 38, 21. See also McDonnell and Martin, above n 127, 27–8; Dodson and McCarthy, above n 45, 7; Evidence to Senate Community Affairs Legislation Committee, Parliament of Australia, Darwin, 21 July 2006, 12 (Ron Levy).

145 Dillon and Westbury, above n 37, 124; Fien *et al.*, above n 50, 25.

146 SLAP maps for each community be accessed through the Bushtel website, above n 7.

147 Fien *et al.*, above n 50, 25.

148 Ibid.

149 Musharbash, above n 14, 21.

150 See, eg, ibid, 152 including n 3, for an example with respect to housing.

151 On ALRA land there were in fact two informal interfaces: between the Land Trust and the ICHO, and between the ICHO and each housing resident. On CLA land, the ICHO may have been either the landowning body or a related body; however, even on CLA land the relationship between the ICHO and each resident has remained informal.

152 Communal property is defined in Chapter 2.

153 Issues with respect to the care of houses are discussed in Chapter 7.

154 Francesca Merlan, 'Explorations towards Intercultural Accounts of Socio-Cultural Reproduction and Change' (2005) 75 *Oceania* 167, 167.

155 Melinda Hinkson and Benjamin Smith, 'Introduction: Conceptual Moves towards an Intercultural Analysis' (2005) 75 *Oceania* 157; Patrick Sullivan, 'Searching for the Intercultural, Searching for the Culture' (2005) 75 *Oceania* 183; Batty, above n 54; Holcombe, 'Luritja Management of the State', above n 18; Holcombe, 'Socio-Political Perspectives', above n 19, 2; Martin, 'Rethinking the Design of Indigenous Organisations', above n 54 Patrick Sullivan, *Belonging Together: Dealing with the Politics of Disenchantment in Australian Indigenous Policy* (Aboriginal Studies Press, 2011) 18–32.

156 Merlan, above n 154.

157 Ibid, 169.

158 Martin, 'Rethinking Aboriginal Community Governance', above n 79, 119.

159 Clarissa Fourie, 'Land Readjustment for Peri-Urban Customary Tenure: The Example of Botswana' in Robert Hume and Hilary Lim (eds), *Demystifying the Mystery of Capital: Land Tenure and Poverty in Africa and the Caribbean* (Routledge Cavendish, 2004) 31, 31.

160 See, eg, ibid, 36; Michael Barry, 'Formalising Informal Land Rights: The Case of Marconi Beam to Jo Slovo Park' (2006) 30 *Habitat International* 628, 630; Jamie Baxter and Michael Trebilcock, ' "Formalizing" Land Tenure in First Nations: Evaluating the Case for Reserve Tenure Reform' (2009) 7(2) *Indigenous Law Journal* 45, 51.

161 Martin, 'Rethinking Aboriginal Community Governance', above n 79, 119.

Bibliography

Books/articles/reports/web pages

Albrecht, Paul, *Relhiperra: About Aborigines* (Bennelong Society, 2008).

Altman, Jon, Craig Linkhorn and Jennifer Clarke, 'Land Rights and Development Reform in Remote Australia' (Discussion Paper No 276/2005, Centre for Aboriginal Economic Policy Research, 2005).

Evidence to Senate Community Affairs Legislation Committee, Parliament of Australia, Darwin, 21 July 2006, 70 (Jon Altman).

Altman, Jon, 'The "National Emergency" and Land Rights Reform: Separating Fact from Fiction' (Briefing paper for Oxfam Australia prepared by the Centre for Aboriginal Economic Policy Research, 7 August 2007).

Arnhem Land Progress Aboriginal Corporation, Submission No 61 to House of Representatives Standing Committee on Aboriginal and Torres Strait Islander Affairs, Parliament of Australia, *Inquiry into Community Stores in Remote Aboriginal and Torres Strait Islander Communities*, 17 February 2009.

Austin-Broos, Diane, *Arrernte Present, Arrernte Past: Invasion, Violence, and Imagination in Indigenous Central Australia* (University of Chicago Press, 2009).

Australian Bureau of Statistics, *4710.0 – Housing and Infrastructure in Aboriginal and Torres Strait Islander Communities, Australia, 2006* (17 April 2007) www.abs.gov.au/AUSSTATS/abs@.nsf/Latestproducts/4710.0Main%20Features42006?opendocument&tabname=Summary&prodno=4710.0&issue=2006&num=&view=.

Australian Government, 'Report on the Northern Territory Emergency Response Redesign Consultations' (2009).

Evidence to Senate Community Affairs Legislation Committee, Parliament of Australia, Darwin, 21 July 2006, 26–7 (David Avery).

Barry, Michael, 'Formalising Informal Land Rights: The Case of Marconi Beam to Jo Slovo Park' (2006) 30 *Habitat International* 628.

Batty, Philip, 'Private Politics, Public Strategies: White Advisers and Their Aboriginal Subjects' (2005) 75(3) *Oceania* 209.

Baxter, Jamie and Michael Trebilcock, ' "Formalizing" Land Tenure in First Nations: Evaluating the Case for Reserve Tenure Reform' (2009) 7(2) *Indigenous Law Journal* 45.

Biddle, Nicholas, 'The Scale and Composition of Indigenous Housing Need, 2001–06' (Working Paper No 47/2008, Centre for Aboriginal Economic Policy Research, 2008).

Evidence to Senate Community Affairs Legislation Committee, Parliament of Australia, Darwin, 21 July 2006, 78 (Dennis Bree).

Central Land Council, 'Communal Title and Economic Development' (Policy Paper, 2005).

Central Land Council, 'The Governance Role of Local Boards: A Scoping Study from Six Communities' (2010).

Central Land Council, Submission No 347 to Senate Standing Committees on Community Affairs, Parliament of Australia, *Inquiry into Stronger Futures in the Northern Territory Bill 2011 and Two Related Bills*, 1 February 2012.

de Soto, Hernando, *The Mystery of Capital: Why Capitalism Triumphs in the West and Fails Everywhere Else* (Black Swan, 2001).

124   Communities on Aboriginal land

Dillon, Michael and Neil Westbury, *Beyond Humbug: Transforming Government Engagement with Indigenous Australia* (Seaview Press, 2007).

Dodson, Michael and Diana McCarthy, 'Communal Land and the Amendments to the *Aboriginal Land Rights (Northern Territory) Act*' (Research Discussion Paper No 19, Australian Institute of Aboriginal and Torres Strait Islander Studies, 2006).

Fien, John *et al.*, 'Towards a Design Framework for Remote Indigenous Housing' (Final Report No 114, Australian Housing and Urban Research Institute, March 2008).

Fourie, Clarissa, 'Land Readjustment for Peri-Urban Customary Tenure: The Example of Botswana' in Robert Hume and Hilary Lim (eds), *Demystifying the Mystery of Capital: Land Tenure and Poverty in Africa and the Caribbean* (Routledge Cavendish, 2004) 31.

Gleeson, Brian, 'Coordinator General for Remote Indigenous Services Six Monthly Report July–November 2009' (Australian Government, 2009).

Habibis, Daphne *et al.*, 'Improving Housing Responses to Indigenous Patterns of Temporary Mobility' (Final Report No 162, Australian Housing and Urban Research Unit, 2011).

Evidence to Senate Standing Committee on Community Affairs (Budget Estimates), Parliament of Australia, Canberra, 28 May 2007, 66 (John Hicks).

Hinkson, Melinda and Benjamin Smith, 'Introduction: Conceptual Moves towards an Intercultural Analysis' (2005) 75 *Oceania* 157.

Holcombe, Sarah, 'Socio-Political Perspectives on Localism and Regionalism in the Pintubi Luritja Region of Central Australia: Implications for Service Delivery and Governance' (Working Paper No 25/2004, Centre for Aboriginal Economic Policy Research, 2004).

Holcombe, Sarah, 'Traditional Owners and "Community-Country" Anangu: Distinctions and Dilemmas' (2004) 2 *Australian Aboriginal Studies* 64.

Holcombe, Sarah, 'Luritja Management of the State' (2005) 75 *Oceania* 222.

House of Representatives Standing Committee on Aboriginal and Torres Strait Islander Affairs, Parliament of Australia, *Everybody's Business: Remote Aboriginal and Torres Strait Community Stores* (2009).

Imanpa Community Council, 'The Intervention and Beyond' (December 2007).

Keys, Catherine, 'The House and the *Yupukarra*, Yuendumu 1946–96' in Peter Read (ed), *Settlement: A History of Australian Indigenous Housing* (Aboriginal Studies Press, 2000).

Keys, Catherine, 'Housing Design Principles from a Study of Warlpiri Women's *Jilmi*' in Paul Memmott (ed), *Take 2: Housing Design in Indigenous Australia* (Royal Australian Institute of Architects, 2003) 64.

Langton, Marcia, 'Anthropology, Politics and the Changing World of Aboriginal Australians' (March 2011) 21(1) *Anthropological Forum* 1.

Evidence to Senate Community Affairs Legislation Committee, Parliament of Australia, Darwin, 21 July 2006, 12 (Ron Levy).

Evidence to Senate Community Affairs Legislation Committee, Parliament of Australia, Darwin, 21 July 2006, 32 (Siobhan McDonnell).

McDonnell, Siobhan and David Martin, 'Indigenous Community Stores in the "Frontier Economy": Some Competition and Consumer Issues' (Discussion Paper No 234/2002, Centre for Aboriginal Economic Policy Research, 2002).

Martin, David, 'Money, Business and Culture: Issues for Aboriginal Economic

Policy' (Discussion Paper No 101/1995, Centre for Aboriginal Economic Policy Research, 1995).

Martin, David, 'Rethinking the Design of Indigenous Organisations: The Need for Strategic Engagement' (Discussion Paper No 248/2003, Centre for Aboriginal Economic Policy Research, 2003).

Martin, David, 'Rethinking Aboriginal Community Governance' in Paul Smyth, Tim Reddel and Andrew Jones (eds), *Community and Local Governance in Australia* (University of New South Wales Press, 2005) 108.

Martin, David, 'Why the "New Direction" in Federal Indigenous Affairs Policy Is as Likely to "Fail" as the Old Directions' (Topical Issue No 05/2006, Centre for Aboriginal Economic Policy Research, 2006).

Martin, David and Julie Finlayson, 'Linking Accountability and Self-Determination in Aboriginal Organisations' (Discussion Paper No 116/1996, Centre for Aboriginal Economic Policy Research, 1996).

Memmott, Paul, Stephen Long and Linda Thomson, 'Indigenous Mobility in Rural and Remote Australia' (Final Report No 90, Australian Housing and Urban Research Institute, 2006).

Memmott, Paul *et al.*, 'Indigenous Home-Ownership on Communal Title Lands' (Final Report No 139, Australian Housing and Urban Research Institute, November 2009).

Memmott, Paul *et al.*, 'Modelling Crowding in Aboriginal Australia' (Positing Paper No 141, Australian Housing and Research Institute, August 2011).

Merlan, Francesca, 'Explorations towards Intercultural Accounts of Socio-Cultural Reproduction and Change' (2005) 75 *Oceania* 167.

Moran, Mark, 'What Job, Which House?: Simple Solutions to Complex Problems in Indigenous Affairs' (March 2009) *Australian Review of Public Affairs* www. australianreview.net/digest/2009/03/moran.html.

Mowbray, Martin, 'Municipalising Land Councils: Land Rights and Local Governance' in Jon Altman, Tim Rowse and Frances Morphy (eds), *Land Rights at Risk? Evaluations of the Reeves Report* (Centre for Aboriginal Economic Policy Research, 1999).

Musharbash, Yasmine, *Yuendumu Everyday: Contemporary Life in Remote Aboriginal Australia* (Aboriginal Studies Press, 2008).

Myers, Fred, *Pintupi Country, Pintupi Self: Sentiment, Place, and Politics among Western Desert Aborigines* (University of California Press, 1991).

Neutze, Max, 'Housing for Indigenous Australians' (2000) 15(4) *Housing Studies* 485.

Northern Land Council, Submission No 13 to the Senate Community Affairs Committee, Parliament of Australia, *Inquiry into Aboriginal Land Rights (Northern Territory) Amendment Bill 2006*, 21 July 2006.

Northern Land Council, Submission No 361 to Senate Standing Committees on Community Affairs, Parliament of Australia, *Inquiry into Stronger Futures in the Northern Territory Bill 2011 and Two Related Bills*, 10 February 2012.

Northern Territory Government, *Northern Territory Government Bushtel* (2007) www.bushtel.nt.gov.au.

Northern Territory Government, 'Maningrida Study' (Department of Regional Development, Primary Industry, Fisheries and Resources, 2008).

Northern Territory Government, 'Market Basket Survey 2008' (Department of Health and Families, 2008).

126 Communities on Aboriginal land

Orr, Andrea, *Remote Indigenous Housing System: A Systems Social Assessment* (PhD Thesis, Murdoch University, 2005).

Peterson, Nicolas, 'Demand Sharing: Reciprocity and the Pressure for Generosity among Foragers' *American Anthropologist* (1993) 95(4) 860.

Peterson, Nicolas, 'Community Development, Civil Society and Local Government in the Future of Remote Northern Territory Growth Towns' (2013) 14(4) *Asia Pacific Journal of Anthropology* 339.

PricewaterhouseCoopers, 'Living in the Sunburnt Country: Indigenous Housing – Findings of the Review of the Community Housing and Infrastructure Programme' (Report to the Department of Families, Community Services and Indigenous Affairs, 2007).

Ranse, Greg, Submission No 50 to House of Representatives Standing Committee on Aboriginal and Torres Strait Islander Affairs, Parliament of Australia, *Inquiry into Community Stores in Remote Aboriginal and Torres Strait Islander Communities*, 20 February 2009.

Reeves, John, 'Building on Land Rights for the Next Generation: The Review of the *Aboriginal Land Rights (Northern Territory) Act 1976*' (Australian Government, 1998).

Rosenman, Nadia and Alex Clunies-Ross, 'The New Tenancy Framework for Remote Aboriginal Communities in the Northern Territory' (2011) 7(24) *Indigenous Law Bulletin* 11.

Evidence to Community Affairs Legislation Committee, Senate, Darwin, 21 July 2006, 26 (David Ross).

Rowse, Tim, 'The Indigenous Sector' in Diane Austin-Broos and Gaynor Macdonald (eds), *Culture, Economy and Governance in Aboriginal Australia* (Sydney University Press, 2005) 213.

Sanders, Will, 'Local Governments and Indigenous Australians: Developments and Dilemmas in Contrasting Circumstances' (Discussion Paper No 84/1995, Centre for Aboriginal Economic Policy Research, 1995).

Sanders, Will, 'Good Governance for Indigenous Communities and Regions: More Diverse Than Unified, as Much Process as Structure' (Paper presented at the Indigenous Governance Conference, Canberra, 3–5 April 2002).

Sanders, Will, 'Dispersal, Autonomy and Scale in Indigenous Community Governance: Some Reflections on Recent Northern Territory Experience' (Paper presented at the North Australian Research Unit, Darwin, 30 October 2003).

Sanders, Will, 'Thinking about Indigenous Community Governance' (Discussion Paper No 262/2004, Centre for Aboriginal Economic Policy Research, 2004).

Sanders, Will, 'Housing Tenure and Indigenous Australians in Remote and Settled Areas' (Discussion Paper No 275/2005, Centre for Aboriginal Economic Policy Research, 2005).

Sanders, Will, 'Being a Good Senior Manager in Indigenous Community Governance: Working with Public Purpose and Private Benefit' (Discussion Paper No 280/2006, Centre for Aboriginal Economic Policy Research, 2006).

Sanders, Will, 'Local Governments and Indigenous Interests in Australia's Northern Territory' (Discussion Paper No 285/2006, Centre for Aboriginal Economic Policy Research, 2006).

Schwab, Robert G., 'The Calculus of Reciprocity: Principles and Implications of Aboriginal Sharing' (Discussion Paper No 100/1995, Centre for Aboriginal Economic Policy Research, 1995).

Smith, Diane, 'From Gove to Governance: Reshaping Indigenous Governance in the Northern Territory' (Discussion Paper No 265/2004, Centre for Aboriginal Economic Policy Research, 2004).

Smith, Diane, 'Indigenous Families, Households and Governance' in Diane Austin-Broos and Gaynor Macdonald (eds), *Culture, Economy and Governance in Aboriginal Australia* (Sydney University Press, 2005) 175.

Steering Committee for the Review of Government Service Provision, 'Overcoming Indigenous Disadvantage: Key Indicators 2009' (Productivity Commission, 2009).

Sullivan, Patrick, 'From Land Rights to the Rights of the People' (1996) 3(85) *Aboriginal Law Bulletin* 16.

Sullivan, Patrick, 'Searching for the Intercultural, Searching for the Culture' (2005) 75 *Oceania* 183.

Sullivan, Patrick, 'The Aboriginal Community Sector and the Effective Delivery of Services: Acknowledging the Role of Indigenous Sector Organisations' (Working Paper No 73, Desert Knowledge CRC, 2010).

Sullivan, Patrick, *Belonging Together: Dealing with the Politics of Disenchantment in Australian Indigenous Policy* (Aboriginal Studies Press, 2011).

Thamarrurr Development Corporation, *About Us*, http://thamarrurr.org.au/index.php/about-us.

Wadeye Aboriginal Community, *Wadeye Council* (1998) www.indiginet.com.au/wadeye/index.htm.

Westbury, Neil and Will Sanders, 'Governance and Service Delivery for Remote Aboriginal Communities in the Northern Territory: Challenges and Opportunities' (Working Paper No 6/2000, Centre for Aboriginal Economic Policy Research, 2000).

Woodward, Edward, 'Aboriginal Land Rights Commission: First Report' (Australian Government, 1973).

Woodward, Edward, 'Aboriginal Land Rights Commission: Second Report' (Australian Government, 1974).

Legislation

Aboriginal Land Rights (Northern Territory) Act 1976 (Cth).
Northern Territory National Emergency Response Act 2007 (Cth).

5 Australian debate about land reform and the new political consensus

5.1 Introduction

This book describes how the Australian Government's enactment of the iconic *Aboriginal Land Rights (Northern Territory) Act 1976* (Cth) (ALRA) reflected a shift in the political consensus of the time. Just a few years earlier the conservative Liberal–Country Party Coalition had opposed the introduction of land rights, and while there remained some resistance on the conservative side of politics, there was also a sufficiently broad middle ground for the ALRA to pass through parliament with bipartisan support. This did not mean that the issue of land rights was thereafter uncontested. Debate was ongoing, particularly with respect to the proper ambit of land rights, and the extent to which the rights of Indigenous land-owners should prevail over the rights of others.

Since 2004 something altogether different has occurred. There has been another shift in the political consensus with respect to Indigenous land, this time led by the Coalition parties. The new consensus takes the form of frequent statements about how existing forms of Indigenous land ownership are holding people back and need to be reformed. This chapter describes the debate out of which the new consensus emerged. It is argued here that that debate has been conducted using vague and ill-defined terminology that is poorly suited to a discussion of the tenure circumstances of communities on Indigenous land. This impacted in several ways. To a considerable degree, it led to the wrong issues being contested. Frequently, debate about communal and individual ownership has been used as a proxy for debate about the role of Indigenous culture and the direction of Indigenous policy. It has also resulted in pertinent issues – such as home ownership and economic development – being debated poorly, and in a manner that was far more divisive and less instructive than was necessary or helpful.

Unsurprisingly, this has had a negative impact on understandings and has contributed to the at times considerable level of confusion that has been demonstrated during implementation of the recent reforms, as described in later chapters. It has also had a broader impact. This chapter describes how debate about land reform has contributed to confusion

Australian debate about land reform 129

about the nature of the issues affecting Indigenous communities and the direction of new policies. The debate has perpetuated an unhelpful dichotomy between 'modern' and 'traditional' culture in a manner that misrepresents day-to-day life in Indigenous communities. It has also enabled recent shifts in the direction of Indigenous policy to be portrayed as a shift towards greater 'individualism', when they are more accurately characterised as a deepening of the role of governments in the lives of Indigenous community residents.

It is significant how and by whom the debate has been conducted. The debate was not initiated by residents of communities on Indigenous land or by the Indigenous landowners for those communities. Nor did it emerge out of a long history of academic research. While there were several Indigenous spokespeople on both sides of the debate, it was primarily conducted at a national level in mainstream forums. It also came to be embraced by a Coalition Government that had for some time been expressing a desire to find new ways of approaching Indigenous policy. Enabling a shift from 'communal ownership' to 'individual ownership' of land came to be presented as a core component of its new approach.

The chapter broadly divides its description of the debate into three parts. Section 5.2 considers the main period of debate – between 2004 and 2007 – as well as the way in which debate emerged. Section 5.3 describes how a new or ancillary narrative, based on a different set of terminology, was used in the period between 2007 and 2013. Section 5.4 sets out more recent developments. The chapter concludes in Section 5.5 with a brief comment on the nature of the new political consensus.

5.2 The first period of debate: communal and individual ownership

Prior to 2004: historical debate about Indigenous land

The three formal reviews of the ALRA

The widespread debate that emerged in late 2004 was a debate about communal and individual ownership of land. It was suggested that 'communal ownership' had become a barrier to economic integration, contributing to poor social and economic conditions in communities on Indigenous land. What is striking, given how prominent that debate quickly became, was how little history there was of such concern. While there had previously been debate about the ownership of Indigenous land, particularly ALRA land in the Northern Territory, its focus was elsewhere. For the most part it was debate about *how* Indigenous land should be owned communally, not *whether*.

There were three formal reviews of the ALRA prior to 2004, which provide some insight into the nature of concerns about Indigenous land

130 *Australian debate about land reform*

ownership during that earlier period. Barry Rowland QC conducted the first review in 1980.[1] Rowland focused mainly on the mining provisions and raised no concerns about the land ownership structure.[2] Justice John Toohey, who had been an Aboriginal Land Commissioner, conducted the second review in 1983.[3] One of Toohey's conclusions was that there was a 'good case for broadening the definition' of 'traditional Aboriginal owners' in the Act. While it had been interpreted in a 'flexible and responsive manner', he found it was drafted too narrowly to capture all those with an ownership interest. However, as so many land claims were still being heard, he concluded that it would create too much uncertainty to alter the definition at that time. He recommended no immediate change, but that a 'fresh look might be taken at the definition' once the hearing of land claims had substantially concluded.[4] Toohey also received a detailed submission from Peter Sutton, one of Australia's most experienced anthropologists, on the ALRA's 'inadequate handling of the relation between what might be called the secular domain and the sacred domain'. Sutton recommended the legislation be amended to create a 'bicameral system of Land Councils', so as to bolster the relative autonomy of spiritual deliberation in a context where 'economic development and rapid cultural change threaten ... the moral basis of a traditional society'. Toohey found that the concept was 'an interesting one' but that it required 'more attention than is possible in this review'.[5]

The concern for Toohey and Sutton was the extent to which the ALRA reflected or distorted ownership of land in accordance with Aboriginal law. It is unsurprising that this would be an issue. As discussed in Chapter 2, the formalisation of a communal property system always involves some element of alteration and regimentation. There has long been discussion about how well the ALRA deals with this issue.[6] This is clearly different from the question of whether communal ownership prevents economic integration.

John Reeves QC conducted a third formal review of the ALRA in 1998.[7] The 'Reeves Report' was the most detailed and wide-ranging of the three, and included several recommendations with respect to land ownership. The most significant was replacing the two largest Aboriginal Land Councils with a number of smaller 'Regional Land Councils' ('RLCs'), which would have far greater freedom to develop their own decision-making procedures. Rather than having to obtain the consent of 'traditional Aboriginal owners', Reeves recommended that RLCs decide for themselves who they should consult with 'in accordance with Aboriginal tradition'.[8]

Again, it can be seen that Reeves was concerned with how land was owned communally rather than whether it should be. He did not consider it necessary to move away from communal ownership, nor did he regard it as preventing economic development. In fact, Reeves devoted a chapter to the related question of 'whether inalienable freehold title ... placed undue restraint on the commercial use of Aboriginal land'.[9] He concluded that it

Australian debate about land reform   131

did not, and supported the retention of inalienable title principally because it was able to prevent loss of ownership.[10] More broadly, Reeves rejected the idea that Aboriginal people's economic future lay in making better use of their land. In his view, the ALRA 'does not, and was not intended to, provide Aboriginal people with economic, or needs-related entitlements'.[11] He was conscious of the marginal economic value of most Aboriginal land, of worldwide changes to the agricultural industry and of the decreasing importance of land as an asset compared to other forms of property. Consequently, he argued, a focus on developing Aboriginal land would lead to an 'economic cul de sac'.[12] As will be seen below, a very different approach has been taken during the debate about land reform in the period since 2004. Reeves also characterised payments for the use of Aboriginal land as being a problem rather than a benefit. He argued that such payments were exacerbating 'dependency on unearned income',[13] and recommended that mining payments and 'all other income from activities on Aboriginal land should be applied … to particular purposes' and not allocated to individuals or families.[14] Again, this can be contrasted with the way in which rent on leases has been more recently presented.

The Reeves Report did nevertheless propose a radical restructuring of land ownership under the ALRA. Its recommendations were supported by the conservative CLP Government of the Northern Territory,[15] but were opposed by a wide range of other people and organisations, including the Land Councils.[16] Following a critical review of the Report by a House of Representatives committee, the Federal Coalition Government effectively shelved it.[17] None of its recommendations was implemented.

Between Reeves and late 2004: emerging concerns about communal ownership

In the period between the Reeves Report and 2004 a small but growing number of people began to argue that the way in which Indigenous land was owned might be preventing economic development. It appears that Hernando de Soto's book *The Mystery of Capital* played some part in this. Noel Pearson, an influential Aboriginal lawyer and public intellectual from Queensland, published a review of the book in 2001, arguing that de Soto's theories in relation to 'dead capital' were relevant to Indigenous land ownership in Australia.[18] He revisited this argument in a further article in 2004.[19] It is significant that Pearson based his argument on the understanding that Indigenous people owned the 'housing, infrastructure, buildings, enterprises etc' in Indigenous communities.[20] He appears to have hoped that land reform would lead to Indigenous people gaining more defined ownership of these assets. During the course of recent reforms, governments have generally taken a different approach to ownership, particularly with respect to housing and government-funded infrastructure. The overwhelming majority of leases and subleases have been granted to

132   *Australian debate about land reform*

government departments, rather than Indigenous people. This is clearly a departure from what Pearson anticipated.

There were a small number of other references to the issue during this period. Productivity Commission Chairman Gary Banks suggested that 'common property ownership' inhibited the 'scope to realise the economic potential of Indigenous land'.[21] Development economist Ron Duncan published a paper setting out the case for the 'individualisation' of 'customary ownership' through the grant of long-term leases,[22] to which economist and anthropologist Jon Altman wrote a reply.[23] Long-term public servant Bob Beadman published a wide-ranging report on issues affecting Aboriginal communities, which included several references to a need for land reform.[24]

In some cases, the people who argued that there were problems with Indigenous land ownership structures also expressed a more general concern with the grant of land rights. For example, Gary Johns and Peter Howson – two of the leading figures associated with the Bennelong Society[25] – both wrote that existing ownership structures inhibited economic development.[26] However, they also argued that the problem with land rights was more fundamental, in that 'there is a direct conflict between land rights, as an expression of separatism, and the prospects of individual Aborigines for advancement'.[27]

While not in the public arena, there was a behind-the-scenes development during this period that was also significant. In early 2004, the Northern Territory Government produced a 'concept paper' on community leasing. It provided a copy to the Northern Territory Aboriginal Land Councils and, more importantly, to the Australian Government.[28] Chapter 6 describes how the model set out in this 'concept paper' formed the basis for the introduction of township leasing by the Australian Government in 2006.

The emergence of a widespread debate

The political context

While prior to December 2004 debate about communal ownership of Indigenous land was not widespread, from then on it increased markedly. As several authors have noted,[29] the political context was significant to how debate unfolded. This section briefly summarises that context.

Federal elections in October 2004 resulted in the Howard Coalition Government being re-elected for a fourth consecutive term and obtaining a majority in both houses of Parliament. This meant that from 1 July 2005, it was for the first time able to amend legislation (such as the ALRA) without having to negotiate with the Opposition or minor parties. The Howard Government had historically taken a more restrictive approach to the recognition of Indigenous rights, including native title. In 1997, Prime Minister John Howard had argued that the High Court's decision in *Wik*

Peoples v Queensland[30] had 'pushed the pendulum too far in the Aboriginal direction'.[31] In order to 'return the pendulum to the centre', his government amended the *Native Title Act 1993* (Cth) to make it easier for non-Indigenous people to carry out activities on land that was subject to native title.[32] The fact that the Howard Government had so recently intervened to reduce Indigenous rights to land led some people to express suspicion when, in December 2004, Howard announced that his government was considering further reforms to Indigenous land. There were also strong continuities between the language of formal equality, which the government had previously employed to explain the need to place limits on Indigenous rights (such as native title), and that of 'normalisation', which became part of the government's explanation for why land reform was required.[33]

Particularly in the period since 2000, the Howard Government had also been making broader changes to the way in which Indigenous programmes were administered.[34] This included the introduction of policies such as 'mutual obligation' and 'shared responsibility' and the mainstreaming of service delivery. As one part of this, in 2004 the government took the final steps in abolishing the Aboriginal Torres Strait Islander Commission (ATSIC), replacing it after the October general elections with an advisory body called the National Indigenous Council (NIC). Members of the NIC were appointed by the government, rather than elected by Indigenous people (as ATSIC commissioners had been). As described below, the NIC was to play an important role in debate about land reform.

During this period, there was also a growing divergence in views between different Indigenous leaders as to how several issues of Indigenous policy should be dealt with. By 2004 some of those divisions had become marked and there was a level of interpersonal animosity.[35] This too had an impact on the debate about land reform. It also had an impact on the way in which that debate was reported, as the divergence in views itself became a media story.

2004–5: the emergence of debate

One 'quiet Sunday' in early December 2004,[36] Warren Mundine – a high-profile Aboriginal man from NSW who had just been appointed to the NIC – issued a media statement on several issues of Indigenous policy. One of those issues was Indigenous land ownership, in relation to which Mundine said 'we need to move away from communal land ownership and non-profit community-based businesses and take up home ownership, economic land development and profit-making businesses'.[37] The NIC was due to meet that week for the first time, and Mundine's statements attracted media attention. It was initially his comments on an apology to the Stolen Generation that were focused upon,[38] but attention soon shifted to his statements about land reform. In the next few days at least two other

134 *Australian debate about land reform*

members of the NIC gave public support to Mundine's comments about land reform.[39] By the end of the week, the Prime Minister added his support and announced that his government was considering a new scheme to allow for 'private ownership' of Indigenous land through the use of 99-year leases.[40]

From that point, debate about Indigenous land reform spread quickly. Several other Indigenous leaders immediately expressed a concern that Indigenous people might lose title to their land or be forced to give up 'communal ownership'.[41] In the ensuing months, the Prime Minister and Minister for Indigenous Affairs made several speeches outlining why they believed reform was necessary.[42] The NIC drafted a set of land reform principles that were made public in June 2005.[43] The issue attracted considerable media attention and comment,[44] particularly in *The Australian* newspaper, which editorialised in favour of reform.[45] It was one of the major issues at that year's *National Native Title Conference*,[46] and in that year's *Native Title Report*.[47] There were also several other journal articles, reports and conference papers on land reform throughout 2005 and into the following year.[48]

The exact nature of the debate during this period is described in greater detail below, in particular the terminology that was used and the issues that were contested. First it is important to clarify how the context for debate changed as the debate progressed, in a way that impacted significantly on how it was conducted.

2006–7: greater urgency

During 2006 there were several events that shifted the nature of public debate about Indigenous policy generally, including debate about land reform. In January of that year, Mal Brough replaced Amanda Vanstone as the Minister for Indigenous Affairs. The new Minister took a far more forceful approach to prosecuting the need for changes in Indigenous policy. Then on 15 May 2006, ABC's *Lateline* programme aired an interview with Alice Springs prosecutor, Nanette Rogers, in which she detailed several shocking cases of sexual assault of Aboriginal children by Aboriginal offenders in the Northern Territory.[49] This was not the first time that higher levels of violence and abuse in Indigenous communities had been reported upon, but there was an unusually potent response to the programme. The issue received ongoing media attention over the following days and weeks and Mal Brough called an urgent summit of State and Territory leaders to tackle violence against and abuse of Indigenous women and children.[50]

The following month, on 21 June 2006, the *Lateline* programme ran a further report, this time detailing more specific allegations of abuse in the community of Mutitjulu.[51] Again there was sustained media interest in the allegations that were raised. In the wake of that second programme,

Australian debate about land reform 135

the Northern Territory Government commissioned an inquiry into child abuse in Aboriginal communities.[52] The report from that inquiry was called *Little Children Are Sacred*,[53] which was finalised in mid-2007 and became the catalyst for the announcement of the Northern Territory Emergency Response (NTER).

For some years there had been an increasing level of media interest in the problems being manifested in Indigenous communities, such as higher rates of welfare dependence, petrol sniffing, violence and abuse. It would be misleading to suggest that events in 2006 put such issues on the front page for the first time; however, the focus was far more sustained than had occurred previously. This led to an atmosphere of emergency in the public political arena, in which context the NTER was introduced. As described in Chapter 6, the NTER was one of the most dramatic and interventionist sets of reforms in recent Australian history.

This framing of the situation in Indigenous communities as constituting a national emergency impacted on debate about land reform in two important ways. It first led to an increased sense of urgency about the need for reform. The new Minister was quick to make an explicit connection between the 'appalling levels of violence and abuse in many of these communities' and the need for land reform.[54] As a corollary, there was less political tolerance for opposition to reform. This clearly had an impact on shifting the political consensus. It is notable that when the first set of reforms – township leasing – was introduced in 2006, the Labor Party opposed them.[55] However, when the NTER was announced in 2007, which included a far more dramatic and problematic set of land reforms, the Labor Party immediately gave its support.[56]

The second consequence of this emergency atmosphere was that less attention was paid to detail at the exact moment that the reforms themselves began. The Australian Government introduced three major sets of land reform during this period: township leasing in 2006, followed by the NTER and housing reforms in 2007.[57] This could have been the point at which the disjuncture between the language used to debate the reforms and the true impact of the reforms themselves was made clear. However, this did not occur. Indeed, the level of public and academic debate about land reform has decreased significantly during the period in which the reforms themselves have been implemented. For those in favour of reform, there was little need to argue. For those who were opposed to or critical of reform, the argument appeared to have been lost. By the end of 2007, both major parties were committed to the introduction of land reform in Indigenous communities.

Subject matter of the debate

The emergency atmosphere alone cannot explain this shift in the political consensus. It was also due to the way in which the issues were framed and

136 *Australian debate about land reform*

land reform was debated. This section clarifies the nature of this debate, by describing the language that was used and the issues that were contested.

The terminology

Overwhelmingly, debate during this period was structured around a dualism between 'communal ownership' and 'individual ownership'. The starting point for reform was described using terms such as communal ownership,[58] while the outcome of reform was referred to as individual ownership[59] or private property.[60] No attempt was made to clarify exactly what these terms meant.[61] 'Communal ownership' was often characterised as a type of free-form collective ownership[62] – a situation where 'everything [is] owned by the community'[63] – rather than a distinct system pursuant to which individuals can acquire rights. As described below, in some cases communal ownership was simply treated as an analogy for communalism or a collectivist ethos.

A number of issues were debated using this language. The two central and recurring issues were home ownership and economic development on Indigenous land; however, it was not these issues alone that animated debate. The concepts of communal and individual ownership were also used to debate a number of broader issues, particularly the role of culture and the direction of Indigenous policy. For some participants, the debate about communal and individual ownership also represented an opportunity to revisit the issue of land rights itself.

A more detailed description of these issues is provided below. As background to this, a comment is first made on the level of generality at which debate occurred, and the impact this had.

High level of generality

Perhaps the most important point for understanding the debate about Indigenous land reform in Australia is that it was conducted at a very high level of generality. Terms such as 'communal ownership' came to be used with respect to several very different circumstances, often without distinction. They were used to describe Indigenous land ownership, sometimes including native title, the tenure arrangements in communities on Indigenous land, the housing system in those communities and the ownership of businesses. This meant that a number of very different issues were debated at the same time, without the distinction between those issues being made clear.

It is often noted that around half of the Northern Territory is now Aboriginal land, the majority being land held under the ALRA. There are also 68 larger residential communities that are situated on either ALRA or community living area (CLA) land. Chapter 4 describes how, in those communities, land and infrastructure have been allocated pursuant to informal

Australian debate about land reform 137

tenure arrangements that reflect the interaction between traditional authority, community authority and government authority. While traditional ownership was important it was also only one part of a broader dynamic.

Two important distinctions arise out of this for the purposes of debate about land reform. The first is between residential communities and other areas of Indigenous land. There is a set of issues that are particular to communities and community tenure, and another set that instead relate to the larger areas of land outside of communities. The issues that are particular to communities include whether council offices, police stations and recreational halls should be subject to a lease, whether they should pay rent and whether informal tenure arrangements have restricted access to finance for enterprises (such as stores, garages and art centres). This is different from the issues affecting land outside of communities. Here, the question is how well, and also how fairly, the collective land ownership system supports the development of such activities as agriculture or tourism. The two sets of issues are distinct. The fact that (some) Indigenous people own large areas of land outside of communities is not evidence that the tenure arrangements inside communities should be formalised or left informal. Conversely, the fact that a community of 800 people does not have a hairdresser is not evidence that the ownership system for land outside of communities is failing. In the same way, each set of issues requires its own set of reforms. Most relevantly, formalising the tenure arrangements in communities does not change the way in which land outside of communities is owned or used.

The second important distinction is between *land ownership* and the *informal tenure arrangements* in communities. Not only are the tenure arrangements in communities distinct from the land ownership system, they are also quite different. For land held under the ALRA, which attempts to provide for formal ownership of land in accordance with Aboriginal land tenure, groups of people have shared rights to areas of country. The informal tenure arrangements in communities instead provide individuals and organisations with exclusive rights to particular land and buildings (something akin to a 'holding'[64]). In other words, the informal tenure arrangements in communities provide for different types of rights. To a considerable extent, the two systems also have different normative bases. The allocation of rights under Aboriginal land tenure is based on Aboriginal law, while the allocation of rights in communities is based on the exigencies of modern-day community life and the need for people living and working in communities (including governments and NGOs) to give order to the way in which land and infrastructure are utilised. While the informal tenure arrangements in communities do display certain distinct cultural features, they are different from the cultural features that characterise Aboriginal land tenure.

For the most part, neither of these distinctions was maintained during debate about land reform. That debate frequently crossed seamlessly

138 Australian debate about land reform

between communities and other areas of land, and between land owner-ship and the ownership of houses and enterprises. This impacted on that debate in three important ways. It led, first, to a number of different issues being conflated. The most obvious example is that the economic issues affecting communities were conflated with those affecting areas of land outside of communities. The existence of large areas of Indigenous land was frequently used to explain the need for a set of reforms that – as detailed in following chapters – affect only the tenure arrangements in communities. Similarly, communal ownership of businesses was often dis-cussed alongside communal ownership of land as if the issues were one and the same. There were in effect several different issues being debated simultaneously, without the boundaries between them being made clear.

A second consequence of debate being conducted in such general terms was that it contributed to confusion about the role of culture and tradi-tion. The starting point for reform – communal ownership – was presented as a manifestation, or even a core component, of traditional culture, from which the introduction of individual ownership or private property was presented as a departure. The failure to recognise a separate set of informal tenure arrangements in communities meant a failure to acknowledge that new forms of property had already evolved in that context. This led to the wrong set of cultural issues being referred to, and to the cultural circum-stances of communities being misrepresented and misunderstood.

A third consequence was that very little attention was given to the space upon which the majority of the proposed reforms were to operate: that is, the existing informal tenure arrangements in communities. While there was concern about protecting 'communal ownership' – which came to be pre-sented as 'underlying communal ownership' – no attention was given to the way in which the reforms would reflect, alter or distort the existing informal arrangements, or what de Soto refers to as the 'social contract'. This also meant that several of the important questions raised by the reforms – such as whether all or just some infrastructure should be leased (or subleased); whether leases should be short-term or long-term and alien-able or inalienable; and the consequences of charging rent – were simply not debated. Those issues would clearly have benefited from greater discus-sion prior to the implementation of reforms.

This high level of generality is important background to understanding how certain issues came to be contested. The following section now describes in greater detail what those issues were, beginning with the two focal issues of home ownership and economic development on Indigenous land.

What is it that was being contested?

Communal ownership preventing economic development

The first of the two focal issues was whether it was necessary to 'move away from communal land ownership' in order to enable economic development on Indigenous land,[65] and assist 'Indigenous Australians to become a part of the real economy'.[66] There were some very different perspectives on this. Hughes and Warin argued that 'communal ownership of land, royalties and other resources is the principal cause of the lack of economic development in remote areas'.[67] Beadman said it was time to admit that measures designed to protect Aboriginal land ownership 'have inhibited economic development'.[68] Towards the other end of the spectrum, Ridgeway said it was 'a furphy to suggest that communal ownership is the barrier to enabling economic development on Indigenous land',[69] and the Central Land Council argued that low levels of economic development were due to 'a significant number of other factors' and not 'communal land ownership'.[70]

This was clearly an area where the failure to distinguish between communities and other areas of Indigenous land had an impact on the debate. A recurring theme was that Indigenous people now owned large areas of land but had little to show for it by way of economic development. For example, *The Australian* described how 'Aboriginal organisations own something like 20 per cent of the continent, but indigenous Australian children in remote communities still suffer from poor living conditions'.[71] NIC Chairwoman, Sue Gordon, said it was necessary to address 'how the now considerable Indigenous land base might be best used to facilitate the economic development of Indigenous people'.[72] Amanda Vanstone asked why 'when Indigenous Australia theoretically controls such a large proportion of the Australian land mass, they are themselves so poor'.[73] Her successor as Minister, Mal Brough, noted that the ALRA had 'been successful in returning land to Aboriginal people', in that 'almost half of the Northern Territory is now Aboriginal land', but it had 'not been successful in facilitating productive use of that land'.[74]

These frequent references to the size of Indigenous landholdings made it easier to argue that there was a clear need for reform, despite the fact that the reforms under discussion did not affect the bulk of that land. It would nevertheless mislead to suggest that there was a widespread belief that land reform would lead to an economic transformation or was all that was required to enable economic development. For example, *The Australian* acknowledged that 'owning property in communities without an economic base [will not] make anybody rich';[75] while Sue Gordon described how there were other more significant 'obstacles to economic independence and to wealth generation on Indigenous land'.[76] Land reform, she argued, should be considered 'a precondition, not a panacea'.[77] For many, this

140 *Australian debate about land reform*

appears to have become the established wisdom. Land reform has come to be seen as something necessary in order to enable economic development, not enough on its own but a *sine qua non* and as good a place as any to start. For example, *The Australian* has editorialised that the 'lack of tradeable property rights under indigenous land title is increasingly recognised as holding back commercial development'.[78] The Chairman of the Productivity Commission has singled out 'an inability to make effective private use of communal land' as a reason for the underrepresentation of Indigenous people in private enterprise.[79] The Coordinator General for Remote Indigenous Service Delivery has argued that land reform is required to 'enable progress in economic development'.[80] And while he was Prime Minister, Kevin Rudd told Parliament that the government was 'driving an aggressive land tenure reform agenda, which is necessary to ... lay the foundations for economic development in remote communities'.[81] This viewpoint is one of the enduring outcomes of debate about land reform.[82]

Communal ownership preventing home ownership

The second of the two focal issues was home ownership. The idea of introducing home ownership into communities on Indigenous land was not new. Several people had written about it previously,[83] and in the 1980s the Queensland Government had introduced just such a programme by way of perpetual leases known as 'Katter leases'.[84] During the debate about Indigenous land reform there was nevertheless a significance increase in the attention given to home ownership. Two things are significant about the way in which the issue was discussed. The first is that people in favour of land reform came to present home ownership as a reason, and a key reason, for the introduction of a broader set of reforms. To clarify, it is not necessary to alter community-wide tenure arrangements, or area-wide land ownership, in order to enable home ownership for particular houses. All that is necessary is that the subject houses have an appropriate form of tenure, such as a long-term and transferable lease. That is not, however, how the issue was presented. The Australian Government in particular argued that in order to enable home ownership it was necessary to introduce a broader set of reforms that would result in a shift from 'communal ownership' to 'individual ownership' across entire communities.[85] As Dillon and Westbury note, this was 'clever politics', in that home ownership was an issue that resonated 'with the aspirations of many Indigenous and non-Indigenous citizens'.[86] Focusing on home ownership as a rationale for land reform helped garner public and political support for land reform generally.

The second significant feature of the way in which home ownership was discussed is the extent to which it came to be framed primarily as a tenure issue. That is, there was among reform proponents a tendency to focus on tenure to the exclusion of other barriers to the introduction of home ownership. To be clear, there were several people (primarily those opposed to reform) who during debate pointed to the significant economic barriers.[87] For the most part, those in favour of reform avoided any discussion of economic issues by presenting home ownership as something people would have the opportunity to aspire to once the issue of tenure had been resolved. This was usually framed in terms of giving people 'a chance to own their own home',[88] which was something that 'all Australians should be able to aspire towards'[89] even though 'not everyone can afford it'.[90] A more forceful version of this approach was to argue that without land reform Indigenous community residents were being 'denied [the right] to own their own home'.[91]

It is significant at this point to note that the Queensland Government's earlier attempt at introducing home ownership through the use of 'Katter leases' did not turn out well.[92] Moran reports that in the community of Kowanyama, houses made the subject of Katter leases 'subsequently deteriorated to an unacceptable standard', to the point where they needed replacing.[93] Moran had previously written about home ownership on several occasions, primarily in the Queensland context, and was of the view that its introduction should be pursued.[94] However, he also cautioned that the failure of Katter leases 'clearly demonstrates the risks of proceeding with home ownership in a simplistic manner'.[95] In 2001, he was part of a team that conducted a survey of interest in home ownership in four Indigenous communities. The researchers again concluded that home ownership should be made available, but also found that the 'complexity surrounding the issues [is] undeniable' and so it 'must be approached with care and rigour'.[96]

In the adversarial climate that surrounded debate about land reform, there was less scope for approaching the issue of home ownership with 'care and rigour'. At times a very high level of animosity was generated. For example, when Aboriginal and Torres Strait Islander Social Justice Commissioner, Tom Calma, expressed concerns about the introduction of home ownership, he was described as a 'hypocrite' because he owned a house in Canberra yet was trying to 'deny' the same choice to other Indigenous people.[97] Over time it became common for home ownership to be characterised not as a complex policy issue but as something remote Indigenous residents were being denied and that land reform would enable.[98]

Chapter 7 describes how this more reductive approach to the issue of home ownership appears to have had an impact on policy development. Between 2006 and 2010, the Australian Government spent more than $10 million on a programme to enable home ownership in communities on Indigenous land. This resulted in just 16 grants of home ownership across Australia. There is also evidence that some houses have been priced in a manner that puts purchasers at risk of economic loss, suggesting that the non-tenure barriers to the creation of effective home ownership schemes have received too little attention.

142 *Australian debate about land reform*

Communal ownership, policy and culture

While economic development and home ownership were the two primary issues around which debate was conducted, they were not necessarily the issues that most animated debate. From the beginning, the debate about land reform was also a debate about culture. In his first reported contribution to the debate, Prime Minister Howard spoke of the need to 'base Aboriginal policy ... on the development of a more entrepreneurial culture'.[99] *The Australian* described the proposed reforms as 'the most determined effort yet to create an enterprise culture within Aboriginal communities'.[100] The NIC spoke not just of economic development but of enabling 'entrepreneurship'.[101] For these and other contributors, the introduction of individual ownership was understood as representing a shift towards a less traditional, more economically integrated culture.

Conversely, Ridgeway argued that the Prime Minister's comments illustrated a 'profound cross-cultural misunderstanding' and were 'drawn purely from a western perspective that prizes individualism'.[102] Dodson and McCarthy argued that privatisation of Indigenous land was 'a simplistic attempt at social engineering',[103] and that the right to self-determination included 'the right to forms of tenure that reflect cultural difference'.[104] Watson argued that the privatisation was 'merely the latest piece of [Howard's] assimilation puzzle',[105] and former Chairman of the NLC, Galarrwuy Yunupingu, was quoted as saying the reforms attacked 'the very basis of Aboriginal culture – communal title'.[106] Grattan characterised the reforms as an attempt by the government to 'inject a greater dose of individualism'.[107] It appears that for a great many people, this is how the introduction of 'individual ownership' was understood.

Some contributors went further, and characterised the existing arrangements as an attempt to bind Indigenous people to a form of atavistic collectivism. Hughes and Warin referred to this as a 'socialist experiment', an attempt to 'create an Aboriginal and Torres Strait Islander hunter-gatherer utopia'.[108] Christopher Pearson described 'inalienable community freehold' as a 'leftover from the Arcadian fantasy era in which our very own noble savages were expected to wander off happily ever after to their dreaming'.[109] Duffy spoke of how Indigenous people had been denied 'private property', and government funds had been used 'to enforce a communal approach'.[110] When presenting the legislation to enable township leasing, Mal Brough described how 'the enforcement of collective rights over individual rights' had been 'an abject failure'.[111]

Connection to debate about welfare

Ancillary to the narrative about the need for a more entrepreneurial culture was the argument that land reform would lessen dependence on welfare. For those in favour of reform, this added weight to their arguments. For

Australian debate about land reform 143

example, *The Australian* said that while 'private ownership of communal assets cannot cure [poverty] it offers an alternative to the collectivised welfare that has done little to help indigenous Australians prosper'.[112] Amanda Vanstone argued that there was 'no romance in communal poverty. It crushes individual motivation and condemns all too passive acceptance of more of the same'.[113] Her government was instead trying to build 'Indigenous wealth, employment and entrepreneurial culture, as these are integral to boosting economic development and reducing poverty and dependence on passive welfare'.[114] Howson identified a need to move away from the 'rentier lifestyle which is connected to land rights',[115] and Hughes described how socialist policies such as the absence of 'private property rights' prevented economic development and necessitated 'social welfare payments that led to welfare-dependence'.[116]

Recontesting land rights

For some, the debate about communal and individual ownership of Indigenous land was an opening to recontest land rights itself. For example, Evans took the opportunity to argue that 'the only reform of the [ALRA] which matters is its repeal'.[117] Howson called for reforms that would make it easier for non-Aboriginal people to get access to Aboriginal land, and in particular remove 'barriers to exploration and mining in the Aboriginal lands'.[118] Unsurprisingly, several authors on the other side of the debate were concerned about the potential for land reform to more generally undermine land rights.[119]

It was in this context that contributors such as Noel Pearson referred to a need to distinguish between 'land reform – which enables community members to own their homes [and] facilitates the development of private enterprises', which is a 'legitimate agenda', and 're-contesting land rights [which] is not'.[120] The government itself was conscious of making this distinction. Prime Minister Howard said he wanted to 'make native title and communal land work better', not 'wind back or undermine native title or land rights'.[121] Pearson argued that people

> should take John Howard's word in good faith: that changes in land title arrangements will be aimed at the development needs of Aboriginal people, not giving governments and third parties more power over land use and access at the expense of Aboriginal rights.[122]

Tension and compromise

During the debate, the need for land reform came to be presented in terms of a need to resolve a fundamental tension between the 'communal nature' of Indigenous society and landholding and 'the imperatives of the modern world'.[123] For example, Pearson argued that 'Aboriginal people are now at

144 *Australian debate about land reform*

a critical juncture'. On the one hand, communal landholding was 'at the core of our heritage … notwithstanding the view of many people that we should simply abandon it as a debilitating encumbrance'.[124] On the other hand, there was the need for greater economic development and engagement. Pearson argued that this called for 'intelligent compromise', whereby 'inalienable Indigenous title to land' was able to coexist with new structures that enabled better economic participation.[125]

When the NIC developed a set of 'land reform principles', they too used the model of tension and compromise. They began by acknowledging that 'the principle of *underlying* communal interests in land is fundamental to Indigenous culture'.[126] Over the top of this, they argued, 'individuals and families' should be given the opportunity 'to acquire and exercise a personal interest in those lands, whether for the purposes of home ownership or business development'.[127] The Australian Government adopted a similar framework. Prime Minister Howard said that he recognised that 'communal interest in and spiritual attachment to land is fundamental to indigenous culture'.[128] His government was committed to preserving this, but wanted to 'add opportunities for families and communities to build economic independence and wealth through use of their communal land assets'.[129]

While the tension between the communal nature of Indigenous societies and a more individualistic mainstream culture is itself an important issue, it is not a particularly useful lens through which to consider issues with respect to land reform in Indigenous communities. It does not help identify why schools and police stations were so rarely subject to a lease – clearly it was not so that these could be 'communally owned'. It does not explain why housing was delivered through a (government-funded) community-housing model – which cannot be attributed to the retention or protection of Indigenous tradition. Nor can it adequately explain why existing enterprises (such as community stores, visitor accommodation and art centres) tended to be owned collectively – it is at least arguable that in many cases this has as much to do with the economic circumstances of communities and the nature of those enterprises, as it does with the 'communal nature' of Indigenous societies.

Further, describing the reforms then under discussion – which was the introduction of township leasing – as a 'compromise' does not capture their true effect. Chapter 6 describes how township leases result in a government entity acquiring full control over community land use and planning. The effect of this is to deepen the role of government in an important aspect of community life, rather than resolve a tension between tradition and modernity.

Discussion and critique

Tenure and culture

As Rowse succinctly noted in 2007, during debate about land reform 'both sides of [the] polarity have attached far too much, sociologically, to forms of title'.[130] This assessment is borne out in the description of the debate provided above. Communal ownership of land was presented – positively and negatively – as being integral to the existence and continuation of a distinct or traditional Indigenous culture. The introduction of individual ownership was presented – positively and negatively – as a mechanism for inducing cultural change. There are profound problems with this type of characterisation.

First, it attributes too much of a determinative role to property. It suggests that 'communal property' is the basis for, or at the least coexistent with, a communal or collectivist ethos; while 'individual ownership' or 'private property' is coexistent with individualism and entrepreneurialism. This is not the case. Cultural features that might be regarded as communal, such as the kinship sharing norms described in Chapter 4, are not *derived* from communal property, nor do they *affect* only communal property. In contemporary Indigenous communities, those sharing norms frequently operate with respect to objects such as cash and vehicles that are often owned by individuals as private property.

This is not to suggest that forms of property have no influence on culture; rather that the relationship is far more complex and less determinative than was so often suggested during debate. Comaroff argues that '[l]and tenure rules do not determine the behaviour of people', but they do 'embody the ideational and organisational framework within which the process of competition for land and status takes place'.[131] This is a useful way of understanding the potential impact of land reform: it can alter the 'ideational and organisational framework' within which competition and cooperation take place. It can also do so in ways that are difficult to predict. The introduction of the cash economy provides an example of this. Martin describes how Aboriginal communities have interpreted the introduction of cash in a particular way, imbuing it with meaning in a manner that reflects 'contemporary indigenous values'.[132] However, just as 'money is transformed within the Aboriginal domain, so too does it transform social, political and economic relationships with profound implications for the manner in which Aboriginal society is produced and reproduced'.[133] In the same way, new forms of land ownership will interact with existing norms and political systems. Even if the outcome of reforms had been private property over land – which in almost all cases it has not[134] – this would not mean the creation of a new social order. Those new property rights would interact with the existing social order in complex and unpredictable ways. They would not simply effect a cultural transition.

146 *Australian debate about land reform*

Further, it is not just that 'far too much, sociologically' was attached to forms of title during debate about land reform; it is also that the wrong form of title was identified. Debate was overwhelmingly conducted on the basis that it was Indigenous land tenure, and consequently traditional Indigenous culture, under discussion. This ignores the fact that Indigenous people living in residential communities had – in the context of their inter-relationship with outsiders (primarily governments and NGOs) – developed new forms of tenure for the use and management of houses and other infrastructure. Inside communities, it was those new forms of tenure that embodied 'the ideational and organisational framework' through which competition for status and resources took place. It was according to those informal arrangements that houses were allocated and that land was made available for an art centre. It was through those informal arrangements that permission was given or refused for a new store to open. And those informal tenure arrangements were already a significant departure from tradition, as indeed are permanent residential communities themselves.

This does not mean that Indigenous land tenure is irrelevant. As described above, it continues to play an important role in community politics, in how people identify and the way authority is allocated, including with respect to land use in communities. It is, however, not the primary basis for ordering day-to-day community life. Indeed, as Sutton notes, there are many aspects of day-to-day community life that instead have a deep impact on Indigenous land tenure, such as 'the diminution of the encompassing power of kinship, the swelling tide of emphasis on private property and consumer goods, and the rising importance of residential community identities'.[135] Nor does it mean that Indigenous culture is irrelevant; rather that the culture that is relevant to the reforms is modern Indigenous culture as it is practised in remote communities. This is a culture that has evolved and will continue to evolve in its adaptive response to changed circumstances.

Tenure, economy and relationships

A useful way of understanding the debate about land reform is in terms of the way in which its impact on *relationships* was depicted. Land reform was often presented as a way of enabling greater interaction between Indigenous community residents and the wider Australian community, particularly the mainstream economy. Conversely, communal ownership was presented as a barrier to such engagement. Some argued that this was deliberate, such as Hughes and Warin who state that the grant of land rights was seen not just as restitution 'but also as the base for customary, communal, socialist societies distinct from the rest of capitalist Australia'.[136] Others said that it was the result of legal complexity, such as Pearson and Kostakidis who argue that existing ownership systems for Indigenous land and assets 'are so complex as to present an effective

Australian debate about land reform 147

barrier to entry into the mainstream economy'.[137] Land reform was presented as the means for removing those barriers. As Prime Minister Howard said, the aim was to 'dismantle the barriers that hinder indigenous Australians from sharing in the bounty that this great country has to offer'.[138] Paul Toohey argued that as a result of the reforms 'ordinary Aboriginal Australia will have friendships and business relationships with ordinary white Australians'.[139]

To date there is no evidence of the recent land reforms enabling new relationships between Indigenous residents and the wider Australian community. It is still the case that the outsiders who have the most contact with communities on Indigenous land are governments and NGOs. And it is on these *existing* relationships that the reforms have had the most impact. In particular, the reforms mean that governments now play a deeper and more institutionalised role in community life. As described below, this is not the way in which the government's new approach to Indigenous policy was characterised or debated.

There is a further point here to do with the impact of land reform on *internal* relationships; that is, relationships between Indigenous community residents. Land reform was presented as a means for putting those relationships on a more commercial footing, whereby individuals would be rewarded for their efforts. Grattan captures this succinctly: she describes how the Australian Government presented land reform as a 'normalisation' of community arrangements, 'by which they really mean an injection of more commercial and market factors and the legal arrangements that go with them'.[140] This is of course central to the way in which the culturally transformative impact of land reform was depicted. Proponents of land reform often presented 'market mechanisms as a primary driver to transform Aboriginal people's values';[141] to induce a shift away from communalism towards 'individual aspiration as a driving force for progress'.[142]

This characterisation is so foreign to the actual impact of the recent land reforms that it is in hindsight remarkable. The reforms have not put the relationship between Aboriginal residents on a more commercial footing. Their potential to do so was wildly exaggerated. They have had a significant – and potentially harmful – impact on the relationship between traditional owners and non-traditional owner residents.[143] Beyond that, they have not had the transformative impact that was suggested.

Tenure and policy

It is argued here that the high reliance on a communal–individual ownership dualism during debate about land reform has had a detrimental impact on the implementation of the recent reforms. It has also had a broader consequence – it has impacted harmfully on debate about and understandings of Indigenous policy. There are two mains reasons for this. The first is that it enabled the perpetuation of an outmoded and harmful

148 *Australian debate about land reform*

dualism between tradition and modernity, a dualism that impedes understandings of the issues affecting Indigenous communities. As described above, this was exemplified by the failure to identify the existence of a set of informal tenure arrangements that have their basis in modern community life. The existing arrangements were instead attributed to 'tradition' and 'culture', and the purported failure of those arrangements was characterised accordingly. Consequently, the solution was presented as a shift towards modernity. This occludes the way in which the lives of Indigenous people are very much a product of their modern-day engagement with Australian society, which, as Austin-Broos emphasises, includes the profound significance of their being socially and economically marginalised by that society.[144]

Second, this terminology provided an incorrect picture of the nature of the shift that was occurring in the direction of Indigenous policy. This is because land reform, and the shift towards 'individual ownership', was presented as part of a broader shift towards policies that targeted Indigenous people as individuals rather than communities. Grattan characterised the reforms as an attempt to 'inject a greater dose of individualism', which was part of a broader government project 'which is to re-tilt the communal and collective approach laid down in Aboriginal affairs policy in the 1970s'.[145] Mal Brough said that earlier governments had 'focused on the collective Aboriginal community at the expense of considering the needs and aspirations of the individuals and families'.[146] He argued the 'new direction' would instead provide individuals with the 'right to choose their own pathway'.[147]

This is not an accurate depiction of the impact of recent land reforms. Rather than experiencing greater individual freedom, residents of Aboriginal communities are now subject to greater government control. This is also true of other shifts in the direction of Indigenous policy. It is difficult to find any area of Australian Government policy in the period since 2005 in which Indigenous people as individuals have been provided with greater opportunity to 'choose their own pathway'. There are instead several areas in which governments are playing a more interventionist role in people's lives. And yet this was not the shift that was debated during the period in which the new policy settings were being developed. There was a great deal of discussion about the need for Indigenous people to engage with the broader community as individuals, particularly the need for economic integration. There was far less discussion about the consequences of governments taking on a greater role in people's lives. It is the latter that has been the far more widespread reform, the consequences of which are likely to be long-term and significant.

Australian debate about land reform   149

5.3 Between 2007 and 2013: a need for 'secure tenure'

A shift in the language

There is no doubt that the most important period of debate was between 2004 and 2007. It was during this period that debate was most widespread, when new understandings were forged and the shift in the political consensus occurred. By the time the Labor Party was elected to government in November 2007 it had reversed its earlier opposition and come to support reform. Over the next six years it continued to implement all of the Coalition's reforms to Aboriginal land in the Northern Territory. Chapter 6 describes how in small ways the Labor Party put its own stamp on the reform process, though not in a way that substantially altered the impact of the reforms. The Labor Party did, however, change the language used to explain the need for reform, especially through its use of the concept of 'secure tenure'.

The new language had a distinctly more technocratic and less provocative tone. This appears to have been a deliberate shift, an attempt to take some of the heat out of the debate. Where the Coalition Government had argued that 'the enforcement of collective rights over individual rights has been an abject failure'[148] and that 'self determination was the biggest mistake',[149] the new Labor Government instead spoke about how '[w]ithout secure long term tenure, ownership of housing assets is uncertain'.[150] As a rhetorical strategy this change appears to have been effective. It is difficult to see why anyone would object to the introduction of 'secure tenure'.

However, this more technical-sounding terminology has not actually been used in its technical sense. As described in Chapter 2, tenure security refers to the degree of certainty experienced by occupiers, their confidence that their rights will be recognised and protected in the event of challenge. That is not the meaning that was given to it by the Labor Government (hence the use here of inverted commas). In fact, the Labor Government never provided a clear definition of 'secure tenure' and used the term to mean several different things.

Its most common usage was in the context of what came to be known as 'secure tenure' policies (see Chapter 6), under which the Australian Government required that tenure arrangements in larger Indigenous communities be formalised, and formalised in a particular manner. For example, the Australian Government has said that it will not fund the construction of new houses in communities on Aboriginal land in the Northern Territory unless all residential housing in the relevant community has been leased to the Department of Housing for at least 40 years. It describes this as requiring 'secure tenure'. Thus, where the former Minister for Indigenous Affairs, Jenny Macklin, explained that 'the certainty of secure tenure' is 'a pre-condition' to government investment in housing,[151] she

150 *Australian debate about land reform*

used the term as shorthand for *the formalisation of tenure in a manner that complies with government policy*. This is a very different thing from tenure security in the true sense of the term.

This is not the only sense in which the term has been used. It has been used to describe *government control over land*, even where tenure has not been formalised, such as where the five-year leases were described as 'providing short-term security of tenure'.[152] It has also been used in the same way that terms such as 'individual ownership' were used previously – to describe the purported beneficial outcomes of land reform in the most general of terms. For example, the former government stated that 'secure tenure reduces transaction costs and provides the commercial certainty that allows a land asset to be used in different ways, whether as security for financing, as a site for business establishment or as a resource to be developed'.[153] It is hard to attribute a single meaning to 'secure tenure' in this sentence.

'Secure tenure' quickly became the primary framework through which the Labor Government came to present the need for land reform in Indigenous communities. This did not mean that terms such as communal and individual ownership were entirely discarded. The government never denounced them as flawed and sometimes still used them.[154] Moreover much of the literature on land reform published during this period still referred to communal and individual ownership rather than 'secure tenure'.[155] It was nevertheless the case that 'secure tenure' terminology was the pervading language used by the Australian Government between 2007 and 2013.

An expanding rationale

This shift in language was accompanied by an incremental expansion in the stated rationale for land reform. For example, Jenny Macklin explained that

> without secure long term tenure, ownership of housing assets is uncertain. Without secure long term tenure, responsibility for the maintenance of facilities and housing is confused. Without secure long term tenure, residents and tenants occupy their homes without any security or certainty. And without secure long term tenure, potential investors have no incentive to invest.[156]

While the last sentence continues the theme of economic development (and attributes a different meaning to 'secure tenure'), the earlier sentences introduce a new concern for certainty, particularly with respect to the maintenance of houses. Certainty and clarity came to be frequently cited as key rationales for reform, despite not being part of the earlier debate. A brochure on 'Reforming Land Tenure Arrangements on Indigenous Held

Land' from this period describes how the purpose of reform was to 'provide certainty for all land users including Government, those investing in business, and to allow for home ownership'.[157]

Interestingly, there was no public commentary on this expanding rationale for land reform and no criticism of the government for its inconsistent and inaccurate use of language. As the concept of tenure security is not one that most people are familiar with, the government was able to use 'secure tenure' terminology flexibly, to explain the need for land reform in an apparently more technical and non-contentious manner. When the Minister explained how 'previous governments' invested in housing and other infrastructure 'with no firm legal basis', while her government insisted 'on secure tenure',[158] it gave the impression that it was doing nothing more than introducing a long-overdue fix to a technocratic issue. The language provided no indication of the type of decisions that were being made, or how particular approaches were being favoured over others.

The following chapters describe how one impact of 'secure tenure' policies has been to make land use more bureaucratic and subject to greater government control. This is very much the opposite of what was suggested by earlier references to 'individual ownership' and 'private property'. It is striking then that 'secure tenure' policies have attracted the support of some of the same people who had earlier argued for the introduction of 'individual ownership'.[159] This indicates the effectiveness of 'secure tenure' as a rhetorical device. One consequence is that this terminology appears to have contributed to less scrutiny and greater confusion during the period in which the real implementation of the reforms was occurring. This made it easier for the government to implement those reforms in the manner of its choosing, without having to justify its decisions.

5.4 Since 2013: a renewed focus on land reform

In many respects, the progression of Indigenous policy in Australia since the 1970s has been seen as belonging on the left side of politics. Over the last decade or so there has been a concerted attempt by some conservative politicians to shift this perception. Notable among them is Tony Abbott. In a 2004 speech, referring to the complex and at times provocative arguments of Noel Pearson, Abbott described how the

> Pearson critique is a serious challenge to the political left and a once-in-a-generation opportunity for the political right. The left has consistently let down indigenous people because of its faith that, despite failing everywhere else, somehow socialism might work in Aboriginal communities.[160]

Abbott was later appointed leader of the Coalition, and following the September 2013 elections became Prime Minister. Consistent with his view

152 *Australian debate about land reform*

that new approaches to Indigenous policy represented an opportunity for the political right, he sought to elevate the Indigenous affairs portfolio by absorbing it into the Department of Prime Minister and Cabinet.

Two areas in which Abbott regards the political right as having an advantage over the 'socialism' of the left are with respect to welfare reform and land reform. While the Labor Party did continue to implement the land reforms during its period in government (2007–13), the Coalition has argued that they did so half-heartedly, that the reforms had 'stalled' because Labor had 'no appetite for changing the status quo'.[161] Consequently, upon their return to power the Coalition promised to reinvigorate land reform processes.[162]

Once again, the new government has made a change to the language it uses to prosecute the case for land reform. It must be noted, however, that while it identifies land reform as a priority area, the government has said relatively little about it in public forums. This is not because it has been doing nothing. It is clear, for example, that renewed effort has been put into the acquisition of township leases over Aboriginal communities in the Northern Territory.[163] There is also evidence of renewed pressure on state governments to reform Indigenous land for which they are responsible.[164] In October 2014, the Council of Australian Governments (COAG) commissioned an 'urgent investigation into Indigenous land administration and use' to find ways of supporting 'Indigenous land owners to leverage their land assets for economic development'.[165] Interest in land reform at a governmental level is also reflected in the attention it receives in more general publications such as the *White Paper on Developing Northern Australia*[166] and commissioned documents such as *The Forrest Review*.[167] However, the government itself has made only a small number of public statements about land reform. It has said little about why it is required or how it will effect change. A few comments can be made about the statements that have been made.

The first is that it appears the new government has dropped the use of 'secure tenure' terminology. This has corresponded with a narrowing of the stated rationale for reform. The former Labor Government had argued that 'secure tenure' was required not just for home ownership and economic development but also so that ownership of assets could be made certain and responsibility for maintenance made clear. In many respects this was more consistent with the actual reforms, in that their impact on home ownership and economic development has clearly been dwarfed by their greater impact on the management or governance of land and infrastructure in Indigenous communities. Despite this, in its public statements the Abbott Government has tended to explain the need for land reform entirely in terms of enabling home ownership and economic development.[168]

While the new government does sometimes still use the concepts of communal and individual ownership,[169] it does not do so nearly as often as it did during the first period of debate (although there has been something of a resurgence in the use of these terms by some other people[170]). Instead, the government tends to talk in more general terms about 'land reform',[171] 'land tenure reform',[172] 'land administration'[173] and creating ways to 'leverage ... land assets to create economic development opportunities'.[174] At other times it simply focuses on promoting township leasing, which is its preferred model of land reform for Aboriginal community in the Northern Territory. In this context, there continues to be a disjuncture between the language of the government and the reforms themselves. For example, on its website the government states that communities with a township lease are advantaged by the creation of 'long term tradeable tenure',[175] while the Minister for Indigenous Affairs has referred to 'long term and transferable subleases' of the type that 'you or I could go to the bank with and get a mortgage on'.[176] As described in later chapters, long-term and tradable tenure has been the rare exception rather than the general rule on township leases, where the focus has instead been on charging rent. This suggests that there may be ongoing confusion about the precise way in which land reform is intended to support economic development.

5.5 Conclusion: the new political consensus

This chapter has described several fundamental flaws in the way that Indigenous land reform has been debated in Australia. It argues that as a consequence, that debate has been harmful for both understandings of land reform and debate about Indigenous policy more generally. Be that as it may, the debate did have a very concrete outcome: it has resulted in a new political consensus with respect to Indigenous land ownership. This chapter concludes by clarifying the exact nature of that new consensus.

Prior to the debate described here, for several decades governments relied on informal tenure arrangements when providing infrastructure and delivering services in communities on Indigenous land. Chapter 4 describes those arrangements in some detail. It is not that debate about land reform led to concern about those arrangements or the belief that they needed to be examined more closely, to see what was working and what need improvement. To the contrary, the debate led to the existing informal tenure arrangements being largely overlooked. What instead emerged from the debate was a political consensus that there was a clear and pressing need for widespread reform. This was a quantum shift, and a lot of ground was passed over without consideration in the process. There was no opportunity for a more targeted discussion about which aspects of the existing informal tenure arrangements most needed attention and which might have actually been well suited to the economic and social circumstances of communities. And perhaps more significantly, there was very little discussion about the exact mechanisms by which land reform would achieve the outcomes suggested.

154 *Australian debate about land reform*

To be clear, it is not argued here that the pre-existing informal tenure arrangements were without fault. If the debate about land reform had led to a closer examination of those arrangements, it is likely that today we would have a clearer picture of their flaws, including the extent to which informality led to confusion or tenure insecurity. However, that is not what occurred. As a result of the way in which land reform was debated, the consensus that emerged was that the need for reform was apparent and there was no need to investigate further. This helps explain the sweeping and at times highly coercive nature of the reforms that are described in the following chapter, as well as some of the confusion that has accompanied the implementation of those reforms.

Notes

1 Barry W. Rowland, 'Examination of the Aboriginal Land Rights (Northern Territory) Act 1976–80' (Department of Aboriginal Affairs, 1980).
2 Diana Perche, 'Dialogue between Past and Present: Policy Evaluation and History' (2011) 57(3) *Australian Journal of Politics and History* 403, 413–15.
3 John Toohey, 'Seven Years On: Report by Mr Justice Toohey to the Minister for Aboriginal Affairs on the *Aboriginal Land Rights (Northern Territory) Act 1976* and Related Matters' (Australian Government, 1983).
4 Ibid, 37–9.
5 Ibid, 47–8. See also Peter Sutton, 'Suggestions for a Bicameral System' (1984) 5(3) *Anthropological Forum* 395.
6 See, eg, Francesca Merlan, 'The Regimentation of Customary Practice: From Northern Territory Land Claims to Mabo' (1995) 6(1/2) *Australian Journal of Anthropology* 64.
7 John Reeves, 'Building on Land Rights for the Next Generation: The Review of the *Aboriginal Land Rights (Northern Territory) Act 1976*' (Australian Government, 1998).
8 Ibid, 210–11.
9 Ibid, 473.
10 Ibid, 482.
11 Ibid, 54.
12 Ibid, v–viii, 479. See also 568–71, 578.
13 Ibid, 361.
14 Ibid, 368.
15 Northern Territory Government, Submission No 61 to the Senate Community Affairs Committee, Parliament of Australia, *Inquiry into the Recommendations of the Reeves Report Review of the Aboriginal Land Rights (Northern Territory) Act 1976*, June 1999.
16 See submissions to the House of Representatives Standing Committee on Aboriginal and Torres Strait Islander Affairs Inquiry into the Reeves Report on the Aboriginal Land Rights (Northern Territory) Act, available at www. aph.gov.au/Parliamentary_Business/Committees/House_of_Representatives_ Committees?url=atsia/reeves/inquiryinf.htm. See also Jon Altman, Frances Morphy and Tim Rowse (eds), *Land Rights at Risk? Evaluations of the Reeves Report* (Centre for Aboriginal Economic Policy Research, 1999); Ian Viner, 'A Review of the Reeves Report: Whither Land Rights in the Northern Territory? Whither Aboriginal Self-determination?' (15 July 1999) *Online Opinion* www.onlineopinion.com.au/view.asp?article=1084&page=0; Paul Albrecht,

Australian debate about land reform 155

'Comments on the Reeves Report' (Paper presented at the Quadrant seminar: Rousseau v Reality – Aborigines and Australian Civilisation, Sydney, 21 August 1999); Peter Sutton, 'Anthropological Submission on the Reeves Review' (1999) 9(2) *Anthropological Forum* 189, 196.

17 Sean Brennan, 'Economic Development and Land Council Power: Modernising the Land Rights Act or Same Old Same Old?' (2006) 10(4) *Australian Indigenous Law Reporter* 1, 24.

18 Noel Pearson, 'Review: *The Mystery of Capital: Why Capitalism Triumphs in the West and Fails Everywhere Else* by Hernando de Soto' (September 2001) *Australian Public Intellectual Network*.

19 Noel Pearson and Lara Kostakidis-Lianos, 'Building Indigenous Capital: Removing Obstacles to Participation in the Real Economy' (Cape York Institute, 2004).

20 Ibid, 2.

21 Gary Banks, 'Indigenous Disadvantage: Assessing Policy Impacts' (Speech delivered at the Pursuing Opportunity and Prosperity Conference, Melbourne Institute of Applied Economic and Social Research/The Australian, Melbourne, 13 November 2003).

22 Ron Duncan, 'Agricultural and Resource Economics and Economic Development in Aboriginal Communities' (2003) 47(3) *Australian Journal of Agricultural and Resource Economics* 307. Duncan's arguments were reported by Alan Wood, 'Individual Enterprise the Key to Progress for Aborigines', *The Australian*, 29 April 2003, 13.

23 Jon Altman, 'Economic Development and Indigenous Australia: Contestations over Property, Institutions and Ideology' (2004) 48(3) *Australian Journal of Agricultural and Resource Economics* 513.

24 Bob Beadman, 'Do Indigenous Youth Have a Dream?' (Menzies Research Centre Ltd, 2004) 3, 16–19, 29–31, and see also Central Land Council (CLC), 'Beadman Report Contributes Nothing' (Media Release, 3 June 2004).

25 The Bennelong Society was a think tank formed in 2001 to promote conservative political perspectives on Indigenous issues. It closed down in 2011; see John Ferguson, 'Lack of Interest Kills Bennelong Society', *The Australian* (online), 22 November 2011 www.theaustralian.com.au/national-affairs/lack-of-interest-kills-bennelong/story-fn59niix-1226201813451.

26 Gary Johns, 'The Poverty of Aboriginal Self-Determination' in Gary Johns (ed), *Waking up to the Dreamtime: The Illusion of Aboriginal Self-Determination* (Media Masters, 2001) 15, 17; Peter Howson, 'Why We Desperately Need New Aboriginal Policies' (Bennelong Society, 10 May 2002) 5; Gary Johns, 'The Gulf between Aboriginal Policies and Aboriginal People in Australia' (Libertad y Desarrollo Institute, 6 June 2003) 16.

27 Johns, *Waking Up to the Dreamtime*, above n 26, 29. See also Peter Howson, 'The Failure of Aboriginal Segregation' (2003) 47(5) *Quadrant* 50, 53; Peter Howson, 'Aborigines Need Economic Assimilation' (Bennelong Society, 31 March 2003); Gary Johns, 'Look for Strength in Mainstream', *The Australian*, 22 November 2001, 11; Gary Johns and Ron Brunton, 'Separate Path to Division', *The Australian*, 12 April 2000, 15; Gary Johns, 'Integration Gives Head Start to Life Chances', *The Australian*, 2 February 2004, 7. A further author opposed to both communal ownership and land rights more generally is Warby; see Michael Warby, *Past Wrongs, Future Rights: Anti-Discrimination, Native Title and Aboriginal and Torres Strait Islander Policy, 1975–1997* (Tasman Institute, 1997) iii; Michael Warby, *What Makes a Third World Country?* (1 January 2001) Institute of Public Affairs www.ipa.org.au/news/520/what-makes-a-third-world-country-/pg/10.

28 See Central Land Council (CLC), 'Communal Title and Economic Development' (Policy Paper, 2005) 2, 18.

156 *Australian debate about land reform*

29 Jon Altman, Craig Linkhorn and Jennifer Clarke, 'Land Rights and Development Reform in Remote Australia' (Discussion Paper No 276/2005, Centre for Aboriginal Economic Policy Research, 2005) 1; Stuart Bradfield, 'Communal Ownership of Indigenous Land and Individual Wealth Creation: The Debate So Far, Identifying Key Questions' (Paper presented at the National Native Title Conference, Coffs Harbour, 1–3 June 2005) 1; Michael Dodson and Diana McCarthy, 'Communal Land and the Amendments to the *Aboriginal Land Rights (Northern Territory) Act*' (Research Discussion Paper No 19, Australian Institute of Aboriginal and Torres Strait Islander Studies, 2006) 5–6.
30 (1996) 187 CLR 1.
31 Quoted in Heather McRae*et al.*, *Indigenous Legal Issues, Commentary and Materials* (Thomson Reuters, 2009) 311.
32 Ibid, and see generally pages 308–19.
33 On the subject of these continuities, see Deidre Howard-Wagner, 'The Denial of Separate Rights: Political Rationalities and Technologies Governing Indigenous Affairs as Practices of Whiteness' (Paper presented at The Australian Sociological Association Annual Conference, Auckland, New Zealand, 4–7 December 2007). With respect to 'normalisation', see Diana Perche, 'Indigenous Land Reform and the Market: Changing Social Constructions in Indigenous Land Policy during the Howard Era' (Paper presented at Australian Political Studies Association Annual Conference, Macquarie University, Sydney, 30 September 2009) 8; Kirsty Howey, ' "Normalising" What? A Qualitative Analysis of Aboriginal Land Tenure Reform in the Northern Territory of Australia' (2014–15) 18(1) *Australian Indigenous Law Review* 4.
34 In relation to these broader changes see the authors referred to at above n 29 and see also Bill Gray and Will Sanders, 'Views from the Top of the "Quiet Revolution": Secretarial Perspectives on the New Arrangements in Indigenous Affairs' (Discussion Paper No 282/2006, Centre for Aboriginal Economic Policy Research, 2006) 1.
35 Sarah Maddison, *Black Politics: Inside the Complexity of Aboriginal Political Culture* (Allen & Unwin, 2009) xxvii–xxxvi.
36 Warren Mundine, 'Aboriginal Governance and Economic Development' (Paper presented at the National Native Title Conference, Coffs Harbour, 1–3 June 2005) 1.
37 Mark Metherell, 'Land System Holds Us Back, Says Mundine', *The Sydney Morning Herald*, 7 December 2004, 6.
38 See, eg, Mark Metherell, 'Sorry Will Not Change Lives, Says Mundine', *The Sydney Morning Herald*, 6 December 2004, 2; AAP, 'Forget "Sorry" Issue, Says Black Leader', *Hobart Mercury* 6 December 2004, 2.
39 See comments of Joseph Elu in Patricia Karvelas, 'Land Rights May Be Privatised', *The Australian*, 10 December 2010, 4, and reference to Wesley Aird in Christopher Pearson, 'Case to Put the Lands Right', *The Weekend Australian*, 11 December 2004, 18.
40 Dennis Shanahan and Patricia Karvelas, 'PM Considers New Land Rights Plan', *The Weekend Australian*, 11 December 2004, 4. See also Stuart Bradfield, 'White Picket Fence or Trojan Horse? The Debate over Communal Ownership of Indigenous Land and Individual Wealth Creation' (Issues Paper No 3, Australian Institute of Aboriginal and Torres Strait Islander Studies Native Title Research Unit, 2005) 3.
41 Bradfield, 'White Picket Fence or Trojan Horse?', above n 40, 3.
42 See John Howard, 'Address to the National Reconciliation Planning Workshop' (Speech delivered at the National Reconciliation Planning Workshop, Canberra, 30 May 2005); Amanda Vanstone, 'Address to National Press Club' (Speech delivered at the National Press Club, Canberra, 23 February 2005);

Amanda Vanstone, 'Address to the Reconciliation Australia Conference' (Speech delivered at the National Reconciliation Planning Workshop, Canberra, 31 May 2005); Amanda Vanstone, 'Beyond Conspicuous Compassion: Indigenous Australians Deserve More Than Good Intentions' (Speech delivered to the Australia and New Zealand School of Government, Australian National University, Canberra, 7 December 2005).

43 National Indigenous Council (NIC), 'Possible Indigenous Land Tenure Principles' (Draft Working Document, National Indigenous Council, 3 June 2005). A copy is attached at Annexure 2 of the 2005 Native Title Report, available at www.hreoc.gov.au/social_justice/nt_report/ntreport05/app. 2.html.

44 In addition to the articles referred to above see, eg, Ashleigh Wilson and Amanda Hodge, 'PM's New Deal for Blacks: Private Homes to Be Allowed on Native Title', *The Australian*, 7 April 2005, 1; Michael Duffy, 'A Good Land Right Is a Good Deed', *The Sydney Morning Herald*, 9 April 2005, 41; Michelle Grattan, 'Howard Tilts at Title Fight', *The Sunday Age* (Melbourne), 10 April 2005, 17; Nassim Khadem, '99-Year Lease Plan for Aboriginal Land', *The Age* (Melbourne), 6 October 2005.

45 Editorial, 'Land Rights Should Apply to Individuals', *The Australian*, 19 February 2005, 13; Editorial, 'Black Revolution: Economic Engagement Is the Path to Prosperity', *The Australian*, 6 October 2005, 18.

46 Bradfield, 'Communal Ownership of Indigenous Land and Individual Wealth Creation', above n 29; Aden Ridgeway, 'Addressing the Economic Exclusion of Indigenous Australians through Native Title' (Paper presented at the Native Title Conference, Coffs Harbour, 1–3 June 2005); Mundine, above n 36.

47 Tom Calma, 'Native Title Report 2005' (Australian Human Rights Commission, 2005) chs 1, 3.

48 In addition to those referred to above see Helen Hughes and Jenness Warin, 'A New Deal for Aborigines and Torres Strait Islanders in Remote Communities' (Issues Analysis No 54, Centre for Independent Studies, 1 March 2005); John McDonnell, 'Land Rights and Aboriginal Development' (2005) 49(6) *Quadrant* 30; Margaret Stephenson, 'Reforms to Indigenous Land in Australia: Some Lessons from Other Jurisdictions' (Paper presented at Australasian Law Teachers Association Annual Conference, Melbourne, 4–7 July 2006); Ray Evans, 'Land Tenure and Impediments to Commercialisation: A Retrospective' (Paper presented at the Bennelong Conference, Melbourne, 10 September 2005); Helen Hughes, 'The Economics of Indigenous Deprivation and Proposals for Reform' (Issue Analysis No 63, Centre for Independent Studies, 23 September 2005); Penny Lee, 'Individual Titling of Aboriginal Land in the Northern Territory: What Australia Can Learn from the International Community' (2006) 29(2) *University of New South Wales Law Journal* 22; and Samantha Hepburn, 'Transforming Customary Title to Individual Title: Revisiting the Cathedral' (2006) 11(1) *Deakin Law Review* 63. Relating to the same period of debate, although published in 2007 were: Margaret Stephenson, 'Individual Title versus Collective Title in Australia: Reflections on the Northern American and New Zealand Experiences of Indigenous Title to Land' in Elizabeth Cooke (ed), *Modern Studies in Property Law, Volume 4* (Hart Publishing, 2007) 295; Lee Godden and Maureen Tehan, 'Translating Native Title to Individual "Title" in Australia: Are Real Property Forms and Indigenous Interests Reconcilable?' in Elizabeth Cooke (ed), *Modern Studies in Property Law, Volume 4* (Hart Publishing, 2007), 263; Lewis Shillito, 'Strata Title Aboriginal Towns? An Alternative to the Town-Leasing Proposal' (2007) 14(3) *Australian Property Law Journal* 201; Michael Dillon and Neil Westbury, *Beyond Humbug: Transforming Government Engagement with Indigenous Australia* (Seaview Press, 2007) 120–74.

49 Australian Broadcasting Corporation, 'Crown Prosecutor Speaks out about Abuse in Central Australia', *Lateline*, 15 May 2006 (Tony Jones and Nanette Rogers).

50 Patricia Karvelas, 'Brough to Hold Radical Talks on Ending Violence', *The Australian*, 18 May 2006, 4.

51 Australian Broadcasting Corporation, 'Sexual Abuse Reported in Indigenous Community', *Lateline*, 21 June 2006 (Suzanne Smith).

52 Northern Territory Government, 'Chief Minister Orders Inquiry into Child Sex Abuse' (Media Release, 22 June 2006).

53 Northern Territory Government, 'Little Children Are Sacred' (Report of the Northern Territory Board of Inquiry into the Protection of Aboriginal Children from Sexual Abuse, 2007).

54 Commonwealth, *Parliamentary Debates*, House of Representatives, 31 May 2006, 5 (Mal Brough).

55 See, eg, Commonwealth, Parliamentary Debates, House of Representatives, 19 June 2006, 83 (Warren Snowdon); Commonwealth, Parliamentary Debates, House of Representatives, 12 June 2007, 91 (Jenny Macklin). There were exceptions: notably, Warren Mundine was National Vice-President of the Labor Party when he began arguing for reform. However, Labor's Indigenous Affairs spokesman, Senator Kim Carr, made it clear that Mundine's comments were his own and did not reflect party policy; see Metherell, 'Land System Holds Us Back', above n 37.

56 Australian Broadcasting Corporation, 'PM Receives Support for His Plan for Aboriginal Communities', *Lateline*, 21 June 2007 (Narda Gilmore).

57 Each set of reforms is described in detail in Chapter 6.

58 Terms used in addition to communal ownership include 'communal title', 'communally held land', 'communally owned land', 'communal land', 'communally titled land', 'communal property', 'inalienable freehold communal title' and 'land held in common by communities'.

59 Terms used in addition to individual ownership include 'individual property', 'individual property rights', 'individual leases', 'individual leasehold interests', 'formal individual title', 'individual title' and 'individualised land tenure'.

60 Terms used in addition to private property include 'private ownership', 'private property rights' and 'private individual ownership'.

61 It was not until 2010 that the four categories of property regime were defined in the context of the Australian debate; see Jude Wallace, 'Managing Social Tenure' in Lee Godden and Maureen Tehan (eds), *Comparative Perspectives on Communal Land and Individual Ownership: Sustainable Futures* (Routledge, 2010) 25, 34.

62 A point made at the time by David Dalrymple, 'Land Rights and Property Rights' (2007) 51(1) *Quadrant* 61, 62.

63 John Howard, quoted in Mark Metherell, 'PM Backs Indigenous Enterprise', *The Sydney Morning Herald*, 10 December 2004, 7.

64 Holdings are described in Chapter 2.

65 Warren Mundine quoted in Metherell, 'Land System Holds Us Back', above n 37.

66 Vanstone, 'Address to Reconciliation Australia', above n 42.

67 Hughes and Warin, above n 48, 15.

68 Beadman, above n 24, 3.

69 Ridgeway, above n 46, 9.

70 CLC, 'Communal Title and Economic Development', above n 28, 4–6.

71 Editorial, 'Land Rights Should Apply to Individuals', above n 45.

72 Quoted in NIC, above n 43.

73 Vanstone, 'Address to Press Club', above n 42.

Australian debate about land reform 159

74 Commonwealth, *Parliamentary Debates*, House of Representatives, 31 May 2006, 5 (Mal Brough).

75 Editorial, 'Land Rights Should Apply to Individuals', above n 45.

76 Quoted in NIC, above n 43.

77 Ibid.

78 Editorial, 'The House and Land Package?', *The Australian*, 18 November 2010, 15.

79 Gary Banks, 'Are We Overcoming Indigenous Disadvantage?' (Speech delivered at Reconciliations Australia's 'Closing the Gap Conversations' Series, Canberra, 7 July 2009) 11.

80 Brian Gleeson, 'Coordinator General for Remote Indigenous Services Six Monthly Report April–September 2011' (Australian Government, 2011) 53.

81 Commonwealth, *Parliamentary Debates*, House of Representatives, 26 February 2009, 2031 (Kevin Rudd).

82 There are a large number of other examples but see, eg, the comments of the CSIRO group executive in Andrew Johnson, 'Unlocking the North', *The Australian*, 14 June 2013, 10; Campbell Newman in Australian Broadcasting Corporation, 'Property Key to Ending Indigenous Welfare Cycle: Newman', *ABC News*, 15 January 2013 (Eric Tlozek); Amos Aikman, 'Land Rights "Block" Aborigines', *The Australian*, 15 July 2014, 2; Amos Aikman, 'Land Rights out of Step?', *The Australian*, 31 July 2014, 9.

83 See, eg, Mark Moran, 'Home Ownership for Indigenous People Living on Community Title Land in Queensland: Scoping Study Report' (Queensland Aboriginal Coordinating Council, Aboriginal and Torres Strait Islander Commission, 1999) and see the various reports referred to on pages 1–2 of that document; Mark Moran*et al.*, 'Home Ownership for Indigenous People Living on Community Title Land in Queensland: Preliminary Community Survey' (Aboriginal Environments Research Centre, University of Queensland, 2001); Reeves, above n 7, 500.

84 See Moran, above n 83, 13–14, 17–18, and see also discussion below.

85 This was particularly the case during debate about the introduction of township leasing: see, eg, Commonwealth, *Parliamentary Debates*, House of Representatives, 19 June 2006, 121 (Mal Brough).

86 Dillon and Westbury, above n 48, 170.

87 See, eg, CLC, 'Communal Title and Economic Development', above n 28, 11; Altman, Linkhorn and Clarke, above n 29, 12; Ridgeway, above n 46, 9; Will Sanders, 'Indigenous Housing Tenure in Remote Areas: Directions and Constraints' (Topical Issue No 6/2008, Centre for Aboriginal Economic Policy Research, 2008) 1.

88 Vanstone, 'Beyond Conspicuous Compassion', above n 42.

89 John Howard quoted in Wilson and Hodge, above n 44.

90 Amanda Vanstone quoted in AAP, 'Indigenous Land Shake-up Announced', *The Age* (online), 5 October 2005 www.theage.com.au/news/national/indigenous-land-shakeup-announced/2005/10/05/1128191763403.html.

91 Commonwealth, *Parliamentary Debates*, House of Representatives, 19 June 2006, 121 (Mal Brough); Mal Brough, 'Historic Agreement for 99 Year Lease in NT' (Media Release, 30 August 2007). See also below n 98.

92 Moran, above n 83, 13–14, 17–18; Moran*et al.*, above n 83, 1, 35–6, 39, 42–3; Mark Moran, *Practising Self-Determination: Participation in Planning and Local Governance in Discrete Indigenous Settlements* (PhD Thesis, University of Queensland, 2006) 301. It should be noted that in recent years, some people have instead characterised Katter leases as a positive initiative that was never given a chance due to a change of government; see, eg, Noel Pearson, 'Hats Off to Katter's Grand Plan', *The Australian*, 7 May 2011, 12;

160 *Australian debate about land reform*

Helen Hughes, Sara Hudson and Mark Hughes, 'Lands Where No One Can Feel at Home', *The Australian*, 25 June 2011, 6.

93 Moran, 'Home Ownership Scoping Study', above n 83, 18.

94 Ibid, 20–1.

95 Ibid, 18.

96 Moran *et al.*, above n 83, 1.

97 Patricia Karvelas, 'Axe Public Housing: Pearson', *The Australian*, 21 February 2007, 15. See also Simon Kearney *et al.*, 'Some "Not Ready" for Aussie Dream', *The Australian*, 21 February 2008, 1.

98 See, eg, Helen Hughes, Mark Hughes and Sara Hudson, 'Private Housing in Indigenous Lands' (Policy Monograph 113, Centre for Independent Studies, 2010), who take a similar approach in several of their other publications on home ownership; Lindsay Murdoch, 'Great Australian Dream Time … a Home to Call Their Own', *The Sydney Morning Herald*, 15 April 2010, 7; Liberal Party of Australia, *Aboriginal Home Ownership* (21 December 2010) www.liberal.org.au/latest-news/2010/12/21/aboriginal-home-ownership-0; Campbell Newman, 'Hope for Indigenous Home Owners' (Media Release, 15 January 2013); Alison Anderson, 'New Measure Brings Us Hope', *NT News* (Darwin), 26 January 2013, 22. See also above n 91.

99 Quoted in Metherell, 'PM Backs Indigenous Enterprise', above n 63.

100 Editorial, 'Black Revolution', above n 45.

101 NIC, above n 43. See also Hughes, above n 48, 9, 11; Calma, above n 47, 7, 10, 11, 13, 116, 118.

102 Ridgeway, above n 46, 8.

103 Dodson and McCarthy, above n 29, 5.

104 Ibid, 5.

105 Nicole Watson, 'Review of Aboriginal Land Titles' (Briefing Paper No 7, Jumbunna Indigenous House of Learning, September 2005) 2. Conversely Howson, who was in favour of reform, argued that assimilation should be their aim, as 'the preservation of Aboriginal culture' through 'separatism' had been such a failure; see Peter Howson, 'Land Rights: The Next Battleground' (2005) 49(6) *Quadrant* 24, 26.

106 Quoted in Grattan, above n 44.

107 Ibid.

108 Hughes and Warin, above n 48, 3.

109 Christopher Pearson, above n 39.

110 Duffy, above n 44.

111 Commonwealth, *Parliamentary Debates*, House of Representatives, 19 June 2006, 121 (Mal Brough).

112 Editorial, 'Land Rights Should Apply to Individuals', above n 45.

113 Vanstone, 'Beyond Conspicuous Compassion', above n 42.

114 Quoted in Calma, above n 47, 7.

115 Howson, 'Land Rights', above n 105, 28.

116 Hughes, above n 48, 10. See also comments of Newman in Australian Broadcasting Corporation, 'Property Key to Ending Indigenous Welfare Cycle', above n 82.

117 Evans, above n 48, 6.

118 Howson, 'Land Rights', above n 105, 25.

119 See, eg, Nicole Watson, 'Howard's End: The Real Agenda behind the Proposed Review of Indigenous Land Titles' (2005) 9(4) *Australian Indigenous Law Reporter* 1; Dodson and McCarthy, above n 29, 10.

120 Noel Pearson, 'Reconciliation a Building Block', *The Australian*, 19 April 2005, 13. See also Dillon and Westbury, above n 48, 146; Bradfield, 'White Picket Fence or Trojan Horse?', above n 40, 6.

121 Howard, above n 42. See also Vanstone, 'Address to Reconciliation Australia', above n 42; Vanstone, 'Beyond Conspicuous Compassion', above n 42.
122 Pearson, 'Reconciliation a Building Block', above n 120.
123 Ibid.
124 Ibid.
125 Pearson and Kostakidis, above n 19.
126 NIC, above n 43 (emphasis added).
127 Ibid.
128 Howard, above n 42.
129 Ibid.
130 Tim Rowse, 'The National Emergency and Indigenous Jurisdictions' in Jon Altman and Melinda Hinkson (eds), *Coercive Reconciliation: Stabilise, Normalise, Exit Aboriginal Australia* (Arena Publications, 2007) 47, 54. Rowse adds 'both believe too strongly in the moral paradigms of "property"'.
131 Comaroff, quoted in Clarissa Fourie, 'Land Readjustment for Peri-Urban Customary Tenure: The Example of Botswana' in Robert Hume and Hilary Lim (eds), *Demystifying the Mystery of Capital: Land Tenure and Poverty in Africa and the Caribbean* (Routledge Cavendish, 2004) 31, 35. Comaroff was writing in relation to customary tenure, but his argument applies more broadly.
132 David Martin, 'Money, Business and Culture: Issues for Aboriginal Economic Policy' (Discussion Paper No 101/1995, Centre for Aboriginal Economic Policy Research, 1995) 4.
133 Ibid, 13. See also Chapter 4.
134 See Chapters 6 and 7.
135 Peter Sutton, 'Stanner and Aboriginal Land Use: Ecology, Economic Change, and Enclosing the Commons' in Melinda Hinkson and Jeremy Beckett (eds), *An Appreciate of Difference: WEH Stanner and Aboriginal Australia* (Aboriginal Studies Press, 2008) 169, 172–3.
136 Hughes and Warin, above n 48, 4.
137 Pearson and Kostakidis, above n 19.
138 Howard, above n 42.
139 Paul Toohey 'A New Lease of Life', *The Weekend Australian Magazine*, 10 January 2009, 14, 14.
140 Grattan, above n 44.
141 David Martin, 'Policy Alchemy and the Magical Transformation of Aboriginal Society' in Yasmine Musharbash and Marcus Barber (eds), *Ethnography & the Production of Anthropological Knowledge: Essays in Honour of Nicolas Peterson* (Australian National University E Press, 2011) 201, 208.
142 Howard, above n 42.
143 This is discussed further in Chapters 7 and 8.
144 See, eg, Diane Austin-Broos, *Arrernte Present, Arrernte Past: Invasion, Violence, and Imagination in Indigenous Central Australia* (University of Chicago Press, 2009) 5 and generally.
145 Grattan, above n 44.
146 Mal Brough, 'Blueprint for Action in Indigenous Affairs' (Speech delivered at the National Institute of Governance, Canberra, 5 December 2006).
147 Ibid.
148 Commonwealth, *Parliamentary Debates*, House of Representatives, 19 June 2006, 121 (Mal Brough).
149 Ibid.
150 Jenny Macklin, 'Closing the Gap: Building an Indigenous Future' (Speech delivered to the National Press Club, Canberra, 27 February 2008).
151 Ibid.

162 Australian debate about land reform

152 See, eg, Australian Government, 'Stronger Futures in the Northern Territory' (Discussion Paper, June 2011) 22. Chapter 5 describes how tenure was not formalised under five-year leases due to their short duration.

153 Australian Government, 'Indigenous Economic Development Strategy 2011–2018' (Department of Families, Housing, Community Services and Indigenous Affairs, 2011) 63.

154 See, eg, Jenny Macklin, 'Address to the NSW Aboriginal Land Council' (Speech delivered to the NSW Aboriginal Land Council, Cessnock, 5 March 2009), in which the Minister refers to 'communal Aboriginal land' and 'individual title'.

155 See Nicole Watson, 'The Abuse of Indigenous Land Tenure as a Tool of Social Engineering' (2008) 1 *Journal of the Australasian Law Teachers' Association* 163; Sanders, above n 87; Sutton, 'Stanner and Aboriginal Land Use', above n 135; Margaret Stephenson, 'To Lease or Not to Lease? The Leasing of Indigenous Statutory Lands in Australia: Lessons from Canada' (2009) 35(3) *Commonwealth Law Bulletin* 545; Sara Hudson, 'From Rhetoric to Reality: Can 99-year Leases Lead to Homeownership for Indigenous Communities?' (Policy Monograph 92, Centre for Independent Studies, 2009); Perche, 'Indigenous Land Reform and the Market', above n 33; Lee Godden and Maureen Tehan, 'Introduction: A Sustainable Future for Communal Lands, Resources and Communities' in Lee Godden and Maureen Tehan (eds), *Comparative Perspectives on Communal Lands and Individual Ownership: Sustainable Futures* (Routledge, 2010) 1; Tom Calma, 'Social Justice, Communal Lands and Sustainable Communities' in Lee Godden and Maureen Tehan (ed), *Comparative Perspectives on Communal Lands and Individual Ownership: Sustainable Futures* (Routledge, 2010) 49; Maureen Tehan, 'Customary Land Tenure, Communal Titles and Sustainability: The Allure of Individual Title and Property Rights in Australia' in Lee Godden and Maureen Tehan (eds), *Comparative Perspectives on Communal Lands and Individual Ownership: Sustainable Futures* (Routledge, 2010) 353; Lee Godden, 'Communal Governance of Land and Resources as a Sustainable Institution' in Lee Godden and Maureen Tehan (eds), *Comparative Perspectives on Communal Lands and Individual Ownership: Sustainable Futures* (Routledge, 2010) 385; Hughes, Hughes and Hudson, above n 98; Don Fuller, Susan Bandias and Darius Pfitzer, 'Utilizing Aboriginal Land in the Northern Territory for Economic and Human Development' (Charles Darwin University, 2011).

156 Macklin, 'Closing the Gap Speech', above n 150.

157 Australian Government, *Reforming Land Tenure Arrangements on Indigenous Held Land* (2012).

158 Jenny Macklin, 'Building the Foundations for Change' (Speech delivered at the Sydney Institute, Sydney, 9 August 2011).

159 See, eg, Editorial, 'A Reward for Quiet Persistence', *The Australian*, 14 June 2012, 13, in which the acquisition of long-term leases by the government is described as 'an important factor in the progress made' with respect to housing.

160 Tony Abbott, 'Seize the Moment' (Speech delivered to the Bennelong Society, Sydney, 3 September 2004).

161 The Liberal Party and The Nationals, 'The Coalition's Policy for Indigenous Affairs' (September 2013) 8.

162 See, eg, Nigel Scullion, '2014 National Native Title Conference Speech' (Speech delivered at the National Native Title Conference, Coffs Harbour, 2 June 2014).

163 See, eg, Nigel Scullion, 'Historic Arnhem Land Lease Agreement' (Media Release, 17 October 2013) and Nigel Scullion, 'Pirlangimpi Township Lease Agreement' (Media Release, 14 March 2014).

Australian debate about land reform 163

164 See Scullion, '2014 National Native Title Conference Speech', above n 162.
165 See Australian Government, Department of Prime Minister and Cabinet, *COAG Investigation into Indigenous Land Administration and Use* (2015) www.dpmc. gov.au/indigenous-affairs/about/jobs-land-and-economy-programme/coag-land-investigation.
166 Australian Government, 'Our North, Our Future: White Paper on Developing Northern Australia' (June 2015).
167 Andrew Forrest, 'The Forrest Review: Creating Parity' (Commonwealth of Australia, 2014).
168 See, eg, Nigel Scullion, 'Land Reform for the Future', *Koori Mail*, 26 March 2014 (available at http://minister.indigenous.gov.au/media/2014-03-26/land-reform-future-published-koori-mail); Scullion, '2014 National Native Title Conference Speech', above n 162.
169 See, eg, Tony Abbott, 'Indigenous Affairs: A Coalition Approach' (Speech delivered at the Sydney Institute, Sydney, 15 March 2013); Australian Government, 'Our North, Our Future', above n 166, 15, 29.
170 See, eg, Forrest, above n 167, 2, 209–15; Editorial, 'How to Turn Indigenous Land Rights into Prosperity', *The Australian*, 21 May 2015, 13; Warren Mundine, 'Shooting an Elephant: Four Giant Steps' (Speech delivered to the Garma Festival Corporate Dinner, 10 August 2013).
171 Scullion, 'Land Reform for the Future', above n 168.
172 The Liberal Party and The Nationals, above n 161, 8.
173 Australian Government, Department of Prime Minister and Cabinet, *Jobs, Land and Economy Programme* (2014) www.dpmc.gov.au/indigenous-affairs/about/jobs-land-and-economy-programme.
174 Ibid.
175 Australian Government, Department of Prime Minister and Cabinet, *Township Leasing on Aboriginal Land in the Northern Territory* (2014) www.dpmc.gov.au/indigenous-affairs/about/jobs-land-and-economy-programme/township-leasing-aboriginal-land-northern-territory.
176 Scullion, '2014 National Native Title Conference Speech', above n 162.

Bibliography

Books/articles/reports/web pages

AAP, 'Forget "Sorry" Issue, Says Black Leader', *Hobart Mercury* 6 December 2004, 2.
AAP, 'Indigenous Land Shake-up Announced', *The Age* (online), 5 October 2005 www.theage.com.au/news/national/indigenous-land-shakeup-announced/2005/10/05/1128191763403.html.
Abbott, Tony, 'Seize the Moment' (Speech delivered to the Bennelong Society, Sydney, 3 September 2004).
Abbott, Tony, 'Indigenous Affairs: A Coalition Approach' (Speech delivered at the Sydney Institute, Sydney, 15 March 2013).
Aikman, Amos, 'Land Rights "Block" Aborigines', *The Australian*, 15 July 2014, 2.
Aikman, Amos, 'Land Rights out of Step?', *The Australian*, 31 July 2014, 9.
Albrecht, Paul, 'Comments on the Reeves Report' (Paper presented at the Quadrant seminar: Rousseau v Reality – Aborigines and Australian Civilisation, Sydney, 21 August 1999).

164 *Australian debate about land reform*

Altman, Jon, 'Economic Development and Indigenous Australia: Contestations over Property, Institutions and Ideology' (2004) 48(3) *Australian Journal of Agricultural and Resource Economics* 513.

Altman, Jon, Craig Linkhorn and Jennifer Clarke, 'Land Rights and Development Reform in Remote Australia' (Discussion Paper No 276/2005, Centre for Aboriginal Economic Policy Research, 2005).

Altman, Jon, Frances Morphy and Tim Rowse (eds), *Land Rights at Risk? Evaluations of the Reeves Report* (Centre for Aboriginal Economic Policy Research, 1999).

Anderson, Alison, 'New Measure Brings Us Hope', *NT News* (Darwin), 26 January 2013, 22.

Austin-Broos, Diane, *Arrernte Present, Arrernte Past: Invasion, Violence, and Imagination in Indigenous Central Australia* (University of Chicago Press, 2009).

Australian Broadcasting Corporation, 'Crown Prosecutor Speaks out about Abuse in Central Australia', *Lateline*, 15 May 2006 (Tony Jones and Nanette Rogers).

Australian Broadcasting Corporation, 'Sexual Abuse Reported in Indigenous Community', *Lateline*, 21 June 2006 (Suzanne Smith).

Australian Broadcasting Corporation, 'PM Receives Support for His Plan for Aboriginal Communities', *Lateline*, 21 June 2007 (Narda Gilmore).

Australian Broadcasting Corporation, 'Property Key to Ending Indigenous Welfare Cycle: Newman', *ABC News*, 15 January 2013 (Eric Tlozek).

Australian Government, 'Stronger Futures in the Northern Territory' (Discussion paper, June 2011).

Australian Government, 'Indigenous Economic Development Strategy 2011–2018' (Department of Families, Housing, Community Services and Indigenous Affairs, 2011).

Australian Government, *Reforming Land Tenure Arrangements on Indigenous Held Land* (2012).

Australian Government, 'Our North, Our Future: White Paper on Developing Northern Australia' (June 2015).

Australian Government, Department of Prime Minister and Cabinet, *Jobs, Land and Economy Programme* (2014) www.dpmc.gov.au/indigenous-affairs/about/jobs-land-and-economy-programme.

Australian Government, Department of Prime Minister and Cabinet, *Township Leasing on Aboriginal Land in the Northern Territory* (2014) www.dpmc.gov.au/indigenous-affairs/about/jobs-land-and-economy-programme/township-leasing-aboriginal-land-northern-territory.

Australian Government, Department of Prime Minister and Cabinet, *COAG Investigation Into Indigenous Land Administration and Use* (2015) www.dpmc.gov.au/indigenous-affairs/about/jobs-land-and-economy-programme/coag-land-investigation.

Banks, Gary, 'Indigenous Disadvantage: Assessing Policy Impacts' (Speech delivered at the Pursuing Opportunity and Prosperity Conference, Melbourne Institute of Applied Economic and Social Research/The Australian, Melbourne, 13 November 2003).

Banks, Gary, 'Are We Overcoming Indigenous Disadvantage?' (Speech delivered at Reconciliations Australia's 'Closing the Gap Conversations' Series, Canberra, 7 July 2009).

Beadman, Bob, 'Do Indigenous Youth Have a Dream?' (Menzies Research Centre Ltd, 2004).

Bradfield, Stuart, 'Communal Ownership of Indigenous Land and Individual Wealth Creation: The Debate So Far, Identifying Key Questions' (Paper presented at the National Native Title Conference, Coffs Harbour, 1–3 June 2005).

Bradfield, Stuart, 'White Picket Fence or Trojan Horse? The Debate over Communal Ownership of Indigenous Land and Individual Wealth Creation' (Issues Paper No 3, Australian Institute of Aboriginal and Torres Strait Islander Studies Native Title Research Unit, 2005).

Brennan, Sean, 'Economic Development and Land Council Power: Modernising the Land Rights Act or Same Old Same Old?' (2006) 10(4) *Australian Indigenous Law Reporter* 1.

Commonwealth, *Parliamentary Debates*, House of Representatives, 31 May 2006, 5 (Mal Brough).

Commonwealth, *Parliamentary Debates*, House of Representatives, 19 June 2006, 121 (Mal Brough).

Brough, Mal, 'Blueprint for Action in Indigenous Affairs' (Speech delivered at the National Institute of Governance, Canberra, 5 December 2006).

Brough, Mal, 'Historic Agreement for 99 Year Lease in NT' (Media Release, 30 August 2007).

Calma, Tom, 'Native Title Report 2005' (Australian Human Rights Commission, 2005).

Calma, Tom, 'Social Justice, Communal Lands and Sustainable Communities' in Lee Godden and Maureen Tehan (ed), *Comparative Perspectives on Communal Lands and Individual Ownership: Sustainable Futures* (Routledge, 2010) 49.

Central Land Council, 'Beadman Report Contributes Nothing' (Media Release, 3 June 2004).

Central Land Council, 'Communal Title and Economic Development' (Policy Paper, 2005).

Dalrymple, David, 'Land Rights and Property Rights' (2007) 51(1) *Quadrant* 61.

Dillon, Michael and Neil Westbury, *Beyond Humbug: Transforming Government Engagement with Indigenous Australia* (Seaview Press, 2007).

Dodson, Michael and Diana McCarthy, 'Communal Land and the Amendments to the *Aboriginal Land Rights (Northern Territory) Act*' (Research Discussion Paper No 19, Australian Institute of Aboriginal and Torres Strait Islander Studies, 2006).

Duffy, Michael, 'A Good Land Right Is a Good Deed', *The Sydney Morning Herald* (Sydney), 9 April 2005, 41.

Duncan, Ron, 'Agricultural and Resource Economics and Economic Development in Aboriginal Communities' (2003) 47(3) *Australian Journal of Agricultural and Resource Economics* 307.

Editorial, 'Black Revolution: Economic Engagement Is the Path to Prosperity', *The Australian*, 6 October 2005, 18.

Editorial, 'The House and Land Package?', *The Australian*, 18 November 2010, 15.

Editorial, 'Land Rights Should Apply to Individuals', *The Australian*, 19 February 2005, 13.

Editorial, 'A Reward for Quiet Persistence', *The Australian*, 14 June 2012, 13.

Editorial, 'How to Turn Indigenous Land Rights into Prosperity', *The Australian*, 21 May 2015, 13/

166 *Australian debate about land reform*

Evans, Ray, 'Land Tenure and Impediments to Commercialisation: A Retrospective' (Paper presented at the Bennelong Conference, Melbourne, 10 September 2005).

Ferguson, John, 'Lack of Interest Kills Bennelong Society', *The Australian* (online), 22 November 2011 www.theaustralian.com.au/national-affairs/lack-of-interest-kills-bennelong/story-fn59niix-1226201813451.

Forrest, Andrew, 'The Forrest Review: Creating Parity' (Commonwealth of Australia, 2014).

Fourie, Clarissa, 'Land Readjustment for Peri-Urban Customary Tenure: The Example of Botswana' in Robert Hume and Hilary Lim (eds), *Demystifying the Mystery of Capital: Land Tenure and Poverty in Africa and the Caribbean* (Routledge Cavendish, 2004) 31.

Fuller, Don, Susan Bandias and Darius Pfitzer, 'Utilizing Aboriginal Land in the Northern Territory for Economic and Human Development' (Charles Darwin University, 2011).

Gleeson, Brian, 'Coordinator General for Remote Indigenous Services Six Monthly Report April–September 2011' (Australian Government, 2011).

Godden, Lee, 'Communal Governance of Land and Resources as a Sustainable Institution' in Lee Godden and Maureen Tehan (eds), *Comparative Perspectives on Communal Lands and Individual Ownership: Sustainable Futures* (Routledge, 2010) 385.

Godden, Lee and Maureen Tehan, 'Translating Native Title to Individual "Title" in Australia: Are Real Property Forms and Indigenous Interests Reconcilable?' in Elizabeth Cooke (ed), *Modern Studies in Property Law, Volume 4* (Hart Publishing, 2007) 263.

Godden, Lee and Maureen Tehan, 'Introduction: A Sustainable Future for Communal Lands, Resources and Communities' in Lee Godden and Maureen Tehan (eds), *Comparative Perspectives on Communal Lands and Individual Ownership: Sustainable Futures* (Routledge, 2010) 1.

Grattan, Michelle, 'Howard Tilts at Title Fight', *The Sunday Age* (Melbourne), 10 April 2005, 17.

Gray, Bill and Will Sanders, 'Views from the Top of the "Quiet Revolution": Secretarial Perspectives on the New Arrangements in Indigenous Affairs' (Discussion Paper No 282/2006, Centre for Aboriginal Economic Policy Research, 2006).

Hepburn, Samantha, 'Transforming Customary Title to Individual Title: Revisiting the Cathedral' (2006) 11(1) *Deakin Law Review* 63.

Howard, John, 'Address to the National Reconciliation Planning Workshop' (Speech delivered at the National Reconciliation Planning Workshop, Canberra, 30 May 2005).

Howard-Wagner, Deidre, 'The Denial of Separate Rights: Political Rationalities And Technologies Governing Indigenous Affairs as Practices Of Whiteness' (Paper presented at The Australian Sociological Association Annual Conference, Auckland, New Zealand, 4–7 December 2007).

Howey, Kirsty, ' "Normalising" What? A Qualitative Analysis of Aboriginal Land Tenure Reform in the Northern Territory of Australia' (2014–15) 18(1) *Australian Indigenous Law Review* 4.

Howson, Peter, 'Why We Desperately Need New Aboriginal Policies' (Bennelong Society, 10 May 2002).

Howson, Peter, 'Aborigines Need Economic Assimilation' (Bennelong Society, 31 March 2003).

Howson, Peter, 'The Failure of Aboriginal Segregation' (2003) 47(5) *Quadrant* 50.

Howson, Peter, 'Land Rights: The Next Battleground' (2005) 49(6) *Quadrant* 24.

Hudson, Sara, 'From Rhetoric to Reality: Can 99-year Leases Lead to Homeownership for Indigenous Communities?' (Policy Monograph 92, Centre for Independent Studies, 2009).

Hughes, Helen, 'The Economics of Indigenous Deprivation and Proposals for Reform' (Issue Analysis No 63, Centre for Independent Studies, 23 September 2005).

Hughes, Helen and Jenness Warin, 'A New Deal for Aborigines and Torres Strait Islanders in Remote Communities' (Issues Analysis No 54, Centre for Independent Studies, 1 March 2005).

Hughes, Helen, Sara Hudson and Mark Hughes, 'Lands Where No One Can Feel at Home', *The Australian*, 25 June 2011, 6.

Hughes, Helen, Mark Hughes and Sara Hudson, 'Private Housing in Indigenous Lands' (Policy Monograph 113, Centre for Independent Studies, 2010).

Johns, Gary, 'The Poverty of Aboriginal Self-Determination' in Gary Johns (ed), *Waking up to the Dreamtime: The Illusion of Aboriginal Self-Determination* (Media Masters, 2001) 15.

Johns, Gary, 'Look for Strength in Mainstream', *The Australian*, 22 November 2001, 11.

Johns, Gary, 'The Gulf between Aboriginal Policies and Aboriginal People in Australia' (Libertad y Desarrollo Institute, 6 June 2003).

Johns, Gary, 'Integration Gives Head Start to Life Chances', *The Australian*, 2 February 2004, 7.

Johns, Gary and Ron Brunton, 'Separate Path to Division', *The Australian*, 12 April 2000, 15.

Johnson, Andrew, 'Unlocking the North', *The Australian*, 14 June 2013, 10.

Karvelas, Patricia, 'Brough to Hold Radical Talks on Ending Violence', *The Australian*, 18 May 2006, 4.

Karvelas, Patricia, 'Axe Public Housing: Pearson', *The Australian*, 21 February 2007, 15.

Karvelas, Patricia, 'Land Rights May Be Privatised', *The Australian*, 10 December 2010, 4.

Kearney, Simon *et al.*, 'Some "Not Ready" for Aussie Dream', *The Australian*, 21 February 2008, 1.

Khadem, Nassim, '99-Year Lease Plan for Aboriginal Land', *The Age* (Melbourne), 6 October 2005.

Lee, Penny, 'Individual Titling of Aboriginal Land in the Northern Territory: What Australia Can Learn from the International Community' (2006) 29(2) *University of New South Wales Law Journal* 22.

Liberal Party of Australia, *Aboriginal Home Ownership* (21 December 2010) www.liberal.org.au/latest-news/2010/12/21/aboriginal-home-ownership-0.

The Liberal Party and The Nationals, 'The Coalition's Policy for Indigenous Affairs' (September 2013).

McDonnell, John, 'Land Rights and Aboriginal Development' (2005) 49(6) *Quadrant* 30.

Commonwealth, Parliamentary Debates, House of Representatives, 12 June 2007, 91 (Jenny Macklin).

168 Australian debate about land reform

Macklin, Jenny, 'Closing the Gap: Building an Indigenous Future' (Speech delivered to the National Press Club, Canberra, 27 February 2008).

Macklin, Jenny, 'Address to the NSW Aboriginal Land Council' (Speech delivered to the NSW Aboriginal Land Council, Cessnock, 5 March 2009).

Macklin, Jenny, 'Building the Foundations for Change' (Speech delivered at the Sydney Institute, Sydney, 9 August 2011).

McRae, Heather *et al.*, *Indigenous Legal Issues, Commentary and Materials* (Thomson Reuters, 2009).

Maddison, Sarah, *Black Politics: Inside the Complexity of Aboriginal Political Culture* (Allen & Unwin, 2009).

Martin, David, 'Money, Business and Culture: Issues for Aboriginal Economic Policy' (Discussion Paper No 101/1995, Centre for Aboriginal Economic Policy Research, 1995).

Martin, David, 'Policy Alchemy and the Magical Transformation of Aboriginal Society' in Yasmine Musharbash and Marcus Barber (eds), *Ethnography & the Production of Anthropological Knowledge: Essays in Honour of Nicolas Peterson* (Australian National University E Press, 2011) 201.

Merlan, Francesca, 'The Regimentation of Customary Practice: From Northern Territory Land Claims to Mabo' (1995) 6(1/2) *Australian Journal of Anthropology* 64.

Metherell, Mark, 'Sorry Will Not Change Lives, Says Mundine', *The Sydney Morning Herald* (Sydney), 6 December 2004, 2.

Metherell, Mark, 'Land System Holds Us Back, Says Mundine', *The Sydney Morning Herald* (Sydney), 7 December 2004, 6.

Metherell, Mark, 'PM Backs Indigenous Enterprise', *The Sydney Morning Herald* (Sydney), 10 December 2004, 7.

Moran, Mark, 'Home Ownership for Indigenous People Living on Community Title Land in Queensland: Scoping Study Report' (Queensland Aboriginal Coordinating Council, Aboriginal and Torres Strait Islander Commission, 1999).

Moran, Mark, *Practising Self-Determination: Participation in Planning and Local Governance in Discrete Indigenous Settlements* (PhD Thesis, University of Queensland, 2006).

Moran, Mark *et al.*, 'Home Ownership for Indigenous People Living on Community Title Land in Queensland: Preliminary Community Survey' (Aboriginal Environments Research Centre, University of Queensland, 2001).

Mundine, Warren, 'Aboriginal Governance and Economic Development' (Paper presented at the National Native Title Conference, Coffs Harbour, 1–3 June 2005).

Mundine, Warren, 'Shooting an Elephant: Four Giant Steps' (Speech delivered to the Garma Festival Corporate Dinner, 10 August 2013).

Murdoch, Lindsay, 'Great Australian Dream Time ... a Home to Call Their Own', *The Sydney Morning Herald* (Sydney), 15 April 2010, 7.

National Indigenous Council, 'Possible Indigenous Land Tenure Principles' (Draft Working Document, National Indigenous Council, 3 June 2005).

Newman, Campbell, 'Hope for Indigenous Home Owners' (Media Release, 15 January 2013).

Northern Territory Government, Submission No 61 to the Senate Community Affairs Committee, Parliament of Australia, *Inquiry into the Recommendations of the Reeves Report Review of the Aboriginal Land Rights (Northern Territory) Act 1976*, June 1999.

Northern Territory Government, 'Chief Minister Orders Inquiry into Child Sex Abuse' (Media Release, 22 June 2006).

Northern Territory Government, 'Little Children Are Sacred' (Report of the Northern Territory Board of Inquiry into the Protection of Aboriginal Children from Sexual Abuse, 2007).

Pearson, Christopher, 'Case to Put the Lands Right', *The Weekend Australian*, 11 December 2004, 18.

Pearson, Noel, 'Review: *The Mystery of Capital: Why Capitalism Triumphs in the West and Fails Everywhere Else* by Hernando de Soto' (September 2001) *Australian Public Intellectual Network*.

Pearson, Noel, 'Reconciliation a Building Block', *The Australian*, 19 April 2005, 13.

Pearson, Noel, 'Hats off to Katter's Grand Plan', *The Australian*, 7 May 2011, 12.

Pearson, Noel and Lara Kostakidis-Lianos, 'Building Indigenous Capital: Removing Obstacles to Participation in the Real Economy' (Cape York Institute, 2004).

Perche, Diana, 'Indigenous Land Reform and the Market: Changing Social Constructions in Indigenous Land Policy during the Howard Era' (Paper presented at Australian Political Studies Association Annual Conference, Macquarie University, Sydney, 30 September 2009).

Perche, Diana, 'Dialogue between Past and Present: Policy Evaluation and History' (2011) 57(3) *Australian Journal of Politics and History* 403.

Reeves, John, 'Building on Land Rights for the Next Generation: The Review of the *Aboriginal Land Rights (Northern Territory) Act 1976*' (Australian Government, 1998).

Ridgeway, Aden, 'Addressing the Economic Exclusion of Indigenous Australians through Native Title' (Paper presented at the Native Title Conference, Coffs Harbour, 1–3 June 2005).

Rowland, Barry W., 'Examination of the Aboriginal Land Rights (Northern Territory) Act 1976–80' (Department of Aboriginal Affairs, 1980).

Rowse, Tim, 'The National Emergency and Indigenous Jurisdictions' in Jon Altman and Melinda Hinkson (eds), *Coercive Reconciliation: Stabilise, Normalise, Exit Aboriginal Australia* (Arena Publications, 2007) 47.

Commonwealth, *Parliamentary Debates*, House of Representatives, 26 February 2009, 2031 (Kevin Rudd).

Sanders, Will, 'Indigenous Housing Tenure in Remote Areas: Directions and Constraints' (Topical Issue No 6/2008, Centre for Aboriginal Economic Policy Research, 2008).

Scullion, Nigel, 'Historic Arnhem Land Lease Agreement' (Media Release, 17 October 2013).

Scullion, Nigel, 'Pirlangimpi Township Lease Agreement' (Media Release, 14 March 2014).

Scullion, Nigel, 'Land Reform for the Future', *Koori Mail*, 26 March 2014.

Scullion, Nigel, '2014 National Native Title Conference Speech' (Speech delivered at the National Native Title Conference, Coffs Harbour, 2 June 2014).

Shanahan, Dennis and Patricia Karvelas, 'PM Considers New Land Rights Plan', *The Weekend Australian*, 11 December 2004, 4.

Shillito, Lewis, 'Strata Title Aboriginal Towns? An Alternative to the Town-Leasing Proposal' (2007) 14(3) *Australian Property Law Journal* 201.

Commonwealth, Parliamentary Debates, House of Representatives, 19 June 2006, 83 (Warren Snowdon).

170 Australian debate about land reform

Stephenson, Margaret, 'Reforms to Indigenous Land in Australia: Some Lessons from Other Jurisdictions' (Paper presented at Australasian Law Teachers Association Annual Conference, Melbourne, 4–7 July 2006).

Stephenson, Margaret, 'Individual Title versus Collective Title in Australia: Reflections on the Northern American and New Zealand Experiences of Indigenous Title to Land' in Elizabeth Cooke (ed), *Modern Studies in Property Law, Volume 4* (Hart Publishing, 2007) 295.

Stephenson, Margaret, 'To Lease or Not to Lease? The Leasing of Indigenous Statutory Lands in Australia: Lessons from Canada' (2009) 35(3) *Commonwealth Law Bulletin* 545.

Sutton, Peter, 'Suggestions for a Bicameral System' (1984) 5(3) *Anthropological Forum* 395.

Sutton, Peter, 'Anthropological Submission on the Reeves Review' (1999) 9(2) *Anthropological Forum* 189.

Sutton, Peter, 'Stanner and Aboriginal Land Use: Ecology, Economic Change, and Enclosing the Commons' in Melinda Hinkson and Jeremy Beckett (eds), *An Appreciate of Difference: WEH Stanner and Aboriginal Australia* (Aboriginal Studies Press, 2008) 169.

Tehan, Maureen, 'Customary Land Tenure, Communal Titles and Sustainability: The Allure of Individual Title and Property Rights in Australia' in Lee Godden and Maureen Tehan (eds), *Comparative Perspectives on Communal Lands and Individual Ownership: Sustainable Futures* (Routledge, 2010) 353.

Toohey, John, 'Seven Years on: Report by Mr Justice Toohey to the Minister for Aboriginal Affairs on the *Aboriginal Land Rights (Northern Territory) Act 1976* and Related Matters' (Australian Government, 1983).

Toohey, Paul, 'A New Lease of Life', *The Weekend Australian Magazine*, 10 January 2009, 14.

Vanstone, Amanda, 'Address to National Press Club' (Speech delivered at the National Press Club, Canberra, 23 February 2005).

Vanstone, Amanda, 'Address to the Reconciliation Australia Conference' (Speech delivered at the National Reconciliation Planning Workshop, Canberra, 31 May 2005).

Vanstone, Amanda, 'Beyond Conspicuous Compassion: Indigenous Australians Deserve More Than Good Intentions' (Speech delivered to the Australia and New Zealand School of Government, Australian National University, Canberra, 7 December 2005).

Viner, Ian, 'A Review of the Reeves Report: Whither Land Rights in the Northern Territory? Whither Aboriginal Self-determination?' (15 July 1999) *Online Opinion* www.onlineopinion.com.au/view.asp?article=1084&page=0.

Wallace, Jude, 'Managing Social Tenure' in Lee Godden and Maureen Tehan (eds), *Comparative Perspectives on Communal Land and Individual Ownership: Sustainable Futures* (Routledge, 2010) 25.

Warby, Michael, *Past Wrongs, Future Rights: Anti-Discrimination, Native Title and Aboriginal and Torres Strait Islander Policy, 1975–1997* (Tasman Institute, 1997).

Warby, Michael, *What Makes a Third World Country?* (1 January 2001) Institute of Public Affairs www.ipa.org.au/news/520/what-makes-a-third-world-country-/pg/10.

Watson, Nicole, 'Howard's End: The Real Agenda behind the Proposed Review of Indigenous Land Titles' (2005) 9(4) *Australian Indigenous Law Reporter* 1.

Watson, Nicole, 'Review of Aboriginal Land Titles' (Briefing Paper No 7, Jumbunna Indigenous House of Learning, September 2005).

Watson, Nicole, 'The Abuse of Indigenous Land Tenure as a Tool of Social Engineering' (2008) 1 *Journal of the Australasian Law Teachers' Association* 163.

Wilson, Ashleigh and Amanda Hodge, 'PM's New Deal for Blacks: Private Homes to Be Allowed on Native Title', *The Australian*, 7 April 2005, 1.

Wood, Alan, 'Individual Enterprise the Key to Progress for Aborigines', *The Australian*, 29 April 2003, 13.

Legislation

Aboriginal Land Rights (Northern Territory) Act 1976 (Cth).
Native Title Act 1993 (Cth).

Cases

Wik Peoples v Queensland (1996) 187 CLR 1.

6 The reforms

6.1 Introduction

It was against the background of this flawed debate that the Australian Government began implementing its Indigenous land tenure reforms. It has ultimately introduced three sets of reforms in the period since 2006. Two are specific to Aboriginal land in the Northern Territory, while the third also affects housing in larger communities on Indigenous land in other jurisdictions. Further to this, and partly in response to pressure from the Australian Government, several state governments have introduced changes to their statutory land rights schemes. The Queensland Government has made a number of amendments to make it easier to grant leases over Indigenous land in that state,[1] and has more recently enacted legislation that enables certain areas of Indigenous land to be divided up and converted to ordinary freehold. The South Australian Government has rewritten the legislation for one of its schemes.[2] That legislation was very old and it was updated for several reasons, including a desire to make it easier to grant leases and other interests.[3] Western Australia does not have statutory land rights as such, but has been investigating options for land tenure reform on its Aboriginal Lands Trust estate.[4]

This chapter describes the four most important of these reforms: the three sets of reforms to Aboriginal land in the Northern Territory and the more recent introduction of legislation to allow for the allotment of Indigenous land in Queensland. The reforms to Aboriginal land in the Northern Territory were the first and are the most developed and wide-ranging. They also have a broader significance in that they represent the vanguard of the Australian Government's efforts at reforming Indigenous land tenure. The recent Queensland legislation is significant for a different reason. Ultimately, all of the other reforms involve more widespread leasing and subleasing on Indigenous land. In some cases those leases are long-term, but underlying ownership remains with the Indigenous landowners. The Queensland amendments represent the first attempt by an Australian government to enable the allotment of Indigenous land (which is also sometimes called 'individuation'), which means that they raise a different set of issues from the other reforms.

The reforms   173

Each section of this chapter is devoted to a separate reform. Section 6.2 describes township leases, the first of the Australian Government's reforms and the one most closely connected to the debate. The government often referred specifically to township leasing when it first announced its intention to introduce land reform, and it is instructive to compare the outcomes of township leasing with the debate. Section 6.3 describes the land reforms included in the Northern Territory Emergency Response, or Intervention. The Intervention was the most dramatic development in Australian Indigenous policy for decades. Among its several significant reforms were four in relation to Aboriginal land tenure. Some of these measures are ongoing, while others – most notably the five-year leases – were subject to a sunset clause that has now come and gone. The five-year leases have nevertheless had an enduring impact on relationships around land use in Aboriginal communities.

Section 6.4 deals with reforms to housing tenure and the related introduction of 'secure tenure' policies, reforms that also extend to communities beyond the Northern Territory. The allotment of Indigenous land in Queensland is described in Section 6.5. The chapter concludes in Section 6.6 with a summary and discussion of the cumulative impact of the reforms.

6.2 Township leasing

Overview

Township leasing is the most complete land reform model that the Australian Government has yet developed. The five-year leases were short-term and have now ended. 'Secure tenure' policies cover only certain infrastructure, albeit the greater portion of all infrastructure. Township leases are long-term and cover entire communities. However, township leasing is also the least widespread of the reforms. To date, there are only three township leases covering six communities, all of which are situated on off-shore islands. There are no township leases on the mainland. This may soon change, as the government has reported that lease negotiations are under way for several further communities.[5] Township leasing also remains the government's reform of choice. It has on a number of occasions said that it would like to see township leases over all major communities, and identifies the negotiation of township leases as one of its key strategies for increasing employment in communities on Aboriginal land.[6] The current Minister has argued that township leasing 'has brought about change unlike any seen before in remote Aboriginal communities'.[7] This means that the significance of township leasing as a reform extends beyond the three existing leases.

174 *The reforms*

Development of the township leasing model

In 2004 the Northern Territory (NT) Government drafted a 'concept paper' on a new leasing model for communities on land held under the *Aboriginal Land Rights (Northern Territory) Act 1976* (Cth) (the ALRA).[8] It provided copies of the paper to each of the Aboriginal Land Councils and later to the Australian Government.[9] When the more widespread debate about Aboriginal land reform began in December 2004, it appears that the Prime Minster was already familiar with the contents of the paper as he specifically referred to a proposal for 99-year leases.[10] The following April, his government announced plans to introduce a new leasing system for 'Aboriginal townships' based on the model proposed by the NT Government.[11] A Bill to enable what by then was called 'township leasing' was presented to Parliament in May 2006.[12] The Bill also provided for several other changes, and collectively represented the most extensive and far-reaching amendments to the ALRA since its introduction.[13] As it held a majority in both Houses, the Howard Government secured passage of the legislation without having to negotiate with the Opposition or minor parties. After a brief Senate inquiry, the *Aboriginal Land Rights (Northern Territory) Amendment Act 2006* (Cth) was enacted in August 2006.[14] Township leasing was enabled through the insertion of a new section 19A into the ALRA; consequently township leases are also sometimes referred to as 'section 19A leases'.

Section 19A

Elements of the township leasing model

In short, township leasing is a particular – and highly exogenous – model for formalising tenure arrangements in communities on Aboriginal land. Its core elements are most easily explained diagrammatically. Chapter 4 describes how previously there have been very few leases in communities on ALRA land and, for the most part, the relationship between the Land Trust and occupiers has been informal. This is depicted in Figure 6.1, which also divides infrastructure into the three categories used in Chapter 4.

As the diagram depicts, with respect to housing for Aboriginal residents ('residential housing') there were in fact two informal interfaces: between the Land Trust and the housing manager (ICHO), and between the housing manager and the residents of each house.

Under a township lease, the entire area of land in and around a community is leased to a statutory body, which has the power to grant subleases and licences over sections of the community without requiring further permission from the landowners. It is formalisation through a two-step process. The first step is for the Land Trust to grant a township lease – which is effectively a head lease – to the statutory body, and the second step is for the statutory body to grant subleases and licences to each

The reforms 175

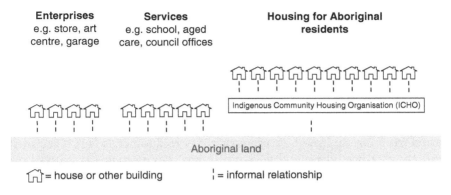

Figure 6.1 The pre-existing tenure arrangements.

occupier, which takes place over a longer period of time. The situation after both stages are complete is depicted in Figure 6.2, which also shows the new arrangements with respect to residential housing that are described below in Section 6.4.

Figure 6.2 shows the basic structure of the township leasing model. In fact, all elements of this model except for preserved rights (see below) could have been implemented through the existing section 19 leasing provisions. It appears that the reason for introducing section 19A was so that core elements of the township leasing model could be embedded in the legislation itself, making them inviolable. The following sections describe how this has been achieved.

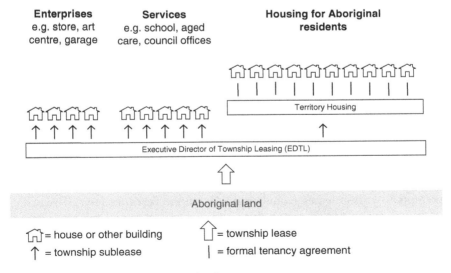

Figure 6.2 Outcome under a township lease.

176 *The reforms*

Restrictions on the terms of a section 19A lease

There are no restrictions on the terms that can be included in a section 19 lease. It simply enables leasing over ALRA land. By contrast, there are three sets of restrictions on leases granted under section 19A. The first is in relation to the period of the lease. A lease under section 19A must be for a period of between 40 and 99 years, and, once agreed to, the period of the lease cannot be reduced, even by further agreement of the parties.[15] Second, section 19A imposes restrictions on the transfer or encumbrance of a township lease. A township lease cannot be mortgaged, and can only be transferred from one approved government entity to another.[16] This reflects its purpose as a head lease and does not in any way prevent the transfer or encumbrance of subleases.

Third, and most importantly, section 19A imposes restrictions on the terms that may be included in a township lease. A township lease cannot contain (a) a term requiring the payment, or non-payment, of rent under a sublease, or (b) a term that requires the consent of any person to the grant of a sublease.[17] This prevents the traditional owners from using the terms of the head lease to retain control over certain decision-making. Restricting the level of traditional owner-control over subleases is one of the key elements of the township leasing model.[18]

The identity of the leaseholder

Whereas a section 19 lease can be granted to any person, in keeping with its purpose a lease under section 19A can only be granted to an 'approved government entity'. Initially, it was intended that the NT Government would create this entity, but in 2006 support for township leasing within the NT Government waned and relations between the two governments soured.[19] This lead to the Australian Government creating its own approved entity through further amendments to the ALRA in 2007.[20] The entity was called the Executive Director of Township Leasing, or EDTL. In 2008, the Rudd Labor Government increased the statutory functions of the EDTL,[21] allowing it to also hold and manage 'housing precinct leases' and subleases over town camp land (see below).

Exemption from certain laws

To make the formalisation process easier and cheaper, section 19A exempts township leases from certain Northern Territory laws. Township leases are exempt from stamp duty and must be accepted for registration on the land titles register despite any irregularities. Further, rules in relation to the subdivision of land do not apply to the grant of a township lease.[22] The Act also empowers the Australian Government to make regulations that modify Northern Territory property law as it applies to township leases.[23] This power was exercised in December 2008 with the passage of regulations that make it easier for the EDTL to formalise the subdivision of infrastructure within a township lease.[24]

The purpose of modifying these laws is to reduce the costs associated with creating smaller land parcels. It does so by circumventing the normal planning procedures, effecting a legal bias in favour of leases and subleases held by the EDTL. Other communities on Aboriginal land have not been extended the same exemptions. The EDTL has reported that, where practical, normal planning procedures have been followed.[25]

Preserved rights and interests

As township leases cover entire communities, they may include areas that are already subject to a section 19 lease or in relation to which the occupant has some other formal or informal right of occupancy. Section 19A allows for those interests to be preserved and to continue for the duration of the township lease as if they were granted by the EDTL in place of the Land Trust.[26] Again, this simplifies and makes easier the formalisation process.

The three existing township leases

The three leases

While section 19A of the ALRA embeds certain elements of township leasing – such as restricting the ability of traditional owners to impose controls over the grant of subleases – it does not set out all elements of the model. Much also depends on the terms of each lease, as well as the policies and activities of the EDTL. This section sets out some of the decisions that have been made with respect to the three existing township leases.

The first township lease was granted on 30 August 2007, for a period of 99 years and over the community of Wurrumiyanga, which at the time was called Nguiu (the 'Wurrumiyanga lease').[27] On 4 December 2008, a second township lease was granted over the three communities of Angurugu, Umbakumba and Milyakburra (the 'Anindilyakwa lease'), for an effective period of 80 years. Attracting less publicity, a third township lease was granted over the communities of Milikapiti and Wurankuwu on 22 November 2011 (the 'Milikapiti lease'), also for a period of 99 years. The Wurrumiyanga and Milikapiti leases are both situated on the Tiwi Islands, which are to the north of Darwin, and their terms are almost identical. The Anindilyakwa lease covers communities on Groote Eylandt and Bickerton Island, which are further to the east off the coast of Arnhem Land. The leases cover all existing infrastructure as well as an area of land surrounding each community.[28]

178 *The reforms*

Rent and other benefits

(A) RENT

Rent under the township leases has a fixed, up-front component and a variable, ongoing component. The variable component is based on the rent received on subleases.[29] The EDTL must record the amount of rent it receives and, after deducting operating expenses, pay the balance as rent on the township lease. Below it is described how the EDTL has pursued policies that mean rent on subleases will exceed expenses in the long term, so traditional owners will receive ongoing rent.

In addition to this, each lease provides for a one-off, up-front payment, the purpose of which is to make township leasing more attractive to landowners. The up-front payment is also the minimum payment for the first 15 years of the lease, meaning that during the first 15 years additional rent will only be paid if the total variable rent exceeds the up-front payment. This has led the Northern Land Council to characterise the up-front payment as a loan.[30] The up-front payment for the Wurrumiyanga lease was $5 million, meaning that landowners will not receive any further rent during the first 15 years unless the total variable rent during that period exceeds $5 million, which is unlikely.[31] For the Anindilyakwa lease, the introductory payment was reduced to $4.5 million, in total, for all three communities.[32] Under the Milikapiti lease, the introductory payment was $1.76 million for Milikapiti and $0.19 million for Wurankuwu.[33]

(B) COMMUNITY BENEFITS

Chapter 4 describes how in most communities on Aboriginal land the majority of residents are not traditional owners for that land. Wurrumiyanga is a good example of this: there are around 250 traditional owners,[34] for a community of between 1,265 and 1,582 residents.[35] Non-traditional owner residents will not directly benefit from rent on the township lease, and so the Australian Government further offered a benefits package for each community. For Wurrumiyanga, the package included 25 new houses, repairs and maintenance on all other houses, $1 million for additional health initiatives, improvements to the cemetery and a community profile study.[36] Dillon and Westbury report that this benefits package was influential in securing support for the lease.[37] For the communities subject to the Anindilyakwa lease, there was also a set of housing, education and training benefits,[38] while for Milikapiti and Wurankuwu the community benefits package was more flexible: amounts of $1.5 million and $160,000 respectively were allocated, with the community having some discretion about how the money was spent.[39]

While these packages are clearly of benefit to the subject communities, it would be misleading to characterise them as a benefit of township leasing.

The reforms 179

They are more in the nature of an inducement, as they represent the allocation of discretionary spending to particular communities on the basis of their adopting the government's preferred approach to land reform.

Subleases and licences

Once a township lease is granted, the EDTL may grant subleases and licences over portions of the lease area without requiring the further consent of the land owners. However, each township lease contains a number of rules that the EDTL must follow when granting subleases (and licences). The two most important are described here.

(A) SUBLEASES ON A COMMERCIAL BASIS

All three township leases contain a rule that subleases must be granted 'on a commercial basis applying sound business principles'.[40] There are potential exceptions to this rule for subleases to a sacred site authority[41] or community benefit organisation.[42] For all other subleases – such as a sublease to a government department, housing authority, home owner or enterprise – the text of the lease suggests that rent must be charged on a 'commercial basis'.

However, this does need to be read in light of section 19A(15) of the ALRA, which provides that a township lease 'must not contain any provision relating to the payment of rent, or the non-payment of rent, in relation to a sublease of the lease'. Both the general rule and the exceptions to it would appear to be provisions 'relating to the payment of rent, or the non-payment of rent, in relation to a sublease', and consequently in breach of section 19A(15). To the extent this is the case, the EDTL is not bound by them. The reason for including a clause that is clearly inconsistent with the ALRA has not been explained. Its effect is to give the impression that landowners have greater control over the subleasing process than is in fact the reality. That said, with the notable exception of subleases over residential housing, the EDTL has pursued a policy of seeking 'commercial' rent on subleases.

(B) RESTRICTIONS ON TRANSFER

The township leases also impose some restrictions on the transfer or alienability of subleases. This is achieved in several ways. The Wurrumiyanga and Milikapiti leases require the EDTL to ensure that sublease holders do not part with or share possession of their sublease other than with a relative, without the prior written consent of the Land Trust and the EDTL.[43] Those leases also include a rule that the grant of a sublease must not 'directly result in the number of Non-Tiwi Permanent Residents of the Township' exceeding 15 per cent of the total population, unless the

180   *The reforms*

Consultative Forum (see below) increases this limit.[44] The EDTL reports that this is not currently an issue in Wurrumiyanga as the percentage of Non-Tiwi Permanents Residents is between 5 and 7 per cent.[45] There is no equivalent provision in the Anindilyakwa lease, which instead contains a rule specific to housing whereby a residential sublease can only be granted to people falling within certain identified categories, although those categories are broad.[46]

All three leases provide that the EDTL must not grant a sublease to any person who is not a 'fit and proper person', and in particular must not grant a sublease to any person convicted of certain sexual offences or crimes against children.[47] To establish this, the EDTL must obtain a national police record check. There are no exceptions to this rule for traditional owners or Aboriginal residents.

Role of the Consultative Forum

The main thing that a township lease does is to give the EDTL control over the process of formalising tenure in the lease area. Within the constraints described above, the EDTL has a broad discretion as to how it does so. There is a single forum for Aboriginal input into the EDTL's decision-making, which is a body called the 'Consultative Forum'. The Consultative Forum is an unincorporated body made up of nominees of the Land Trust and the EDTL, with the majority being nominees of the Land Trust.[48] It meets about twice a year.[49]

The three leases prescribe several situations where the EDTL is required to consult with the Consultative Forum in the course of decision-making. In almost all cases the EDTL must 'have due regard to' its recommendations, but is not required to follow its directions. For example, the EDTL must consult with the Consultative Forum about the grant of a sublease over residential housing to Territory Housing,[50] but is not bound by its recommendations.[51] There are two relatively minor exceptions in the Wurrumiyanga and Milikapiti leases, where the EDTL does need the consent of the Consultative Forum. The EDTL cannot allow the construction of buildings above a certain height or too close to the water without the consent of the Consultative Forum.[52] Further, only the Consultative Forum may increase the limit of 15 per cent with respect to non-Tiwi permanent residents.[53] In all other circumstances, the Consultative Forum makes only recommendations.

Consultative Forum members are effectively appointed by the traditional owners, rather than by community residents as a whole. There is no additional forum for input by community residents, except where they form part of 'the public'.[54] The outcome is that the only local Aboriginal input into decision-making under the township lease is by representatives of the traditional owners through the Consultative Forum, and in most instances the EDTL is only required to 'have due regard to' their recommendations. The EDTL has stated that the role of the Consultative Forum is to provide advice 'about issues of importance to the Township' and keep the EDTL 'aware of emerging issues'.[55] Actual responsibility for decision-making belongs to the EDTL.

Policies and practices of the EDTL

In short, the EDTL has considerable discretion with respect to the formalisation process. There are certain rules that must be followed, but it is the EDTL that ultimately determines to whom subleases are granted, for how long they are granted and (as a result of section 19A(15) of the ALRA) the amount of rent that is sought. This section details how the EDTL has approached these decisions.

The allocation of subleases

(A) PROCESS FOR THE GRANT OF SUBLEASES

One of the more important steps in any formalisation process is deciding to whom formal rights are granted. In communities on Aboriginal land, the majority of infrastructure is already occupied and for the most part the EDTL has simply contacted existing occupiers and told them of the need to obtain a sublease. Residential housing is an exception, in that the sublease has been granted to Territory Housing rather than directly to residents. This is part of the new housing policies described below.

The process is more involved with respect to land or infrastructure that is unoccupied. The EDTL has developed certain procedures to deal with this. For example, it has published a 'Residential Sublease Application Form'[56] and a 'Commercial Sublease Application Form',[57] which detail the sort of information required of applicants. Applicants for a commercial sublease must provide such information as a business plan, a description of the entity's ownership structure and the details of any proposed infrastructure. The form provides some guidance as to the principles against which applications will be assessed. The EDTL has described some of the challenges in applying these principles, such as assessing whether additional competition is likely to be helpful or harmful to the community.[58] In most communities, land is abundant but there are limits on the availability of serviced lots. This means that the EDTL can be required to weigh the question of which applicants should be given priority.[59] To date, the EDTL has involved the Consultative Forum in these decisions.

What emerges from this description is that the EDTL operates in the manner that might be expected of any bureaucratic agency. There are forms, procedures and policies, some of which have been published. There is consultation with stakeholders, in particular the Consultative Forum. And due to the way in which subleases have been granted, the role of the

182   *The reforms*

EDTL is ongoing. It is not simply a matter of finalising subleases and step-
ping back. Certain ongoing management is required, such as approving (or
refusing to approve) the transfer of a sublease.

(B) TO WHOM HAVE SUBLEASES BEEN GRANTED?

The Wurrumiyanga township lease was the first to be granted and most of
the community has now been subleased, making it the most useful site for
a study of sublease holders. It cannot be considered an 'average' community as the circumstances of communities vary too much. With its population of between 1,265 and 1,582 residents, Wurrumiyanga is also one of
the largest communities. It does nevertheless provide some indication as to
what might be expected in other communities on Aboriginal land. The
table in Figure 6.3 describes all recorded subleases for Wurrumiyanga,
using the groupings (residential housing, service providers, enterprises) set
out in Chapter 4.[60]

As the table demonstrates, residential housing is by far the single largest
form of infrastructure in Aboriginal communities – as it is in most places.
Wurrumiyanga has the most advanced home ownership programme of any
community on Indigenous land in Australia, the outcome of a multi-million
dollar programme that is detailed in Chapter 7. However, home ownership
still represents only a small proportion of all residential housing. Around 5
per cent of Aboriginal households have purchased a home, while the
remaining 95 per cent remain in social housing. For the moment, the level
of home ownership has also plateaued. Most grants occurred in 2009 and
there have been no further grants since November 2010. It appears that
some initial saturation point has been reached.

Beyond this there have been no subleases to individuals or families. That
is, there has been no 'individual ownership' beyond the 15 home ownership grants. The largest holders of subleases are the NT Government, the
Regional Council and the Catholic Church. A smaller number have been
granted to service providing NGOs and enterprises. The table also provides
a clear picture of the nature of economic activity in remote communities
on Aboriginal land. It is an economy dominated by government-funded
service provision. This has consequences for land reform. When we talk
about community-wide reforms to tenure arrangements, we are mainly
talking about arrangements for service providers and for residential
housing. While so often the focus of debate has been on enterprises, in
reality that is a small part of the story.

The terms of subleases

The EDTL has developed two sets of standard terms to assist with the
drafting of subleases.[61] The first is for residential subleases, which means
staff housing and home ownership rather than social housing. Social

Sublease holder	Duration	Number of lots
Residential Housing		
Territory Housing	60 years	281
Home owners	99 years	15
Total number of residential housing lots		296
Service providers		
Catholic Church	20 years	26
Tiwi Islands Regional Council	20 years	22
Northern Territory Government	20 years	17
Bathurst Island Housing Association	20 years	10
Indigenous Essential Services (NT Government-owned corporation responsible for power, water and sewerage)	20 years	8
Calvary Home Care Services	20 years	2
Tiwi Training and Employment Ltd	20 years	2
Menzies School of Health	20 years	1
Red Cross	20 years	1
Northern Territory General Practice Education Limited	20 years	1
Total number of service provider lots		93
Enterprises		
Mantiyupwi Pty Ltd (owned by traditional owners)	20 years	8
	5 years	2
Nguiu Ullintjinni Association (store and garage)	20 years	7
Tiwi Design (art centre)	20 years	3
Nguiu Club Association (licensed bar)	20 years	2
Ngaruwanajirri Artists (art centre)	20 years	1
Tiwi Enterprises Pty Ltd	20 years	1
Renhe (Australia) Investment Group (property developer)	20 years	1
Wulirankuwu Trust	20 years	1
Total number of enterprise lots		26
TOTAL		415

Figure 6.3 Table of Wurrumiyanga subleases.

housing has been subleased to Territory Housing pursuant to the new housing policy described in Section 6.4. The second set of standard terms is for commercial premises.[62] Of note is the approach that has been taken to alienability. The law around this is complex, as it involves the intersection between sublease terms, legislation and case law, but in summary the standard sublease terms provide only a limited right of alienability.

Specifically, the standard terms provide that a sublease holder cannot transfer or share possession – other than to or with a relative[63] – without the prior written consent of the EDTL.[64] For commercial premises, the consent of the Land Trust is also required.[65] This is subject to a statutory

184　*The reforms*

rule (which applies to any lease or sublease) that 'consent is not to be unreasonably withheld'.[66] There is a great deal of case law about what amounts to an unreasonable withholding of consent.[67] It is not yet clear how that case law will apply to the rather particular circumstances of a township sublease. What is clear is that the standard terms attempt to create a right of alienability that is limited, so that the EDTL and in some cases the Land Trust retain some control over the reallocation of subleases.

Rent on subleases

One of the most enduring impacts of township leasing has been with respect to rent. With the notable exception of Territory Housing, sublease holders are now expected to pay rent, which is a development that has spread to communities without a township lease (see below). The extent of the change has been significant. Prior to the township lease in Wurrumiyanga, only $2,000 per year was being collected in rent. By 2014 this had increased to $642,000 per year.[68]

The office of the EDTL has developed sophisticated processes for determining the appropriate rent for each sublease. It has engaged a valuation company from Darwin to provide advice on 'what you might call a market price, bearing in mind that there is not really a market'.[69] This figure can be modified to take into account the fact that an occupier has contributed to existing infrastructure,[70] as well as the purpose for which the land is being used.[71] If an NGO relies on government funding but is not currently funded for the payment of rent, a period of grace might be provided.[72] Occupiers can try to negotiate a lesser amount; however, the EDTL holds a monopoly over community land and its publications suggest that a firm line is usually taken. For most occupiers the obligation to pay rent is ongoing. Home ownership subleases are the exception, where buyers pay an up-front purchase price but do not pay ongoing rent.[73]

There is scope for diverging views about whether the introduction of rent should be seen as a positive development. It has been characterised as a means for enabling economic development but also as a harmful form of unearned income. The consequences of rent for traditional owners and communities are explored in following chapters.

Freehold-like or leasehold-like?

The EDTL has said that 'township lease arrangements aim to approximate ordinary freehold title to the greatest extent possible'.[74] The Australian Government has on several occasions made similar statements.[75] Despite this, the terms of existing subleases do not reflect an attempt to approximate freehold. To the contrary, most existing subleases are distinctly leasehold-like. Freehold – and more particularly the fee simple – is the broadest form of ownership available under Australian law. While it is not possible for a lease or sublease to replicate fee simple, it is possible to approximate it. A commonly cited example is the Australian Capital Territory, where 'landowners' acquire a form of unrestrictive, alienable and long-term leasehold. Such a lease might be described as 'freehold-like'; however, this is different from what has been occurring on township leases.

Township subleases are subject to certain restrictions on alienability, which is not a characteristic of fee simple ownership. The majority of subleases are also subject to annual rental. The EDTL has argued that '[p] aying appropriate rent ... is an essential element' of trying to 'approximate ordinary freehold'.[76] This statement reflects the at times high level of confusion that has accompanied the implementation of these reforms. Paying rent is a distinctly leasehold-like characteristic, and not like ordinary freehold. Further, while it is possible for the EDTL to grant subleases that run for the duration of the township lease, with the exception of home ownership subleases it has not done so. In Wurrumiyanga, the majority of subleases have been for 20 years, including those to enterprises.

Nor are these the only conditions imposed by township subleases. The standard sublease terms referred to above are lengthy and prescriptive. The standard commercial terms contain 44 clauses, each with numerous subclauses, and together with annexures comprise 60 pages. Many of those clauses impose restrictions on the activities of the sublease holder. A sublease may only be used for a specified permitted use,[77] and the written permission of the EDTL is required for any development or construction.[78] There are restrictions on the use of signage and introduction of flora and fauna.[79] The standard terms also refer to activities that are already prohibited by law, thereby making a breach of those laws a breach of the sublease.[80] The Land Trust, Land Council and EDTL all have certain rights of entry,[81] and the sublease holder may be issued with a condition report, required to maintain and insure improvements or remove new improvements upon expiration of the sublease.[82] A breach of these terms may result in termination of the sublease.[83] While these sort of clauses might not be unusual in a commercial sublease, they reflect an attempt to provide sublease holders with a contained set of tenure rights, rather than a set of rights that approximate a fee simple.

Home ownership subleases are an exception to this rule, in that they are significantly more freehold-like than other subleases. As well as being for a longer period, they are paid for up-front and are not subject to ongoing rental. Somewhat surprisingly, even home ownership subleases are subject to restrictions on alienability, as well as many of the other restrictive terms referred to above.

I do not suggest that township subleases *should* approximate freehold to the greatest extent possible, as the EDTL and the Australian Government have stated. That depends very much on the circumstances and the aims of reform. Chapter 8 introduces a framework for considering whether

186   *The reforms*

and in what circumstances leases and subleases should be 'freehold-like' or 'leasehold-like'. However, the substantial disjuncture between the statements of the EDTL and Australian Government and the terms of subleases reflects a high level of confusion about the form that subleases should take. Existing frameworks for debating land reform – in terms of communal–individual ownership or the introduction of 'secure tenure' – have not helped with this. Indeed references to approximating freehold title suggest that the communal–individual ownership debate in particular has instead contributed to confusion.

The cost of township leasing

Township leasing has not been cheap. First, there is the up-front rent, which in total for the three existing leases has been $11.45 million. That rent has been paid out of the Aboriginal Benefits Account,[84] in other words out of funds that have already been set aside for the benefit of Aboriginal people, a development that has attracted criticism.[85] In addition, there are the ongoing costs of the EDTL, which is based in Canberra and has staff in Darwin. For the six years from 2008 to 2014 those costs totalled $6,377,827.[86] This is a considerable sum of money, against which any benefits of township leasing have to be assessed.

6.3 The Northern Territory Emergency Response

The Northern Territory Emergency Response (NTER) in 2007 was one of the most significant and dramatic events in the history of Australian Indigenous policy. Eight years later it remains controversial. Also known as the Intervention, the NTER involved the Australian Government in a unilateral assertion of control over Aboriginal communities. It included the introduction of income management, a licensing regime for community stores and the extension of restrictions on alcohol. It also included four land tenure reforms, which are the focus here.

The NTER was initially conceived of as a five-year project and that five-year period ended in August 2012. In fact, certain of the reforms introduced as part of the NTER are ongoing, such as the majority of reforms to the permit system. Others have been revoked or allowed to lapse, such as statutory rights and the five-year leases. In 2011 the Australian Government began to develop a new set of reforms to replace the NTER after its expiry. Those new reforms are called Stronger Futures, and they contain one further land reform which is also described here.

Announcement of the NTER

The NTER was introduced in the context of increasing concern about high levels of child abuse in Aboriginal communities. That concern had been

The reforms   187

building for some time, especially since the airing of a series of media reports in 2006. In response to those reports, on 8 August 2006 the NT Government set up an inquiry into the protection of Aboriginal children from sexual abuse. Rex Wild and Pat Anderson were appointed to the Board of Inquiry, and their report – called *Little Children Are Sacred* – was returned at the end of April 2007.[87] There was a delay of around six weeks while the NT Government prepared a response and arranged for publication, and so it was not until 15 June that it was released.[88] When it was released, the Chief Minister committed to 'implementing the key action areas' and providing a full response to the report's 97 recommendations at the August sittings of Parliament.[89]

The following week, however, Prime Minister John Howard and Federal Minister for Indigenous Affairs Mal Brough called a joint press conference in which they declared a 'national emergency in relation to the abuse of children in indigenous communities in the Northern Territory'.[90] They said that the *Little Children Are Sacred* report had identified disturbing and widespread levels of abuse and that the NT Government was taking too long to respond. Consequently, they announced that the Australian Government was introducing its own set of emergency measures. In fact, those measures were not based on the recommendations of the report, but were a set of measures that the Australian Government had itself been working on.

Among the measures announced that day were the 'acquiring' of prescribed 'townships' through five-year leases and the 'scrapping' of the permit system for 'common areas, road corridors and airstrips for prescribed communities on Aboriginal land'.[91] Minister Brough also told the NT Government that it was expected to immediately resume all town camp leases where housing associations were in breach of the lease conditions, and if they did not do so urgently the Australian Government would itself take action.[92] Legislation to implement the NTER was introduced to Parliament on 7 August 2007 and, after a one-day Senate inquiry, was passed by both houses on 17 August 2007.[93] The final version of the legislation included two further land reforms: provision for a new form of occupancy called 'statutory rights' and the creation of a new power to compulsorily acquire town camp land.

Five-year leases

History and relevance

The most widespread of the land-related NTER measures was the compulsory acquisition of five-year leases over 64 remote Aboriginal communities. Of those communities, 47 were on ALRA land and 16 were on community living area (CLA) land, while one was on Crown land subject to a land claim.[94] All formed part of the identified list of 73 remote Aboriginal

188 *The reforms*

communities with a population of greater than 100. Smaller communities – known as outstations or homelands – were not acquired.

The five-year leases were a very dramatic and intrusive reform, far more so than township leasing. Township leases require the consent of traditional owners, while five-year leases were imposed without any form of consultation. They also expired on 17 August 2012.[95] They are nevertheless of ongoing relevance for two reasons: they embody important aspects of the Australian Government's approach to tenure in Aboriginal communities during recent years; and they appear to have had an ongoing impact on social relations in remote Aboriginal communities.

Lease terms

While they are described in the *Northern Territory National Emergency Response Act 2007* (Cth) (the NTNER Act) as a 'lease', due to their compulsory nature the five-year leases were unlike any conventional form of leasehold. The acquisition process allowed the Commonwealth to determine the lease boundaries at its discretion. It took a broad and inclusive approach. In addition to the subject communities, many five-year leases included such surrounding areas as airstrips, rubbish dumps, bores, gravel pits and nearby outstations, as well as large areas of vacant land.[96] After it had acquired the leases, the Commonwealth conducted a more comprehensive ground-based survey and in 2009 reduced the lease areas by more than half to 'exclude areas which are not essential to support the delivery of services as part of the NTER'.[97] The terms of the five-year leases were also determined entirely by the Commonwealth, and those terms provided the Commonwealth with exclusive possession and quiet enjoyment, subject to the preservation of certain existing rights and interests.[98]

Rent

The NTNER Act was drafted so that the Commonwealth was not required to pay rent,[99] and only required to pay compensation to the extent that it was constitutionally obliged to do so.[100] There was at the time some doubt about this, and the former Coalition Government sent mixed signals as to whether it would nevertheless pay compensation.[101] This issue ultimately came before the High Court, which found that just terms compensation was required,[102] although by that point the new Labor Government had committed to paying 'reasonable rent' for the leases.[103]

It was not until 25 May 2010 – nearly three years into the leases – that the Commonwealth was able to announce that it had begun paying rent.[104] Even then, there was ongoing disputation between the Commonwealth and the Central Land Council (CLC) and Northern Land Council (NLC) about the appropriate amount of rent.[105] This is partly because it was a novel situation, with scope for different views as to how the land should be

The reforms   189

valued. There are no public records of the total amount of rent that was ultimately paid for the five-year leases. Reports suggest that it was tens of millions of dollars.

Occupiers

The effect of the five-year leases was to give the Commonwealth direct control over land use in subject communities. This also meant that the Commonwealth was suddenly responsible for such matters as the reallocation of infrastructure and giving permission for new developments. It had no previous experience with this and was required to set up an additional bureaucracy to deal with the role. Due to the short time frame, no attempt was made to issue occupiers with formal rights. Rather, the Commonwealth created a system of rules for occupiers to follow. Activities such as construction, demolition or changing occupiers required the permission of the Commonwealth.[106] Approval was not required for the continuation of an existing use.[107]

Expiry of the five-year leases

Upon expiry of the five-year leases legal arrangements reverted to those that existed prior to their acquisition. This means that since 17 August 2012, the Australian Government has relinquished legal control over land use in affected communities. Instead, it has focused on 'securing leases over social housing and Commonwealth assets on five-year lease communities' as part of its 'secure tenure' policies.[108] As described below, hundreds of leases have now been granted under those policies.

While in a legal sense the five-year leases have come and gone, their impact is ongoing. The CLC states that the leases 'damaged relations between the Australian Government and Aboriginal people in remote communities'.[109] They have also contributed to an alteration in the approach that landowners and land users take to the use of community land, including a loss of faith in the reliability of informal tenure arrangements. Later chapters describe how this has narrowed the potential for alternative approaches to land reform.

Permit reforms

The permit system, which regulates access to ALRA land, has long been one of its more controversial aspects (there is no permit system on CLA or town camp land). When John Reeves QC reviewed the ALRA in 1998, he concluded that permits should be abolished and access to ALRA land instead regulated by the same laws that apply to other land: a common law implied licence to enter for lawful purposes, as modified by trespass law.[110] Reeves gave several reasons for this. He found that 'Aboriginal custom did

190 *The reforms*

not appear to include a commonly acknowledged right to exclude others from lands, except sacred sites',[111] and argued that the permit system did not have the 'general support of the Aboriginal people'.[112] He was also concerned about the impact of permits on non-Aboriginal people, arguing that they were 'racially discriminatory to all other Territorians'.[113] The Commonwealth parliamentary committee set up to consider the Reeves Report rejected his recommendations in relation to permits and noted that, contrary to the Report, 'the vast majority of Aboriginal people told the Committee that they wanted the permit system to remain'.[114]

Eight years later, the Australian Government announced a review of the permit system for different reasons. In late 2006, Minister Brough advised that the government could 'no longer allow the situation where children are being abused' in circumstances 'where the full glare of Australia's public, through its media, cannot be brought to bear so that Australians [can] demand this no longer occur'.[115] The next month, his department issued a discussion paper on permits and invited submissions from the public.[116] In addition to reiterating concerns about the 'monopoly of silence', the discussion paper argued that permits isolated Aboriginal communities economically and socially and had failed to stop the scourge of drug trafficking, violence and abuse. The discussion paper attracted around 100 submissions; however, there was no formal response and the submissions were not made public.[117] Instead the government introduced changes to the permit system as part of the NTER the following year.[118] While introduced as part of the NTER, these reforms are ongoing.

Most of the recent Indigenous land tenure reforms in Australia affect only the land in larger residential communities. Some of the permit reforms are an exception to this in that they affect any area of ALRA land, although their impact is relatively minor. Those reforms enable a slightly wider group of people to access Aboriginal land without a permit,[119] and state that a permit can only be revoked by the person who issued it.[120] Prior to this, traditional owners could revoke a permit issued by a Land Council and vice versa.[121] This can no longer occur; moreover where one traditional owner issues a permit, it cannot be revoked by another.

All other amendments to the permit system only affect residential communities. The amendments provide that any member of the public may enter ALRA land to attend a public court hearing.[122] More broadly, all members of the public now have a right to access roads and 'common areas' inside communities,[123] and may gain access to such communities through a nearby aerodrome or landing.[124] The minister may also declare an access road open to the public,[125] although no declarations have yet been made. Where a person leaves a 'common area' to enter premises with the permission of someone who appears to be the occupier, they have a complete defence against a charge of failing to obtain a permit.[126]

The continuation of the permit reforms – when other elements of the NTER expired in August 2012 – has attracted little public attention.[127]

The reforms 191

This stands in stark contrast to the very heated public debate that preceded their introduction. It would appear that the permit reforms have had a less significant impact than either side of that debate suggested they would. They have not resulted in a significant influx of visitors to communities on ALRA land, to either their benefit or detriment.[128]

Statutory rights

A further NTER reform was an amendment to the ALRA to enable 'statutory rights'.[129] Their purpose was to provide governments with an ongoing and rent-free right to exclusive possession of land on which government-funded infrastructure had been built, as an alternative to leasing. The provisions required landowner consent, were never used and were repealed in 2012.[130] Their inclusion reflects the Australian Government's emerging concern with acquiring greater control over government-funded infrastructure.

Power to compulsorily acquire town camp land

It is described below how in 2007 the Commonwealth began implementing new policies with respect to social housing in Indigenous communities. It is in this context that it began negotiating for the Alice Springs town camp housing associations to relinquish their leases over the camps, thereby allowing the land to revert to Crown land, or to sublease all housing areas to Territory Housing for 99 years, in return for housing upgrades to the value of $70 million. For the housing associations, this meant losing ownership and control of the camps, and the offer was rejected.[131]

When the NTER was introduced a few months later, it included two sets of provisions with respect to town camp land. The first enabled the Commonwealth to take action to forfeit town camp leases where the housing association was in breach of lease conditions,[132] while the second simply made it easier for the Commonwealth to compulsorily acquire town camp land.[133] The first set of provisions was never used, but the second was to prove significant.

During this same period, the Commonwealth was engaged in more successful negotiations with the town camp housing associations in Tennant Creek. In August 2007 they agreed to a sublease to Territory Housing in return for $30 million of upgrades and additional infrastructure.[134] However, the Alice Springs housing associations continued to resist and instead began work on an alternative proposal, based on a sublease to a community housing body (rather than Territory Housing).[135] Negotiations continued under the new Labor Government and in July 2008 the parties entered into an 'Agreed Work Plan'.[136] The plan committed the parties to a third option, which was a 40-year sublease to the EDTL.[137] This represented a slight expansion in the role of the EDTL, beyond just township leasing.

192 *The reforms*

The agreement broke down when the parties began negotiating sublease terms, at which point the housing associations renewed their push for a sublease to a community housing body.[138] The Commonwealth would not agree to this and on 24 May 2009 announced that it would negotiate no further and was instead taking the first steps towards compulsorily acquiring the land, using the provisions introduced as part of the NTER.[139] To avoid compulsory acquisition, the town camp associations ultimately agreed to a sublease to the EDTL on the terms required by the Commonwealth.[140] The EDTL then entered into a 'housing management agreement' with Territory Housing, which enables housing in the town camps to be run as public housing.[141]

There was an exception to this process for the town camp known as Ilpeye Ilpeye. Most residents of that camp are also native title holders for Alice Springs, and a different agreement was reached. In 2010, the Commonwealth acquired the fee simple for Ilpeye Ilpeye, in return for which the native title holders received compensation and an undertaking to work towards enabling home ownership.[142] Three years later the Commonwealth announced that an agreement had been reached whereby 'the Aboriginal land owners' were granted a vacant area of land inside the town camp as freehold, to enable them to use that land for home ownership.[143] The announcement did not specify how home ownership is to be financed or which 'Aboriginal land owners' will be allocated land.[144] All other housing at Ilpeye Ilpeye has been transferred to Territory Housing to be managed as public housing (as has occurred on the other town camps).[145]

These are the only land reforms that have targeted town camps. They are again instructive for what they reflect about the Australian Government's approach to land reform in recent years. It was not prepared to accept a deal under which tenure arrangements were formalised through a sublease to a community housing body. It was the increase in government control rather than the formalisation of tenure arrangements it was most concerned with. Its actions with respect to the Alice Springs town camps also reflect the extent to which the Australian Government has been prepared to act coercively in achieving its preferred outcome.

After the NTER: Stronger Futures

The rules for granting leases on CLA land have always been far more restrictive than those for ALRA land. This has become increasingly problematic as a result of the 'secure tenure' policies detailed below. In some cases, the intersection between these new policies and restrictive leasing provisions has resulted in communities on CLA land being denied new infrastructure or being required to build infrastructure on adjacent land.[146] While it has received little public attention, this is a significant problem and a clear policy failure.

For several years, the two major Land Councils (the CLC and NLC) have been in discussion with the NT and Australian governments about how this problem might be resolved. One option is to simply give CLA associations the power to grant leases by removing existing restrictions. The CLC and NLC have argued that this would be problematic as CLA associations do not have the 'resources or capacity' to play such a role.[147] They have instead proposed the creation of bodies called 'CLA Land Trusts', which would operate in a similar way to Aboriginal Land Trusts under the ALRA, except that the ownership group would be members of the existing CLA association.[148]

CLA land is regulated by Northern Territory law and reforms require amendments to that law. It appears that by 2012, the Australian Government had lost patience with waiting for the NT Government to make such reforms. When legislation to implement Stronger Futures – the reform package that replaced the NTER – was introduced, it included a provision that enables the Australian Government, by regulation, to 'modify any law of the Northern Territory relating to' CLA land.[149] Regulations passed in 2013 give CLA associations the authority to grant leases over their land to a corporation or person for any purpose that is permitted under a planning scheme for the community.[150] This is an unusual reform, in that it is rare for the Commonwealth to override laws of the Northern Territory.

6.4 Housing reforms and 'secure tenure' policies

Introduction

A third set of reforms has received much less attention in public forums and academic research. It is at times more difficult to source information about them, as they did not require legislation and so have not been debated by Parliament. And while they are often the subject of passing reference in government publications, there is no single or detailed public document that sets out their rationale or parameters. The reforms referred to here are the introduction of 'secure tenure' policies, initially with respect to housing and then more broadly. The term 'secure tenure' is used here in inverted commas to indicate that it is not being used in its technical sense. 'Secure tenure' policies have more to do with formalisation than tenure security. At other times they are simply about government control. They might be summarised as a new policy requiring tenure arrangements for certain infrastructure in communities on Aboriginal land to be formalised in a manner consistent with rules set down by the Australian Government. This section tracks the development and implementation of those policies, starting with their application to housing.

194 *The reforms*

Reforms to residential housing

A change in housing policy

Chapter 4 describes how in the past housing for Aboriginal residents in communities on Aboriginal land has been a type of informal community housing. Bodies called Indigenous Community Housing Organisations (ICHOs) were responsible for the management of housing, but did so informally in that they did not own or lease the houses. In 2006, the Australian Government commissioned PricewaterhouseCoopers (PWC) to conduct a review of the programme under which ICHOs were funded.[151] PWC recommended a number of sweeping changes, including the fostering of home ownership and a graduated shift from community housing to mainstream public housing.[152]

In May 2007, the Howard Coalition Government announced that it was instigating new arrangements for the funding of Indigenous housing across the country, based substantially on the recommendations of the PWC report.[153] It was during this period that it began negotiations with town camp housing associations in Alice Springs and Tennant Creek. It also commenced discussions with the NT Government about how the new funding arrangements would operate, particularly with respect to remote communities. This culminated in September 2007 with a memorandum of understanding between the two governments (the MoU).[154] The MoU embodies all three of the key elements of the new approach to remote Indigenous housing: the division of communities into categories of priority for the purposes of funding; government 'ownership' of housing, with provision also made for home ownership; and the shift from a community housing to a public housing model.

While it occurred during a period of intense debate about Aboriginal land reform, the significance of the MoU was barely noted at the time. A press release in relation to the MoU referred mainly to the amount of funding involved, noting in passing that the 'Australian Government's intention is to introduce normal public housing arrangements in the communities'.[155] Despite this low-key beginning, the changes reflected in the MoU have become the most widespread of the recent land reforms.

Priority communities

This book has on several occasions referred to a list of 73 larger Aboriginal communities in the Northern Territory. Those communities have been the primary target of recent land reforms. They are also connected to the introduction of 'priority community' policies. The MoU refers to them as the '73 emergency response communities' (due to their connection to the NTER) and locates them for funding purposes as falling between 'main urban centres' and 'outstation communities'.[156] It then divides the list into

The reforms   195

two, distinguishing between 'larger/strategically placed growth communities' and 'the balance of the 73 emergency response communities'.[157] The significance of the distinction is that 'growth communities' were eligible for new housing while 'the balance' would receive only repairs and upgrades.[158] Outstations would ultimately be eligible for neither. In April of the following year, the new Federal Labor Government clarified the make-up of each group, naming 16 communities to 'receive major capital works' and 57 to receive only maintenance and repairs to existing houses.[159]

The effect of priority community policies is to allocate a greater proportion of funding to certain larger or strategically placed communities at the expense of other communities. Over the last decade they have become more widespread. The Australian Government has extended such an approach to all remote Indigenous housing funding, as well as certain other service delivery.[160] It also connects the allocation of funding to land reform and the availability of 'appropriate land tenure arrangements ... for home ownership'.[161] The NT Government introduced its own list of priority communities, called 'growth towns' or 'service hubs'.[162] More recently the Western Australian Government went further, suggesting that it might shut down up to 150 of the state's 274 remote Aboriginal communities, although this was partly an attempt to put funding pressure on the Australian Government.[163]

Government 'ownership' of housing

The MoU provided that all new housing in Aboriginal communities would be 'owned by Territory Housing' and that 'existing housing will transfer to publicly owned Territory Housing' over time.[164] This 'ownership' was to be achieved through long-term leases. It later came to describe this as requiring 'secure tenure' and clarified the rules as to what was required of those leases. They have to be for a period of at least 40 years, cover all residential housing (existing houses as well as the houses to be built) and must enable Territory Housing to implement new tenancy management arrangements without requiring the further consent of landowners or the community.[165] These leases to government housing departments over housing areas have been termed 'housing precinct leases',[166] to distinguish them from township leases.

This policy has since been extended beyond the Northern Territory. As part of the *National Partnership Agreement on Remote Indigenous Housing*, pursuant to which the Australian Government has committed $4.7 billion in funding over 10 years,[167] the construction of new houses in any state or territory is 'conditional on secure land tenure being settled',[168] which (except in the handful of places where the government already owns the land) means a housing precinct lease to the relevant department of housing.[169] The Australian Government has also said that those leases must

196   *The reforms*

be rent-free, in 'recognition of the significant government investment in housing set to follow' from their grant.[170]

Where landowners refuse to grant a housing precinct lease, a community does not receive new housing. The CLC reports that this has resulted in a 'sense of being blackmailed', which is one of 'six key reasons why communities have been reluctant to enter into' housing precinct leases 'despite the offer of ... new housing'.[171] Other reasons include the 'ill-feeling caused by ... the five-year leases', 'reservations about the capacity of Territory Housing' and the 'loss of community control over important housing management issues'.[172] Faced with limited choice, however, most landowners have ultimately agreed and there are now at least 21 housing precinct leases for communities in the CLC region alone.[173]

On a township lease, there is instead a housing precinct sublease to Territory Housing, which has the same effect. Where a house is made the subject of home ownership, which has been uncommon, it must first be removed from the housing precinct lease or sublease so that a longer grant can be made directly to the home owner.

Public housing model

The third element of the new arrangements is a shift from community housing to mainstream public housing. That is, responsibility for housing management has shifted from ICHOs to Territory Housing. This is closely connected to the housing precinct leases, but is also a separate development. The leases give the government greater control over housing and the ability to choose the housing manager. If there is a change of policy during the term of the lease, it is still possible to revert to community housing. The housing precinct leases give the government more direct control over such decisions.

The mainstreaming of housing management has meant a dramatic increase in the role of Territory Housing. Previously it was responsible only for public housing inside the larger towns (such as Darwin and Alice Springs). It is now responsible for town camps and all 73 larger remote communities. This has been accompanied by a mainstreaming of management practices, frequently described as a 'normalisation' of tenancy arrangements. As part of this, residents of town camps and remote communities are now required to enter into formalised tenancy agreements, which are regulated under the *Housing Act 1982* (NT) and *Residential Tenancies Act 1999* (NT).[174] This involves the imposition of more exacting tenancy standards. As the former Minister for Indigenous Affairs, Jenny Macklin, put it, 'under "normalised" tenancy agreements, tenants will be expected to pay fair market rents, pay their rents on time, cover the cost of any damage and not interfere with the peace of their neighbours'.[175] The government presents the reforms as a shift away from the special or more accommodating treatment that was previously given to Indigenous housing residents. One consequence of this is that tenants face greater risk of sanction, and if they 'wilfully fail to meet' their obligations they 'will face eviction'.[176]

Rosenman and Clunies-Ross argue that under new arrangements the residents of remote communities are subject to rules 'that go well beyond those imposed by ... most tenancy agreements'.[177] For example, remote tenants are not allowed to keep unregistered or defective vehicles on their premises or use their premises to make 'substantial repairs'. Nor are they allowed to have toxic or flammable items such as diesel. The authors state that 'arguably, these rules are being used to engender behavioural change by imposing conditions' that go beyond those normally imposed on tenants.[178] This suggests that the tenancy reforms go beyond 'normalisation', and impose higher standards on remote residents. Rosenman and Clunies-Ross also note that 'unlike urban public housing tenants who are offered fixed term leases, tenants in remote houses are offered only periodic (monthly) tenancies with *no security of tenure*'.[179] That is because, despite what the government has sometimes suggested,[180] the purpose of housing reforms is not to provide greater tenure security for Aboriginal residents. To the contrary, their purpose is to implement a strategic *reduction* in tenure security for Aboriginal residents, the rationale for which is considered in Chapter 7.

Broader 'secure tenure' policies

'Secure tenure' beyond housing

Over time, 'secure tenure' policies were extended beyond housing to include certain other infrastructure in communities on Indigenous land. The exact boundaries of these policies are difficult to ascertain, simply because governments have published very little about them, and then only in the most general of terms. It is clear that they extend to infrastructure that is occupied by the Australian or NT Government.[181] It appears that they also encompass infrastructure constructed using government funding.[182]

It is less clear whether the policies extend beyond this – to, for example, other infrastructure occupied by NGOs that receive government funding – however, in a practical sense the point is becoming moot, at least in the Northern Territory. A consequence of 'secure tenure' policies, in combination with the other reforms, has been a shift in attitudes to leasing, including among traditional owners and Land Councils. Consequently, what started as a government policy is now being embraced as Land Council practice, not least because most leases provide for the payment of rent. As the CLC states, 'the Australian Government and the Northern Territory Government are now committed to a "secure tenure" policy, which stipulates that those operating on Aboriginal land should hold a formal legal

198 *The reforms*

interest ... in the land on which their assets are located'. Consequently, they advise people who 'have assets located on Aboriginal land [to] apply for a lease or licence over that land as soon as possible'.[183]

This has led to a massive increase in the number of leases being granted in communities on Aboriginal land. In June 2012, the NLC reported that over the previous two years a total of 459 leases had been granted across its region.[184] In October 2013, the CLC stated that it had overseen the grant of 478 leases and was currently processing a further 511 applications.[185] The CLC also gave more specific figures for two of the communities in its region. They reported that in Lajamanu 81 per cent of serviced lots had been leased, with that figure expected to soon reach 95 per cent. In Alekarenge, it was 71 per cent and expected to reach 82 per cent on existing applications.[186] The shift has occurred quickly. Until 2010, no one had ever applied for a lease in Alekarenge.[187] It is likely that process has been slower in other communities; however, the consequence is that in time most (if not all) occupiers of land and infrastructure in communities on Aboriginal land will be required to obtain a lease. This is depicted in Figure 6.4.

In some respects, this is similar to outcomes under a township lease. From a tenant's perspective, there is little difference between a lease and a sublease. The available evidence suggests that the terms and conditions tend to be similar, and the EDTL and Land Councils take a similar approach to the setting of rent. The key difference of course is with respect to control over the formalisation process. Under a township lease it is the EDTL that manages this, while in communities without a township lease it is the Land Councils and traditional owners.

It should be noted, however, that even in a community without a township lease governments have significant input into the leasing process. They are ultimately responsible for funding most services in remote communities. As negotiations around housing demonstrate, the Australian

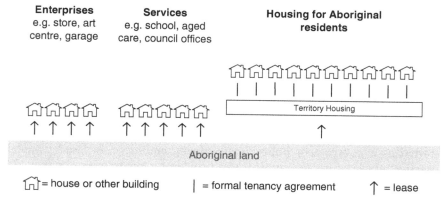

Figure 6.4 Outcome under 'secure tenure' policies.

Government is willing to withhold funding if it does not approve of an outcome. It has nevertheless continually expressed a preference for township leases and treats the broader implementation of 'secure tenure' policies on communities without a township lease as a short-term compromise. Not all of its arguments for doing so appear to be well founded. For example, it argues that without a township lease 'leases are applied for, consulted on and, if agreed, granted on a case by case basis'.[188] This is clearly not the case. The reason the CLC and NLC have been able to grant so many leases in recent years is because they consult upon and process leases in large batches. It might be argued that township leasing is more streamlined, particularly as Aboriginal landowners do not have to be consulted, but the difference is not as great as the government suggests. The government also states that township leases create 'arrangements that deliver the transferability of ordinary freehold title' and that communities with a township lease are advantaged 'because the long term tradeable tenure is a suitable platform for Government investment, including in social housing'.[189] These statements are also incorrect. As set out above, there have been very few freehold-like or long-term and tradable subleases. Meanwhile, the CLC and the NLC continue to express concerns about township leases because of the loss of traditional owner control. The last year has seen something of a revival in contestation about township leasing.[190]

Rent

While the Australian Government has said that housing precinct leases should be rent-free, it has taken a different approach to other leases on Aboriginal land. Since at least 2009, it has agreed in principle that governments should pay rent for the use of Aboriginal land, and not just in communities subject to a township lease.[191] Ultimately, the NT Government has come to accept this position, although not without resistance. It has stated that across the Territory its rent will initially 'be in the order of $3 million per year and will rise to around $5 million per year when all parcels are surveyed and leased'.[192]

Significantly, the CLC states that there 'is now an expectation amongst traditional owners that fair rent will be paid by people or entities seeking leases or licences over Aboriginal land'.[193] This primarily affects service providers, and the CLC notes that the Australian and NT governments have 'acknowledged that their commitment to the secure tenure policy will necessitate them funding third party service providers working on Aboriginal communities such that they can pay rent for the land on which their assets are located'.[194] An application form prepared by the CLC sets out a formula for the calculation of 'fair rent',[195] which appears to have been developed in consultation with the EDTL.[196] The CLC also advises those organisations instead seeking a peppercorn rent to detail the 'community

200 *The reforms*

benefit' that they intend to provide, so that this information can be presented to the traditional owners.[197]

What is striking about this is the shift in emphasis with respect to rent. In a 2005 publication, the CLC noted that in the past leases 'for a community purpose' and 'for government infrastructure' had attracted only peppercorn rent, and supported the continuation of this practice (noting that ultimately the decision belongs to the traditional owners, not the Land Council).[198] In their more recent publications, the CLC instead state that traditional owners expect to be paid rent. This shift is a direct result of the recent reforms, and its consequences are discussed in Chapter 7.

6.5 Allotment of Indigenous land in Queensland

Indigenous land rights in Queensland

Queensland has one of the most complex land rights systems in Australia.[199] One reason for this is that during the 1970s and 1980s, the conservative Bjelke-Petersen Government opposed any move towards the introduction of a Northern Territory-style land rights scheme in Queensland,[200] as part of which it instead created its own schemes. In 1978, for two communities it granted a 50-year lease to the local shire council.[201] In the early 1980s, it created a new form of title called Deed of Grant in Trust (DOGIT), under which trustees own land for the benefit of Aboriginal or Torres Strait Islander residents.[202] Most (but not all) Indigenous reserves were converted to DOGIT land, with the local Aboriginal or Torres Strait Islander council appointed trustee. The key differences between DOGIT land and ALRA land are that DOGIT land is subject to greater government control and is owned for the benefit of residents rather than traditional owners. Then in 1991, the new Goss Labor Government finally introduced a statutory land rights scheme.[203] The scheme allows for reserve land, DOGIT land and the shire leases to be converted to Aboriginal land or Torres Strait Islander land. Depending on the terms of the grant, that land is then owned for the native title holders or for Indigenous people 'particularly concerned with the land', which includes people with either a traditional connection or a residential connection.[204]

In a number of places this already complex situation is made more complicated by native title. Where Indigenous land is owned for the benefit of residents rather than traditional owners, and native title has not been extinguished, then the interests of native title holders must be considered separately. Where, for example, the trustees for DOGIT land wish to grant a lease over land that is subject to native title, they will first need to engage with the future act provisions of the *Native Title Act*.[205] In practice, this usually means obtaining the agreement of native title holders through an Indigenous Land Use Agreement.[206] This issue does not arise on land that is owned traditionally, such as ALRA land, because there is an alignment between land ownership and native title.[207]

The reforms   201

Leasing Indigenous land in Queensland

Queensland legislation has long allowed for the grant of leases over DOGIT land, Aboriginal land and Torres Strait Islander land. In the last few decades, however, leasing has not been widespread. The interaction between land ownership and native title is one reason for this, as is the fact that leasing processes were relatively complicated and restrictive. In recent years there have been several attempts to simplify those procedures through legislative amendment, and the number of leases is increasing. To some extent, this parallels the implementation of 'secure tenure' policies in the Northern Territory.[208]

Beginning in 2014, the updated leasing provisions have also been used for home ownership. While this has often been referred to as a 'first',[209] there had in fact previously been a home ownership scheme in some communities on Indigenous land in Queensland, by way of what are commonly known as 'Katter leases'. It would be unfortunate if this was forgotten, as there were significant problems with Katter leases and their introduction is generally regarded as a failure.[210] Nevertheless, the recent grants of home ownership are the first in more than two decades. While the numbers are currently small they may grow over time.

The issues with respect to home ownership and the leasing of Indigenous land in Queensland are similar to those for the Northern Territory, and so they are not described here in any detail. Of greater significance is a recent development that may result in the allotment of Indigenous land for the first time in Australia.

Allotment

Step one: a freehold instrument

The *Aboriginal and Torres Strait Islander Land (Providing Freehold) and Other Legislation Amendment Act 2014* (Qld), which commenced on 1 January 2015, enables DOGIT land, Aboriginal land and Torres Strait Islander land in 'urban areas'[211] to be divided into smaller lots and converted to ordinary freehold. Up to 34 communities are affected by the amendments;[212] however, as will become clear, if and when they are used the amendments will affect only certain areas of land within communities rather than entire communities.

There are a number of steps required before a conversion of land can occur. The landholding body must first enact a freehold instrument, comprising a freehold schedule setting out the areas of land that will be available for grant (which can be in the form of a map),[213] and a freehold policy setting out matters such as the eligibility criteria, the pricing policy and the details of how the community will be consulted on the allocation process. There are also detailed provisions about how the trustee must consult on

202   *The reforms*

the freehold instrument itself. It must first set down a consultation plan and then follow that plan, keeping records of its consultations.[214] There are rules about what the consultation plan must include, such as consulting with the native title holders, notifying the community and allowing people sufficient opportunity to express their views.[215]

Once consultations are complete, and the trustee has created a freehold instrument, it must then have that instrument approved. The approval process depends on whether the instrument only covers land for which there is already an 'interest holder' – that is, over which there is a lease, lease entitlement, sublease, residential tenancy agreement or statutory occupancy right[216] – or includes land for which there is no existing interest holder.[217] The process is simpler where the instrument only covers land for which there is already an interest holder; the freehold instrument is sent directly to the Minister for approval.[218] Where the instrument includes other areas, the trustee must first ask the relevant local council to attach the freehold instrument to its planning scheme.[219] The local council then issues a call for written submission from the public, as a result of which it may make changes to the instrument. When this process is finalised, the local council sends a report to the minister summarising the issues raised in public submissions and how it has responded to them.[220] Ultimately all freehold instruments are received by the minister for approval, who is required to take certain matters into account when making a decision. The minister can approve or reject the instrument, or to approve it subject to amendment.[221]

This is a long process, involving several rounds of consultation and approval, especially for land over which there is no existing interest holder. As such, it likely to be some time before the first freehold instrument is enacted.

Step two: granting freehold

Once a freehold instrument is in place, people who are eligible can then start applying to the trustee for a grant of freehold. The only people who are eligible are Aboriginal people and Torres Strait Islanders, and their spouses and former spouses.[222] A grant cannot be made to the government or a corporation of any kind. It is also possible for a freehold instrument to further limit eligibility through additional criteria.[223] For example, a trustee might limit eligibility to those people who have lived in the community for a certain period of time. There are no set parameters or guidelines as to what the additional criteria might include. Of course, once a grant of freehold has been made it can then be sold to any person, corporation or entity. It is only the initial grant that is restricted.

It would be problematic and potentially unjust if people were able to apply for a grant of freehold over land that someone else already has an interest in. Consequently, the legislation again draws a distinction between land for which there is already an interest holder and other areas of land. Where there is an interest holder, that person is the only one who can apply for the freehold. This means that where the interest holder is the government or a corporate entity of any kind (including NGOs), no one is eligible to apply. This clearly limits the potential scope of the legislation. Most, if not all, infrastructure other than social housing will currently be occupied by the government, the local council or a corporate entity (NGOs, enterprises), none of which are eligible to apply for freehold. If and when allotment does occur, it will most likely be contained to social housing and vacant land (unless the legislation is further amended).

Where there is no interest holder, the trustee must engage in a detailed process to ensure that the allocation process is fair. It must first publicise its intention to allocate the land and call for applications from eligible persons.[224] The publication notice must detail the allocation method (with a choice of auction, ballot or tender[225]), the reserve or price and the deposit (if any) that will be required to participate further. The trustee must also appoint a probity officer to monitor the allocation process and certify that it was undertaken correctly.[226] When applications are received, they are processed according to the allocation method and the successful applicant is given the opportunity to complete the purchase.

The legislation imposes an addition step with respect to social housing. Where an application relates to land upon which there is a dwelling of any kind, the trustee must give notice to the housing department.[227] The housing department must then advise whether the dwelling is social housing, and if it is social housing whether it can be sold. If it can be sold, the trustee must set the value of the house using a valuation methodology that has been agreed with the housing department.[228] The same rules apply where home ownership instead occurs by way of a 99-year home ownership lease,[229] which has been the method to date for communities on Indigenous land in Queensland.[230]

Impact on native title

As described above, most of the Indigenous land that is potentially affected by these reforms is owned for the benefit of residents rather than traditional owners. In a number of communities, however, native title still subsists over at least part of the land. Significantly, a grant of freehold will permanently extinguish native title. In practical terms, this means that trustees will need to enter into an Indigenous Land Use Agreement (ILUA) prior to or as part of the process for enacting a freehold instrument, under which the native title holders consent to extinguishment. The government does not provide any funding for trustees to compensate native title holders, describing the process as 'self-funding'.[231] This means that the trustees must find a way to provide compensation themselves, or native

204 *The reforms*

title holders must be persuaded to forgo their rights without compensation. This may be an impediment to allotment going ahead, at least in some communities.

Comment

In some respects, these recent amendments to enable the allotment of Indigenous land in Queensland are the most radical of the recent Australian reforms. They raise a broader set of issues than the formalisation of tenure arrangements through leasing and subleasing. However, they are both contained in their application and subject to several obstacles. The most significant obstacle is that the processes required for allotment are time-consuming and expensive. This is exacerbated by the fact that the Queensland Government has not agreed to provide any funding other than setting aside \$75,000 to help 'pilot communities undertake community consultation'.[232] Beyond this, it states that 'any costs incurred by the trustee [are] to be recovered through the freehold land purchase price'.[233] It assists that most infrastructure in Indigenous communities has now been surveyed.[234] However, trustees will need to compensate native title holders and pay the costs of community consultation (once the pilot programme funds have been expended) and for the engagement of a probity officer. Where there is no sealed road or essential services, they will also need to find money for those expenses.[235]

There is a curiously emphatic tone to the Queensland Government's statements about its lack of funding for the reforms. It presents the fact that they are 'self-funding' as a virtue. The consequence is that the amendments are less likely to be utilised. Where they are utilised, as explained above, they will not result in entire communities being converted to freehold. Initial grants can only be made to individuals and not to corporate entities (which includes corporations owned by Aboriginal and Torres Strait Islanders). Most, if not all, existing enterprises and service providers are either corporate entities or governments, and the infrastructure they occupy will not be included. The only existing infrastructure likely to be affected is social housing, in which case the provisions are effectively an alternative to home ownership through 99-year leases. They might also be used with respect to new areas of land, for which there is no existing interest holder, once the more onerous consultation and planning procedures have been complied with.

6.6 Summarising the reforms

The creation of individual ownership?

During public debate, a number of people have presented the outcome of land reform as the introduction of 'individual ownership' or 'private property'. This was particularly common during the early period of debate, when the political consensus was shifting. But how well does this reflect the actual outcome of the reforms? To date, the only reported instances of 'individual ownership' have been for home ownership, and home ownership has been very much a rarity. As at October 2014, there were only 25 grants of home ownership on Indigenous land across Australia.[236] Meanwhile, thousands of houses have instead been leased or subleased to state and territory housing departments. Beyond housing, there are no reports of any individual acquiring a lease or sublease for commercial purposes. For the most part, leases and subleases for commercial purposes are instead being granted to those same organisations that previously occupied the same infrastructure informally.

Describing this as 'individual ownership' or 'private property' is clearly misleading. In many instances, the reforms are more accurately described as a shift towards 'state property', with its consequent increase in government ownership and control. In the Northern Territory, five-year and township leases effect a shift towards state property at an underlying level. They result in the Commonwealth, or a Commonwealth statutory body (the EDTL), acquiring control over land use and the formalisation process in subject communities. The shift to state property is not complete, in that the five-year leases were short-term and under a township lease the traditional owners retain certain ownership benefits, most notably rent. However, this increase in government control is the very purpose for which these reforms were introduced.

There has also been a shift towards state property with respect to specific infrastructure. The most pronounced example of this is the housing precinct leases, which represent a shift to state property for the 40-plus year duration of the lease. Again, the effect of this is to increase government control over housing. This increase in government control is the very opposite of what is suggested by terms such as 'individual ownership' and 'private property'.

The recent Queensland amendments are a limited exception to this. Allotment does effect a shift to private property and will result in ownership of land by individuals and families. This raises a broader set of issues to formalisation through leasing and subleasing. It may be some time before the provisions enabling allotment are utilised as the process is expensive and involved. If and when they are utilised, they will affect only certain areas of community land rather than entire communities. Even in those communities, more widespread will be the grant of leases to governments, including leases to the housing department over social housing.

The introduction of secure tenure?

Between 2008 and 2013, the Australian Government would often instead describe the need for land reform in terms of enabling 'secure tenure'. This

206　*The reforms*

is also misleading. With respect to housing – the initial focus of 'secure tenure' policies – the reforms do not provide occupiers with greater tenure security. To the contrary, they represent a strategic and targeted reduction in tenure security. The Government argues that tenants have been too secure, and that one reason the reforms are necessary is to increase the threat of sanction for those tenants who fail to comply with tenancy rules.

With respect to other infrastructure, the tenure security impact of the reforms is more difficult to gauge. Across Australia, most enterprises and service providers in communities on Indigenous land historically occupied infrastructure under informal arrangements. In the Northern Territory, they are now being made to obtain a lease or sublease. For those occupiers who previously experienced tenure insecurity, this may be a positive development. For others – and the description provided in Chapter 4 suggests that most occupiers experienced relatively secure tenure – the impact will be more equivocal. As well as now being required to pay rent, their leases and subleases will also periodically come to an end. Their tenure has gone from being flexible and negotiated to fixed and bounded. It is significant that for several years the NT Government and shire councils resisted signing up to leases and subleases. This suggests that the pre-existing informal arrangements suited them sufficiently well and that they regarded the costs of having a lease or sublease as outweighing the benefits.

Mandatory formalisation

If not individual ownership or secure tenure – what then are we to make of the reforms, particularly the more extensive and advanced reforms in the Northern Territory? There are the five-year leases, which have come and gone, and which were exclusively to do with government control. They did not lead to any formalisation for occupiers as they were too short. They did involve the Australian Government engaging with community tenure arrangements in a far greater way than it had previously. There are the permit reforms, which also to some extent stand alone. They make it easier for non-Aboriginal people to access certain areas of ALRA land, primarily in communities. And then there are township leases and 'secure tenure' policies (including as they impact on town camps). Rather than 'secure tenure', both of these reforms are better described as a type of formalisation – and more particularly, a highly exogenous and often mandatory formalisation programme. It is not that occupiers are being given the *opportunity* to acquire formalised rights, or to do so more easily. It is that they are *required* to. These are the most widespread and enduring reforms. But what is their rationale? And what are their consequences? Are they better or worse than allotment? And are there other options? These and related questions are considered in the following two chapters.

Notes

1 For an overview of the amendments to 2009, see Tom Calma, 'Native Title Report 2009' (Australian Human Rights Commission, 2009) 166–76. There have been additional amendments since 2009 to further streamline the leasing process.
2 Government of South Australia, Department of the Premier and Cabinet, *Review of the Aboriginal Lands Trust Act 1966* (2013) http://dpc.sa.gov.au/review-aboriginal-lands-trust-act-1966.
3 Government of South Australia, Department of the Premier and Cabinet, 'Aboriginal Lands Trust Act Review Discussion Paper: Key Issues' (2008) 8–9. See also Calma, above n 1, 177.
4 Public information about this process is scarce, but see Commonwealth Scientific and Industrial Research Organisation (CSIRO), 'Land Tenure in Northern Australia: Opportunities and Challenges for Investment' (June 2013) 7; Calma, above n 1, 179–81; Brian Gleeson, 'Coordinator General for Remote Indigenous Services Six Monthly Report April 2011–September 2011' (Australian Government, 2011) 57.
5 See, eg, Nigel Scullion, 'Historic Arnhem Land Lease Agreement' (Media Release, 17 October 2013); Nigel Scullion, 'Pirlangimpi Township Lease Agreement' (Media Release, 14 March 2014).
6 Australian Government, Department of Prime Minister and Cabinet, *Jobs, Land and Economy* (2014) www.indigenous.gov.au/jobs-land-and-economy.
7 Nigel Scullion, 'Land Reform for the Future', *Koori Mail*, 26 March 2014 (available at http://minister.indigenous.gov.au/media/2014-03-26/land-reform-future-published-koori-mail).
8 Central Land Council (CLC), 'Communal Title and Economic Development' (Policy Paper, 2005) 1.
9 Ibid, 1, 15.
10 Dennis Shanahan and Patricia Karvelas, 'PM Considers New Land Rights Plan', *The Weekend Australian*, 11 December 2004, 4.
11 Michelle Grattan, 'Howard Tilts at Title Fight', *The Sunday Age* (Melbourne), 10 April 2005, 17.
12 Commonwealth, *Parliamentary Debates*, House of Representatives, 31 May 2006, 5 (Mal Brough).
13 See generally Sean Brennan, 'Economic Development and Land Council Power: Modernising the *Land Rights Act* or Same Old Same Old?' (2006) 10(4) *Australian Indigenous Law Reporter* 1.
14 Ibid, 1.
15 *Aboriginal Land Rights (Northern Territory) Act 1976* (Cth) ss 19A(4), (4A).
16 Ibid, ss 19A(8), (8A), (9).
17 Ibid, ss 19A(14), (15).
18 Michael Dillon and Neil Westbury, *Beyond Humbug: Transforming Government Engagement with Indigenous Australia* (Seaview Press, 2007) 151.
19 Ibid, 144–6.
20 *Aboriginal Land Rights (Northern Territory) Amendment (Township Leasing) Act 2007* (Cth). The website of the EDTL can be viewed at www.otl.gov.au.
21 *Indigenous Affairs Legislation Amendment Act 2008* (Cth).
22 *Aboriginal Land Rights (Northern Territory) Act 1976* (Cth) ss 19C, 19D.
23 Ibid, s 19E.
24 *Aboriginal Land Rights (Northern Territory) Amendment Regulations (No. 2) 2008* (Cth). For clarity, the distinction between this regulation and ss 19D and 20SA(4) (described above) is that the regulations apply to subleases under a township lease while the latter apply to a township lease itself.

208 *The reforms*

25 Pat Watson, 'Executive Director of Township Leasing Annual Report 2009–2010' (Australian Government, 2010) 7.
26 *Aboriginal Land Rights (Northern Territory) Act 1976* (Cth) ss 19A(10), (11), (12).
27 Copies of the leases are available through a title search at the Northern Territory Land Titles Office. The Wurrumiyanga lease is lease number 662214. The Anindilyakwa lease is lease number 692818. The Milikapiti lease is lease number 760828.
28 The respective area of each lease is 454 hectares for Wurrumiyanga, 150 hectares for Angurugu, 314 hectares for Umbakumba, 510 hectares for Milyakburra, 840 hectares for Wurankuwu and 544 hectares for Milikapiti; see *Aboriginal Land Rights (Northern Territory) Regulations 2007* (Cth) regs 5, 5A, 6.
29 See definition of 'Income' in cl 1.1. of the Wurrumiyanga lease. Where clauses are common to all three leases, references to the Wurrumiyanga lease only are provided.
30 Northern Land Council, 'Poster Ire', *Land Rights News – Northern Edition* (Darwin), October 2014, 8.
31 Wurrumiyanga lease, cl 5.1(b)(i)(A).
32 Anindilyakwa lease, item 5 of the Schedule.
33 Milikapiti lease, cls 5.1(b)(i)(A) and 5.1(b)(ii)(A).
34 See Wurrumiyanga lease, Annexure 6.
35 Brian Gleeson, 'Coordinator General for Remote Indigenous Services Six Monthly Report July–November 2009' (Australian Government, 2009) 30.
36 Mal Brough, 'Historic Agreement for 99 Year Lease in NT' (Media Release, 30 August 2007). See also Tom Calma, 'Social Justice, Communal Lands and Sustainable Communities' in Lee Godden and Maureen Tehan (eds), *Comparative Perspectives on Communal Lands and Individual Ownership: Sustainable Futures* (Routledge, 2010) 49, 55–6.
37 Dillon and Westbury, above n 18, 150.
38 See Anindilyakwa lease, cl 5 and Annexure 3.
39 This is detailed in a letter from the Minister dated 17 November 2011, a copy of which is attached to the Milikapiti lease. That letter states that Milikapiti will also 'receive an additional $1.5 million' of housing funding.
40 Wurrumiyanga lease, cl 10.1.
41 Ibid, cl 10.14.
42 Ibid, cl 10.7.
43 Ibid, cl 10.1(f). Section 19A(14) of the ALRA provides that a township lease 'must not contain any provision requiring the consent of any person to the grant of a sublease'; however, it does not prohibit provisions requiring the consent of the Land Trust to the *transfer* of a sublease. Consequently, this clause would appear to be valid.
44 Ibid, cl 10.5.
45 Greg Roche, 'Executive Director of Township Leasing Annual Report 2010–2011' (Australian Government, 2011) 27.
46 The categories include government agencies, a broad group of Aboriginal people as well as people who work in the community or have lived there for more than 12 months; see cl 10.6 of the Anindilyakwa lease.
47 Wurrumiyanga lease, cl 10.6, and see also definition of 'Sexual or Crime Against Children Offence' in cl 1.1.
48 Wurrumiyanga lease, cl 23.1 and see also Anindilyakwa lease, cl 21.1.
49 Roche, above n 45, 21.
50 Territory Housing is the NT Government's public housing body.
51 Wurrumiyanga lease, cls 6.3(e), 23.5.

The reforms 209

52 Wurrumiyanga lease, cl 17.2. This must be considered in light of s 134(2) of the *Law of Property Act 2000* (NT), which states that in

> a lease that contains a covenant ... against the making of improvements without ... consent, the covenant ... is, despite any express term in the lease to the contrary, to be taken to be subject to the qualification that the ... consent is not to be unreasonably withheld.

53 Wurrumiyanga lease, cl 10.5(b).
54 For example cl 11.8(b) of the Wurrumiyanga lease provides that the EDTL 'must notify the public of any proposal to vary the Permitted Use of a Township Licence. Members of the public must have sufficient opportunity to comment or object to such variation'.
55 Australian Government Office of Township Leasing, *About the Office of Township Leasing* (2010) Commonwealth of Australia www.otl.gov.au/about.htm#5.
56 Australian Government Office of Township Leasing, *Residential Sublease Application Form* (2009) Commonwealth of Australia www.otl.gov.au/docs/residential_sublease.pdf.
57 Australian Government Office of Township Leasing, *Commercial Sublease Application Form* (2009) Commonwealth of Australia www.otl.gov.au/docs/commercial_sublease.pdf.
58 Watson discusses this with respect to two actual sublease applications; see Evidence to Council of Territory Co-operation, Legislative Assembly of the Northern Territory, Darwin, 14 April 2010, 13 (Pat Watson), and see also pages 20–1, 27.
59 See, eg, Roche, above n 45, 18, 21.
60 The table is based on a title search of NT Portion 1640 conducted on 16 July 2014, supplemented by published reports of the Office of Township Leasing. Some figures are approximated.
61 Both the Wurrumiyanga and Milikapiti leases attach a set of standard terms for the EDTL to use in subleases. The standard terms developed by the EDTL are somewhat different from these. The EDTL reports that modifications were taken to the Consultative Form for approval; see Evidence to Council of Territory Co-operation, Legislative Assembly of the Northern Territory, Darwin, 14 April 2010, 19 (Pat Watson).
62 The documents are called 'Township Sublease Residential Premises' (the 'standard residential terms') and 'Township Sublease Commercial (non-retail)' (the 'standard commercial terms'). They have not been published, but were provided on request by the Office of Township Leasing.
63 This exception only applies to residential subleases; see standard residential terms, cl 11(b).
64 Standard residential terms, cl 11.
65 Standard commercial terms, cl 9.
66 *Law of Property Act 2000* (NT) s 134(2).
67 Peter Butt, *Land Law* (Lawbook Co, 6th ed, 2009) 365–70.
68 AAP, 'Final Tiwi Community to Sign 99-Year Lease', *SBS News* (online), 14 March 2014, www.sbs.com.au/news/article/2014/03/14/final-tiwi-community-sign-99-year-lease.
69 Evidence to Council of Territory Co-operation, Legislative Assembly of the Northern Territory, Darwin, 14 April 2010, 19 (Pat Watson).
70 Ibid, 10–11, 19.
71 Ibid, 7, 19–20.
72 Ibid, 42.
73 Pat Watson, 'Executive Director of Township Leasing Annual Report 2008–2009' (Australian Government, 2009) 9.

210   *The reforms*

74 Australian Government Office of Township Leasing, *Sublease Rental Payments* (2010) Commonwealth of Australia www.otl.gov.au/site/sublease_rental_OOD.asp.

75 Australian Government, 'Indigenous Home Ownership Issues Paper' (Department of Families, Housing, Community Services and Indigenous Affairs, May 2010) 17; Australian Government Department of Families, Housing, Community Services and Indigenous Affairs, Submission to South Australian Department of the Premier and Cabinet, *Review of the Aboriginal Lands Trust Act 1966*, 2009, 2; Australian Government, Department of the Prime Minister and Cabinet, *Frequently Asked Questions about Township Leasing* (2014) www.dpmc.gov.au/indigenous-affairs/about/jobs-land-and-economy-programme/frequently-asked-questions-about-township-leasing.

76 Office of Township Leasing, above n 74.

77 Standard commercial terms, cls 10.9, 14.1.

78 Ibid, cl 16.1.

79 Ibid, cls 14.5 and 17.6 respectively.

80 Including a breach of the planning scheme (cl 14.1) or an alcohol management plan (cl 14.2). There are further activities that may already be restricted by other laws, such as in relation to nuisances (cl 15.1) and hazardous waste (cl 17.1).

81 Standard commercial terms, cl 6.3.

82 Ibid, cls 26, 27, 28, 34, 43.2.

83 Ibid, cl 38.

84 *Aboriginal Land Rights (Northern Territory) Act 1976* (Cth) s 64(4A)(b).

85 See, eg, Calma, 'Social Justice, Communal Lands and Sustainable Communities', above n 36. For a contrary view see Dillon and Westbury, above n 18, 141.

86 The costs of the EDTL are published in annual reports that are available at Australian Government Office of Township Leasing, *Publications*, Commonwealth of Australia www.otl.gov.au/site/publications.asp. An unknown portion of these expenses relate to housing precinct leases, town camp subleases and the ongoing efforts of the EDTL to assist traditional owners with economic development, as described in Chapter 7.

87 Northern Territory Government, 'Ampe Akelyernemane Meke Mekarle: Little Children Are Sacred' (Report of the Northern Territory Board of Inquiry into the Protection of Aboriginal Children from Sexual Abuse, 2007).

88 Northern Territory Government, *Inquiry into the Protection of Aboriginal Children from Sexual Abuse* (2007) www.inquirysaac.nt.gov.au.

89 Northern Territory Government, 'Inquiry Report' (Media Release, 15 June 2007).

90 John Howard and Mal Brough, 'Indigenous Emergency' (Joint Press Conference, 21 June 2007) http://parlinfo.aph.gov.au/parlInfo/search/display/display.w3p;query=Id%3A%22media%2Fpressrel%2F8XFN6%22.

91 Mal Brough, 'National Emergency Response to Protect Aboriginal Children in the NT' (Media Release, 21 June 2007).

92 Ibid.

93 Melinda Hinkson, 'Introduction: In the Name of the Child' in Jon Altman and Melinda Hinkson (eds), *Coercive Reconciliation: Stabilise, Normalise, Exit Aboriginal Australia* (Arena Publications, 2007) 1, 2–3.

94 *Northern Territory National Emergency Response Act 2007* (Cth) sch 1, pts 1, 2, 3.

95 Ibid, s 31(2)(b).

96 Central Land Council, *Australian Government Briefing* (14 December 2007) 8 www.clc.org.au/files/pdf/CLC_Australian_Government_Intervention_Briefing_-_Dec_2007.pdf.

The reforms 211

97 Jenny Macklin, 'Government Finalises Five-Year Lease Boundaries in NT Indigenous Communities' (Media Release, 27 February 2009).
98 *Northern Territory National Emergency Response Act 2007* (Cth) s 35.
99 Ibid.
100 Ibid, s 134.
101 Sean Brennan, '*Wurridjal v Commonwealth*: The Northern Territory Intervention and Just Terms for the Acquisition of Property' (2009) 33 *Melbourne University Law Review* 957, 964–5.
102 *Wurridjal v Commonwealth* (2009) 237 CLR 309.
103 Jenny Macklin, 'Compulsory Income Management to Continue as Key NTER Measure' (Media Release, 23 October 2008).
104 Jenny Macklin and Warren Snowdon, 'Rent Payments for NTER Five-Year Leases' (Media Release, 25 May 2010).
105 Central Land Council (CLC), 'Land Reform in the Northern Territory: Evidence Not Ideology' (2013) 15.
106 Australian Government, 'Five-Year Leased Communities' (Closing the Gap Information Sheet).
107 Australian Government, 'Closing the Gap in the Northern Territory Monitoring Report July–December 2009 Part Two' (Department of Families, Housing, Community Services and Indigenous Affairs, 2010) 48–9.
108 Australian Government, 'Closing the Gap, End of Five Year Leases' (Information Sheet, 2012) 1.
109 CLC, 'Land Reform in the Northern Territory', above n 105, 15.
110 John Reeves, 'Building on Land Rights for the Next Generation: The Review of the *Aboriginal Land Rights (Northern Territory) Act 1976*' (Australian Government, 1998) 304–7. Reeves said that trespass law would need to be modified to take account of large tracts of Aboriginal land; see page 307.
111 Ibid, 305.
112 Ibid, 306.
113 Ibid, 304. See also iii, viii, 67, 306–8. See also Brennan, 'Economic Development and Land Council Power', above n 13, 3.
114 House of Representatives Standing Committee on Aboriginal and Torres Strait Islander Affairs, *The Report of the Inquiry into the Reeves Review of the Aboriginal Land Rights (Northern Territory) Act 1976* (1999) 116.
115 Mal Brough, 'Permit System for Indigenous Communities' (Media Release, 12 September 2006). See also Mal Brough, 'Permit System No Protection for the Vulnerable' (Media Release, 14 September 2006).
116 Mal Brough, 'Discussion Paper on Indigenous Permit System Released' (Media Release, 4 October 2006).
117 Jon Altman, 'The "National Emergency" and Land Rights Reform: Separating Fact from Fiction' (Briefing paper for Oxfam Australia prepared by the Centre for Aboriginal Economic Policy Research, 7 August 2007) 6.
118 See *Families, Community Services and Indigenous Affairs and Other Legislation Amendment (Northern Territory National Emergency Response and Other Measures) Act 2007* (Cth) sch 4.
119 See *Aboriginal Land Rights (Northern Territory) Act 1976* (Cth) s 70(2A).
120 Ibid, s 74AA.
121 *Aboriginal Land Act 1980* (NT) s 5.
122 *Aboriginal Land Rights (Northern Territory) Act 1976* (Cth) s 70G.
123 Ibid, ss 70E, 70F. Common area is defined as 'an area that is generally used by members of the community concerned, but does not include: (a) a building; or (b) a sacred site; or (c) an area prescribed by the regulations'; s 70F(20).
124 Ibid, ss 70C, 70D.
125 Ibid, s 70B. Many of the roads to Aboriginal communities are already public

212   *The reforms*

roads. This provisions applies only to those roads that were not previously public roads.

126 Ibid, ss 70(2D)–(2E). The provisions refer to permission of an 'occupier', which includes 'a person present at the premises who is in apparent control of the premises'.

127 Though Land Councils have argued that the reforms should be revoked and the old system reinstated; see, eg, Aboriginal Peak Organisations of the Northern Territory, 'Response to Stronger Futures' (Submission to the Australian Government on Stronger Futures, August 2011) 11.

128 The CLC does argue that there have been consumer scams in Central Australia since the permit reforms; see Australian Broadcasting Corporation, 'Rip-offs Spark Plea to Return Aboriginal Land Permits', *ABC News*, 30 August 2012 (Allyson Horn).

129 Inserted into the ALRA by the *Families, Community Services and Indigenous Affairs and Other Legislation Amendment (Northern Territory National Emergency Response and Other Measures) Act 2007* (Cth).

130 *Stronger Futures in the Northern Territory (Consequential and Transitional Provisions) Act 2012* (Cth) sch 2 item 3.

131 See Mal Brough, 'Major Howard Government Investment in Alice Springs Indigenous Accommodation' (Media Release, 13 March 2007); Tangentyere Council, 'Town Camp Residents Determined to Keep Their Land' (Media Release, 19 April 2007); Mal Brough, 'Alice Springs Town Camps' (Media Release, 18 April 2007); Mal Brough, 'Minister Disappointed by Decision on Alice Springs Town Camps' (Media Release, 23 May 2007).

132 *Northern Territory National Emergency Response Act 2007* (Cth) ss 43–6.

133 Ibid, s 47. This is in addition to the process available to the Commonwealth under the *Lands Acquisition Act 1989* (Cth).

134 Mal Brough, 'Historic 99 Year Town Camp Sub-Leases Agreed in Tennant Creek' (Media Release, 7 August 2007).

135 Calma, 'Native Title Report 2009', above n 1, 156.

136 Jenny Macklin, '$5.3 Million Upgrade for Tangentyere Housing' (Media Release, 10 July 2008).

137 Calma, 'Native Title Report 2009', above n 1, 156–7.

138 Ibid, 157.

139 Ibid.

140 The subleases were finalised in December 2009; see Jenny Macklin, Paul Henderson and Warren Snowdon, 'Work to Start on the Transformation of the Alice Springs Town Camps' (Media Release, 3 December 2009).

141 Roche, above n 45, 18.

142 Jenny Macklin, Karl Hampton and Warren Snowdon, 'New Housing Opportunities in Ilpeye Ilpeye' (Media Release, 29 January 2010).

143 Jenny Macklin and Warren Snowdon, 'Landmark Agreement Paves the Way for Home Ownership in the Ilpeye-Ilpeye Town Camp' (Media Release, 21 June 2013).

144 Ibid. The media release does not specify whether the freehold has been granted to individuals or to a representative body, but does state that the process will lead to 'individual land titles'.

145 Ibid.

146 Central Land Council (CLC), Submission No 347 to Senate Standing Committees on Community Affairs, Parliament of Australia, *Inquiry into Stronger Futures in the Northern Territory Bill 2011 and Two Related Bills*, 1 February 2012, 8–9.

147 Ibid, 8, and see Northern Land Council (NLC), Submission No 361 to Senate Standing Committees on Community Affairs, Parliament of Australia, *Inquiry*

The reforms 213

into Stronger Futures in the Northern Territory Bill 2011 and Two Related Bills, 10 February 2012, 3–4.

148 CLC, Submission No 347, above n 146, 10; NLC, Submission No 361, above n 147, 4.

149 *Stronger Futures in the Northern Territory Act 2012* (Cth) ss 32–5.

150 *Stronger Futures in the Northern Territory Regulation 2013* (Cth).

151 PricewaterhouseCoopers, 'Living in the Sunburnt Country: Indigenous Housing – Findings of the Review of the Community Housing and Infrastructure Programme' (Report to the Department of Families, Community Services and Indigenous Affairs, 2007).

152 Ibid, 16, 23–5.

153 Dillon and Westbury, above n 18, 168–9.

154 Australian Government and Northern Territory Government, 'Memorandum of Understanding: Indigenous Housing, Accommodation and Related Services' (17 September 2007).

155 Mal Brough, 'Funding for Major Indigenous Housing Projects' (Media Release, 18 September 2007), and see also Mal Brough, 'Government Delivers Long-Term Commitment to Housing Jobs, Health and Police as Part of Long Term Commitment to NT' (Media Release, 18 September 2007).

156 Australian and Northern Territory Governments, above n 154, cl 15.

157 Ibid.

158 Ibid, cl 15, 17.

159 Jenny Macklin, Paul Henderson and Warren Snowdon, 'Landmark Housing Project for NT Indigenous Communities' (Media Release, 12 April 2008).

160 Calma, 'Native Title Report 2009', above n 1, 142–8.

161 Scullion, 'Land Reform for the Future', above n 7.

162 Calma, 'Native Title Report 2009', above n 1, 149–50.

163 Australian Broadcasting Corporation, '150 WA Communities May Close', *Lateline*, 20 November 2014 (Caitlyn Gribbin).

164 Australian and Northern Territory Governments, above n 154, cl 13.

165 Jenny Macklin, 'Address to the NSW Aboriginal Land Council' (Speech delivered to the NSW Aboriginal Land Council, Cessnock, 5 March 2009); Calma, 'Native Title Report 2009', above n 1, 132, 164.

166 Australian Government and Northern Territory Government, *What Are the Different Types of Leases in Remote Communities?* (November 2009) Territory Housing www.housing.nt.gov.au/__data/assets/pdf_file/0012/123411/rfs45_rhnt_typesofleases_Jan12.pdf.

167 Council of Australian Governments, *National Partnership Agreement on Remote Indigenous Housing* (2008) cl 28.

168 Ibid, cl 15.

169 Calma, 'Native Title Report 2009', above n 1, 166–84.

170 Ibid, 139. Despite this, it appears that in Queensland the Department of Housing does pay a 'lease charge' to the landowing trustee; see Australian Government and Queensland Government, *Home Ownership on Indigenous Communal Lands: Councils' Roles and Responsibilities*, 2 www.hpw.qld.gov.au/SiteCollectionDocuments/CouncilsFinal.pdf.

171 Central Land Council (CLC), 'Community Leasing: An Alternative Proposal' (Discussion Paper, December 2010) 3.

172 Ibid.

173 Greg Roche, 'Executive Director of Township Leasing Annual Report 2013–2014' (Australian Government, 2014) 20. In the CLC region housing precinct leases have been granted to the EDTL, which then grants a ten-year sublease to Territory Housing. The CLC states that this is to retain the 'possibility that the EDTL/Australian Government could provide the second

214 *The reforms*

ten-year sublease to an alternative service provider'; CLC, 'Community Leasing: An Alternative Proposal', above n 171, 3.

174 Northern Territory Government, Department of Housing, *Remote Public Housing Management Framework* (20 September 2012) www.housing.nt.gov. au/remotehousing/managing_and_maintaining_housing.

175 Jenny Macklin, 'Speech to Cape York Institute Leadership Academy' (Speech delivered to the Cape York Institute Leadership Academy, Cairns, 22 July 2008).

176 Commonwealth, *Parliamentary Debates*, House of Representatives, 26 February 2009, 2031 (Kevin Rudd).

177 Nadia Rosenman and Alex Clunies-Ross, 'The New Tenancy Framework for Remote Aboriginal Communities in the Northern Territory' (2011) 7(24) *Indigenous Law Bulletin* 11, 14.

178 Ibid.

179 Ibid (emphasis added). The same point was also made more recently: see Aboriginal Peak Organisations of the Northern Territory, 'New NT Aboriginal Housing Body to Tackle Aboriginal Housing Crisis in the NT' (Media Release, 16 March 2015).

180 Macklin, 'Speech to Cape York Institute', above n 175.

181 See Malarndirri McCarthy, 'Historic Decision to Pay the Rent to Lease Aboriginal Land' (Media Release, 23 November 2011).

182 See, eg, Brian Gleeson, 'Coordinator General for Remote Indigenous Services Six Monthly Report September 2010–March 2011' (Australian Government, 2011) 42.

183 Central Land Council, *Applying for a Lease, Licence or Other Interest in Aboriginal Land* (2012) www.clc.org.au/articles/cat/leasing-aboriginal-land.

184 Northern Land Council (NLC), 'Record Number of Lease Agreements Approved by NLC Full Council' (Media Release, 1 June 2012).

185 CLC, 'Land Reform in the Northern Territory', above n 105, 18.

186 Ibid, 3, 19–23.

187 Ibid, 22.

188 Australian Government, Department of the Prime Minister and Cabinet, *Frequently Asked Questions about Township Leasing*, above n 75.

189 Ibid.

190 See, eg, Northern Land Council, *Land Rights News – Northern Edition* (Darwin), October 2014, 1, 3–9.

191 Calma, 'Native Title Report 2009', above n 1, 139–40.

192 McCarthy, above n 181.

193 CLC, *Application for a Lease, Licence or Other Interest in Aboriginal Land*, above n 183.

194 Ibid.

195 Based on 7 per cent and 10 per cent of the unimproved value of the land for residential and non-residential purposes respectively; ibid.

196 Greg Roche, 'Executive Director of Township Leasing Annual Report 2011–2012' (Australian Government, 2012) 18.

197 CLC, *Application for a Lease, Licence or Other Interest in Aboriginal Land*, above n 183.

198 CLC, 'Communal Title and Economic Development', above n 8, 21, 24.

199 For an overview of the various Queensland schemes see Garth Nettheim, Gary Meyers and Donna Craig, *Indigenous Peoples and Governance Structures: A Comparative Analysis of Land and Resource Management Rights* (Aboriginal Studies Press, 2002) 271–81.

200 Frank Brennan, *Land Rights Queensland Style: The Struggle for Aboriginal Self-Management* (University of Queensland Press, 1992) 11–13.

The reforms 215

201 Ibid.
202 Ibid, 90.
203 Ibid, chs 5, 6.
204 See *Aboriginal Land Act 1991* (Qld) ss 3, 38. Here and elsewhere below there are parallel provisions in the *Torres Strait Islander Land Act 1991* (Qld). To avoid repetition, only the *Aboriginal Land Act* is referenced.
205 *Native Title Act 1993* (Cth).
206 See, eg, Agreements, Treaties and Negotiated Settlements Project (ATNS), *Palm Island Improved Land Management Practices Indigenous Land Use Agreement* (6 December 2011) www.atns.net.au/agreement.asp?EntityID=5481.
207 This is formally recognised in ss 210, 233(3) of the *Native Title Act 1993* (Cth).
208 See Calma, 'Native Title Report 2009', above n 1, 166–8.
209 See, eg, Tim Mander, Greg Elmes and Nigel Scullion, 'Delivering Home Ownership for Yarrabah Families' (Media Release, 8 October 2014).
210 This is described in Chapter 7.
211 *Aboriginal Land Act 1991* (Qld) s 32B (definitions of 'urban area' and 'urban purposes').
212 Explanatory Notes, Aboriginal and Torres Strait Islander Land (Providing Freehold) and Other Legislation Amendment Bill 2014 (Qld) 4.
213 *Aboriginal Land Act 1991* (Qld) s 32D.
214 Ibid, s 32I(1).
215 Ibid, s 32I(3).
216 Ibid, s 32B (definition of 'interest holder'). Statutory occupancy rights refer to the rights of governments to remain on land that they occupied when it was made Indigenous land; see s 199. Equivalent provisions in the Northern Territory ALRA are described in Chapter 4.
217 *Aboriginal Land Regulation 2011* (Qld) reg 50B.
218 *Aboriginal Land Act 1991* (Qld) s 32J(2)(a).
219 Ibid, s 32J(2)(b).
220 Ibid, s 32K.
221 Ibid, s 32L.
222 Ibid, s 32B (definition of 'eligible person').
223 Ibid, s 32D(6).
224 Ibid, ss 32Z, 32ZA.
225 Ibid, s 32B (definition of 'allocation method').
226 Ibid, s 32ZB.
227 Ibid, s 32R.
228 Any money that the trustee receives for a social housing dwelling must be set aside and used only for housing services; ibid, s 288.
229 Ibid, s 128.
230 See Australian Broadcasting Corporation, 'Home Ownership Dreaming', *Background Briefing*, 1 February 2015 (Ian Townsend) www.abc.net.au/radionational/programs/backgroundbriefing/2015-02-01/6052302.
231 Queensland, *Parliamentary Debates*, Legislative Assembly, 8 May 2014, 1434 (Andrew Cripps).
232 Explanatory Notes, Aboriginal and Torres Strait Islander Land (Providing Freehold) and Other Legislation Amendment Bill 2014 (Qld) 11. It was reported in May 2015 that seven communities have signed up to the pilot programme; see Michael McKenna, 'Communities Embrace New Property Frontier', *The Australian*, 21 May 2015, 2. However, several practitioners from Queensland have told the author that concern about the programme is widespread and movement on the reforms is likely to be slow, particularly on land subject to native title.

216 The reforms

233 Queensland, *Parliamentary Debates*, Legislative Assembly, 8 May 2014, 1434 (Andrew Cripps).
234 Evidence to Agriculture, Resources and Environment Subcommittee, Legislative Assembly, Queensland Parliament, Cherbourg, 29 July 2014, 4 (Andrew Luttrell, Director, Policy, Department of Natural Resources and Mines).
235 Ibid.
236 Indigenous Business Australia, 'Home Ownership on Indigenous Land Now a Reality in Yarrabah' (Media Release, 22 October 2014). See also Chapter 7.

Bibliography

Books/articles/reports/web pages

AAP, 'Final Tiwi Community to Sign 99-Year Lease', *SBS News* (online), 14 March 2014, www.sbs.com.au/news/article/2014/03/14/final-tiwi-community-sign-99-year-lease.

Aboriginal Peak Organisations of the Northern Territory, 'Response to Stronger Futures' (Submission to the Australian Government on Stronger Futures, August 2011).

Aboriginal Peak Organisations of the Northern Territory, 'New NT Aboriginal Housing Body to Tackle Aboriginal Housing Crisis in the NT' (Media Release, 16 March 2015).

Agreements, Treaties and Negotiated Settlements Project (ATNS), *Palm Island Improved Land Management Practices Indigenous Land Use Agreement* (6 December 2011) www.atns.net.au/agreement.asp?EntityID=5481.

Altman, Jon, 'The "National Emergency" and Land Rights Reform: Separating Fact from Fiction' (Briefing paper for Oxfam Australia prepared by the Centre for Aboriginal Economic Policy Research, 7 August 2007).

Australian Broadcasting Corporation, 'Rip-offs Spark Plea to Return Aboriginal Land Permits', *ABC News*, 30 August 2012 (Allyson Horn).

Australian Broadcasting Corporation, '150 WA Communities May Close', *Lateline*, 20 November 2014 (Caitlyn Gribbin).

Australian Broadcasting Corporation, 'Home Ownership Dreaming', *Background Briefing*, 1 February 2015 (Ian Townsend).

Australian Government, 'Closing the Gap in the Northern Territory Monitoring Report July–December 2009 Part Two' (Department of Families, Housing, Community Services and Indigenous Affairs, 2010).

Australian Government, 'Indigenous Home Ownership Issues Paper' (Department of Families, Housing, Community Services and Indigenous Affairs, May 2010).

Australian Government, 'Closing the Gap, End of Five Year Leases' (Information Sheet, 2012).

Australian Government, 'Five-Year Leased Communities' (Closing the Gap Information Sheet).

Australian Government Department of Families, Housing, Community Services and Indigenous Affairs, Submission to South Australian Department of the Premier and Cabinet, *Review of the Aboriginal Lands Trust Act 1966*, 2009.

Australian Government, Department of the Prime Minister and Cabinet, *Jobs, Land and Economy* (2014) www.indigenous.gov.au/jobs-land-and-economy.

Australian Government, Department of the Prime Minister and Cabinet, *Frequently*

Asked Questions about Township Leasing (2014) www.dpmc.gov.au/indigenous-affairs/about/jobs-land-and-economy-programme/frequently-asked-questions-about-township-leasing.

Australian Government and Northern Territory Government, 'Memorandum of Understanding: Indigenous Housing, Accommodation and Related Services' (17 September 2007).

Australian Government and Northern Territory Government, *What Are the Different Types of Leases in Remote Communities?* (November 2009) Territory Housing www.housing.nt.gov.au/__data/assets/pdf_file/0012/123411/rfs45_rhnt_typesofleases_Jan12.pdf.

Australian Government Office of Township Leasing, *Commercial Sublease Application Form* (2009) Commonwealth of Australia www.otl.gov.au/docs/commercial_sublease.pdf.

Australian Government Office of Township Leasing, *Residential Sublease Application Form* (2009) Commonwealth of Australia www.otl.gov.au/docs/residential_sublease.pdf.

Australian Government Office of Township Leasing, *About the Office of Township Leasing* (2010) Commonwealth of Australia www.otl.gov.au/about.htm#5.

Australian Government Office of Township Leasing, *Sublease Rental Payments* (2010) Commonwealth of Australia www.otl.gov.au/site/sublease_rental_OOD.asp.

Australian Government Office of Township Leasing, *Publications*, Commonwealth of Australia www.otl.gov.au/site/publications.asp.

Australian Government and Queensland Government, *Home Ownership on Indigenous Communal Lands: Councils' Roles and Responsibilities* www.hpw.qld.gov.au/SiteCollectionDocuments/CouncilsFinal.pdf.

Brennan, Frank, *Land Rights Queensland Style: The Struggle for Aboriginal Self-Management* (University of Queensland Press, 1992).

Brennan, Sean, 'Economic Development and Land Council Power: Modernising the *Land Rights Act* or Same Old Same Old?' (2006) 10(4) *Australian Indigenous Law Reporter* 1.

Brennan, Sean, '*Wurridjal v Commonwealth*: The Northern Territory Intervention and Just Terms for the Acquisition of Property' (2009) 33 *Melbourne University Law Review* 957.

Commonwealth, *Parliamentary Debates*, House of Representatives, 31 May 2006 (Mal Brough).

Brough, Mal, 'Permit System for Indigenous Communities' (Media Release, 12 September 2006).

Brough, Mal, 'Permit System No Protection for the Vulnerable' (Media Release, 14 September 2006).

Brough, Mal, 'Discussion Paper on Indigenous Permit System Released' (Media Release, 4 October 2006).

Brough, Mal, 'Major Howard Government Investment in Alice Springs Indigenous Accommodation' (Media Release, 13 March 2007).

Brough, Mal, 'Alice Springs Town Camps' (Media Release, 18 April 2007).

Brough, Mal, 'Minister Disappointed by Decision on Alice Springs Town Camps' (Media Release, 23 May 2007).

Brough, Mal, 'National Emergency Response to Protect Aboriginal Children in the NT' (Media Release, 21 June 2007).

218   The reforms

Brough, Mal, 'Historic 99 Year Town Camp Sub-Leases Agreed in Tennant Creek' (Media Release, 7 August 2007).

Brough, Mal, 'Historic Agreement for 99 Year Lease in NT' (Media Release, 30 August 2007).

Brough, Mal, 'Funding for Major Indigenous Housing Projects' (Media Release, 18 September 2007).

Brough, Mal, 'Government Delivers Long-Term Commitment to Housing Jobs, Health and Police as Part of Long Term Commitment to NT' (Media Release, 18 September 2007).

Butt, Peter, *Land Law* (Lawbook Co, 6th ed, 2009).

Calma, Tom, 'Native Title Report 2009' (Australian Human Rights Commission, 2009).

Calma, Tom, 'Social Justice, Communal Lands and Sustainable Communities' in Lee Godden and Maureen Tehan (ed), *Comparative Perspectives on Communal Lands and Individual Ownership: Sustainable Futures* (Routledge, 2010) 49.

Central Land Council (CLC), 'Communal Title and Economic Development' (Policy Paper, 2005).

Central Land Council, *Australian Government Briefing* (14 December 2007) www.clc.org.au/files/pdf/CLC_Australian_Government_Intervention_Briefing_-_Dec_2007.pdf.

Central Land Council (CLC), 'Community Leasing: An Alternative Proposal' (Discussion Paper, December 2010).

Central Land Council (CLC), *Application for a Lease, Licence or Other Interest in Aboriginal Land* (2012) www.clc.org.au/files/pdf/Leasing_application_form.pdf.

Central Land Council (CLC), *Applying for a Lease, Licence or Other Interest in Aboriginal Land* (2012) www.clc.org.au/articles/cat/leasing-aboriginal-land.

Central Land Council (CLC), Submission No 347 to Senate Standing Committees on Community Affairs, Parliament of Australia, *Inquiry into Stronger Futures in the Northern Territory Bill 2011 and Two Related Bills*, 1 February 2012.

Central Land Council (CLC), 'Land Reform in the Northern Territory: Evidence Not Ideology' (2013).

Commonwealth Scientific and Industrial Research Organisation (CSIRO), 'Land Tenure in Northern Australia: Opportunities and Challenges for Investment' (June 2013).

Council of Australian Governments, *National Partnership Agreement on Remote Indigenous Housing* (2008).

Queensland, *Parliamentary Debates*, Legislative Assembly, 8 May 2014, 1434 (Andrew Cripps).

Dillon, Michael and Neil Westbury, *Beyond Humbug: Transforming Government Engagement with Indigenous Australia* (Seaview Press, 2007).

Explanatory Notes, Aboriginal and Torres Strait Islander Land (Providing Freehold) and Other Legislation Amendment Bill 2014 (Qld).

Gleeson, Brian, 'Coordinator General for Remote Indigenous Services Six Monthly Report July–November 2009' (Australian Government, 2009).

Gleeson, Brian, 'Coordinator General for Remote Indigenous Services Six Monthly Report September 2010–March 2011' (Australian Government, 2011).

Gleeson, Brian, 'Coordinator General for Remote Indigenous Services Six Monthly Report April 2011–September 2011' (Australian Government, 2011).

Government of South Australia, Department of the Premier and Cabinet, 'Aboriginal Lands Trust Act Review Discussion Paper: Key Issues' (2008).

Government of South Australia, Department of the Premier and Cabinet, *Review of the Aboriginal Lands Trust Act 1966* (2013) http://dpc.sa.gov.au/review-aboriginal-lands-trust-act-1966.

Grattan, Michelle, 'Howard Tilts at Title Fight', *The Sunday Age* (Melbourne), 10 April 2005, 17.

Hinkson, Melinda, 'Introduction: In the Name of the Child' in Jon Altman and Melinda Hinkson (eds), *Coercive Reconciliation: Stabilise, Normalise, Exit Aboriginal Australia* (Arena Publications, 2007) 1.

House of Representatives Standing Committee on Aboriginal and Torres Strait Islander Affairs, *The Report of the Inquiry into the Reeves Review of the Aboriginal Land Rights (Northern Territory) Act 1976* (1999).

Howard, John and Mal Brough, 'Indigenous Emergency' (Joint Press Conference, 21 June 2007).

Indigenous Business Australia, 'Home Ownership on Indigenous Land Now a Reality in Yarrabah' (Media Release, 22 October 2014).

Evidence to Agriculture, Resources and Environment Subcommittee, Legislative Assembly, Queensland Parliament, Cherbourg, 29 July 2014 (Andrew Luttrell, Director, Policy, Department of Natural Resources and Mines).

McCarthy, Malarndirri, 'Historic Decision to Pay the Rent to Lease Aboriginal Land' (Media Release, 23 November 2011).

McKenna, Michael, 'Communities Embrace New Property Frontier', *The Australian*, 21 May 2015, 2.

Macklin, Jenny, '$5.3 Million Upgrade for Tangentyere Housing' (Media Release, 10 July 2008).

Macklin, Jenny, 'Speech to Cape York Institute Leadership Academy' (Speech delivered to the Cape York Institute Leadership Academy, Cairns, 22 July 2008).

Macklin, Jenny, 'Compulsory Income Management to Continue as Key NTER Measure' (Media Release, 23 October 2008).

Macklin, Jenny, 'Government Finalises Five-Year Lease Boundaries in NT Indigenous Communities' (Media Release, 27 February 2009).

Macklin, Jenny, 'Address to the NSW Aboriginal Land Council' (Speech delivered to the NSW Aboriginal Land Council, Cessnock, 5 March 2009).

Macklin, Jenny and Warren Snowdon, 'Rent Payments for NTER Five-Year Leases' (Media Release, 25 May 2010).

Macklin, Jenny and Warren Snowdon, 'Landmark Agreement Paves the Way for Home Ownership in the Ilpeye-Ilpeye Town Camp' (Media Release, 21 June 2013).

Macklin, Jenny, Karl Hampton and Warren Snowdon, 'New Housing Opportunities in Ilpeye Ilpeye' (Media Release, 29 January 2010).

Macklin, Jenny, Paul Henderson and Warren Snowdon, 'Landmark Housing Project for NT Indigenous Communities' (Media Release, 12 April 2008).

Macklin, Jenny, Paul Henderson and Warren Snowdon, 'Work to Start on the Transformation of the Alice Springs Town Camps' (Media Release, 3 December 2009).

Mander, Tim, Greg Elmes and Nigel Scullion, 'Delivering Home Ownership for Yarrabah Families' (Media Release, 8 October 2014).

Nettheim, Garth, Gary Meyers and Donna Craig, *Indigenous Peoples and*

Governance Structures: A Comparative Analysis of Land and Resource Management Rights (Aboriginal Studies Press, 2002).

Northern Land Council, Submission No 361 to Senate Standing Committees on Community Affairs, Parliament of Australia, *Inquiry into Stronger Futures in the Northern Territory Bill 2011 and Two Related Bills*, 10 February 2012.

Northern Land Council, 'Record Number of Lease Agreements Approved by NLC Full Council' (Media Release, 1 June 2012).

Northern Land Council, 'Poster Ire', *Land Rights News – Northern Edition* (Darwin), October 2014, 8.

Northern Territory Government, *Inquiry into the Protection of Aboriginal Children from Sexual Abuse* (2007) www.inquirysaac.nt.gov.au.

Northern Territory Government, 'Inquiry Report' (Media Release, 15 June 2007).

Northern Territory Government, 'Ampe Akelyernemane Meke Mekarle: Little Children Are Sacred' (Report of the Northern Territory Board of Inquiry into the Protection of Aboriginal Children from Sexual Abuse, 2007).

Northern Territory Government, Department of Housing, *Remote Public Housing Management Framework* (20 September 2012) www.housing.nt.gov.au/remote-housing/managing_and_maintaining_housing.

PricewaterhouseCoopers, 'Living in the Sunburnt Country: Indigenous Housing – Findings of the Review of the Community Housing and Infrastructure Programme' (Report to the Department of Families, Community Services and Indigenous Affairs, 2007).

Reeves, John, 'Building on Land Rights for the Next Generation: The Review of the *Aboriginal Land Rights (Northern Territory) Act 1976*' (Australian Government, 1998).

Roche, Greg, 'Executive Director of Township Leasing Annual Report 2010–2011' (Australian Government, 2011).

Roche, Greg, 'Executive Director of Township Leasing Annual Report 2011–2012' (Australian Government, 2012).

Roche, Greg, 'Executive Director of Township Leasing Annual Report 2013–2014' (Australian Government, 2014).

Rosenman, Nadia and Alex Clunies-Ross, 'The New Tenancy Framework for Remote Aboriginal Communities in the Northern Territory' (2011) 7(24) *Indigenous Law Bulletin* 11.

Commonwealth, *Parliamentary Debates*, House of Representatives, 26 February 2009, 2031 (Kevin Rudd).

Scullion, Nigel, 'Historic Arnhem Land Lease Agreement' (Media Release, 17 October 2013).

Scullion, Nigel, 'Pirlangimpi Township Lease Agreement' (Media Release, 14 March 2014).

Scullion, Nigel, 'Land Reform for the Future', *Koori Mail*, 26 March 2014 (available at http://minister.indigenous.gov.au/media/2014-03-26/land-reform-future-published-koori-mail).

Shanahan, Dennis and Patricia Karvelas, 'PM Considers New Land Rights Plan', *The Weekend Australian*, 11 December 2004, 4.

Tangentyere Council, 'Town Camp Residents Determined to Keep Their Land' (Media Release, 19 April 2007).

Watson, Pat, 'Executive Director of Township Leasing Annual Report 2008–2009' (Australian Government, 2009).

Watson, Pat, 'Executive Director of Township Leasing Annual Report 2009–2010' (Australian Government, 2010).
Evidence to Council of Territory Co-operation, Legislative Assembly of the Northern Territory, Darwin, 14 April 2010 (Pat Watson).

Legislation and subordinate legislation

Aboriginal and Torres Strait Islander Land (Providing Freehold) and Other Legislation Amendment Act 2014 (Qld).
Aboriginal Land Act 1980 (NT).
Aboriginal Land Act 1991 (Qld).
Aboriginal Land Regulation 2011 (Qld).
Aboriginal Land Rights (Northern Territory) Act 1976 (Cth).
Aboriginal Land Rights (Northern Territory) Amendment Act 2006 (Cth).
Aboriginal Land Rights (Northern Territory) Amendment (Township Leasing) Act 2007 (Cth).
Aboriginal Land Rights (Northern Territory) Amendment Regulations (No 2) 2008 (Cth).
Aboriginal Land Rights (Northern Territory) Regulations 2007 (Cth).
Families, Community Services and Indigenous Affairs and Other Legislation Amendment (Northern Territory National Emergency Response and Other Measures) Act 2007 (Cth).
Housing Act 1982 (NT).
Indigenous Affairs Legislation Amendment Act 2008 (Cth).
Lands Acquisition Act 1989 (Cth).
Law of Property Act 2000 (NT).
Native Title Act 1993 (Cth).
Northern Territory National Emergency Response Act 2007 (Cth).
Residential Tenancies Act 1999 (NT).
Stronger Futures in the Northern Territory (Consequential and Transitional Provisions) Act 2012 (Cth).
Stronger Futures in the Northern Territory Act 2012 (Cth).
Stronger Futures in the Northern Territory Regulation 2013 (Cth).
Torres Strait Islander Land Act 1991 (Qld).

Cases

Wurridjal v Commonwealth (2009) 237 CLR 309.

7 Making sense of the reforms

7.1 Introduction

It is clear that the reforms described in the previous chapter do not do what it was said they would during debate that preceded their introduction. Rather than individual ownership or private property, the most common outcome has been a shift towards state property, quite the opposite to what was suggested. The significance of this should not be understated; it calls into question the very rationale for introducing the reforms. There is, however, no reason to believe that this was the result of a deliberate deception, that debate about communal and individual ownership was manufactured to conceal some ulterior motive. Whatever their flaws, these reforms do not share with the 19th-century reforms to indigenous land in the United States and New Zealand the aim of divesting Aboriginal people of their land. Indeed, one consequence of the reforms is that governments are now paying far more rent on Aboriginal land. The Australian reforms walk different ground, and raise different issues.

To consider those issues, this chapter continues the practice of distinguishing between categories of infrastructure. Section 7.2 considers the reforms as they affect residential housing, the houses that Aboriginal community residents live in. Residential housing has been a focus of reform efforts across Australia, and these reforms have an immediate and direct impact on community residents. They are considered here in some detail. Section 7.3 considers the reforms to infrastructure beyond residential housing – the offices, staff housing and purpose-built infrastructure occupied by service providers and enterprises. The two most significant developments here have been the introduction of rent and the altering of relationships around land use. In this context, this chapter also clarifies what the reforms do *not* do. For the most part, they have not led to the creation of 'land markets' and their economic impact is not only more contained than was predicted during debate about land reform, it is also very different. In the Northern Territory, rather than land reform paving the way for investors to establish enterprises more easily, it has given *landowners* the licence to exploit their position for commercial ends. This is

Making sense of the reforms   223

not the economic transformation that was sometimes suggested. It is never-theless a significant development with several consequences, not all of which are positive. At several points the chapter compares the Northern Territory reforms with the allotment of Indigenous land in Queensland. While the amendments to enable allotment have not yet been used, the contrast between the two sets of reforms helps clarify what is particular about each.

7.2 Residential housing

Dillon and Westbury describe it as 'blindingly apparent' that the 'pre-existing policy frameworks for the provision of Indigenous housing ... have not delivered solutions, particularly in remote Australia'.[1] This is an important backdrop for the critique of the housing reforms provided here. While this section details several problems with the recent reforms, it would be disingenuous to do so without acknowledging the extent to which the pre-existing arrangements had also attracted concern. The two reforms to housing – the housing precinct leases and the (limited) introduc-tion of home ownership – are very much responses to those concerns. They are also two very different responses and understanding this difference helps to understand their likely impact over time.

Home ownership

The implementation of home ownership

Chapter 5 describes how one consequence of home ownership being con-nected to the broader – and at times acrimonious – debate about land reform is that it often came to be characterised reductively. Rather than a complex policy issue with several facets, and one that required 'care and rigour',[2] it frequently came to be presented as something existing tenure arrangements were preventing and that land reform would enable. As Dillon and Westbury note, this was clever politics.[3] It enabled people in favour of land reform – including the government – to present the need for reform in terms that all Australians could relate to.[4] It appears, however, that this approach has come at a cost in terms of policy development. Other issues with respect to home ownership, particularly economic issues, have not received the attention they deserve.

This is reflected in the outcomes of the Home Ownership on Indigenous Land (HOIL) Program. Created by the Australian Government in 2006 to 'complement and give substance to' the introduction of township leasing, the HOIL Program provides additional financial support for prospective home owners on Indigenous land.[5] This included low-interest loans, grants, mortgage co-payments and assistance with meeting the purchase price.[6] The HOIL Program was initially allocated $107.4 million over four years

224 *Making sense of the reforms*

to provide 460 loans to homebuyers on Indigenous land across Australia.[7] The Australian National Audit Office (ANAO) conducted a review of the Program in 2010, and found that only 15 grants of home ownership had been made, all in the Northern Territory. Fourteen of those were in Wurrumiyanga, with a fifteenth elsewhere on the Tiwi Islands.[8] That is, at the end of four years the programme had achieved less than 4 per cent of its target outcome. In doing so, it had incurred administrative costs of $9.9 million (in addition to the $2.7 million lent to purchasers).[9] Nor has the rate of uptake increased since then. As of October 2014, there were only 25 reported grants of home ownership on Indigenous land across the country.[10]

By any measure, the HOIL Program has been an expensive failure. The ANAO attributes this failure primarily to delays in implementing appropriate tenure arrangements.[11] This is a surprising conclusion. As part of the Program, the Commonwealth constructed 49 houses for sale to residents in the Northern Territory – 29 in Wurrumiyanga and 10 each in the outstations of Wudapulli and Nama, near Wadeye.[12] Four of the houses in Wudapulli and Nama were the subjects of a special ministerial announcement in 2007.[13] Those four houses cost a total of $3,434,224 to construct,[14] and were ultimately transferred to Territory Housing for use as public housing because 'to be affordable for residents, prospective purchasers would have required a level of subsidisation beyond what was available under the HOIL program'.[15] In other words, the problem here was poor economic modelling, not tenure. In total, of the 49 houses constructed by government only three had been sold to purchasers by 2010, while 45 had instead been transferred to Territory Housing.[16] Again, this was not the result of problems with tenure. Instead, it appears that there was insufficient demand for those houses at the prices at which they were being offered.

The subsidies available under the HOIL Program, while relatively generous, represent only a fraction of the costs of building new houses in remote communities. For example, in 2008 an Aboriginal couple in Wurrumiyanga engaged a builder to construct a '$341,000 two-storey' house.[17] After subsidies, the couple were still left with a mortgage of $282,700.[18] As the couple reportedly have an unusually high combined income of $140,000 p.a.,[19] this is currently affordable. However, another significant issue has not been addressed, being the potential resale value of houses. It is by no means certain that the couple would be able to recover their outlay if they were to sell. This is considered further below; the point here is that there is clearly a need for more sophisticated economic modelling, to ensure that such purchasers do not suffer economic loss. This is an important issue, and it is striking that the ANAO fails to identify it.

It is also striking that until recently the Australian Government had failed to address this issue in any of its publications. There are tentative signs this may be shifting. In March 2013, the Council of Australian

Governments (COAG) Select Council on Housing and Homelessness released an 'Indigenous Home Ownership Paper' that takes a broader approach to the impediments to home ownership in remote Indigenous communities.[20] In particular, the document identifies problems associated with 'limited secondary markets'.[21] This compares favourably to earlier Australian Government publications.[22] It is, however, nearly a decade since the government first began trying to introduce home ownership in communities on Indigenous land, and the more recent publication – while an improvement – does not represent a significant advance on the research that authors in Queensland were producing several years earlier.[23] Many of the same issues are still being raised, with no new answers being provided. It appears that the practice of characterising home ownership as primarily a tenure issue – and as something that land reform would enable – has impeded the development of more sophisticated understandings about how to deal with the full range of issues that home ownership gives rise to.

What form of tenure is required for home ownership?

(A) OPEN, CLOSED AND REGULATED MARKETS

While there are several, significant non-tenure barriers to home ownership in Indigenous communities, it does not mean that tenure is irrelevant. Home ownership does require an appropriate form of tenure (for subject houses – not for entire communities), and there are several matters with respect to tenure that need to be addressed in communities on Indigenous land. It is not clear that all of these matters have been adequately addressed to date.

One of the more important issues for home ownership is whether there should be an open, closed or regulated market. Where markets are open – that is, where there are no restrictions on who can buy houses – there is an increased risk that houses will be lost from Indigenous ownership. This could have a harmful impact on Indigenous communities and consequently several people have argued that markets should be closed.[24] Many communities on Indigenous land are so remote that the issue of open and closed markets may appear irrelevant. That is not the case. There may be circumstances where a development such as a mine results in greater external interest, although this will be uncommon. In most communities, the main 'external' demand will come from governments, NGOs and enterprises, all of which require staff housing. If a market were open, the purchase of houses by these agencies – which are often better resourced than individuals – might result in a loss of housing for Indigenous residents.[25] Some communities might regard this as acceptable, others might see it as harmful; what is most important is that participating communities have the opportunity to arrive at a consensus *prior* to a scheme commencing.

226 *Making sense of the reforms*

This cannot be left ambiguous, as to do so would be to set up a situation of conflict at the point where a home owner wishes to sell to an outsider contrary to the wishes of others.

Creating a closed market is more complex than it first appears, as it means giving formal definition to the eligible group. In some areas, people might choose to do this by reference to a particular language group. This is one part of the market boundaries in Wurrimiyanga, where there are restrictions on the transfer of subleases to 'non-Tiwi'. On the mainland, where there is greater mixing between language groups, this approach might be too narrow. Alternatively, eligibility might be extended to Indigenous people generally, such as occurs with respect to home ownership leases on Indigenous land in Queensland (see below). Some might instead consider this too inclusive. Once a decision is made to close a market, there are further decisions to be made about *how* it should be closed. Again, it is important for participating communities to have the opportunity to deal with this from the outset.

An alternative approach is for the market to be centrally regulated – that is, for the transfer of houses to require the consent of a central authority. This avoids the need to formally define boundaries as the authority can use its discretion. It also gives rise to the question of who it is that should decide and upon what basis. Below it is described how there can also be legal obstacles to providing an authority with this type of discretion.

(B) TOWNSHIP SUBLEASES

Home ownership on land held under the *Aboriginal Land Rights (Northern Territory) Act 1976* (Cth) (the ALRA) does not require a community-wide lease such as a township lease. It can occur through a transferable section 19 lease, such as would have been used if the development at Wudapuli and Nama had been successful. The focus of efforts under the HOIL Program, however, has been on communities with a township lease and particularly Wurrumiyanga, where more than half of all reported grants are to be found.[26]

Home ownership subleases in Wurrumiyanga create a market that is partly closed and partly regulated. It is closed to the extent that a sublease holder cannot transfer a sublease where to do so would result in the permanent non-Tiwi population exceeding 15 per cent.[27] And it is regulated to the extent that the consent of the Executive Director of Township Leasing (EDTL) is required for the transfer of a sublease, which is subject to a statutory rule that consent must not be 'unreasonably withheld'.[28] These arrangements do not necessarily prevent the sale of houses to outsiders. The EDTL reports that the permanent non-Tiwi population of Wurrumiyanga is 5–7 per cent,[29] which means that the 15 per cent rule is currently not a barrier. It is not clear whether the EDTL would withhold consent to the sale of a house to an outsider, nor is it clear whether such a withholding would be considered 'unreasonable' for the purposes of the statutory rule. There is no case law that deals with such a particular situation.[30] Beyond this, it is not clear whether the issue of open and closed markets was appropriately addressed at a community level prior to the introduction of home ownership.

(C) HOME OWNERSHIP IN QUEENSLAND

In 2014, it was announced that a resident from Yarrabah had been granted home ownership through a 99-year lease,[31] which was the first grant of home ownership on Indigenous land in Queensland since the 'Katter leases' in the 1980s. The 99-year home ownership leases can only be transferred to a person who would have been eligible for the grant of such a lease, which in most places will be Aboriginal people or Torres Strait Islanders and their spouses and former spouses.[32] If a community takes up the option of allotment, a 99-year home ownership lease might be converted to ordinary freehold. If that were to occur, there would be no restrictions on its further transfer. It would simply be an open market.

Housing precinct leases and the shift to public housing

The second and more widespread reform to housing is the housing precinct leases, which result in an increase in government control over housing management and a concurrent decrease in community control. The leases are being used to implement a shift to public housing, which means that mainstream housing departments have replaced Indigenous Community Housing Organisations (ICHOs) as housing managers and more centralised and uniform management practices have been introduced. For tenants, this has meant stricter and more formalised tenancy management. They are required to sign up to written tenancy agreements under which there is less scope for ambiguity and greater threat of sanction.

This is clearly a very different reform to home ownership, yet the two have certain things in common. As set out below, they both reflect an attempt to do more than just alter the way in which people occupy houses. They have been presented as being part of a broader normative shift. The way in which they each attempt this is very different. The following section draws out the similarities and differences between the two reforms by describing how they respond to the four most commonly expressed concerns with earlier housing arrangements: that houses were not well cared for; that tenure arrangements narrowed supply options; that houses were unable to be used as collateral; and that government-funded community housing had become a type of harmful welfare.

228 *Making sense of the reforms*

Historic problems with housing in remote Indigenous communities

Houses not sufficiently well cared for

(A) NATURE OF THE PROBLEM

One concern with the earlier arrangements is that houses in Indigenous communities have not been sufficiently well cared for. This has *contributed* to houses having shorter lifespans and providing a poorer level of amenity for residents. The size of the problem is considerable: in 2006, it was estimated that of the 14,812 houses managed by ICHOs in remote and very remote regions across Australia, 1,233 were in need of replacement and 3,355 were in need of major repair.[33] The word 'contributed' is important here – other reasons for houses falling into disrepair include poor construction standards, design problems, relatively harsh climatic conditions and high occupancy levels placing greater pressure on housing components.[34]

The exact relationship between tenure and responsibility for the care of houses needs to be unpacked a little. The housing system in communities prior to the recent reforms was a type of community housing. Being a rental model, this meant that responsibility for the care of houses was shared between landlords (ICHOs) and tenants. Consequently, a failure to maintain houses might be the fault of either ICHOs or tenants (or both). Following a detailed empirical study of remote Indigenous housing, Torzillo *et al.* found that 'only 10% of ... house items requiring repair were due to vandalism or misuse' by tenants, while 65 per cent were due to a lack of 'routine maintenance' and 25 per cent due to faulty installation or equipment.[35] This might be thought to indicate that it is ICHOs, rather than residents, who have failed in their responsibilities. However, not all 'routine maintenance' is the responsibility of landlords, and the authors do not clarify whether the deficient maintenance was a landlord or tenant matter, or whether due to confusion over the division of responsibility.

(B) HOME OWNERSHIP AS A SOLUTION

Home ownership results in a transfer of ownership to occupiers, or more accurately to certain core occupiers. This has several consequences. It ends the division of responsibility for care by shifting it entirely to (core) occupiers, which lessens the scope for ambiguity and results in (core) occupiers bearing a higher maintenance burden. As noted below, some authors have concerns about the consequences of this shift. Home ownership might also provide (core) occupiers with a greater incentive to maintain, repair and prevent damage to houses. There are two main strands to the reasoning behind this. The first is that home owners acquire greater *tenure security* and a set of *alienable rights*. According to the theory set out in Chapter 2,

Making sense of the reforms 229

there are several reasons why this might lead to owners having a greater incentive to maintain their houses. However, a careful application of that theory suggests that any improvement *on this basis* (but see below) is likely to be minimal. It appears that core occupiers of residential housing already experience a high level of tenure security, so any increase will be small. With respect to alienable rights: where owners can sell their property they have an additional incentive to invest, as they may be able to recoup their investment upon sale. Platteau describes this as the 'realisability effect'.[36] This effect will be more pronounced where house prices are high relative to construction costs, as then owners are likely to recover a greater proportion of their investment. As discussed below, it does not appear that house prices in remote Indigenous communities will be high relative to construction costs. In all, the land reform theory described in Chapter 2 would suggest that home ownership will have only a modest impact on care for houses.

There is, however, a second, more complex reason why home ownership might give occupiers a greater incentive to maintain houses, to do with removing a different type of disincentive. The housing system in Aboriginal communities was not simply community housing, it was *government-funded* community housing. The involvement of government alters the dynamics of responsibility, particularly in communities where it has been observed that 'passivity and dependency characterise the relationship' of residents to government.[37] A shift to home ownership can alter this dynamic, although not necessarily.

This might be explained by reference to what the Cape York Institute (CYI) describes as a 'sense of ownership', a somewhat elusive but important concept. It includes (but is not limited to) the feeling of being responsible for something, which is the focus here. The point for present purposes is that legal ownership does not necessarily equate to a sense of ownership (and vice versa). The CYI argues that 'many families and individuals will only develop a strong *sense of ownership* of their homes if they have invested significant personal effort into the acquisition or development of their home'.[38] If this is correct it is relevant to pricing, which is the point that the CYI makes. It is also relevant beyond this. O'Brien argues that a benefit of self-build approaches is that participants in the construction process 'display a sense of "ownership" that has nothing to do with ... legal entitlement'.[39] That is, in and of itself, participation in design and construction can lead to a stronger sense of ownership. The CYI also argues that untidy buildings and neighbourhoods can undermine people's sense of ownership and recommends 'pride of place' programmes that include small co-contributions to building improvements.[40]

The introduction of home ownership into remote communities has not always resulted in improved house care. In Kowanyama, Queensland, the introduction of 'Katter leases' – a perpetual lease over houses – in the 1980s resulted in (or did not prevent) a large number of houses falling into

230   *Making sense of the reforms*

disrepair.[41] More recently in Meekathara, a remote Western Australian town, several of the houses made the subject of home ownership have reportedly been abandoned.[42] The CYI argues that one reason for the failure of 'Katter leases' was that 'families were not required to make any financial or other commitments' and so their 'sense of responsibility and ownership remained unchanged',[43] which may understate the level of financial contribution required of participants.[44] The CYI also argues that a further reason for the failure of the scheme was that houses were 'in poor condition and nearing the end of their lifespan'.[45]

(C) HOUSING PRECINCT LEASES AS A SOLUTION

The housing precinct leases (and concurrent shift to public housing) represent a very different response to this problem. The rental model is retained but modified in important respects. ICHOs are replaced by mainstream housing departments, on the understanding that they are better equipped to maintain houses. On the other side of the ledger, tenants are subject to stricter conditions and face greater sanction if they fail to maintain their house or allow it to be damaged. And the relationship between landlord and tenant has been formalised, to reduce scope for ambiguity and to provide housing departments with the legal means to enforce tenancy rules. The significance of this approach is discussed below.

Tenure arrangements restrict supply options

A second concern for some authors is that tenure arrangements have restricted housing supply, preventing 'people exercising any option other than to wait for government to build them a house'.[46] This argument is presented most strongly by Hughes, Hughes and Hudson, who suggest that a 'million dollars spent supporting private housing would save billions of "social" housing expenditure'.[47] To clarify, selling *existing* houses does not increase housing supply (although if it means houses last longer it will lead to an overall increase in stock over time[48]). 'Enabling private housing' will only increase housing supply where it leads to new construction, for either home ownership or private rental. Several people have noted that a significant barrier to this is the combination of high construction and maintenance costs and low income levels in remote Indigenous communities.[49] Hughes, Hughes and Hudson disagree, arguing that the private sector will construct houses far more cheaply than governments have.[50] If this does occur, there is a risk that cost reductions might be achieved through lower quality and less robust housing. Memmott *et al.* argue that, due to additional pressures on housing in remote communities, lower-cost housing would be more expensive in the long term.[51] They also caution that home ownership should not be seen 'as a means to relieve pressure on funding for new houses'.[52]

Making sense of the reforms 231

To date, reforms to Aboriginal land in the Northern Territory have resulted in only a marginal increase in the supply of houses, and have done so in a way that is concerning. When the ANAO reviewed the HOIL Program in 2010, it found that of the 15 grants of home ownership (at that time), seven were for new houses: three constructed by the government for sale, and four constructed by a builder engaged by the new owner.[53] For houses in this last category, there were some delays and difficulties with contract management, and two organisations raised concerns to the ANAO about construction quality.[54] One couple who engaged a builder experienced delays to the point that in 2010 they told a journalist they regretted signing up.[55] Consequently, the use of a project manager is now mandatory under the Program.[56] This is likely to improve construction standards but may add to costs.

Even with the subsidies available under the HOIL Program, buyers of new houses take on a significant mortgage. Of the 15 home owners in Wurrumiyanga, half have taken on mortgages of over $200,000 (which appears to correspond with those purchasing new houses).[57] The highest is for $300,000. This may be well above the resale price of those houses. The CYI has suggested that the 'market price' in remote Indigenous communities in Queensland is likely to be around $100,000.[58] Based on similar properties in nearby towns, the Queensland Department of Housing values houses in remote communities at between $80,000 and $150,000.[59] Following a case study of five families in Mapoon, Queensland, World Vision suggests median sale prices need to be around $150,000 in order to be affordable.[60] If this is true, purchasers of new houses in Wurrumiyanga are at risk of significant loss if they sell. This will not just be a problem for them; it will affect participation in the scheme. For this reason, the CYI recommends new houses be subsidised to a level that matches their market price,[61] while Memmott *et al.* argue consideration should be given to buyback schemes.[62] Neither has been implemented to date and both are likely to be expensive.

This suggests that home ownership will require greater subsidisation than is currently provided. This is a point of some significance. It means that both social housing and home ownership rely on government financial assistance. While it is a different type of government benefit to social housing, subsidised home ownership is still a type of government benefit. This characterisation should not be shied away from. The ongoing role of governments in remote communities needs to be accepted and incorporated into understandings. This theme is developed further below, in relation to social housing as harmful welfare, and discussed again in Chapter 8.

Use of houses as collateral

A related argument is that earlier arrangements prevented housing from being used as collateral, creating a 'dead capital (poverty) trap'.[63] It is in

232   *Making sense of the reforms*

this context that de Soto's theories are most relevant, and in particular his argument that the 'single most important source of funds for new businesses in the United States is a mortgage on the entrepreneur's house'.[64] For houses in remote Aboriginal communities to help fund new businesses, however, there would need to be not just home ownership but also appropriate market conditions. More particularly, home owners must be in the position of having a *meaningful* level of *recognisable* surplus capital in their house. It must be recognisable in the sense that a financial institution would be willing to lend on the security of a mortgage, which requires a reasonable level of market predictability. And it must be meaningful in that the amount of credit would contribute in a real way to an enterprise. This is much less likely where house prices are low, and impossible where mortgage levels exceed resale prices. Further, for capitalisation to provide the positive benefits predicted by de Soto, credit must then be used towards a productive investment, and not an unproductive investment or consumption. As described in Chapter 2, this does not always occur, and where poor decisions are made about the use of such credit the impact on housing may instead be negative.

Social housing as harmful welfare

A more significant criticism of the pre-existing housing arrangements is that they formed 'a core component of the welfare state provisioning in remote Indigenous communities'.[65] That is, government-funded community housing was not only less well cared for, its provision – in conjunction with other forms of welfare – has had a harmful impact on individual and group norms, resulting in 'welfare dependency'[66] or 'passivity'.[67]

This forms part of a broader debate about welfare in Aboriginal communities.[68] Initially the focus of that debate was on social security payments and employment programmes, but it has now expanded to include other types of government benefit. Noel Pearson and the CYI have played a significant role in this expansion,[69] and some (but not all) of their arguments have been adopted by the Australian Government. They argue that government-funded community housing can be harmful because: it requires little or no responsibility from occupiers, who come to expect that 'governments will provide, maintain and in the end replace their housing'; rents tend to be lower than those charged in other locations or set by the 'market'; poor behaviours attract too little sanction and good behaviours are not rewarded; and while in other places social housing is the exception, for people in special circumstances, in Indigenous communities it has become the norm.[70]

Significantly, some of these can be characterised as facets of the way in which housing has been managed, rather than an incident of social housing per se. This includes rents being lower and poor behaviour attracting too little sanction (to the extent this has been the case). This is the aspect of the

CYI's reasoning that has been adopted by the Australian Government, in the course of explaining the housing precinct leases. The former Minister argued that pre-existing housing arrangements 'in most Indigenous communities [were] at odds with the overarching goal of personal responsibility'.[71] The new and 'more robust tenancy management arrangements'[72] mean that tenants are required to 'sign up to, and adhere to, normal tenancy agreements – an important lever in our drive to rebuild positive community values and behaviour'.[73]

The government has also argued that the new tenancy arrangements are a step towards home ownership, in that they require tenants 'to pay regular and standardised rent and meet care of property requirements' which 'is part of developing the personal responsibility and individual financial resilience and discipline that is also required to purchase and pay off a home'.[74] Nevertheless, these arrangements are not home ownership and do not lessen the involvement of governments nor alter the fact that social housing will remain dominant. They instead increase and make more direct the role of governments in housing. In this respect, they depart significantly from the recommendations of the CYI. Writing of the housing reforms in Queensland, Pearson argues that apart 'from the fact that this public housing model is the embodiment of passive welfare', the shift from 'control by communities to management by the Queensland Department of Housing' is 'completely inconsistent with the nature and culture of the remote communities that I know'.[75] He argues that housing areas in Indigenous communities are not

> anonymous places where the housing department bureaucrat can allocate families indiscriminately on the basis of some housing allocation formula.... My father grew up under that poinsettia.... My great uncle gave my parents this block in the 1960s. These were and are still villages: not housing estates.[76]

This evocatively captures the *reduction* in ownership by residents that the reforms effect, the rationale for which is discussed in the next section.

Laying bare the role of government, laying bare assumptions as to value

Of the concerns identified here, the two that appear to have most shaped the recent reforms are that houses have been insufficiently well cared for and that social housing contributes to welfare dependence. The two housing reforms respond to these concerns very differently. The introduction of home ownership shares much common ground with the land reform theory described in Chapter 2. (Core) occupiers are provided with more secure tenure, a set of alienable rights and responsibility for the care of their own houses, on the understanding that this removes barriers to

234 *Making sense of the reforms*

people advancing their own, long-term self-interest. The housing leases are based on something of an inversion of this approach. They result in a contained or strategic *reduction* in tenure security, and to the extent that it previously existed, the *removal* of a right to devise (transfer through inheritance). Tenants face greater sanction if they fail to comply with new and more onerous standards. While the government has argued this will help residents develop 'personal responsibility', 'individual financial resilience' and 'discipline', the mechanism for this needs to be made clear. It relies on externally imposed discipline, rather than enabling people to further their own self-interest. It effects a reduction of autonomy rather than an enhancement. And arguing that community organisations (ICHOs) have been ineffective in imposing the necessary discipline, the government itself has now taken on that role.

The government has frequently said residents will be subject to an increased duty to care for and maintain houses. But to whom is the duty owed? Under the new arrangements, it is owed to the leaseholder and housing manager, being the department of housing. And perhaps more importantly, on what is the duty based? Does it rely on residents having or developing a sense of obligation to housing departments greater than what they experienced towards ICHOs? Or does it rely on the threat or experience of sanction? From the quotations referred to above, it appears to be the latter. This raises questions on both sides of the equation: about the willingness of residents to meet expectations, and about the ability of governments to effectively perform the role of duty-enforcer.

Writing in relation to the Mardu people of Western Australia, Myrna and Robert Tonkinson argue that a 'striking feature of desert people is their extraordinarily high levels of tolerance for discomfort, frustration, inconvenience and hardship'.[77] They also observe that Mardu place a 'very high value' on their autonomy – an observation frequently made of Aboriginal communities – and also that they understand autonomy differently. 'For the Mardu, autonomy is about making decisions and choices as one sees fit, being accountable to no one, albeit within the bounds of [Aboriginal law].'[78] This combination of factors leads them to conclude that 'efforts by governments to goad such peoples into action through "carrot and stick" schemes, aimed at enticing Aborigines into conformity' are unlikely to work.[79] Peterson makes a similar point, but goes further. He asks: 'What is the future of such communities as social environments if the majority of the long-term inhabitants are alienated from any involvement in and responsibility for the future of their communities?'[80] He discusses this in relation to the dissolution of local councils and their replacement with large regional shires, which he argues has led to alienation. This must surely be a risk with the housing leases, which institutionalise government ownership of and responsibility for large sections of communities.

The introduction of home ownership relies on a different set of assumptions as to value. As noted above, home ownership takes effect by removing the disincentives to people acting in their own long-term interest. However, as Martin so neatly puts it, 'incentives almost by definition are not culture or value free'.[81] It is not suggested that home ownership is somehow *incompatible* with Indigenous culture in remote communities. That does not appear to be the case. The allocation of houses to individuals is certainly nothing new. Nevertheless, home ownership in remote communities will take place in a different cultural context and rely on a different set of incentives from those found elsewhere.[82] Houses will be valued, used, bought and sold differently. Among other things, this will have an impact on pricing and the behaviour of housing markets.

Ultimately there is no neutral way of governments engaging with remote Aboriginal communities with respect to housing. Those communities do, and will continue to, require government assistance, and understandings of the way in which this should occur are fundamental to a land reform model, a theme returned to in Chapter 8.

7.3 Infrastructure occupied by enterprises and service providers

Mandatory formalisation

In the Northern Territory, the key to understanding the reforms as they affect infrastructure beyond residential housing is that formalisation is being made mandatory. Service providers (governments, councils and NGOs) and enterprises (community stores, art centres, garages, etc) are required to obtain a lease or sublease, whether they want to or not. This is a complete paradigm shift – from widespread reliance on informal tenure arrangements to a complete intolerance for it. Indeed, the Australian Government does not recognise the existence of a functional set of informal tenure arrangements in its publications.

To reiterate, these reforms go beyond making it *easier* for occupiers to obtain formal tenure. They make it *compulsory* to do so. On a township lease, it is not an option for a youth work organisation or an art centre to continue to rely on informal arrangements. The EDTL requires all occupiers to obtain a sublease. They might resist – in Wurrumiyanga, the Northern Territory Government and Shire Council resisted for some time, due to concerns about rent, but ultimately agreed. If an occupier outright refused, and there are no reports of this occurring, they might be given notice to leave by the EDTL. Beyond township leases, mandatory formalisation applies to all organisations affected by 'secure tenure' policies. Without 'secure tenure', they may be ineligible for government funding. And even for infrastructure that is not directly affected by either a township lease or 'secure tenure' policies, Land Councils are now indicating that traditional owners expect occupiers to apply for a lease. On their present trajectory, these reforms will result in most, if not all, tenure arrangements in

236 *Making sense of the reforms*

communities on Aboriginal land in the Northern Territory being formalised. This is a big and expensive project.

The two most important consequences of this development are the increase in the amount of rent payable by occupiers and the formalisation and alteration of relationships around land use. Both are discussed below, together with the impact that the reforms have on economic development.

Rent

A significant increase in rent

Residential housing tenants have always been required to pay some kind of rent; however, that rent was paid to the ICHO rather than landowners. As such it was not rent in the sense that is relevant here. The payment of rent *to landowners* has historically been uncommon, even where a lease has been granted, particularly where the lease was 'for a community purpose'.[83] For example, there were 15 leases in Wurrumiyanga prior to the grant of a township lease, with a combined rent of just $2,000 per year.[84] An exception has been with respect to stores, especially in the Northern Land Council region, where the amount of rent paid to landowners has sometimes been considerable.[85]

The reforms have significantly altered this. There has been no change with respect to housing – while tenants may pay more rent, this continues to go to the housing manager rather than landowners. The change is to other occupiers, those enterprises and service providers who previously paid no rent. In the majority of cases they are now required to do so. There is also a third type of rent that has come into play, which is that paid for by governments on whole-of-community leases, whether township leases or five-year leases. This is slightly different again because it is not paid for by occupiers.

The Australian Government's approach to rent has shifted on several occasions. When legislation to enable township leasing was introduced in 2006, it provided that landowners were not allowed to use the terms of a township lease to require that rent be charged on subleases.[86] Yet the following year the government agreed to exactly such a term in the first township lease, which requires the EDTL to grant subleases on a 'commercial basis'. Legislation implementing the five-year leases provided that the Commonwealth was not required to pay rent and was only required to pay compensation to the extent that it was constitutionally necessary. Ultimately the government agreed to pay 'fair rent' for the five-year leases. The government then said that rent must not be charged on housing precinct leases in 'recognition of the significant government investment in housing set to follow'.[87] However, when 'secure tenure' policies were extended beyond housing it instead said that rent should be paid. This diversity of approaches suggests that that government itself is conflicted. Having

Making sense of the reforms   237

entered into these reforms with no useful set of guiding principles, it has been unclear how best to deal with the issue. Nevertheless, over time a clear trend has emerged – most enterprises and service providers are now required to pay rent.

The consequences of rent

(A) RENT AS AN INCREASE IN THE COSTS OF DOING BUSINESS

One of the more technocratic arguments for the introduction of township leases was that they would avoid the 'high transaction costs involved in negotiating s. 19 leases'.[88] The government has also said that one aim of its 'secure tenure' policies was to reduce 'transaction costs' while providing 'commercial certainty' so as to allow land to be used 'as security for financing, as a site for business establishment or as a resource to be developed'.[89] Contrary to what these arguments suggest, both township leasing and 'secure tenure' policies result in an *increase* in costs for the majority of occupiers and investors, rather than a decrease, primarily because they are now required to pay rent. In other words, as a result of new policies it is now more expensive to establish or carry on a business in Aboriginal communities. Over time, the consequence of this may be a reduction in investment.

However, the size of this disincentive will depend on the extent to which rent represents a real increase in costs. The costs of operating in remote Aboriginal communities are already high and rent, particularly small amounts of rent, may represent only a marginal increase. For example, it has been reported that the Tiwi Islands Regional Council will be required to pay rent of around $200,000 per year.[90] This sounds significant, but less so when considered against the size of the council's operations and its annual budget of over $18 million.[91] The Northern Territory Government has estimated that its total rent will be around $5 million per year; again, a small fraction of its overall costs.[92] The disinvestment impact of introducing rent should not be overstated. If it does have an impact, it is likely to be small and incremental rather than sudden or dramatic.

(B) RENT AS LANDOWNER INCOME

Conversely, the benefit of rent is that it provides a source of income for landowners. As in Wurrumiyanga, rent might be reinvested in the community. In conjunction with other forms of support (see below), this can lead to some increase in enterprise development. Here too the size of the increase should not be overstated, as to date it has been modest. Alternatively rent might be invested in community development projects, as supported by the Central Land Council (CLC).[93] This will instead result in a modest increase in social investment.

238   *Making sense of the reforms*

Not all rent will be invested in community projects or enterprise development. Some will instead be distributed to individuals and used for consumption (including where rent is invested and the profits are later distributed). It is at this point that issues around the characterisation of these payments come into play, whether as harmful welfare or constructive income. Beadman, for example, has criticised the introduction of rent as creating 'a passive "royalty" flow for Traditional Owners'.[94] However, this requires far greater consideration. Why should the payment of rent be regarded as harmful welfare in Aboriginal communities, while it is so commonly regarded as constructive income in other contexts? This is considered further in Chapter 8.

This discussion indicates that rent will have both a positive and negative impact on investment in communities on Aboriginal land, although in both cases the impact is likely to be small. The positive impact is more immediate and visible, while the negative impact will be incremental and long term. This may have influenced the government's decision to ultimately favour the introduction of rent. Whether or not it consciously understood the problem in these terms, it was faced with choosing between trying to create an optimal investment environment for occupiers, knowing that the impact would be minimal, and trying to immediately stimulate economic activity through the introduction of greater rent, which also fosters landowner goodwill. It has for the most part opted to follow the latter path.

A market reform?

This is a good point to consider claims about the market nature of the Northern Territory reforms. Dillon and Westbury argue that one of the advantages of township leases is that they 'facilitate the development of a real estate market'.[95] In a similar vein, the EDTL states that township leasing is the 'best option for Aboriginal communities ... to build a sustainable market for future generations'.[96] More recently, the Minister for Indigenous Affairs has said that an advantage of township leases is that they 'support long term and transferable subleases' of the type that 'you or I could go to the bank with and get mortgage on'.[97] However, with the exception of home ownership subleases (of which there have been very few), the existing township leases have not actually created a real estate market. This is primarily because subleases have been drafted to maximise rent, rather than create a valuable form of tenure for sublease holders. Consequently, the subleases themselves are not in the nature of a marketable commodity. The Commonwealth Bank confirmed this when provided with a copy of the standard commercial sublease terms and asked to advise whether they might be used to support a mortgage. They said they would not, as the terms were 'so onerous at to make the [sublease] near to valueless' and arguably 'a business liability rather than an asset'.[98]

The EDTL has alternatively argued that township leases can help move communities 'from a situation where [they are] almost totally reliant on Commonwealth and Northern Territory Government capital injections for economic development to one that more closely aligns to a market-based approach'.[99] This suggests that township leasing might be considered a market reform in a different sense, despite not creating a land market, because it results in greater rent. However, the charging of rent by a monopoly provider is not a market reform in any meaningful sense and the introduction of rent does not actually lessen reliance on the Commonwealth and Northern Territory governments. The overwhelming majority of rent will ultimately be paid for by them, either directly as occupiers or indirectly through the funding of service providers. The CLC reports that the two governments have 'acknowledged that their commitment to the secure tenure policy will necessitate them funding third party service providers [to] pay rent'.[100] This rent is still an 'injection' of government funds, although in a different form.

The key point is that the use of market language elides the primary mechanism that the government is using to stimulate economic development in Aboriginal communities. It has elected to focus on creating an income stream for landowners, even though this comes at a cost to investors and occupiers. The use of market language also gives the impression that the reforms do more than they actually do, that there has been some fundamental transformation. That has not been the case.

It is here that recent developments in Queensland are potentially significant. Where Indigenous land is divided up and converted to ordinary freehold, this will create a land market. The creation of a 'normal' land market appears to be one of the reasons why the amendments to allow allotment were introduced, when Queensland legislation already allowed for long-term leasing over Indigenous land. However, if and when it occurs, allotment will not affect entire communities. Restrictions in the legislation mean that it will initially be contained to home ownership and vacant land.[101] It will not result in community-wide land markets. It is argued in Chapter 8 that there are compelling reasons for such restrictions.

New enterprises in township lease communities

One of the good news stories of the Northern Territory reforms has been a small increase in enterprise activity in communities with a township lease, especially Wurrumiyanga. This is a development that has been keenly promoted by supporters of township leasing. The Tiwi Land Council and the EDTL report that the traditional owners for Milikapiti and Wurankuwu agreed to a township lease because they had 'observed, and now seek to replicate the quite outstanding ... economic development opportunities flowing from' the township lease in Wurrumiyanga.[102] The Minister for Indigenous Affairs has said that township leases have paved 'the way for

240 *Making sense of the reforms*

new businesses, jobs and home ownership', bringing about changes that are 'unlike any seen before in remote Aboriginal communities'.[103] Consequently, one of the Australian Government's top priorities with respect to encouraging employment and economic development is to '[n]egotiate more township leases'.[104]

It is important, then, to be clear about what it is that has led to these developments. Is it the result of new tenure arrangements? Or does it have another cause? And does it actually require a township lease? To consider this issue, it is useful to first identify the exact nature of the new enterprises, which fall into two categories. In the first category are the investments traditional owners have made using rent, particularly the up-front rent they have received upon the grant of a township lease. For example, the up-front rent for the Wurrumiyanga lease was $5 million, which has been used to purchase the tourist operator Tiwi Tours, establish a car-rental business, buy a truck,[105] construct a house as part of a joint venture with a food van operator,[106] and part-fund the construction of a super-market complex. In the second category are property developments. In Wurrumiyanga, the traditional owners (through their investment body, Mantiyupwi Pty Ltd) have obtained a total of 10 subleases over land in the community.[107] The two most significant of these have been the purchase of a temporary contractors' camp, which has been upgraded to provide short-term accommodation,[108] and the construction of a supermarket complex that includes four small retail spaces.[109] This was partly financed through the up-front rental payment, but also through a loan from a commercial bank that was secured by a mortgage.[110]

There are several things to note about these developments. The first is the role played by rent. In fact several of the new, or newly acquired, enterprises have nothing to do with land reform or tenure per se – they are simply the investment of up-front rent by traditional owners. That rent is paid for out of the Aboriginal Benefits Account (ABA), money that was already set aside for the benefit of Aboriginal people in the Northern Territory. Many of these projects – such as the shopping complex – might have been directly eligible for ABA funding, which is frequently used to support Aboriginal enterprises. There are, however, important differences between direct grants of funding and payments mediated through rent. The traditional owners have greater control over rent, and from everyone's perspective it is their money rather than government money.

Significantly, all new and newly acquired enterprises are owned by traditional owners, who in Wurrumiyanga make up less than one-fifth of the population. This is one of several ways in which the recent reforms transform the relationship between traditional owners and (other) residents, as described below. Further, the traditional owners are the one group that already had legal ownership of land. They have always had the ability to grant leases on whatever terms they wanted, and to mortgage those leases, but rarely have they done so *in communities*. This has been the real change: it is not that traditional owners have finally acquired a form of ownership that is useful, rather they have been given social licence to exploit their land ownership in a way that they did not have previously.

Despite what is sometimes suggested, township leasing has not led to widespread mortgaging of commercial subleases. In fact, the supermarket complex at Wurrumiyanga is the only reported example of this so far. Importantly, it was only possible because the terms of that sublease are exceptional rather than the norm. As described above, most commercial subleases are in the nature of a liability rather than a marketable asset. The sublease for the supermarket is on more favourable terms because it was granted to the traditional owners. There is nothing to indicate that mortgaging of commercial subleases will become widespread.

It is also significant that none of the new enterprises are owned by individuals or families; they are all owned collectively by traditional owners. Collectively owned enterprises are hardly a new phenomenon in remote Aboriginal communities. Indeed, during debate it was said by some that land reform would lead to a move away from 'communal ownership' of businesses. This is a complex issue, more complex than was suggested during debate; however, it is important that individuals are given opportunities to develop enterprises and tenure arrangements should support this. Chapter 8 describes how this requires a more strategic and targeted approach to land reform.

A final point needs to be made about the broader impact of township leasing. Part of the aim of the discussion above is to make it clear that the recent developments in Wurrumiyanga do not depend on there being a township lease. For example, the traditional owners could have set up the arrangements for the supermarket complex without a township lease. And yet these developments *have* occurred on communities subject to a township lease more than in other communities. Why is that? There appears to be three reasons. The first is rent, particularly the up-front rental payment. That same money could have been transferred to traditional owners by other mechanisms, such as a direct grant of funding, but not in a way that replicates the autonomy and authority that traditional owners have with respect to rent. The second reason is the social licence given to traditional owners to exploit their land ownership inside communities. Both rent and this social licence have an impact on non-traditional owner residents in ways that can be problematic, an issue considered further in Chapter 8. A third reason appears to be the support provided by the EDTL, whose office has been active in working with traditional owners to find new ways to exploit their land ownership for commercial gain. As there are only a small number of township lease communities, the EDTL has been able to work relatively intensively with them. There is no reason why similar support could not be provided in communities without a township lease, except of course that it would require additional funding.

242   *Making sense of the reforms*

There have been a number of myths and misconceptions about the way in which the Northern Territory reforms contribute to economic development. When presenting the enabling legislation to Parliament, former Minister Brough said township leases would create a new tenure system 'that will allow individuals to have property rights' as it is 'individual property rights that drive economic development'.[111] This would 'make it significantly easier for individuals to ... establish businesses'.[112] However, this is not what has occurred. As the EDTL more recently put it, township leases have been used 'to regularise land tenure arrangements within the townships and to facilitate a commercial return for Traditional Land Owners'.[113] It is not the case that new businesses have sprung up – individual or otherwise – because people who were previously unable to gain access to land are now able to. Nor is it the case that existing enterprises have grown because they now have a more valuable form of property rights; to the contrary, a greater proportion of enterprises are now required to pay rent. And rather than communities becoming less reliant on government injections, it is more accurate to say that some government payments are now mediated through rent, a development that has positive and negative consequences.

The impact of the reforms on relationships

During debate, land reform has sometimes been presented as a way of lessening isolation and enabling new relationships, particularly greater economic interaction between Indigenous community residents and the wider Australian community. As Paul Toohey put it, 'ordinary Aboriginal Australia will have friendships and business relationships with ordinary white Australians'.[114] There is no evidence of the reforms having this impact; however, they have had a profound impact on *existing* relationships, particularly those around land use.

Prior to the reforms, land and infrastructure were allocated and occupied under informal tenure arrangements. Those arrangements were the negotiated product of the relationship between residents, traditional owners and governments. The essence of this relationship was that traditional owners made land available to community residents, and community residents invited government agencies, NGOs, enterprises, etc. into their community. This depended on a certain amount of goodwill. Whether grudgingly or willingly, in most cases traditional owners made their land available for free. To some extent this reflected a historical reality: many communities were already established by the time the land was formally made Indigenous land. The residents had a clear right to be there.

In the Northern Territory, this has changed as a result of township leasing, 'secure tenure' policies, five-year leases and reforms to local government. The most obvious change is an increase in government control. While governments have always played a role in decision-making around

Making sense of the reforms 243

land use, their role is now more active, institutionalised and authorial. This is most apparent under township and five-year leases, but is also the effect of 'secure tenure' policies. Arguably, one of the reasons the Australian Government was willing to forgo legal control when five-year leases ended was that it can exert sufficient influence for its purposes through other means, such as control over funding. It has very much set the agenda for how formalisation is to occur and now that the process has commenced it no longer relies on the legal control that the five-year leases provided.

A further change has been the marginalisation of community decision-making. Previously, community bodies – particularly the local council – played the dominant role in the informal tenure arrangements. Today governments deal directly with landowners. This explains a somewhat paradoxical feature of township leases – they result in traditional owners losing legal control, yet are often presented as giving them 'true' owner-ship. Minister Brough told Parliament that a 'senior traditional owner' said '[w]e will now be legally entitled to play a direct role in the administration and development of our town ... We have not been in that position since Nguiu was first established nearly 100 years ago'.[115] *The Australian* reports a traditional owner saying it was 'about time the right people got their say in this town'.[116] The EDTL quotes a traditional owner as saying township leases help them get 'power back', that while they always owned the land now they 'actually [have] it on paper'.[117]

These statements reflect the way township leases shift power from non-traditional owner residents to traditional owners. John Hicks, CEO of the Tiwi Land Council, argues that during the period of 'local government control' traditional owners were not appropriately recognised, while through township leasing they have 'written themselves into the script'.[118] The description is apt: it is traditional owners who receive rent, sit on the Consultative Forum and own the new enterprises. There are no such forums or ongoing benefits for non-traditional owner residents. Traditional owners have increased their political and economic power at the expense of non-traditional owner residents. To some extent this must also be true in communities affected by 'secure tenure' policies.[119] Again, it is tradi-tional owners who receive rent, and under ALRA leasing processes it is traditional owners who have the most say over the grant of leases.

The government and EDTL present the statements referred to above as being an Aboriginal imprimatur for the reforms. To those less familiar with community dynamics – being most Australians – these quotations appear to be an endorsement by 'senior' people with 'traditional' author-ity. Interestingly, they are very much at odds with earlier statements by Minsters Vanstone and Brough, who argued that one reason land reform was necessary was so that non-traditional owner residents could escape the 'arbitrary' control of 'feudal' traditional owners.[120] As Dodson and McCarthy point out, these provocative statements were always incorrect: non-traditional owner residents were not subject to 'arbitrary' control by

244 *Making sense of the reforms*

traditional owners.[121] They were subjects of informal arrangements in which they themselves played a key role. But what is their situation today? What does it mean to be a non-traditional owner resident growing up in Wurrumiyanga? The single most important community forum for decision-making – the local council – has been disbanded and replaced by a regional shire council. Legal control over land use has been transferred to the EDTL, who consults with and pays rent to the traditional owners. Housing has been transferred to Territory Housing. They very much risk being 'alienated from any involvement in and responsibility for the future of their communities'.[122]

Coincident with this shift has been a loss of goodwill and the emergence of more defined position taking. This was an inevitable consequence of the government's heavy-handed approach to reform, particularly the five-year leases. An example of this is to be found in the CLC's statements in relation to rent – in 2005, they indicated that leases for 'government infrastructure' were likely to attract only peppercorn rent, while by 2010 they reported 'an expectation among traditional owners' that 'fair' rent be paid by all occupiers.[123] Another example emerged when the five-year leases ended: one community wrote to the Northern Territory Government demanding its employees leave or face prosecution for trespass.[124] Happily it appears that no attempt was made to carry out this threat. That it was made reflects a change to the way in which tenure is understood.

This element of more defined position taking is the most concerning aspect of rent. While its investment impact will be both positive and negative, and while it has both positive and negative characteristics as a form of benefit, it is of great consequence that it is paid only to traditional owners. This will inevitably accentuate the significance of the distinction between those people who fall within the definition of 'traditional owners' and those who do not, in circumstances where the making of that distinction is already complicated. The risk of conflict must be high.

One of the striking features of the allotment reforms in Queensland is that, if and when they are used, they take the opposite approach to resolving the tension between traditional ownership and residence. A grant of ordinary freehold results in the extinguishment of native title, meaning there is no ongoing role for traditional owners with respect to that land. There is a complete shift to the resident who is granted the freehold. This effectively means, however, that in places where native title subsists the introduction of allotment will require the agreement of native title holders through an Indigenous Land Use Agreement. This may be a barrier to its introduction.

The advantages of formalised tenure

There are of course advantages to formal tenure and to the widespread formalisation of the tenure arrangements in communities. There can be benefits for occupiers, particularly those who experienced some level of tenure insecurity under informal arrangements. Some might now find it quicker and easier to negotiate the formal tenure they always preferred. For other occupiers the impact will be more equivocal. In addition to now paying rent, their rights have gone from being indeterminate and negotiated to fixed and bounded. At some point their lease or sublease will end, and they will have to obtain a new one, at which point they might be vulnerable to displacement. This is, however, speculative – there are no reports considering how the new arrangements are experienced by occupiers. What is clear is that their interests have not been paramount. They do not obtain the formal tenure they would prefer: naturally, any occupier would prefer a lease or sublease that was rent-free, long-term and unrestrictive, but for most that is not what they are getting. And in the Northern Territory, many no longer have the option of continuing to rely on informal tenure.

Another benefit to widespread formalisation is that it can provide greater clarity about who is responsible for what infrastructure. The government has argued this is one reason why 'secure tenure' policies are required: for example, former Minister Macklin said that for 'housing and other infrastructure' the government insists on 'secure tenure' without which 'ownership of housing assets is uncertain [and] responsibility for maintenance and repairs is unclear'.[125] While there is no research that identifies the extent of uncertainty created by the earlier arrangements, it is likely to have been less than is suggested by the Minister. If there was a widespread issue, it is surprising that it was not identified until recently. It would also be surprising if there weren't quicker, easier and cheaper ways of clarifying responsibility for maintenance than requiring that all tenure arrangements be formalised.

7.4 Conclusion: was it necessary to be so interventionist?

The reforms described here did not arise out of a long history of Aboriginal landowners or community residents raising concerns about the tenure arrangements in their communities. They instead arose out of a debate conducted in mainstream public forums primarily among political elites, using terminology and concepts that were ill-suited to describing the tenure arrangements in communities. Those reforms were then introduced to – and in some cases imposed upon – communities after they had been developed. This chapter concludes by considering whether it was really necessary to take such a unilateral and intrusive approach. What have the reforms really achieved? And are they worth the cost, both financially and in terms of the disempowering impact of such processes?

246 *Making sense of the reforms*

Reforms to residential housing

The reforms to residential housing raise a slightly different set of issues to reforms to enterprise and service infrastructure. This chapter describes two reforms – home ownership and the housing precinct leases – and how they differ. Perhaps the key point with respect to home ownership is that it could have been introduced in a far less aggressive and divisive manner. Home ownership does not require widespread land reform or the formalisation of entire communities. It requires only an appropriate form of lease or sublease for participating houses, which is in fact what occurs in Queensland. On ALRA land, home ownership can be achieved through a section 19 lease equally as well as a township sublease (provided in both cases that landowners consent). It might be thought that introducing home ownership without some wider reform – such as a township lease – would limit or weaken the home ownership market. That is not the case. Home ownership leases or subleases are their own market. Indeed, as has been described above, there is no 'land market' on the existing township leases beyond the limited grants of home ownership.

In other words, it was not necessary for the Australian Government to take such a hard-line approach to land reform in order to introduce home ownership. Further, it seems that through taking such an approach it neglected to fully work through all of the issues involved. The results of this are evident in the description of the HOIL Program provided above. Not only have there been few grants, the way in which some of those grants have been made is troubling. If the government had approached home ownership as something that communities might wish to consider, rather than characterising it as something 'communal ownership' was preventing, the outcome might have been different. Through discussion with community residents, landowners and Aboriginal organisations, it might have better identified the issues and clarified the areas that require further attention. If that had been the case, it is likely that home ownership on Aboriginal land would be better understood by now. It might even be more common.

The second and more widespread housing reform has been housing precinct leases and the shift to public housing. These reforms are inherently interventionist, in that they deliberately impose a greater role for governments and a lesser role for community organisations. Whether this level of intervention is regarded as necessary will depend on views as to the appropriateness of the new arrangements. The discussion in this chapter provides further clarity as to the exact nature of the role that governments have taken upon themselves.

Making sense of the reforms 247

Reforms to service and enterprise infrastructure

One of the striking things about 'secure tenure' policies as they extend beyond housing is how little the government has said about them. It has only ever articulated their rationale in the most general of terms. This makes them both easier and more difficult to critique. It is possible – and disturbingly easy – to select from the limited statements that the government has made and point out mistakes. In one of its few information sheets on 'Reforming land tenure', the government states that land reform supports 'economic development and home ownership' by making it possible to 'create long term interests in land'.[126] It argues that the 'ability to create long term interests in land [is] crucial to attracting outside investment, which is a prerequisite to any expansion in employment opportunities'.[127] The disjuncture between these sort of statements and the recent reforms themselves is remarkable. It has always been possible to 'create long term interests' on ALRA land. The impact of the reforms has not been to create this ability, but to make formalisation compulsory. And they have done so in a way that makes it more expensive for investors, not cheaper. To the (limited) extent that the reforms have supported economic development, it has been through providing landowners with rent and the social licence to exploit their ownership, rather than through attracting 'outside investment'.

The impact of the reforms is not only economic; the shift towards formalisation has had two other consequences. First, it has resulted in greater regularity around land use. The Australian Government argues that the formalisation of tenure enables governments to 'retain control over assets built on Aboriginal land so as to ensure [they are] used for their intended public benefit, and are maintained over time'.[128] There are clearly benefits to regularising land use in communities through more formal mechanisms. The extent of those benefits is difficult to assess, because there is no research that identifies the extent to which this was previously an issue. It was not identified as such until the reform process had begun and very much has the appearance of a rationale given to explain the need for a set of reforms that were already in train. This does not mean that benefits of regularising land use are not real – but that it is difficult to assess whether those benefits outweigh the costs, being both the financial costs and the consequences of introducing a more formal and therefore more bureaucratic system.

The second major consequence of greater formalisation has been its impact on relationships around land use. In the Northern Territory, this is most pronounced on a township lease but also occurs in any community subject to 'secure tenure' policies. In short, there has been a significant decrease in community-level control over land use, a development exacerbated by the replacement of local councils with regional shires. There has been a commensurate increase in government control and a shift

248 *Making sense of the reforms*

in authority from non-traditional owner residents to traditional owners. This does not appear to be the implementation of a well-thought-out and deliberate, long-term strategy. It instead appears to reflect the outcome of a haphazard and at times erratic process, a consequence of the Australian Government commencing a set of wholesale and dramatic reforms without clearly understanding what it was doing.

This was not the only possibility. It always was, and to some extent remains, open to the government to pursue land reform in a more considered and strategic manner. The exact mechanism for this is discussed in the following chapter, which sets out a framework for developing alternative approaches to land reform.

Notes

1 Michael Dillon and Neil Westbury, *Beyond Humbug: Transforming Government Engagement with Indigenous Australia* (Seaview Press, 2007) 157.
2 Mark Moran *et al.*, 'Home Ownership for Indigenous People Living on Community Title Land in Queensland: Preliminary Community Survey' (Aboriginal Environments Research Centre, University of Queensland, 2001) 1.
3 Dillon and Westbury, above n 1, 170.
4 Ibid.
5 Auditor-General, 'Home Ownership on Indigenous Land Program' (Audit Report No 23 2010–11, Australian National Audit Office, 21 December 2010) 16. On 1 July 2012 the HOIL Program was amalgamated with another programme to form the Indigenous Home Ownership Program.
6 Ibid, 17.
7 Ibid, 18.
8 Ibid.
9 Ibid, 19.
10 Indigenous Business Australia, 'Home Ownership on Indigenous Land Now a Reality in Yarrabah' (Media Release, 22 October 2014).
11 Auditor-General, above n 6, 18–19.
12 Ibid, 59–62.
13 Mal Brough, 'Four Indigenous Families Take the Road to Home Ownership in NT' (Media Release, 3 May 2007). See also Australian Broadcasting Corporation, 'Housing Sector Wary of Wadeye Home-Owner Plans', *The World Today*, 4 May 2007 (Anne Barker).
14 Australian Government, Department of Families, Housing, Community Services and Indigenous Affairs, *Answers to Estimates Questions on Notice, Output Group: 1.2 Question No: 040*, Senate Community Affairs Committee, May 2007, 108. See also Patricia Karvelas, 'Cost Blowout for NT houses', *The Australian*, 3 June 2008, 1.
15 Auditor-General, above n 5, 60.
16 Ibid, 18. It appears that a fourth house was later sold to purchasers.
17 Natasha Robinson, 'Serious Delays Stymie Remote Housing', *The Australian*, 11 December 2010, 5.
18 A copy of the registered mortgage was obtained through a title search.
19 Robinson, above n 17.
20 Council of Australian Governments, Select Council on Housing and Homelessness, 'Indigenous Home Ownership Paper' (2013).
21 Ibid, 13.

Making sense of the reforms 249

22 See especially Australian Government, 'Indigenous Home Ownership Issues Paper' (Department of Families, Housing, Community Services and Indigenous Affairs, May 2010) 14–17.

23 Mark Moran, 'Home Ownership for Indigenous People Living on Community Title Land in Queensland: Scoping Study Report' (Queensland Aboriginal Coordinating Council, Aboriginal and Torres Strait Islander Commission, 1999); Moran *et al.*, above n 2.

24 Cape York Institute for Policy & Leadership (CYI), 'From Hand out to Hand up' (Cape York Welfare Reform Project Design Recommendations, May 2007) 113; Moran, above n 23, 4; Paul Memmott *et al.*, 'Indigenous Home Ownership on Communal Title Lands' (Positioning Paper No 112, Australian Housing and Urban Research Institute, January 2009) 8; Sara Hudson, 'Right Idea, Wrong Approach' (Policy Forum, Centre for Independent Studies, 30 November 2012).

25 It is also possible that norms might develop that would militate against such practices. This is difficult to predict.

26 Of the 25 reported grants, 15 have been in Wurrumiyanga.

27 See cl 10.5 of the Wurrumiyanga lease, described in Chapter 6.

28 *Law of Property Act 2000* (NT) s 134(2).

29 Greg Roche, 'Executive Director of Township Leasing Annual Report 2010–2011' (Australian Government, 2011) 27.

30 See Peter Butt, *Land Law* (Lawbook Co, 6th ed, 2009) 366–70.

31 Tim Mander, Greg Elmes and Nigel Scullion, 'Delivering Home Ownership for Yarrabah Families' (Media Release, 8 October 2014).

32 *Aboriginal Land Act 1991* (Qld) ss 119, 124 and *Torres Strait Islander Land Act 1991* (Qld) ss 84, 89.

33 Dillon and Westbury, above n 1, 159.

34 Ibid, 161, 164; John Fien *et al.*, 'Towards a Design Framework for Remote Indigenous Housing' (Final Report No 114, Australian Housing and Urban Research Institute, March 2008) 26; PricewaterhouseCoopers, 'Living in the Sunburnt Country: Indigenous Housing – Findings of the Review of the Community Housing and Infrastructure Programme' (Report to the Department of Families, Community Services and Indigenous Affairs, 2007) 19–20; Max Neutze, 'Housing for Indigenous Australians' (2000) 15(4) *Housing Studies* 485, 486–8.

35 Paul Torzillo *et al.*, 'The State of Health Hardware in Aboriginal Communities in Rural and Remote Australia' (2008) 32(1) *Australian and New Zealand Journal of Public Health* 7, 7–10.

36 See Chapter 2. The realisability effect operates as an *incentive*. For improvements to the *capacity* of occupiers to maintain properties through collateralisation, see discussion below.

37 Myrna Tonkinson and Robert Tonkinson, 'The Cultural Dynamics of Adaptation in Remote Aboriginal Communities: Policy, Values and the State's Unmet Expectations' (2010) 52 *Anthropologica* 67, 69.

38 CYI, above n 24, 109 (emphasis added). Cf Helen Hughes, Mark Hughes and Sara Hudson, 'Private Housing in Indigenous Lands' (Policy Monograph 113, Centre for Independent Studies, 2010) vii, who argue that existing tenants should be given the option of ownership at no cost to 'kick start private property rights'.

39 David O'Brien, 'Home to Own: Potential for Indigenous Housing by Indigenous People' (2011) (1) *Australian Aboriginal Studies* 65, 74.

40 CYI, above n 24, 115–17. It appears that this has been implemented in some Queensland communities; see Nicholas Rothwell, 'Desire to End the Welfare Drip-feed Takes Pride of Place', *The Australian*, 25 August 2012, 17.

250   *Making sense of the reforms*

41 Moran, above n 23, 13, 17–18; CYI, above n 24, 109.
42 Andrew Beer *et al.*, 'The Drivers of Supply and Demand in Australia's Rural and Regional Centres' (Final Report No 165, Australian Housing and Urban Research Institute, 2011) 34, 104–6.
43 CYI, above n 24, 109.
44 Which was reportedly between $2,000 and $10,000, with most being in the $2–3,000 range; see Moran *et al.*, above n 2, 35.
45 CYI, above n 24, 109. Moran *et al.* make the same argument; see Moran *et al.*, above n 2, 43.
46 Mal Brough, 'Blueprint for Action in Indigenous Affairs' (Speech delivered at the National Institute of Governance, Canberra, 5 December 2006).
47 Hughes *et al.*, above n 38, vii. For a more considered analysis see O'Brien, above n 39.
48 Memmott *et al.*, above n 24, 5.
49 Jon Altman, Craig Linkhorn and Jennifer Clarke, 'Land Rights and Development Reform in Remote Australia' (Discussion Paper No 276/2005, Centre for Aboriginal Economic Policy Research, 2005) 11–12; Central Land Council (CLC), 'Communal Title and Economic Development' (Policy Paper, 2005) 12; Council of Australian Governments, above n 20, 12.
50 See, eg, Hughes *et al.*, above n 38, 12–13.
51 Memmott *et al.*, above n 24, 11–12.
52 Paul Memmott *et al.*, 'Indigenous Home-Ownership on Communal Title Lands' (Final Report No 139, Australian Housing and Urban Research Institute, November 2009) 6.
53 Auditor-General, above n 5, 58.
54 Ibid, 62–3.
55 Robinson, above n 17.
56 Auditor-General, above n 5, 62–3.
57 Copies of all mortgages were obtained through a title search.
58 CYI, above n 24, 110–11.
59 Tony Koch and Sarah Elks, 'Making Great Aussie Dream Come True', *The Australian*, 7 December 2010, 7.
60 AAP, 'Mapoon Land "Too Expensive" For Locals', *The Sydney Morning Herald* (online), 4 September 2009 http://news.smh.com.au/breaking-news-national/mapoon-land-too-expensive-for-locals-20090904-faot.html.
61 CYI, above n 24, 110–11.
62 Memmott *et al.*, 'Indigenous Home Ownership' (Positioning Paper), above n 24, 11. See also Council of Australian Governments, above n 20, 13.
63 Noel Pearson, 'Review: *The Mystery of Capital: Why Capitalism Triumphs in the West and Fails Everywhere Else* by Hernando de Soto' (September 2001) *Australian Public Intellectual Network*; Mark Moran *et al.*, 'Indigenous Home Ownership and Community Title Land: A Preliminary Household Survey' (2002) 20(4) *Urban Policy and Research* 357, 357.
64 Hernando de Soto, *The Mystery of Capital: Why Capitalism Triumphs in the West and Fails Everywhere Else* (Black Swan, 2001) 7.
65 CYI, above n 24, 14.
66 Ibid, 23.
67 Ibid, 14.
68 See, eg, several of Pearson's articles and speeches in Noel Pearson, *Up From the Mission: Selected Writings* (Black Inc, 2009); Jon Altman, Matthew Gray and Will Sanders, 'Indigenous Australians Working for Welfare: What Difference Does It Make?' (2000) 33(4) *Australian Economic Review* 355; David Martin, 'Is Welfare Dependency "Welfare Poison"? An Assessment of Noel Pearson's Proposals for Aboriginal Welfare Reform' (Discussion Paper No

Making sense of the reforms 251

213/2001, Centre for Aboriginal Economic Policy Research, 2001); Anne Daly, 'The Winner's Curse? Indigenous Australians in the Welfare System' (2000) 33(4) *Australian Economic Review* 349; Will Sanders, 'Equality and Difference Arguments in Australian Indigenous Affairs: Examples from Income Support and Housing' (Working Paper No 38/2008, Centre for Aboriginal Economic Policy Research, 2008); Anne Daly and Diane Smith, 'The Role of Welfare in the Economy of Two Indigenous Communities' (2000) 33(4) *Australian Economic Review* 363.

69 See, eg, CYI, above n 24, 13, 107; Noel Pearson, 'Social Housing Model Rips the Heart out of Indigenous Communities', *The Weekend Australian*, 6 February 2010, 13.

70 CYI, above n 24, 107.

71 Jenny Macklin, 'Speech to Cape York Institute Leadership Academy' (Speech delivered to the Cape York Institute Leadership Academy, Cairns, 22 July 2008).

72 Ibid.

73 Jenny Macklin, 'Speech to John Curtin Institute of Public Policy' (Speech delivered at the John Curtin Institute of Public Policy, Perth, 21 April 2009).

74 Australian Government, above n 22, 14.

75 Pearson, 'Social Housing Model Rips the Heart out of Indigenous Communities', above n 69.

76 Ibid.

77 Tonkinson and Tonkinson, above n 37, 69.

78 Ibid.

79 Ibid.

80 Nicolas Peterson, 'Community Development, Civil Society, and Local Government in the Future of Remote Northern Territory Growth Towns' (A paper presented at 60 Years of ANU Anthropology: Contesting Anthropology's Futures Conference, Australian National University, September 2011) 5.

81 David Martin, 'Why the "New Direction" in Federal Indigenous Affairs Policy Is as Likely to "Fail" as the Old Directions' (Topical Issue No 05/2006, Centre for Aboriginal Economic Policy Research, 2006) 8.

82 See, eg, Memmott *et al.*, 'Indigenous Home Ownership' (Final Report), above n 52, generally; Tonkinson and Tonkinson, above n 37, 71–2.

83 CLC, above n 49, 21. See also Northern Land Council (NLC), Submission No 13 to the Senate Community Affairs Committee, Parliament of Australia, *Inquiry into Aboriginal Land Rights (Northern Territory) Amendment Bill 2006*, 21 July 2006, 13, 16.

84 Roche, above n 29, 16.

85 NLC, above n 83, 21.

86 *Aboriginal Land Rights (Northern Territory) Act 1976* (Cth) s 19A(15).

87 Tom Calma, 'Native Title Report 2009' (Australian Human Rights Commission, 2009) 139.

88 See Dillon and Westbury, above n 1, 124, and see also 133 and 144. See also Evidence to Senate Community Affairs Legislation Committee Inquiry into Aboriginal Land Rights (Northern Territory) Amendment Bill 2006, Parliament of Australia, Darwin, 21 July 2006, 78 (Dennis Bree).

89 Australian Government, 'Indigenous Economic Development Strategy 2011–2018' (Department of Families, Housing, Community Services and Indigenous Affairs, 2011) 63.

90 Bob Beadman, 'Northern Territory Coordinator-General for Remote Services: Report No 1 May to November 2009' (Northern Territory Government, 2009) 32.

252 *Making sense of the reforms*

91 See Tiwi Islands Regional Council, *Annual Reports*, http://tiwiislands.org.au/AnnualReport.html.

92 Malarndirri McCarthy, 'Historic Decision to Pay the Rent to Lease Aboriginal Land' (Media Release, 23 November 2011).

93 Central Land Council, 'Community Leasing: an Alternative Proposal' (Discussion Paper, December 2010) 7, 9–11.

94 Bob Beadman, 'Northern Territory Coordinator-General for Remote Services: Report No 2 December 2009 to May 2010' (Northern Territory Government, 2010) 74.

95 Dillon and Westbury, above n 1, 150.

96 Greg Roche, 'Executive Director of Township Leasing Annual Report 2011–2012' (Australian Government, 2012) 4.

97 Nigel Scullion, '2014 National Native Title Conference Speech' (Speech delivered at the National Native Title Conference, Coffs Harbour, 2 June 2014).

98 Beadman, 'Coordinator-General for Remote Services: Report No 2', above n 94, 74–7.

99 Pat Watson, 'Executive Director of Township Leasing Annual Report 2009–2010' (Australian Government, 2010) 10, and see Australian Government, 'Indigenous Home Ownership Issues Paper', above n 22, 16.

100 Central Land Council, *Application for a Lease, Licence or Other Interest in Aboriginal Land* (2012) www.clc.org.au/files/pdf/Leasing_application_form.pdf.

101 This is because initial grants can only be made to Aboriginal people and Torres Strait Islanders, and their spouses and former spouses; see Chapter 6.

102 Tiwi Land Council, 'Annual Report 2010/2011' (2011); Roche, 'EDTL Annual Report 2011–2012 Report', above n 96, 10–11.

103 Nigel Scullion, 'Land Reform for the Future', *Koori Mail* (online), 26 March 2014 http://minister.indigenous.gov.au/media/2014-03-26/land-reform-future-published-koori-mail.

104 Australian Government, Department of Prime Minister and Cabinet, *Jobs, Land and Economy* (2014) www.indigenous.gov.au/jobs-land-and-economy.

105 Watson, above n 99, 13. See also Roche, 'EDTL Annual Report 2010–2011', above n 29, 3–4, 16, 22–4; Roche, 'EDTL Annual Report 2011–2012', above n 96, 11, 23–5.

106 Roche, 'EDTL Annual Report 2010–2011', above n 29, 25, and see also 3, 22.

107 These subleases are detailed in Chapter 6.

108 Australian Government, Department of Prime Minister and Cabinet, *Answers to Estimates Questions on Notice, Question Reference Number 290*, Senate Finance and Public Administration Legislation Committee, Budget Estimates, 26 May–6 June 2014.

109 Greg Roche, 'Executive Director of Township Leasing Annual Report 2012–2013' (Australian Government, 2013) 13–14.

110 Ibid. The mortgage to Westpac Banking Corporation appears on a title search of the township.

111 Commonwealth, *Parliamentary Debates*, House of Representatives, 31 May 2006, 5 (Mal Brough).

112 Ibid.

113 Roche, 'EDTL Annual Report 2010–2011', above n 29, 15, and see also 8.

114 Paul Toohey, 'A New Lease of Life', *The Weekend Australian Magazine*, 10 January 2009, 14, 14.

115 Commonwealth, *Parliamentary Debates*, House of Representatives, 24 May 2007, 10 (Mal Brough) and see also Mal Brough, 'On the Federal Govern-

116 Toohey, above n 114, 14.
117 See, eg, Roche, 'EDTL Annual Report 2011–2012', above n 96, ii, 28.
118 Quoted in Toohey, above n 114, 17.
119 See, eg, Jonathon Kneebone, Kirsty Howey and Shanti Rama, 'Unlocking Potential: Is Communal Title Really to Blame?' (Paper presented at the National Native Title Conference, Alice Springs, 4 June 2013), wherein lawyers for the NLC state that the practical effect of these policies 'may be to increase [traditional owners'] governance and control of land in communities'.
120 See, eg, Amanda Vanstone, 'Beyond Conspicuous Compassion: Indigenous Australians Deserve More Than Good Intentions' (Speech delivered to the Australia and New Zealand School of Government, Australian National University, Canberra, 7 December 2005); Commonwealth, *Parliamentary Debates*, House of Representatives, 31 May 2006, 5 (Mal Brough).
121 Michael Dodson and Diana McCarthy, 'Communal Land and the Amendments to the *Aboriginal Land Rights (Northern Territory) Act*' (Research Discussion Paper No 19, Australian Institute of Aboriginal and Torres Strait Islander Studies, 2006) 7.
122 Peterson, above n 80, 5.
123 This is detailed in Chapter 6.
124 Amos Aikman, ' "Trespass" Threat as Leases Expire', *The Australian*, 24 August 2012, 3.
125 Jenny Macklin, 'Building the Foundations for Change' (Speech delivered at the Sydney Institute, Sydney, 9 August 2011).
126 Australian Government, Office of Township Leasing, *Reforming Land Tenure Arrangements on Indigenous Held Land* (2015) www.otl.gov.au/site/township_leasing_factsheet_1.html.
127 Ibid.
128 Ibid.

Bibliography

Books/articles/reports/web pages

AAP, 'Mapoon Land "Too Expensive" For Locals', *The Sydney Morning Herald* (online), 4 September 2009, http://news.smh.com.au/breaking-news-national/mapoon-land-too-expensive-for-locals-20090904-faot.html.

Aikman, Amos, ' "Trespass" Threat as Leases Expire', *The Australian*, 24 August 2012, 3.

Altman, Jon, Matthew Gray and Will Sanders, 'Indigenous Australians Working for Welfare: What Difference Does It Make?' (2000) 33(4) *Australian Economic Review* 355.

Altman, Jon, Craig Linkhorn and Jennifer Clarke, 'Land Rights and Development Reform in Remote Australia' (Discussion Paper No 276/2005, Centre for Aboriginal Economic Policy Research, 2005).

Auditor-General, 'Home Ownership on Indigenous Land Program' (Audit Report No 23 2010–11, Australian National Audit Office, 21 December 2010).

Australian Broadcasting Corporation, 'Housing Sector Wary of Wadeye Home-Owner Plans', *The World Today*, 4 May 2007 (Anne Barker).

254 *Making sense of the reforms*

Australian Government, 'Indigenous Home Ownership Issues Paper' (Department of Families, Housing, Community Services and Indigenous Affairs, May 2010).

Australian Government, 'Indigenous Economic Development Strategy 2011–2018' (Department of Families, Housing, Community Services and Indigenous Affairs, 2011).

Australian Government, Department of Families, Housing, Community Services and Indigenous Affairs, *Answers to Estimates Questions on Notice, Output Group: 1.2 Question No: 040*, Senate Community Affairs Committee, May 2007, 108.

Australian Government, Department of Prime Minister and Cabinet, *Answers to Estimates Questions on Notice, Question Reference Number 290*, Senate Finance and Public Administration Legislation Committee, Budget Estimates, 26 May–6 June 2014.

Australian Government, Department of Prime Minister and Cabinet, *Jobs, Land and Economy* (2014) www.indigenous.gov.au/jobs-land-and-economy.

Australian Government, Office of Township Leasing, *Reforming Land Tenure Arrangements on Indigenous Held Land* (2015) www.otl.gov.au/site/township_leasing_factsheet_1.html.

Beadman, Bob, 'Northern Territory Coordinator-General for Remote Services: Report No 1 May to November 2009' (Northern Territory Government, 2009).

Beadman, Bob, 'Northern Territory Coordinator-General for Remote Services: Report No 2 December 2009 to May 2010' (Northern Territory Government, 2010).

Beer, Andrew *et al.*, 'The Drivers of Supply and Demand in Australia's Rural and Regional Centres' (Final Report No 165, Australian Housing and Urban Research Institute, 2011).

Evidence to Senate Community Affairs Legislation Committee Inquiry into Aboriginal Land Rights (Northern Territory) Amendment Bill 2006, Parliament of Australia, Darwin, 21 July 2006 (Dennis Bree).

Commonwealth, *Parliamentary Debates*, House of Representatives, 31 May 2006, 5 (Mal Brough).

Brough, Mal, 'Blueprint for Action in Indigenous Affairs' (Speech delivered at the National Institute of Governance, Canberra, 5 December 2006).

Brough, Mal, 'Four Indigenous Families Take the Road to Home Ownership in NT' (Media Release, 3 May 2007).

Commonwealth, *Parliamentary Debates*, House of Representatives, 24 May 2007, 10 (Mal Brough).

Brough, Mal, 'On the Federal Government's Intervention into Northern Territory Indigenous Communities' (Speech delivered at the Alfred Deakin Lecture, University of Melbourne, 2 October 2007).

Butt, Peter, *Land Law* (Lawbook Co, 6th ed, 2009).

Calma, Tom, 'Native Title Report 2009' (Australian Human Rights Commission, 2009).

Cape York Institute for Policy & Leadership, 'From Hand out to Hand up' (Cape York Welfare Reform Project Design Recommendations, May 2007).

Central Land Council, 'Communal Title and Economic Development' (Policy Paper, 2005).

Central Land Council, 'Community Leasing: An Alternative Proposal' (Discussion Paper, December 2010).

Making sense of the reforms 255

Central Land Council, *Application for a Lease, Licence or Other Interest in Aboriginal Land* (2012) www.clc.org.au/files/pdf/Leasing_application_form.pdf.

Council of Australian Governments, Select Council on Housing and Homelessness, 'Indigenous Home Ownership Paper' (2013).

Daly, Anne, 'The Winner's Curse? Indigenous Australians in the Welfare System' (2000) 33(4) *Australian Economic Review* 349.

Daly, Anne and Diane Smith, 'The Role of Welfare in the Economy of Two Indigenous Communities' (2000) 33(4) *Australian Economic Review* 363.

de Soto, Hernando, *The Mystery of Capital: Why Capitalism Triumphs in the West and Fails Everywhere Else* (Black Swan, 2001).

Dillon, Michael and Neil Westbury, *Beyond Humbug: Transforming Government Engagement with Indigenous Australia* (Seaview Press, 2007).

Dodson, Michael and Diana McCarthy, 'Communal Land and the Amendments to the *Aboriginal Land Rights (Northern Territory) Act*' (Research Discussion Paper No 19, Australian Institute of Aboriginal and Torres Strait Islander Studies, 2006).

Fien, John *et al.*, 'Towards a Design Framework for Remote Indigenous Housing' (Final Report No 114, Australian Housing and Urban Research Institute, March 2008).

Hudson, Sara, 'Right Idea, Wrong Approach' (Policy Forum, Centre for Independent Studies, 30 November 2012).

Hughes, Helen, Mark Hughes and Sara Hudson, 'Private Housing in Indigenous Lands' (Policy Monograph 113, Centre for Independent Studies, 2010).

Indigenous Business Australia, 'Home Ownership on Indigenous Land Now a Reality in Yarrabah' (Media Release, 22 October 2014).

Karvelas, Patricia, 'Cost Blowout for NT houses', *The Australian*, 3 June 2008, 1.

Kneebone, Jonathon, Kirsty Howey and Shanti Rama, 'Unlocking Potential: Is Communal Title Really to Blame?' (Paper presented at the National Native Title Conference, Alice Springs, 4 June 2013).

Koch, Tony and Sarah Elks, 'Making Great Aussie Dream Come True', *The Australian*, 7 December 2010, 7.

McCarthy, Malarndirri, 'Historic Decision to Pay the Rent to Lease Aboriginal Land' (Media Release, 23 November 2011).

Macklin, Jenny, 'Speech to Cape York Institute Leadership Academy' (Speech delivered to the Cape York Institute Leadership Academy, Cairns, 22 July 2008).

Macklin, Jenny, 'Speech to John Curtin Institute of Public Policy' (Speech delivered at the John Curtin Institute of Public Policy, Perth, 21 April 2009).

Macklin, Jenny, 'Building the Foundations for Change' (Speech delivered at the Sydney Institute, Sydney, 9 August 2011).

Mander, Tim, Greg Elmes and Nigel Scullion, 'Delivering Home Ownership for Yarrabah Families' (Media Release, 8 October 2014).

Martin David, 'Is Welfare Dependency "Welfare Poison"? An Assessment of Noel Pearson's Proposals for Aboriginal Welfare Reform' (Discussion Paper No 213/2001, Centre for Aboriginal Economic Policy Research, 2001).

Martin, David, 'Why the "New Direction" in Federal Indigenous Affairs Policy Is as Likely to "Fail" as the Old Directions' (Topical Issue No 05/2006, Centre for Aboriginal Economic Policy Research, 2006).

256 *Making sense of the reforms*

Memmott, Paul *et al.*, 'Indigenous Home Ownership on Communal Title Lands' (Positioning Paper No 112, Australian Housing and Urban Research Institute, January 2009).

Memmott, Paul *et al.*, 'Indigenous Home-Ownership on Communal Title Lands' (Final Report No 139, Australian Housing and Urban Research Institute, November 2009).

Moran, Mark, 'Home Ownership for Indigenous People Living on Community Title Land in Queensland: Scoping Study Report' (Queensland Aboriginal Coordinating Council, Aboriginal and Torres Strait Islander Commission, 1999).

Moran, Mark *et al.*, 'Home Ownership for Indigenous People Living on Community Title Land in Queensland: Preliminary Community Survey' (Aboriginal Environments Research Centre, University of Queensland, 2001).

Moran, Mark *et al.*, 'Indigenous Home Ownership and Community Title Land: A Preliminary Household Survey' (2002) 20(4) *Urban Policy and Research* 357.

Neutze, Max, 'Housing for Indigenous Australians' (2000) 15(4) *Housing Studies* 485.

Northern Land Council, Submission No 13 to the Senate Community Affairs Committee, Parliament of Australia, *Inquiry into Aboriginal Land Rights (Northern Territory) Amendment Bill 2006*, 21 July 2006.

O'Brien, David, 'Home to Own: Potential for Indigenous Housing by Indigenous People' (2011) (1) *Australian Aboriginal Studies* 65.

Pearson, Noel, 'Review: *The Mystery of Capital: Why Capitalism Triumphs in the West and Fails Everywhere Else* by Hernando de Soto' (September 2001) *Australian Public Intellectual Network*.

Pearson, Noel, *Up from the Mission: Selected Writings* (Black Inc, 2009).

Pearson, Noel, 'Social Housing Model Rips the Heart out of Indigenous Communities', *The Weekend Australian*, 6 February 2010, 13.

Peterson, Nicolas, 'Community Development, Civil Society, and Local Government in the Future of Remote Northern Territory Growth Towns' (A paper presented at 60 Years of ANU Anthropology: Contesting Anthropology's Futures Conference, Australian National University, September 2011).

PricewaterhouseCoopers, 'Living in the Sunburnt Country: Indigenous Housing – Findings of the Review of the Community Housing and Infrastructure Programme' (Report to the Department of Families, Community Services and Indigenous Affairs, 2007).

Robinson, Natasha, 'Serious Delays Stymie Remote Housing', *The Australian*, 11 December 2010, 5.

Roche, Greg, 'Executive Director of Township Leasing Annual Report 2010–2011' (Australian Government, 2011).

Roche, Greg, 'Executive Director of Township Leasing Annual Report 2011–2012' (Australian Government, 2012).

Roche, Greg, 'Executive Director of Township Leasing Annual Report 2012–2013' (Australian Government, 2013).

Rothwell, Nicholas, 'Desire to End the Welfare Drip-feed Takes Pride of Place', *The Australian*, 25 August 2012, 17.

Sanders, Will, 'Equality and Difference Arguments in Australian Indigenous Affairs: Examples from Income Support and Housing' (Working Paper No 38/2008, Centre for Aboriginal Economic Policy Research, 2008).

Scullion, Nigel, 'Land Reform for the Future', *Koori Mail* (online), 26 March 2014 http://minister.indigenous.gov.au/media/2014-03-26/land-reform-future-published-koori-mail.

Scullion, Nigel, '2014 National Native Title Conference Speech' (Speech delivered at the National Native Title Conference, Coffs Harbour, 2 June 2014).

Tiwi Islands Regional Council, *Annual Reports*, http://tiwiislands.org.au/Annual-Report.html.

Tiwi Land Council, 'Annual Report 2010/2011' (2011).

Tonkinson, Myrna and Robert Tonkinson, 'The Cultural Dynamics of Adaptation in Remote Aboriginal Communities: Policy, Values and the State's Unmet Expectations' (2010) 52 *Anthropologica* 67.

Toohey, Paul, 'A New Lease of Life', *The Weekend Australian Magazine*, 10 January 2009, 14.

Torzillo, Paul *et al.*, 'The State of Health Hardware in Aboriginal Communities in Rural and Remote Australia' (2008) 32(1) *Australian and New Zealand Journal of Public Health* 7.

Vanstone, Amanda, 'Beyond Conspicuous Compassion: Indigenous Australians Deserve More Than Good Intentions' (Speech delivered to the Australia and New Zealand School of Government, Australian National University, Canberra, 7 December 2005).

Watson, Pat, 'Executive Director of Township Leasing Annual Report 2009–2010' (Australian Government, 2010).

Legislation

Aboriginal Land Act 1991 (Qld).
Aboriginal Land Rights (Northern Territory) Act 1976 (Cth).
Law of Property Act 2000 (NT).
Torres Strait Islander Land Act 1991 (Qld).

8 Alternative approaches?

8.1 Introduction

This penultimate chapter now turns to the development of alternative approaches to land reform in communities on Indigenous land. This is not a situation where careful analysis is able to identify a single form of best practice, because views as to what constitutes best practice will vary depending on certain fundamental understandings. Part of the work of this chapter is to identify those understandings and clarify their relationship to land reform. Rather than suggesting a particular land reform model, the chapter describes a framework for deciding how an alternative model might be developed.

This is presented as a two-step process, as set out in Section 8.2. The first step is to identify the main variables, or *what* it is that requires decision, while the second step deals with the question of *how* those variables should be decided upon. The main variables are the identity of the 'underlying land-use authority', the approach taken to the allocation of land and the form of tenure granted to occupiers. In terms of how these variables should be approached, there are three sets of issues – referred to here as the 'three cardinal issues' – that are most important. The three cardinal issues are an assessment of market conditions, understandings of benefit provision and models of governance. Their exact meaning is explained further below.

Ideally, these three cardinal issues need to be addressed *before* a land reform model is developed, rather than during or after. This is a departure from existing approaches in Australia, where land reform itself has been treated as the starting point, perhaps in the hope that through the 'resolution' of tenure the answer to other, more difficult questions might become clearer. It is argued here that this approaches the task from the wrong direction. Land reform is not a precursor or preliminary step; it is the implementation of a development model, the key elements of which are determined by the 'three cardinal issues'. The preferred approach to these issues needs to be made clear so that land reform can be implemented in a manner that is consistent with, and not undermining of, long-term development goals.

Alternative approaches? 259

It is because market conditions vary, and because such different approaches might be taken to governance and benefit provision, that a single best practice model cannot be identified. It is, however, possible to make some suggestions as to the parameters of an ideal model. This is provided in Section 8.3, which draws some conclusions in relation to such matters as in whose interest the underlying land-use authority should act and in what circumstances the aim of land reform should be the creation of 'land markets'.

It is useful before going further to clarify the exact scope of this chapter. It considers alternative reform models for remote communities – that is, those larger residential communities on Indigenous land. It is not concerned with the far larger areas of Indigenous land outside of communities. Communities are a special case, and several of the arguments presented here – such as those in relation to rent – are particular to them. The issues with respect to other areas of Indigenous land, and developments such as exploration and mining, are very different from those considered here. Further, the purpose of this chapter is to provide a clearer picture of the consequences of different land reform outcomes so as to enable better decision-making. It does not directly address the process by which land reform should be introduced, or the exact means by which traditional owners and Indigenous community residents are given input into the government processes that lead to reform.

8.2 Framework for developing a land reform model

A two-step approach

This section sets out a two-step framework for developing a land reform model, regardless of whether that model is a minor shift from the status quo or a significant restructure. In order to deal with the additional complexity that arises, much of the discussion explicitly considers the situation where land is owned on behalf of traditional owners rather than community residents. In the Northern Territory, this is the situation for all land held under the *Aboriginal Land Rights (Northern Territory) Act 1976* (Cth) (the ALRA) and for some community living area (CLA) land.[1] In South Australia it describes all land held under the *Anangu Pitjantjatjara Yankunytjatjara Land Rights Act 1981* (SA) and *Maralinga Tjarutja Land Rights Act 1984* (SA). In Queensland, a somewhat similar dynamic arises with respect to Indigenous land that is also subject to native title.

The first of the two steps is to identify the main variables, those matters that need to be decided upon in the course of reform. Those variables coalesce around: the identity of the 'underlying land-use authority'; the approach taken to allocation; and the form of tenure provided to occupiers. The second step is to identify the factors that determine what approach should be taken to these variables. This is where the three cardinal issues

260 *Alternative approaches?*

come in. These might be considered in the form of three questions: what are the market conditions in the subject community? what is the most helpful and least harmful way of providing government benefits? and what is the model of community governance being implemented? It is the answer to these three questions that determines more than anything else how the main variables should be decided upon.

Alternative models that have been suggested by others

This book is not the first Australian publication to consider alternative models of land reform. Several others have done so, particularly with respect to communities on Aboriginal land in the Northern Territory. As far back as 1998, John Reeves QC recommended community-wide leases to the local council,[2] a suggestion that was supported by Peter Sutton.[3] The Central Land Council (CLC) has published three papers on alternatives to township leasing: the first in 2005,[4] a second in 2010[5] and a third in 2013.[6] In 2006, the Thamarrurr Council proposed a head lease to a 'town corporation',[7] while in 2007 Lewis Shillito published an article considering the potential for strata title.[8] That same year, former Northern Land Council (NLC) Chairman Galarrwuy Yunupingu negotiated a different model (which was never implemented) for the community of Gunyangara/Ski Beach;[9] while in 2009 Sara Hudson, from conservative think tank The Centre for Independent Studies, wrote an article on enabling home ownership, in which she recommended head leases that 'operate like company title'.[10] During 2011, the CLC and NLC developed a proposal specifically for CLA land,[11] and in 2012 Crabtree *et al.* considered the potential for 'community land trusts'.[12] Rather than exhaustively describing and critiquing each of these alternative models, the discussion in Section 8.3 identifies how they address certain of the decisions that need to be made. This provides a clearer picture of what other people have suggested while avoiding repetition.

One thing that all of these alternative models have in common is that they do not alter underlying ownership by the Indigenous landowners. In this respect, the recent amendments to enable the allotment of Indigenous land in Queensland are a significant departure. The consequences of allotment as an alternative model are also considered here.

Step one: the main variables

The underlying land-use authority

The term 'underlying land-use authority', or 'underlying authority', is used here to refer to that body, or those bodies, whose role it is to allocate land and infrastructure to particular occupiers and to determine the form of tenure they are given. It does not need to be a single organisation; under pre-existing arrangements on ALRA land this role was to some extent shared between community organisations (particularly the local council), traditional owners and governments. On Deed of Grant in Trust (DOGIT) land in Queensland that is subject to native title, there can be some sharing of the role between the trustees and native title holders. One of the consequences of recent reforms in the Northern Territory has been an increase in Australian Government involvement at this level. The result of a township lease is to make the Executive Director of Township Leasing (EDTL) the underlying authority. The result of the five-year leases was to make the Commonwealth the underlying authority. These are in fact good examples for describing what an underlying authority is.

There are several things that need to be decided in this context. The most obvious is the identity of the body (or bodies) that will play the primary role (as well as the question of who decides this). Then there is the question of how that body is constituted, its structures and processes, with whom it is required to consult (traditional owners, community residents, governments, other occupiers), whether there are checks and balances on the exercise of power and who it is that has ultimate control. Included in this is the issue of autonomy – where the underlying authority is a body other than government, whether or in what circumstances governments will intervene or prescribe outcomes. As described in earlier chapters, through 'secure tenure' policies the Australian Government is now playing a more interventionist role in land-use decision-making. The scope for autonomy has been lessened.

The allocation of land and infrastructure

The second variable is selecting which people or organisations are allocated land and infrastructure. Of course, in communities on Indigenous land in Australia most infrastructure has already been allocated. The medical clinic is already occupied by a health service provider, the store building is already occupied by a store association. In practical terms, the issues with respect to allocation are: how vacated infrastructure is reallocated, how competing claims to existing infrastructure are adjudicated upon, how unoccupied land is made available for development and whether, or in what circumstances, an existing occupier might be asked to leave.

During debate about land reform it was assumed by some that reform would result in land and infrastructure being allocated to new types of occupiers, such as individuals or profit-making businesses. For the most part this has not been the case. Formal tenure has been granted to the same organisations that previously occupied informally. Section 8.3 provides a more detailed discussion of this issue and whether the current approach should change.

262   *Alternative approaches?*

The form of tenure granted to occupiers

The final variable is the form of tenure granted to occupiers. A threshold question here is whether or in what circumstances tenure should be formalised, and when (if at all) it might be allowed to remain informal. Then there is the question of whether occupiers should be granted a freehold through allotment or leasehold. Where leasehold, there is the question of whether leases (or subleases) should be short- or long-term, restrictive or unrestrictive, alienable or inalienable, and whether or not subject to the payment of rent. More broadly, there is the question of whether the form of tenure should be prescribed – that is, whether there should be a high reliance on fixed precedents and set rules – or whether space should be allowed for individual negotiation.

Deciding upon the most appropriate form of tenure is one of the more complicated issues for a land reform process. It is also an area where the reform theory described in Chapter 2 can be of some use, and in Section 8.3 some of that theory is used to methodically consider what forms of tenure are possible and what their consequences might be. While technical and possibly a little dry, this discussion is ultimately very useful, particularly with respect to the key question of whether the aim of land reform should be the creation of a land market. It is argued here that in some cases marketable forms of tenure will be more problematic than helpful and that a more refined and selective approach will be of greater benefit to communities.

While they are initially presented here discretely, there is a high level of interconnection between these three variables. Most obviously, the ongoing role of the underlying land-use authority depends on the form of tenure that is granted to occupiers. If occupiers are granted freehold, or even 'freehold-like' tenure – such as a lease that is long-term, alienable and unrestrictive – the underlying authority plays less of an ongoing role. Where rent is charged, particularly on an ongoing basis, then the underlying authority has an expanded role. At the same time, the underlying authority decides what form of tenure is granted to occupiers in the first place. This element of circularity means that these issues need to be considered holistically. This relates to a broader point discussed in Section 8.4, which is that any land reform model needs to be considered as part of a cohesive development policy for communities.

Step two: factors determining the approach taken to these variables

Having identified the main variables, or the matters that need to be decided upon, this section now considers the main issues, or what it is that determines *how* these matters should be decided upon. This is presented in terms of the three cardinal issues.

Market conditions

The first cardinal issue is that of market conditions. Put simply, in order to consider the likely impact of any land reform it is necessary to make some assessment of the market circumstances or economic environment in which the reforms will operate. Market conditions constrain what is possible: for example, if incomes are low, then people will pay less for land; and if land prices are low then the benefits of mortgaging land will be smaller. Market conditions also determine the nature of certain risks: for example, if there is a high level of outside interest in the subject land, then the risks of land loss are greater, and where there are monopoly conditions this will impact on the way in which prices are reached.

In most remote communities the economic environment is dominated by governments, who are ultimately responsible for the majority of payments that come into communities. One of the arguments presented here is that the potential economic impact of land reform should not be exaggerated and that land reform cannot be relied upon to escape the conundrum of having communities that rely on government assistance. This is a reality that needs to be accepted and dealt with, rather than avoided or put off in the hope that land reform will somehow clarify things or make it easier to resolve. This is fundamental to the second cardinal issue, understandings of benefit provision.

Understandings of benefit provision

The second cardinal issue is understandings of benefit provision. The term 'benefit provision' is used here to describe the way in which governments and other organisations provide different types of goods, services and payments to individuals and families to help them meet their needs. Benefits in this context take a variety of forms. They include social security or transfer payments, free and subsidised services such as social housing, schools, kindergartens, public transport and health services, and in some cases free or subsidised goods such as food or clothing. In a wealthy country such as Australia, the provision of benefits – particularly by governments – is widespread. Also widespread is the view that in some situations the provision of benefits can be harmful, and not just helpful. It can lead to what is often referred to as 'welfare dependence' or 'passivity', which undermines individual resilience and harms community norms. This is a highly controversial area, and one riven with ideology.

There is nevertheless now a broad political consensus that welfare dependency is one of the more significant problems affecting remote Indigenous communities. This has resulted inter alia in bipartisan political support at a federal level for 'income management' in the Northern Territory and welfare reform trials in Cape York communities in Queensland. At the same time, there is also a broad political consensus that Indigenous

264 *Alternative approaches?*

communities are in some respects under-resourced, that residents live in relative poverty and that there are 'gaps' that governments need to address. It is in this context that governments have committed to 'Closing the Gap in Indigenous Disadvantage'.[13] This results in a tension; governments are at the same time wanting to better resource communities (provide benefits) and avoid the harms of welfare dependence. Resolving this tension requires taking a particular approach to what it is about benefit provision that is harmful. The recent reforms to housing in remote communities provide a good example of the Australian Government trying to resolve this tension. As part of those reforms, the Australian Government is making an 'unprecedented' commitment of $5.5 billion over 10 years to remote Indigenous housing across Australia.[14] In doing so, it makes the release of funding conditional on implementation of the new housing arrangements detailed in previous chapters. The Minister has argued that this is necessary because the earlier housing arrangements were 'at odds with the overarching goal of personal responsibility'.[15] The new housing arrangements implement a new approach to benefit provision.

The term 'understandings of benefit provision' is used here to refer to understandings of what it is about the provision of benefits that can be harmful and how this harm can be minimised or avoided. This is a very complicated issue and one of considerable significance to remote Indigenous communities. The existing literature on it is complex and diverse.[16] The aim here is not to review that literature and put forward a particular perspective but to clarify the relationship between understandings of benefit provision and land reform. This is an important issue, as there has been – and continues to be – considerable confusion in this area.

There are three main areas where understandings of benefit provision are important, although in none of these areas is it the only issue. As indicated above, the first is with respect to housing. Whether (subsidised) home ownership is seen as preferable to social housing, and whether public housing is seen as preferable to community housing, depend to a considerable extent on understandings of benefit provision. The second is with respect to rent and whether the payment of rent to landowners should be characterised as a type of constructive income or harmful welfare. The third is with respect to enterprises. Replacing collectively owned enterprises with ones that are individually owned is not as easy as was sometimes suggested during debate. However, there will be situations in which it is necessary to decide which form of enterprise ownership is to be given preference. For example, should the opportunity to construct offices and lease them profitably to the government be granted to an individual, private company or community-owned enterprise? Understandings of benefit provision are one of the issues to be considered here. To reiterate, in none of these situations is benefit provision the only issue.

During debate about land reform, it has on a number of occasions been suggested that reforms might have a broader impact on welfare. For example, *The Australian* described the introduction of 'private ownership of communal assets' as 'an alternative to the collectivised welfare that has done little to help'.[17] Similarly, former Minister Vanstone described how 'communal poverty' had crushed 'individual motivation', condemning all to 'passive acceptance of more of the same'.[18] The former Premier of Queensland, Campbell Newman, said it was necessary to sort out tenure arrangements in Indigenous communities 'once and for all – so that people can buy a block of dirt, so they can establish a business and have a real life away from welfare'.[19]

These statements suggest that land reform has a role – even a significant role – to play in *solving* the problem of harmful welfare, by transforming either the cultural or economic circumstances of communities. This overstates the potential impact of land reform. Land reform is far more likely to alter the mode of benefit provision than remove the need for benefits. The introduction of home ownership is a good example of this. As described in Chapter 7, current attempts to introduce home ownership have involved a high level of government expenditure, on both administration and the provision of subsidies. And with respect to new houses, it appears that the current level of subsidisation is too low to support home ownership (putting aside other barriers). The need for government benefits does not disappear as a result of tenure arrangements that enable home ownership. Presenting land reform as a way of removing the need for welfare is problematic as it detracts attention from the real work of finding ways to deliver government benefits in the most effective and least harmful way to Indigenous residents of remote communities.

Governance

The third cardinal issue is governance. The term 'governance' as it is used here has two interrelated elements.[20] It refers to the way in which communities govern themselves, and the way that governments exercise their authority in communities. Both elements are relevant to land reform. Indeed it is argued in previous chapters that one of the more pronounced consequences of the recent reforms has been their impact on governance. Despite this, those governance consequences have gone almost unremarked. The Australian Government itself does not use the term governance in this context. The term does, however, need to be used, and the intended governance framework explicitly identified. The importance of this is illustrated by the fact that if tenure arrangements in communities were formalised 15 years ago there is little doubt they would have been formalised very differently. Community organisations such as local councils would have been given a far greater role. In the Northern Territory, those local councils no longer exist. Understandings of governance have shifted and will shift again; great care needs to be taken when embedding a particular approach.

266 *Alternative approaches?*

The importance of governance is most apparent with respect to the identity and processes of the underlying land-use authority. It is similarly clear how governance is relevant to selecting the most appropriate body to own or lease community housing (whether the department of housing, a community housing body, the EDTL, etc). However, understandings of governance will also be embedded in several other ways. The conditions included in a lease or sublease determine the extent to which the underlying land-use authority or the occupier have control over certain decision-making, such as changing the use towards which land may be put. This too is largely an issue of governance. With respect to the delivery of services such as childcare and youth services, and the management of enterprises such as art centres and community stores, understandings of governance will influence whether preference is given to particular types of organisations (local or regional, larger or smaller, Indigenous-managed or mainstream, etc), and whether those organisations are given a form of tenure that embeds their position in a community.

While the governance consequences of recent land reforms have received little attention, there is a considerable body of research that considers governance issues in Indigenous communities more generally.[21] Some of this research critiques the broader shifts in government policy that the recent land reforms reflect. For example, the shift to public housing is one component of a broader 'mainstreaming' of Indigenous service delivery.[22] The increase in government control over land-use decision-making is one part of more 'coercive' or interventionist governance policies,[23] or what Sanders describes as a re-emergence of guardianship as a guiding principle.[24] Again, the aim here is not to review that literature and propose a particular approach to governance but to set out more clearly how understandings of governance are relevant to the development of a land reform model.

What about culture?

Market conditions, benefit provision, governance – these are somewhat dry-sounding terms that might seem detached from the highly particular context in which they are being considered. Specifically, it might be thought that this approach pays too little attention to the distinct cultural environment in Indigenous communities and that culture itself should be a fourth seminal issue. Instead, culture is treated here as being embedded in the other three. With respect to market conditions, cultural preferences and practices will impact on such matters as the amount that people are willing to pay for houses and the way they wish to go about economic development.[25] With respect to benefit provision, culture is very relevant to the way in which Indigenous people interpret and incorporate benefits provided by governments.[26] And with respect to governance, there is a great deal of research that identifies the need for governance arrangements to

Alternative approaches? 267

take account of distinct cultural values and practices, although approaches vary as to how this should be done.[27] The intention here is to treat culture as something that is integrated rather than distinct.

8.3 Defining the parameters of an ideal model

It will by now be clear why it is not possible to set out a single best-practice alternative model of land reform. To do so would require making certain judgements – such as deciding upon the best approach to community governance – whose proper consideration is beyond the scope of the book. That is why Section 8.2 instead describes a framework for developing an alternative model. It is nevertheless possible to make some claims as to what constitutes best practice. For example, it is argued below that there are advantages to having an underlying authority that acts in the interest of all community residents. This conclusion enables a far more targeted discussion about the most appropriate governance arrangements for the underlying authority. The aim of this section is to set out some parameters for best practice. It does so by looking more closely at each of the main variables referred to above: the underlying land-use authority, approaches to allocation and forms of tenure.

Parameters with respect to the underlying land-use authority

Acting in the interest of community residents

It is argued here that there are advantages to having an underlying land-use authority that acts in the interest of all Indigenous community residents, rather than in the interests of traditional owners, one section of the community, governments or some other group. To be clear, it is not the role of a book such as this to prescribe outcomes for Indigenous communities, nor is it the intention here to deny the legitimate claims to land of traditional owners and native title holders. There is, however, a tension between community interests and the rights of traditional owners and native title holders that needs to be recognised rather than ignored. There is no single solution to how that tension can be resolved. Often its resolution will require a deep familiarity with localised issues and a single or one-off act is unlikely to resolve it once and for all. Nevertheless, as the CLC has stated, one objective of land reform should be to 'clarify the relationship between community residents and traditional owners' and to do so constructively.[28] It appears that some of the recent reforms in the Northern Territory have made this more difficult.

Chapter 4 describes the informal tenure arrangements in communities on Aboriginal land prior to the recent reforms. While underlying land-use authority was dispersed, and the concept of community interest was inevitably contested, those arrangements were based on a general understanding

268   *Alternative approaches?*

that the interests of community residents were paramount in most circumstances. This made it possible for informal arrangements to be relied upon relatively effectively for such a long period of time. The recent reforms have changed this. On a township lease it is the traditional owners (and not community residents) who are consulted, who receive rent and who own new enterprises. And in communities without a township lease, it is now far less likely that informal arrangements will deliver stable tenure in a way that prioritises the interest of residents. The government's heavy-handed approach to land reform – particularly the compulsory acquisition of five-year leases – has damaged goodwill and reduced confidence in the reliability of informal arrangements. Dealings with respect to tenure have become more adversarial, one element of which is that traditional owners are more likely to expect rent.[29] In addition to this, the local councils that played such a central role in representing the community interest no longer exist.

Consequently, for communities on ALRA land there will be advantages to introducing a new underlying land-use authority through a mechanism such as a head lease to a body that acts in the interest of (all) community residents. This requires the agreement of traditional owners, which in turn requires that their interests and expectations be addressed. There are certain aspects of land use – such as sacred site protection, and planned new developments on their land – where traditional owners will need to play an ongoing role. In some communities, there will be traditional owners who wish to use the leasing process to increase their authority in other areas. This is an expectation that the recent reforms have encouraged. It is also now likely that in the majority of communities traditional owners will expect rent. These are matters that need to be negotiated in each case. This has been recognised by the CLC, who in their more recent proposal also recommend a head lease to a community body. They suggest that the 'negotiated settlement' between traditional owners and residents should 'be reflected in the headlease'.[30]

While it is not for this book to prescribe how those negotiations take place, it is argued here that there are advantages to: (a) containing the ongoing role of traditional owners (in their formal capacity as traditional owners) to issues such as site protection and the planning of new developments on their land, rather than giving them an enhanced role as has occurred on township leases; and (b) avoiding the situation where ongoing rent is paid to traditional owners. The reasons for this are made clearer below.

Avoiding an anti-commons

The role of the underlying authority includes making land available to investors and providing them with a form of tenure that is suitable to their needs. This is a situation where it is important to avoid the creation of an 'anticommons', where too many discrete decision-makers have the ability

Alternative approaches? 269

to prevent a development or activity. For example, if the grant of a lease to a construction firm required the consent of every community resident, not only would this be time-consuming, there is a good chance that at least one resident might say 'no'. This can lead to chronic underinvestment, or a 'tragedy of the anticommons', a concept popularised by Michael Heller.[31]

It is fragmented decision-making that leads to the creation of an anti-commons, rather than collective ownership per se.[32] Where multiple owners make binding decisions in a single forum, the risk of an anticommons tragedy can be avoided.[33] It is where several processes are required, each of which might result in a refusal, that an anticommons can occur. The relevance of this is that the decision-making processes used by the underlying land-use authority should be designed so as to avoid the situation where there are too many discrete opportunities for refusal. To the extent possible, processes should be streamlined and decisions made in a single forum that enables clear outcomes to be arrived at.

The distinction between constituency and membership

Writing in relation to Indigenous associations, Martin describes how there is value in 'deliberately emphasising the distinction between the constituency or clients of an incorporated association and its formal membership'.[34] This chapter argues that there are advantages in making community residents the 'constituency' of the underlying land-use authority. However, as the quotation from Martin makes clear, that is only the first step. There is still the question of how the body is composed and what processes it must follow. Suggesting that the underlying authority should act in the interests of residents is not the same thing as saying it should simply be composed of, or composed solely of, community residents. There might be scope for drawing on external expertise, or engaging in regional structures where appropriate. There is also the need to avoid the situation where one family or group acquires control of the forum and usurps its function for their own benefit.

What have others suggested?

This is a useful point at which to consider the alternative models that other people have suggested. In varying degrees of detail, those models all address the issue of the underlying land-use authority in some way (albeit not using this term). Reeves simply recommended a head lease to a local council 'or some other suitable body'.[35] Hudson suggested that head leases be granted to 'communities', perhaps through the use of 'company title arrangements'.[36] Thamurrur Council proposed a head lease to a body called a 'town corporation' that would be 'controlled by the traditional owners'.[37] Shillito set out a model based on strata title under which management vests in bodies called 'Community Management Groups', the

270 *Alternative approaches?*

exact make-up of which 'would vary for each township'.[38] The agreement negotiated by Galarrwuy Yunupingu provided for an area of land that included the community of Gunyangara to be leased to a corporation owned by the Gumatj clan, which would then sublease the community itself to the Australian Government.[39] Crabtree *et al.*, who focus particularly on housing, suggest the use of bodies called 'Community Land Trusts' (CLTs), a popular community housing structure in some part of the United States and United Kingdom.[40]

Two proposals stand out in this area, for their detail and for the fact that they have been put forward by Land Councils. The first is in relation to CLA land. In recent years there has been a lot of discussion about enabling leasing on CLA land. The CLC and NLC argue that CLA associations do not have the 'resources or capacity' to manage the leasing process on their own.[41] They have instead proposed a model based on the ALRA, under which CLA associations could voluntarily elect to become 'CLA land trusts', which would hold land on behalf of the members of the former CLA association, meaning that there was no change to the beneficial ownership group but that different processes would apply. CLA land trusts would grant leases only when directed to by the relevant Land Council, and the Land Council could only provide a direction with the consent of the ownership group.[42] It appears that to date the government has rejected this model.

The second is in relation to ALRA land. In 2010 the CLC proposed that for communities on ALRA land there should be a head lease to a 'community land corporation', which would be a 'decision-making body comprising Aboriginal residents'.[43] This actually reflects a shift in the CLC's policy. Five years earlier it had argued occupiers should apply for leases directly from the traditional owners.[44] Its more recent proposal supports 'shifting decision-making power from ... traditional owners to Aboriginal community residents, whether traditional owners or not'.[45] The CLC does, however, make an exception with respect to rent, saying that it supported 'the rights of traditional owners to receive leasing income and decide how it is spent'.[46]

It should be noted that the concept of an underlying land-use authority only applies in an ongoing sense where formalisation occurs through leasing or subleasing. Where there is instead an allotment of land ownership, the role of the underlying land-use authority ceases. The risks and benefits of this are considered further below.

Clarifying the decisions to be made with respect to allocation

Residential housing

In order to clarify the decisions to be made with respect to allocation, it is again useful to distinguish between the categories of land use identified in Chapter 4 – residential housing, enterprises and service providers. The first considered here is residential housing, where a threshold issue is deciding between home ownership and social housing. This has already been discussed in some detail in Chapter 7, where it is suggested that some of the arguments in favour of home ownership – that it will lead to an increase in housing supply, or give entrepreneurs greater access to credit – are not compelling. This does not mean that home ownership should not be considered, rather that the more persuasive arguments for home ownership are based on understandings of benefit provision and concerns about the harmful welfare impact of social housing.

While this does help clarify consideration of this issue, there are also several other matters that also need to be taken into account. There is the question of whether, in the long term, subsidised home ownership or social housing is the cheaper method of meeting the housing needs of Indigenous community residents. There is the impact of selling existing houses on the availability of social housing for those people who need it. There are even such matters as the risk of 'individuals and households [becoming] "entrapped" in low value housing' if a settlement experiences economic decline.[47] Again, none of this means that home ownership should not be considered. It does mean that its introduction in remote and economically marginalised communities is a lot more complex than simply enabling 'individual ownership'.

With respect to social housing, there is a further allocation issue that Noel Pearson has referred to. Chapter 4 described how previously the allocation of social housing to particular individuals was based on not just need but the 'exigencies of community social life and politics'.[48] The new arrangements deliberately remove any element of community control over allocation. While this can reduce the risk of conflict and decisions being influenced by nepotism, there is also a downside to criteria-based allocation. As Pearson describes it, Indigenous communities are 'villages not housing estates'.[49] He argues that they are 'not anonymous places where the housing department bureaucrat can allocate [houses to] families indiscriminately on the basis of some ... formula'.[50] Mechanistic approaches to allocation can reduce people's autonomy and ignore the historical, cultural and relational consequences of where people live.

Who should own enterprises?

One of the initial reasons for introducing land reform was to enable new forms of enterprise ownership. For example, former Minister Mal Brough said that township leasing would 'make it significantly easier for individuals to ... establish businesses'.[51] However, township leasing has not led to individuals establishing businesses, nor have the other reforms. For the most part it is simply that existing enterprises have been granted a lease or sublease. Any new enterprises created on township leases are owned not by individuals but by the traditional owners collectively. Part of the

272 *Alternative approaches?*

problem here is that during debate about land reform 'communal owner-ship' of land was equated with collective ownership of enterprises, and 'individual property rights' were equated with 'individuals' having the opportunity to own businesses. Clearly the relationship is more complex.

The issue of giving preference to particular forms of enterprise does arise, but it arises differently and in a far more modest way than was suggested during debate. There will be, as there has always been, situations in which existing infrastructure (such as the store building or an art centre studio) becomes vacant, or unoccupied land is made available for development. In those circumstances, a number of questions arise: should there be an auction or tender process or can land be allocated to the first applicant? Should preference be given to local Indigenous enterprises? To individuals instead of corporations?

There are several interrelated issues requiring consideration here. One is the market conditions affecting remote communities, which sometimes result in monopolies or duopolies, most notably with respect to community stores. There are also enterprises that are arguably more useful to communities where they combine their commercial activities with what is effectively the provision of a community service, such as where art centres try to maximise the amount of employment they provide or community stores subsidise healthy food.

A further issue is the consequences of having enterprises owned collectively, particularly at the point where they deliver benefits to individual owners. This is where understandings of benefit provision are relevant in their broader sense. Right at the beginning of debate about land reform, Warren Mundine argued that it was necessary for Aboriginal communities to shift away from 'non-profit community-based businesses' to 'profit-making businesses'.[52] But are profit-making businesses actually better at delivering benefits to individuals? Is it better for profitable collective enterprises to pay out dividends to shareholders rather than, for example, make needs-based payments through a charitable structure? This is certainly not something that can be assumed.

These issues with respect to forms of enterprise ownership are complex. Presenting them in terms of a communal–individual ownership dualism does not help clarify them. It instead gives the impression that what is at stake is a structural tension between culture and enterprise. It is suggested here that there are good reasons why certain enterprises are better owned collectively. At the same time, there is also value in trying to maximise opportunities for individual Indigenous residents to set up other enterprises – such as a hairdressing salon, bakery, mechanical workshop or clothes shop – at least in some larger communities. It would be naive to rely on the 'market' to provide such individuals with the infrastructure and form of tenure they require. This needs to be addressed more deliberately. This is tied to the argument that land reform should be approached as part of a cohesive development strategy.

Who should provide services?

With respect to service providers, there are allocation decisions around whether priority should be given to particular types of organisations, such as government or NGO, Indigenous or non-Indigenous, local or regional. This has previously been, and will continue to be, primarily a funding issue. The organisation providing youth services will generally be the organisation that is funded to do so. The real issue here is how this interacts with arrangements with respect to tenure. If a particular service provider is granted a long-term and rent-free sublease over, say, staff housing and a set of offices, then it will be more difficult to replace them with another service provider in the next round of funding. This will be far less of an issue where service providers are required to pay rent, as has been the case under most recent reforms.

Who should decide?

There is a further point that emerges from this discussion of enterprises and service providers. It is the underlying land-use authority who decides, for example, who is given the opportunity to develop vacant land or take over staff housing that is no longer being used. These are clearly decisions that are ideally made in the best interest of the community, which is one reason why the underlying land-use authority should act in the interest of all community residents. Related to this is the issue of how land and infrastructure are *reallocated* after the initial allocation has been made. This will depend on whether or not occupiers have been granted a freehold-like/marketable form of tenure, as discussed in the next section.

What form of tenure should be granted to occupiers?

Should all tenure arrangements be formalised?

The first issue with respect to forms of tenure is whether it should be formal or informal, or more particularly whether occupiers should be *prevented from*, *allowed to* or *required to* obtain formal tenure. Historically on CLA land, occupiers were prevented from obtaining formal tenure due to the legal constraints on the grant of leases. At the other end of the spectrum, on a township lease the EDTL requires all occupiers to obtain a sublease. In between these two positions, it is possible to give occupiers the option of obtaining a lease where they believe it is in their best interest to do so, or to only require them to obtain a lease in certain circumstances. It is argued here that there are advantages to this intermediate approach (where this is still possible).

Whatever their shortcomings, the pre-existing informal arrangements in communities on Indigenous land were cheap. They were inexpensive for

274 *Alternative approaches?*

occupiers, the majority of whom did not have to pay rent, and they were inexpensive to administer, in that they did not require the drawing up of legal agreements or the registration of dealings with land titles offices. By comparison, the recent reforms have been very expensive to implement. The EDTL alone has cost a total of $6,377,827 over the last six financial years, to administer just a handful of communities.[53] The cost of implementing 'secure tenure' policies has not been reported but must be even greater. Implementing these policies across all infrastructure in all communities is expensive.

Under current approaches, some occupiers will be worse off as a result of reform, primarily because they are now required to pay rent. To the extent that the introduction of rent is a deliberate outcome of the reforms, this will not be seen as a problem. However, where rent is not made a priority, an alternative and lower-cost approach is possible that would bring the benefits of formalised tenure to those who want it in a more targeted manner. This would be to allow the majority of occupiers (but not all – see below) to decide for themselves whether obtaining a formal grant of tenure is in their best interest. Of course, if they applied for a formal grant of tenure they may not get it on the terms that they want. That is a matter for negotiation between them and the underlying authority, as discussed in the next section.

It is important here that the benefits of formal tenure are not overstated. For those occupiers who would like a set of alienable or marketable rights, clearly formal tenure is required. And for those occupiers who are worried about their tenure security, a lease may be a useful way of addressing their concerns. However, for others – such as an art centre that knows it enjoys community support, or a service provider with a long-standing status – they may be happy to rely on cheaper, informal tenure arrangements, as they did for so many years previously. This would not only reduce their expenses, it can also avoid some of the costs of formalisation and result in a system that is cheaper to administer. It is at least arguable that a key reason that informal tenure arrangements subsisted for decades in Indigenous communities across Australia is because in their particular circumstances it was economically rational to do so. While there are clearly drawbacks to informal tenure, the benefits may have outweighed the costs.

However, this presupposes not only that occupiers are given a choice as to whether they obtain a lease (and pay rent), but also the existence of informal tenure arrangements that are sufficiently stable and secure. It appears that this did tend to be the case previously, but it is far less likely as a result of the disruptive impact of recent reforms, particularly in the Northern Territory. To some extent, this might be rectified by transferring underlying land-use authority to a body representing the community interest. However, this alone may no longer be sufficient. Many occupiers will have lost confidence in informal arrangements as a result of recent events.

Alternative approaches? 275

While there are advantages to this decentralised and responsive approach to decision-making, it also has its limits. The CLC notes that leasing negotiations have made apparent a 'difficult class of assets' that 'at present, no one wants to accept ongoing responsibility for', such as pools and recreation halls.[54] For such infrastructure, there may be no single 'occupier' who is motivated to apply for a lease, and this type of shared infrastructure is precisely the type that is at risk of being poorly maintained due to unclear lines of responsibility. If a more flexible approach to formalisation is followed, it will also be necessary to identify such problem infrastructure and deal with the issue of who should be made responsible for its maintenance, possibly through a sublease. The CLC suggests that the EDTL may have a role to play in this area.[55]

What sort of formal tenure?

Where a decision is made to grant formal tenure to occupiers, there are several decisions to be made about the terms of that grant. Those terms are usefully divided into two categories: those that relate to the allocation of control over decision-making between the underlying authority and the occupier, and the question of rent.

(A) THE ALLOCATION OF CONTROL BETWEEN THE UNDERLYING LAND-USE AUTHORITY AND OCCUPIERS

Landlords use conditions in leases to retain control over certain decision-making. Common examples include clauses that restrict the transfer of a lease or the use to which the property may be put. The more the restrictions, the greater the extent to which the landlord retains control. For communities on Indigenous land, it is a question of which decisions should be made by the underlying authority and which by occupiers themselves. Often this is simply an issue of community governance. For example, whether the underlying authority should be able to prevent a sublease holder from putting up signs, erecting new infrastructure or changing the use towards which land is put depends on whether it is thought that they should play this sort of planning role, which in turn depends on what other planning systems there are in place.[56] There will of course be economic consequences to this; a sublease that can only be used for a particular purpose will be less valuable.

There is a more particular set of issues that arise with respect to restrictions on transfer or alienability. This is a complex and at times technical area, but also a situation in which the land reform theory described in Chapter 2 can be useful. Put simply, the issue in this context in whether control over the reallocation of land and infrastructure should be *centralised* or *decentralised*. Where the underlying authority imposes restrictions on transfer, then control over reallocation remains centralised. This can

276 *Alternative approaches?*

occur in one of two ways – through a condition prohibiting the transfer of a sublease,[57] or through keeping the period of a sublease short (as when a sublease ends it falls to the underlying authority to reallocate, whether to the existing occupier or another). Conversely, where land is converted to ordinary freehold through allotment, or where a sublease is long-term and may be alienated, it falls to the occupier to decide to whom it is transferred. This is sometimes referred to as *market allocation*, and it brings into play the benefits and risks of alienability, which fall into two groups. First there are the potential economic benefits for occupiers, namely access to further credit (through 'collateralisation') and the ability to recoup investment costs (the 'realisability effect'). More broadly, there is the impact of decentralised decision-making on the way in which property is allocated to different people. Both are considered below.[58]

(B) THE ECONOMIC BENEFITS OF ALIENABILITY FOR OCCUPIERS

A right of alienability can enable *collateralisation*, whereby occupiers are able to access additional sources of credit through the use of their property as collateral. Importantly, collateralisation can only occur where market conditions are suitable. It requires a market that is sufficiently *strong* for property to have a meaningful value and sufficiently *stable* for credit providers to be willing to lend on the security of a mortgage. Where property values are low, sales infrequent or prices unstable, collateralisation is unlikely have a significant impact on credit. Further, for collateralisation to have a positive rather than negative impact, credit must be used productively: either through enabling the occupier to remain liquid during a period of hardship, or through enabling them to make productive investments.

It is unlikely that service providers, whether government or NGO, will wish to make much use of collateralisation. For governments this is simply because they access funds through means other than mortgaging property. It is similar for NGOs, who are far more likely to address their ongoing financial needs by applying for funding than taking on the risks associated with an unfunded mortgage. It is instead enterprises that are more likely to be interested in the benefits of collateralisation. Here, the issue will be the extent to which market conditions allow for those benefits to be realised. Enterprises themselves are well placed to make an assessment of this, as they can seek advice on the matter directly from credit providers. This suggests that, provided surrounding circumstances allow enterprises to have some control over the negotiation process, this is an area where a flexible approach to tenure negotiations will result in better-adapted outcomes.

Alienable property rights can also enable an increase in investment as a result of the 'realisability effect', where owners can 'realise' their investment, or a meaningful proportion thereof, through a relative increase in the value of the property when they sell.[59] Again, the impact of the realisability effect will depend on market conditions. Where construction costs are high and property values are low or uncertain, the impact will be far less.

(C) THE IMPACT OF ALIENABILITY ON HOW PROPERTY IS ALLOCATED

Alienable property rights also mean that property will be reallocated in a decentralised manner through individual transactions. In a sufficiently large and functional market, this can lead to a more efficient allocation, a phenomenon sometimes referred to as 'allocative efficiency'. However, as documented in Chapter 2, market allocation does not always result in greater overall efficiency and where it does it can do so at the expense of equity and access to land by the poor.

Importantly, the factors that determine *optimal allocation* for service providers are different from those which determine optimal allocation among enterprises. With respect to enterprises, a functional market is able to lead to a more efficient allocation because (and to the extent that) the most efficient user will be willing to pay the highest price. That is, allocative efficiency is based on willingness to pay being an accurate indicator of the usefulness (efficiency) of an enterprise. This is not the case for service providers in Indigenous communities, where the optimal service provider is the one that provides its service effectively, efficiently and responsively, rather than profitably. The service provider able to pay the highest purchase price for land will not necessarily be the best service provider for a community. A centralised system is able to reallocate infrastructure to service providers more strategically.[60] This requires a well-functioning underlying authority, and one that acts not only in the interests of community residents but of *all* community residents. In other words, it relies on having an underlying authority that is able to effectively deal with conflict and prevent decisions being made for the benefit of one group only.

And as discussed above, there are also enterprises that are more useful to the community where they are not simply profit-driven. Again, in those situations, the enterprise that is willing to pay the highest price for land may not be the best enterprise for the community. An art centre that maximises community employment and financial returns for artists may be less competitive than an art centre that maximises profit. A community store that subsidises healthy food will be less profitable than one that does not. For other undertakings that are potentially profitable, such as a property development, a well-resourced outside organisation may outbid a local Indigenous enterprise. This suggests that even with respect to enterprises there will be some situations where the risks of unregulated market allocation may outweigh the benefits.

It was noted earlier that imposing restrictions on transfer was only one of two ways in which the underlying authority retains control over

278 *Alternative approaches?*

reallocation. The other is by only making grants for a short period of time. When a sublease expires, the underlying authority decides who receives a further sublease. This gives rise to an additional set of issues. A sublease for too short a time might deter an occupier from making an investment that it would otherwise have made. Shortening the term also reduces the value of the grant, in turn reducing the potential for collateralisation and the realisability effect (to the extent that such potential exists). Again, this is something that occupiers can themselves identify and ask to have taken into account where a flexible approach is taken to forms of tenure.

This somewhat dry and technical discussion illustrates an important point. It has been argued that the 'main goal' of land reform should be the 'creation of a long-term property market' so as to enable economic development.[61] That is after all what happens off Indigenous land. However, a careful consideration of the market conditions affecting remote Indigenous communities suggests that the issue is more complex. The creation of a land market through allotment or by making all subleases long-term and alienable could have negative consequences, particularly with respect to reallocation. Further, the positive consequences of alienability will not be as extensive as they might first appear.

(D) RENT

The second major decision with respect to sublease terms is that of rent. To clarify, the rent referred to here is the rent that enterprises and service providers pay to landowners (not, for example, the rent that tenants pay to housing managers for community housing). This 'rent' might be a one-off or up-front payment – in the nature of a purchase price – in which case the challenge for the underlying authority is to anticipate the market price for the property and then decide whether the initial grant should be at, above or below that price. Or rent might be charged on a regular basis, such as annually, as has generally been the case under the recent reforms (with the exception of home ownership). The consequences of this are discussed in some detail in Chapter 7, but it is worth recapping them here. In terms of investment, rent represents an additional cost for occupiers and investors. This may lead to a decrease in investment over time. Rent is also landowner income, and where that income is invested in communities – either in enterprises, as has occurred in Wurrumiyanga, or in community development projects, as suggested by the CLC – it will result in some increase in investment. As the amount of rent is currently modest, both the investment and disinvestment impacts will be small.

Concerns have also been raised about whether rent payments to landowners should be considered a type of harmful welfare. This requires a judgement based on understandings of benefit provision. In this context, it should be noted that rent has positive as well as negative characteristics. It is different from a government payment such as a funding grant in that

Alternative approaches? 279

it is mediated by exchange – that is, there is an element of 'reciprocity'[62] – and because landowners have a higher degree of autonomy with respect to its use.[63] Where it is an ongoing income stream, it does not have the problem of being a short-term distortion.[64] However, it is also earned collectively. This can lead to contestation about how it is used; moreover, at the point where it is paid out to individuals (if and when this occurs) the degree of reciprocity may have altered. Further, the characteristics of rent as a type of benefit cannot be considered in isolation, particularly to the extent that communities continue to rely on government benefits. It is not enough to simply dismiss rent as a potentially harmful benefit; the more important question is whether it is better or worse than the alternatives it replaces.

However, there is a further consequence of rent that is more concerning. Rent on ALRA land is paid not to or for the benefit of community residents but 'to or for the benefit of the traditional Aboriginal owners'.[65] This makes the distinction between traditional owners and (other) community residents more significant. There is a real risk that over time this will lead to an increase in conflict and contestation, or perhaps the marginalisation of non-traditional owner residents. There are strategies available to minimise these risks; notably, the CLC 'is committed to encouraging traditional owners to distribute large or regular sums of money for community benefit only'.[66] While Land Councils might do as well as they can, there is also a problem here that is structural.

Final comments on the parameters of an ideal model

Under current approaches to land reform in the Northern Territory there is a tension between two objectives: maximising the economic benefits for traditional owners on the one hand and making it cheaper and easier for organisations to operate in Aboriginal communities on the other. The problem is not that there is a tension, but that this is the *wrong* tension. It is not the case that occupiers should automatically get what they want. Naturally, given the choice any occupier will want the broadest set of rights possible, i.e. either freehold or a long-term, unrestrictive and alienable sublease, preferably at no cost. As the discussion above illustrates, that would not necessarily be in the best interest of the community. What is wrong with the current structure is not that the desires of occupiers need to be weighed up or balanced, rather than acquiesced to, but that they are weighed up against the interests of traditional owners. It would be preferable if their interest were instead weighed up against those of community residents as a whole. That is a better framework for negotiating not just rent but all sublease terms.

The various arguments presented above might be summarised in three principles. It is argued here that there are advantages to: (a) having a flexible approach to tenure negotiations, where those negotiations are

280 *Alternative approaches?*

conducted by an underlying land-use authority that (b) acts in the interest of all Indigenous community residents and (c) is well-functioning, responsive and well-advised. As a corollary to this, it is argued that there are advantages to containing the ongoing role of traditional owners in the underlying authority (in their capacity as traditional owners) to issues such as site protection and the planning of new developments, and avoiding the situation where traditional owners receive ongoing rent.

This is not to suggest that the traditional owners do not have the right to receive rent. As landowners, they clearly do. This is not an argument against their rights. It is a conclusion as to the best arrangements for communities (which does not carry over to other areas of Indigenous land). As a consequence of this conclusion, it is suggested that a better approach is to negotiate some type of one-off settlement that enables the boundaries between community land and other areas of land to be clarified and the interests of traditional owners to be respected within the above parameters. This might take the form of a one-off up-front payment, what Peterson has described as 'buying out' their interests.[67] It might instead (or additionally) involve traditional owners being allocated certain areas of community land. In those communities where traditional owners have historically received rent from the community store, provision might be made for this to continue. This was never a simple issue, and it can only have been made more difficult by the fact that under township leases and 'secure tenure' policies traditional owners are now receiving ongoing rent.

8.4 Conclusion: the need for a detailed, realistic and integrated land reform policy

One of the remarkable things about the Australian reforms is how little attention has been paid to clarifying their purpose. During the initial period of debate – about communal and individual ownership – the objects of reform were identified as enabling home ownership and economic development. It was understood that there was a set of secondary objectives behind this, to do with changing the culture of remote communities, but the primary objectives were presented in the most simple of terms. While implementing the reforms, the government has at times articulated a slightly broader set of objectives, which accompanied the introduction of 'secure tenure' policies. In addition to the earlier aims, the government has argued that 'land tenure reform' will 'support better public housing' and lead to improvements in the maintenance of infrastructure.[68] Again, these objectives have been set out in only the broadest of terms.

Such brevity would be less of a problem if there was a single type of land reform or if there were only a small number of straightforward decisions to be made in the course of reform. As this book demonstrates, this is not the case. The decisions to be made are several and complex. There are, for example, different approaches that might be taken to enabling economic development. Ultimately, the Australian Government has taken an approach based on increasing economic returns for landowners. This was not the only option and it was not decided upon following a transparent process or considered debate. It followed on from the awkward and at times confused way in which the reforms were implemented.

The final argument presented by this chapter is that the implementation of reforms should be supported by a detailed land reform policy. So as to avoid some of the waste and confusion that have accompanied the existing reforms, that policy should set out the objectives of reform in far greater detail, addressing not just the aims in general terms but how those aims might be achieved. This is part of approaching the task of land reform from the right direction. For example, one aim of land reform might be to make it as easy as possible for individual community residents to establish a business. To achieve this aim, it will be necessary to identify the infrastructure needs of those entrepreneurs (office space, retail space) and the form of tenure most suitable to their circumstances, which is likely to be low-cost rental. It is not sufficient to naively rely on land reform in general terms or the creation of a land market to deliver this infrastructure or the most useful form of tenure.

This example also illustrates why a land reform policy needs to be integrated, in the sense that there needs to be consistency between it and other government policies. Those individuals who wish to start a business will need more than just a useful form of tenure. They will require other types of support, including quite possibly access to alternative forms of credit. No matter how well land reform itself is implemented, it will not achieve this objective unless there are complementary policies in place. The implementation of land reform is also connected to planning processes. The need to integrate land reform and planning law has been recognised with respect to township leases, where exemptions have been granted to make the formalisation process cheaper and easier.[69]

It is also critical that a land reform policy is realistic. Land reform cannot be relied upon to avoid the fact that communities will continue to require government support. Providing that support in the most beneficial and least harmful manner is a challenge that cannot be avoided or put off, nor will its resolution become clearer once land reform has been implemented. Rather, each model of land reform will implement a particular approach to what it is that can make benefit provision harmful.

Perhaps most importantly, that policy needs to be responsive to the needs of particular communities. To be very clear: producing a more comprehensive land reform policy does not mean that governments alone are responsible for decision-making. To the contrary, it means making clear the role and importance of community decision-making for land reform. It means writing Indigenous landowners and community residents – their needs and aspirations – into the reform process. To date, this has not been a feature of the Australian Government's approach to land reform. It has

282   *Alternative approaches?*

been very much a government-led, and at times government-imposed, approach to reform. It is becoming increasingly clear in hindsight how unnecessary and counter-productive this has been.

Notes

1 See Chapter 4.
2 See John Reeves, 'Building on Land Rights for the Next Generation: The Review of the *Aboriginal Land Rights (Northern Territory) Act 1976*' (Australian Government, 1998) 498–500.
3 Peter Sutton, 'Anthropological Submission on the Reeves Review' (1999) 9(2) *Anthropological Forum* 189, 196.
4 Central Land Council (CLC), 'Communal Title and Economic Development' (Policy Paper, 2005).
5 Central Land Council (CLC), 'Community Leasing – an Alternative Proposal' (Discussion Paper, 2010).
6 Central Land Council (CLC), 'Land Reform in the Northern Territory: Evidence Not Ideology' (Discussion Paper, 2013).
7 Tom Calma, 'Native Title Report 2005' (Australian Human Rights Commission, 2005) 53.
8 Lewis Shillito, 'Strata Title Aboriginal Towns? An Alternative to the Town-Leasing Proposal' (2007) 14(3) *Australian Property Law Journal* 201.
9 For an overview of the agreement and list of references see Agreements, Treaties and Negotiated Settlements Project (ATNS), *Memorandum of Understanding between Galarrwuy Yunupingu and the Commonwealth of Australia* (15 October 2007) www.atns.net.au/agreement.asp?EntityID=4010.
10 Sara Hudson, 'From Rhetoric to Reality: Can 99-Year Leases Lead to Home-ownership for Indigenous Communities?' (Policy Monograph 92, Centre for Independent Studies, 2009) vii.
11 Central Land Council (CLC), Submission No 347 to Senate Standing Committees on Community Affairs, Parliament of Australia, *Inquiry into Stronger Futures in the Northern Territory Bill 2011 and Two Related Bills*, 1 February 2012, 9; Northern Land Council (NLC), Submission No 361 to Senate Standing Committees on Community Affairs, Parliament of Australia, *Inquiry into Stronger Futures in the Northern Territory Bill 2011 and Two Related Bills*, 10 February 2012, 4.
12 Louise Crabtree *et al.*, 'Principles and Practices of an Affordable Housing Community Land Trust Model' (Research Paper, Australian Housing and Urban Research Institute, January 2012); Louise Crabtree *et al.*, 'Community Land Trusts and Indigenous Housing Options' (Final Report No 185, Australian Housing and Urban Research Institute, March 2012).
13 Council of Australian Governments, *Closing the Gap in Indigenous Disadvantage* (2012) www.coag.gov.au/closing_the_gap_in_indigenous_disadvantage.
14 Jenny Macklin, 'Importance of Delivering Remote Indigenous Housing in an Efficient and Affordable Way' (Speech delivered at Parliament House, Canberra, 15 September 2009).
15 Jenny Macklin, 'Speech to Cape York Institute Leadership Academy' (Speech delivered to the Cape York Institute Leadership Academy, Cairns, 22 July 2008). See also Chapter 7.
16 See, eg, Noel Pearson, *Up from the Mission: Selected Writings* (Black Inc, 2009); David Martin, 'Is Welfare Dependency "Welfare Poison"? An Assessment of Noel Pearson's Proposals for Aboriginal Welfare Reform' (Discussion

Alternative approaches? 283

Paper No 213/2001, Centre for Aboriginal Economic Policy Research, 2001); Will Sanders, 'Equality and Difference Arguments in Australian Indigenous Affairs: Examples from Income Support and Housing' (Working Paper No 38/2008, Center refor Aboriginal Economic Policy Research, 2008); David Johnson, 'Introduction to Policy Forum on Welfare Reform' (2001) 34(1) *Australian Economic Review* 81; Jon Altman, Matthew Gray and Will Sanders, 'Indigenous Australians Working for Welfare: What Difference Does It Make?' (2000) 33(4) *Australian Economic Review* 355; Anne Daly, 'The Winner's Curse? Indigenous Australians in the Welfare System' (2000) 33(4) *Australian Economic Review* 349; Anne Daly and Diane Smith, 'The Role of Welfare in the Economy of Two Indigenous Communities' (2000) 33(4) *Australian Economic Review* 363; Nerelle Poroch, 'Welfare Reform and Indigenous Empowerment' (2006) 1 *Australian Aboriginal Studies* 3; Francesca Merlan, 'More Than Rights', *Inside Story*, 11 March 2009 http://inside.org.au/more-than-rights; Diane Austin-Broos, 'Places, Practices, and Things: The Articulation of Arrernte Kinship with Welfare and Work' (February 2003) 30(1) *American Ethnologist* 118; Ciaran O'Faircheallaigh, 'Use and Management of Revenue from Indigenous-Mining Company Agreements: Theoretical Perspectives' (Agreements, Treaties and Negotiated Settlements Project, Working Paper Series, 2011); Tim Rowse, 'McClure's "Mutual Obligation" and Pearson's "Reciprocity": Can They Be Reconciled?' (August 2002) 37(3) *Australian Journal of Social Issues* 263; Patrick McCauley, 'Two Hand Blessing' (2007) 51(10) *Quadrant* 64.

17 Editorial, 'Land Rights Should Apply to Individuals', *The Australian*, 19 February 2005, 13.

18 Amanda Vanstone, 'Beyond Conspicuous Compassion: Indigenous Australians Deserve More Than Good Intentions' (Speech delivered to the Australia and New Zealand School of Government, Australian National University, Canberra, 7 December 2005).

19 Australian Broadcasting Corporation, 'Property Key to Ending Indigenous Welfare Cycle: Newman', *ABC News*, 15 January 2013 (Eric Tlozek). See also Andrew Johnson, 'Unlocking the North', *The Australian*, 14 June 2013, 10.

20 A definition of governance is provided in Chapter 1.

21 In addition to those referred to below see, eg, Neil Westbury and Will Sanders, 'Governance and Service Delivery for Remote Aboriginal Communities in the Northern Territory: Challenges and Opportunities' (Working Paper No 6/2000, Centre for Aboriginal Economic Policy Research, 2000); Bruce Walker, Douglas Porter and Ian Marsh, 'Fixing the Hole in Australia's Heartland: How Government Needs to Work in Remote Australia' (Desert Knowledge Australia, 2012); Diane Austin-Broos and Gaynor Macdonald (eds), *Culture, Economy and Governance in Aboriginal Australia* (Sydney University Press, 2005); Diane Smith, 'From Gove to Governance: Reshaping Indigenous Governance in the Northern Territory' (Discussion Paper No 265/2004, Centre for Aboriginal Economic Policy Research, 2004); Will Sanders, 'Thinking about Indigenous Community Governance' (Discussion Paper No 262/2004, Centre for Aboriginal Economic Policy Research, 2004); Philip Batty, 'Private Politics, Public Strategies: White Advisers and Their Aboriginal Subjects' (2005) 75(3) *Oceania* 209; Sarah Holcombe, 'Socio-political Perspectives on Localism and Regionalism in the Pintubi Luritja Region of Central Australia: Implications for Service Delivery and Governance' (Working Paper No 25/2004, Centre for Aboriginal Economic Policy Research, 2004).

22 See, eg, Patrick Sullivan, *Belonging Together: Dealing with the Politics of Disenchantment in Australian Indigenous Policy* (Aboriginal Studies Press, 2011) 33–47.

284 *Alternative approaches?*

23 See, eg, Greg Marks, 'Coercive Governance and Remote Indigenous Communities: The Failed Promise of the Whole of Government Mantra' (2008) 12(1) *Australian Indigenous Law Review* 2.

24 Will Sanders, 'Experimental Government in Australian Indigenous Affairs: from Coombs to Pearson via Rowse and the Competing Principles' (Discussion Paper No 291/2014, Centre for Aboriginal Economic Policy Research, 2014).

25 See, eg, David Trigger, 'Mining Projects in Remote Aboriginal Australia: Sites for the Articulation and Contesting of Economic and Cultural Features' in Diane Austin-Broos and Gaynor Macdonald (eds), *Culture, Economy and Governance in Aboriginal Australia* (Sydney University Press, 2005) 41; David Martin, 'Policy Alchemy and the Magical Transformation of Aboriginal Society' in Yasmine Musharbash and Marcus Barber (eds), *Ethnography & the Production of Anthropological Knowledge: Essays in Honour of Nicolas Peterson* (Australian National University E Press, 2011) 201, 203–7; Marcia Langton, 'Anthropology, Politics and the Changing World of Aboriginal Australians' (March 2011) 21(1) *Anthropological Forum* 1.

26 See, eg, David Martin, 'Money, Business and Culture: Issues for Aboriginal Economic Policy' (Discussion Paper No 101/1995, Centre for Aboriginal Economic Policy Research, 1995); Myrna Tonkinson and Robert Tonkinson, 'The Cultural Dynamics of Adaptation in Remote Aboriginal Communities: Policy, Values and the State's Unmet Expectations' (2010) 52 *Anthropologica* 67, 69.

27 See, eg, David Martin, 'Rethinking the Design of Indigenous Organisations: The Need for Strategic Engagement' (Discussion Paper No 248/2003, Centre for Aboriginal Economic Policy Research, 2003); Patrick Sullivan, 'Indigenous Governance: The Harvard Project on Native American Economic Development and Appropriate Principles of Governance for Remote Australia' (Research Discussion Paper No 17, Australian Institute of Aboriginal and Torres Strait Islanders Studies, February 2006) 11–12.

28 CLC, 'Community Leasing: an Alternative Proposal', above n 5, 6.

29 See Chapter 7.

30 CLC, 'Community Leasing: an Alternative Proposal', above n 5, ii.

31 See, eg, Michael Heller, 'The Tragedy of the Anticommons: Property in the Transition from Marx to Markets' (1998) 111(3) *Harvard Law Review* 622.

32 See Larissa Katz, 'Red Tape and Gridlock' in D. Benjamin Barros (ed), *Hernando de Soto and Property in a Market Economy* (Ashgate, 2010) 109, 122.

33 One of Heller's solutions to an anticommons tragedy is to combine fragmented decision-making into a single forum; see, eg, Michael Heller, *The Gridlock Economy: How Too Much Ownership Wrecks Markets, Stops Innovation and Costs Lives* (Basic Books, 2008) 119 (discussion of Land Assembly districts) and 125 (reference to using a limited liability company).

34 Martin, 'Rethinking the Design of Indigenous Organisations', above n 27, 11–12.

35 Reeves, above n 2, 500.

36 Hudson, above n 10, 14.

37 With respect to the Wadeye proposal, see Calma, above n 7.

38 Shillito, above n 8, 217.

39 See ATNS, above n 9. This agreement was never implemented.

40 See both reports by Crabtree *et al.* at above n 12.

41 CLC, Submission No 347, above n 11, 8.

42 Ibid, 10; NLC, Submission No 361, above n 11, 4. See also Central Land Council, Submission to the Department of Families, Community Services and Indigenous Affairs, *Discussion Paper on Community Living Area Land Reform in the Northern Territory*, 2013, 3.

Alternative approaches? 285

43 CLC, 'Community Leasing: an Alternative Proposal', above n 5, 6.
44 CLC, 'Communal Title and Economic Development', above n 4.
45 CLC, 'Community Leasing: an Alternative Proposal', above n 5, ii.
46 Ibid, 11.
47 Andrew Beer and Selina Tually, 'Forgotten But Not Gone: The Housing Markets of Australia's Country Towns' (Paper presented at The Sustainability of Australia's Country Towns Conference, La Trobe University, 1 October 2010) 6.
48 Michael Dillon and Neil Westbury, *Beyond Humbug: Transforming Government Engagement with Indigenous Australia* (Seaview Press, 2007) 162.
49 Noel Pearson, 'Social Housing Model Rips the Heart out of Indigenous Communities', *The Weekend Australian*, 6 February 2010, 13.
50 Ibid.
51 Commonwealth, *Parliamentary Debates*, House of Representatives, 31 May 2006, 5 (Mal Brough).
52 Warren Mundine quoted in Mark Metherell, 'Land System Holds Us Back, Says Mundine', *The Sydney Morning Herald*, 7 December 2004, 6.
53 The costs of the EDTL are published in annual reports that are available at Australian Government Office of Township Leasing, *Publications*, Commonwealth of Australia www.otl.gov.au/site/publications.asp. An unknown portion of these expenses relate to housing precinct leases, town camp subleases and the ongoing efforts of the EDTL to assist traditional owners with economic development, as described in Chapter 7.
54 CLC, 'Community Leasing: an Alternative Proposal', above n 5, 10.
55 Ibid.
56 These examples are all drawn from existing township subleases; see Chapter 6.
57 There are legal issues around how this must occur that do not need to be elaborated upon here.
58 The focus here is on service providers and enterprises, as the same issues with respect to home ownership and community housing have already been discussed in Chapter 7.
59 This is separate to the relationship between tenure security and investment. An inalienable sublease might provide tenure security, but only an alienable sublease gives rise to the realisability effect.
60 Noting again that this will contine to be primarily determined by funding.
61 Bob Beadman, 'Northern Territory Coordinator General for Remote Services: Report No 2 December 2009 to May 2010' (Northern Territory Government, 2010) 75.
62 A term frequently used by Pearson; see, eg, Pearson, *Up from the Mission*, above n 16, 143.
63 Which is more consistent with the 'community development' approach described by Danielle Campbell and Janet Hunt, 'Community Development in Central Australia: Broadening the Benefits from Land Use Agreements' (Topical Issue No 7/2010, Centre for Aboriginal Economic Policy Research, 2010).
64 A potential issue with respect to mining payments, see, eg, O'Faircheallaigh, above n 16, 8–9.
65 This is the rule with respect to rent paid under a section 19 lease; see *Aboriginal Land Rights (Northern Territory) Act 1976* (Cth) s 35(4). See also 35(4B) for rent paid on a section 19A lease.
66 CLC, 'Community Leasing: an Alternative Proposal', above n 5, 10.
67 Nicolas Peterson, 'Community Development, Civil Society, and Local Government in the Future of Remote Northern Territory Growth Towns' (A paper presented at 60 Years of ANU Anthropology: Contesting Anthropology's Futures Conference, Australian National University, September 2011) 12.

286 *Alternative approaches?*

68 Australian Government, Office of Township Leasing, *Reforming Land Tenure Arrangements on Indigenous Held Land* (2015) www.otl.gov.au/site/township_leasing_factsheet_1.html.
69 See Chapter 6.

Bibliography

Books/articles/reports/web pages

Agreements, Treaties and Negotiated Settlements Project (ATNS), *Memorandum of Understanding between Galarrwuy Yunupingu and the Commonwealth of Australia* (15 October 2007) www.atns.net.au/agreement.asp?EntityID=4010.

Altman, Jon, Matthew Gray and Will Sanders, 'Indigenous Australians Working for Welfare: What Difference Does It Make?' (2000) 33(4) *Australian Economic Review* 355.

Austin-Broos, Diane, 'Places, Practices, and Things: The Articulation of Arrernte Kinship with Welfare and Work' (February 2003) 30(1) *American Ethnologist* 118.

Austin-Broos, Diane and Gaynor Macdonald (eds), *Culture, Economy and Governance in Aboriginal Australia* (Sydney University Press, 2005).

Australian Broadcasting Corporation, 'Property Key to Ending Indigenous Welfare Cycle: Newman', *ABC News*, 15 January 2013 (Eric Tlozek).

Australian Government Office of Township Leasing, *Publications*, Commonwealth of Australia, www.otl.gov.au/site/publications.asp.

Australian Government, Office of Township Leasing, *Reforming Land Tenure Arrangements on Indigenous Held Land* (2015) www.otl.gov.au/site/township_leasing_factsheet_1.html.

Batty, Philip, 'Private Politics, Public Strategies: White Advisers and Their Aboriginal Subjects' (2005) 75(3) *Oceania* 209.

Beadman, Bob, 'Northern Territory Coordinator General for Remote Services: Report No 2 December 2009 to May 2010' (Northern Territory Government, 2010).

Beer, Andrew and Selina Tually, 'Forgotten But Not Gone: The Housing Markets of Australia's Country Towns' (Paper presented at The Sustainability of Australia's Country Towns Conference, La Trobe University, 1 October 2010).

Commonwealth, *Parliamentary Debates*, House of Representatives, 31 May 2006, 5 (Mal Brough).

Calma, Tom, 'Native Title Report 2005' (Australian Human Rights Commission, 2005).

Campbell, Danielle and Janet Hunt, 'Community Development in Central Australia: Broadening the Benefits from Land Use Agreements' (Topical Issue No 7/2010, Centre for Aboriginal Economic Policy Research, 2010).

Central Land Council, 'Communal Title and Economic Development' (Policy Paper, 2005).

Central Land Council, 'Community Leasing: An Alternative Proposal' (Discussion Paper, 2010).

Central Land Council, Submission No 347 to Senate Standing Committees on Community Affairs, Parliament of Australia, *Inquiry into Stronger Futures in the Northern Territory Bill 2011 and Two Related Bills*, 1 February 2012.

Central Land Council, Submission to the Department of Families, Community Services and Indigenous Affairs, *Discussion Paper on Community Living Area Land Reform in the Northern Territory*, 2013.

Central Land Council, 'Land Reform in the Northern Territory: Evidence Not Ideology' (Discussion Paper, 2013).

Council of Australian Governments, *Closing the Gap in Indigenous Disadvantage* (2012) www.coag.gov.au/closing_the_gap_in_indigenous_disadvantage.

Crabtree, Louise *et al.*, 'Principles and Practices of an Affordable Housing Community Land Trust Model' (Research Paper, Australian Housing and Urban Research Institute, January 2012).

Crabtree, Louise *et al.*, 'Community Land Trusts and Indigenous Housing Options' (Final Report No 185, Australian Housing and Urban Research Institute, March 2012).

Daly, Anne, 'The Winner's Curse? Indigenous Australians in the Welfare System' (2000) 33(4) *Australian Economic Review* 349.

Daly, Anne and Diane Smith, 'The Role of Welfare in the Economy of Two Indigenous Communities' (2000) 33(4) *Australian Economic Review* 363.

Dillon, Michael and Neil Westbury, *Beyond Humbug: Transforming Government Engagement with Indigenous Australia* (Seaview Press, 2007).

Editorial, 'Land Rights Should Apply to Individuals', *The Australian*, 19 February 2005, 13.

Heller, Michael, 'The Tragedy of the Anticommons: Property in the Transition from Marx to Markets' (1998) 111(3) *Harvard Law Review* 622.

Heller, Michael, *The Gridlock Economy: How Too Much Ownership Wrecks Markets, Stops Innovation and Costs Lives* (Basic Books, 2008).

Holcombe, Sarah, 'Socio-political Perspectives on Localism and Regionalism in the Pintubi Luritja Region of Central Australia: Implications for Service Delivery and Governance' (Working Paper No 25/2004, Centre for Aboriginal Economic Policy Research, 2004).

Hudson, Sara, 'From Rhetoric to Reality: Can 99-Year Leases Lead to Homeownership for Indigenous Communities?' (Policy Monograph 92, Centre for Independent Studies, 2009).

Johnson, Andrew, 'Unlocking the North', *The Australian*, 14 June 2013. 10.

Johnson, David, 'Introduction to Policy Forum on Welfare Reform' (2001) 34(1) *Australian Economic Review* 81.

Katz, Larissa, 'Red Tape and Gridlock' in D. Benjamin Barros (ed), *Hernando de Soto and Property in a Market Economy* (Ashgate, 2010) 109.

Langton, Marcia, 'Anthropology, Politics and the Changing World of Aboriginal Australians' (March 2011) 21(1) *Anthropological Forum* 1.

McCauley, Patrick, 'Two Hand Blessing' (2007) 51(10) *Quadrant* 64.

Macklin, Jenny, 'Speech to Cape York Institute Leadership Academy' (Speech delivered to the Cape York Institute Leadership Academy, Cairns, 22 July 2008).

Macklin, Jenny, 'Importance of Delivering Remote Indigenous Housing in an Efficient and Affordable Way' (Speech delivered at Parliament House, Canberra, 15 September 2009).

Marks, Greg, 'Coercive Governance and Remote Indigenous Communities: The Failed Promise of the Whole of Government Mantra' (2008) 12(1) *Australian Indigenous Law Review* 2.

288 *Alternative approaches?*

Martin, David, 'Money, Business and Culture: Issues for Aboriginal Economic Policy' (Discussion Paper No 101/1995, Centre for Aboriginal Economic Policy Research, 1995).

Martin, David, 'Is Welfare Dependency "Welfare Poison"? An Assessment of Noel Pearson's Proposals for Aboriginal Welfare Reform' (Discussion Paper No 213/2001, Centre for Aboriginal Economic Policy Research, 2001).

Martin, David, 'Rethinking the Design of Indigenous Organisations: The Need for Strategic Engagement' (Discussion Paper No 248/2003, Centre for Aboriginal Economic Policy Research, 2003).

Martin, David, 'Policy Alchemy and the Magical Transformation of Aboriginal Society' in Yasmine Musharbash and Marcus Barber (eds), *Ethnography & the Production of Anthropological Knowledge: Essays in Honour of Nicolas Peterson* (Australian National University E Press, 2011) 201.

Merlan, Francesca, 'More Than Rights', *Inside Story*, 11 March 2009 http://inside.org.au/more-than-rights.

Metherell, Mark, 'Land System Holds Us Back, Says Mundine', *The Sydney Morning Herald* (Sydney), 7 December 2004, 6.

Northern Land Council, Submission No 361 to Senate Standing Committees on Community Affairs, Parliament of Australia, *Inquiry into Stronger Futures in the Northern Territory Bill 2011 and Two Related Bills*, 10 February 2012.

O'Faircheallaigh, Ciaran, 'Use and Management of Revenue from Indigenous-Mining Company Agreements: Theoretical Perspectives' (Agreements, Treaties and Negotiated Settlements Project, Working Paper Series, 2011).

Pearson, Noel, *Up from the Mission: Selected Writings* (Black Inc, 2009).

Pearson, Noel, 'Social Housing Model Rips the Heart out of Indigenous Communities', *The Weekend Australian*, 6 February 2010, 13.

Peterson, Nicolas, 'Community Development, Civil Society, and Local Government in the Future of Remote Northern Territory Growth Towns' (A paper presented at 60 Years of ANU Anthropology: Contesting Anthropology's Futures Conference, Australian National University, September 2011).

Poroch, Nerelle, 'Welfare Reform and Indigenous Empowerment' (2006) 1 *Australian Aboriginal Studies* 3.

Reeves, John, 'Building on Land Rights for the Next Generation: The Review of the *Aboriginal Land Rights (Northern Territory) Act 1976*' (Australian Government, 1998).

Rowse, Tim, 'McClure's "Mutual Obligation" and Pearson's "Reciprocity": Can They Be Reconciled?' (August 2002) 37(3) *Australian Journal of Social Issues* 263.

Sanders, Will, 'Thinking about Indigenous Community Governance' (Discussion Paper No 262/2004, Centre for Aboriginal Economic Policy Research, 2004).

Sanders, Will, 'Equality and Difference Arguments in Australian Indigenous Affairs: Examples from Income Support and Housing' (Working Paper No 38/2008, Center for Aboriginal Economic Policy Research, 2008).

Sanders, Will, 'Experimental Government in Australian Indigenous Affairs: From Coombs to Pearson via Rowse and the Competing Principles' (Discussion Paper No 291/2014, Centre for Aboriginal Economic Policy Research, 2014).

Shillito, Lewis, 'Strata Title Aboriginal Towns? An Alternative to the Town-Leasing Proposal' (2007) 14(3) *Australian Property Law Journal* 201.

Smith, Diane, 'From Gove to Governance: Reshaping Indigenous Governance in the Northern Territory' (Discussion Paper No 265/2004, Centre for Aboriginal Economic Policy Research, 2004).

Sullivan, Patrick, 'Indigenous Governance: The Harvard Project on Native American Economic Development and Appropriate Principles of Governance for Remote Australia' (Research Discussion Paper No 17, Australian Institute of Aboriginal and Torres Strait Islanders Studies, February 2006).

Sullivan, Patrick, *Belonging Together: Dealing With the Politics of Disenchantment in Australian Indigenous Policy* (Aboriginal Studies Press, 2011).

Sutton, Peter, 'Anthropological Submission on the Reeves Review' (1999) 9(2) *Anthropological Forum* 189.

Tonkinson, Myrna and Robert Tonkinson, 'The Cultural Dynamics of Adaptation in Remote Aboriginal Communities: Policy, Values and the State's Unmet Expectations' (2010) 52 *Anthropologica* 67.

Trigger, David, 'Mining Projects in Remote Aboriginal Australia: Sites for the Articulation and Contesting of Economic and Cultural Features' in Diane Austin-Broos and Gaynor Macdonald (eds), *Culture, Economy and Governance in Aboriginal Australia* (Sydney University Press, 2005) 41.

Vanstone, Amanda, 'Beyond Conspicuous Compassion: Indigenous Australians Deserve More Than Good Intentions' (Speech delivered to the Australia and New Zealand School of Government, Australian National University, Canberra, 7 December 2005).

Walker, Bruce, Douglas Porter and Ian Marsh, 'Fixing the Hole in Australia's Heartland: How Government Needs to Work in Remote Australia' (Desert Knowledge Australia, 2012).

Westbury, Neil and Will Sanders, 'Governance and Service Delivery for Remote Aboriginal Communities in the Northern Territory: Challenges and Opportunities' (Working Paper No 6/2000, Centre for Aboriginal Economic Policy Research, 2000).

Legislation

Aboriginal Land Rights (Northern Territory) Act 1976 (Cth).
Anangu Pitjantjatjara Yankunytjatjara Land Rights Act 1981 (SA).
Maralinga Tjarutja Land Rights Act 1984 (SA).

9 Conclusion

9.1 A striking contrast

During the same period in which it was implementing Aboriginal land reform in Australia, the Australian Government – through its aid agency AusAID – was also actively engaged with customary land reform in the Pacific. In 2008, after several years of preparatory work, AusAID released a 500-page, two-volume report called *Making Land Work* as 'as an information resource for countries undertaking land policy reform'.[1] The report drew on the assistance of 80 experts in land reform and development.[2] Key terminology – such as formal tenure, tenure security and customary land – is carefully defined.[3] The distinction between tenure formality and tenure security is explicitly identified, as is the fact that 'secure tenure can exist or cease to exist with respect to any landownership structure'.[4] The report makes frequent reference to the fact that land reform is a 'complex and sensitive issue',[5] and concludes that governments should 'intervene only if it is necessary, ensure land policies reflect local needs and circumstances ... actively involve stakeholders rather than only informing them ... balance the interests of landowners and land users [and] provide safeguards for vulnerable groups'.[6] It includes 16 case studies 'of how other countries ... have dealt with land administration and customary tenure issues while promoting economic and social development'.[7] Somewhat ironically, one of those case studies is the 'role of the Central Land Council in Aboriginal land dealings', which it describes in positive terms.[8]

The contrast between this and the Australian Government's approach to Indigenous land reform in Australia could hardly be more stark. In Australia, it did not engage expert advice or seek clarification of the issues. There was no report or consultation period, no case studies and no attempt to define the terminology. After a decade it has never even published an Indigenous land reform policy. It has used the term 'secure tenure' inconsistently and in a manner at odds with its technical meaning (as defined in the AusAID report). It has presented the need for reform as obvious and straightforward rather than complex. It has intervened often and dramatically rather than 'only if it is necessary'. And rather than seeking to balance 'the interests of landowners and land users', it has sought to use the select endorsement of traditional owners as evidence of the efficacy or legitimacy of its reforms.

This book – which relies to a considerable extent on the same body of international research that informed the AusAID report – reflects a deliberate attempt to remove discussion about Indigenous land reform from the ideological sphere and recast it as primarily a technical issue, and a technical issue of such complexity that it cannot be adequately comprehended on the basis of mere intuition. In the course of so doing, it draws three major conclusions.

9.2 Major conclusions of this book

Conclusion one: the wrong debate

The first major conclusion is that Indigenous land reform in Australia has been debated using the wrong terminology. During the most important period of debate, between 2004 and 2007, debate was conducted around the opposing concepts of communal and individual ownership. These (and similar) terms contributed to a very high level of confusion about what it was that was being debated. This was partly because different issues were conflated. The term 'communal ownership' was applied without distinction to a variety of circumstances, such as Indigenous land ownership, the tenure arrangements in communities, ownership of enterprises, native title and the distribution of royalties. It was also because the terms were not defined. Communal ownership was frequently characterised as a type of laissez-faire collectivism, in which 'everybody owns assets',[9] rather than a system for allocating rights over land and infrastructure to particular individuals and organisations. This contributed to the way in which the nature of community life was misconstrued. Conversely, frequent use of the term 'individual ownership' led people to expect that the outcome of land reform would be ownership of land and businesses by individuals.

Perhaps more importantly, this communal–individual ownership dualism resulted in debate coalescing around the wrong issues or themes. 'Communal ownership' was presented as integral to the maintenance of a distinct traditional Indigenous culture. Some people also presented it as a manifestation of 'separatist' policies that had kept Indigenous people structurally apart from mainstream Australia, to their detriment. Reform proponents presented the introduction of 'individual ownership' as a means of enabling greater economic integration and a more entrepreneurial culture. In this respect, the debate was not only misleading, it was also harmful. It perpetuated the use of a destructive modern–traditional dichotomy, under which Indigenous people must either demonstrate that they have retained a 'traditional' culture and identity or accept their position as undifferentiated Australians.

292   *Conclusion*

This also led to debate about land reform being conducted in a far more hostile and divisive manner than was necessary or helpful. This book describes how there is an alternative set of terminology that not only enables issues to be identified more accurately, it avoids the need to use words that are now more loaded than informative.[10] Indeed, it might be said that some passages of the book are rather technical and dry – far more so than much of literature produced during debate about land reform. That is part of its value. For example, describing the pre-existing tenure circumstances in communities on Indigenous land as 'informal tenure arrangements' rather than 'communal ownership' is less evocative, and deliberately so. The earlier language resulted in the evocation of too much emotion, and the paying of too little attention to the details of reforms that have a real and significant impact on the lives of Indigenous community residents.

Between 2008 and 2013, the communal–individual ownership dualism was supplemented by government statements about the need for 'secure tenure'. This represented a step away from the inflammatory language that had characterised the earlier period of debate. In that respect it was a positive development but in other respects it too has been problematic. 'Secure tenure' terminology has been used inconsistently and inaccurately and has added to confusion about the rationale for and consequences of reform.

One outcome of the debate (particularly the first period of debate) has been the emergence of a political consensus that there is a pressing need for widespread reform to the tenure arrangements in communities on Indigenous land. This book demonstrates the flaws in this consensus. The pre-existing informal tenure arrangements in Indigenous communities were not perfect but nor were they fundamentally flawed and in need of immediate overhaul. In some respects they worked well, and potentially represented a well-adapted and efficient response to the modern-day needs of communities. Neither stage of debate allowed for this more nuanced reading of the existing arrangements. This meant that rather than engage in a thorough examination of those arrangements, of what was working and what required attention, the government proceeded directly to implementing a series of widespread, expensive and often invasive reforms.

Further, the terminology used to debate the reforms has provided almost no guidance with respect to how they should be implemented. When it came to answering real questions – such as whether subleases should be short- or long-term, whether rent should be paid, in which circumstances subleases should be alienable – the policy-makers responsible for implementing the reforms could find no assistance in the concepts of communal and individual ownership or 'secure tenure' terminology. The confusion that this resulted in is apparent in some of the statements that have been made about the reforms, several examples of which have been provided in earlier chapters. This relates to the second major conclusion of the book.

Conclusion two: flawed reforms

The second major conclusion is that the existing reforms are in several respects flawed. They are flawed because they have been unnecessarily heavy-handed, most notably the compulsory acquisition of five-year leases. This has led to resentment and conflict and has destroyed some of the goodwill that underpinned earlier arrangements. Rather than landowners and community residents being given the opportunity to identify and resolve problems with the earlier arrangements, they have been forced to respond to yet another government-led initiative that arose out of a public debate well detached from their circumstances. They are also flawed because their implementation began well before all of their consequences were considered. The application of 'secure tenure' policies to community living area (CLA) land in the Northern Territory is a good example of this. Those policies – which require a lease or sublease before infrastructure will be funded – were put into place before a means of enabling leasing on CLA land was established. The Central Land Council states that this has resulted in communities being denied new infrastructure and in facilities instead being built on adjacent land. It also reports 'anecdotal evidence' of service providers choosing not to base themselves in communities on CLA land because of concerns about the ongoing implications of 'secure tenure' policies.[11]

The reforms have also been unnecessarily expensive. Township leasing has already cost several million dollars to administer for just a handful of communities. While the full costs of the five-year leases and implementing 'secure tenure' policies have not been published, they must be even greater. A more targeted approach to reform could have avoided some of these costs. There are also problems with the approach that the reforms take to economic development. Rather than identifying the facilities and tenure arrangements that would best enable community residents to engage in enterprise development, the current approach appears to reflect a naive hope that land reform will automatically create a more conducive environment for economic development. The exact mechanism by which this will occur has not been articulated in any detail. To date, the main contribution of the reforms to economic development has been through rent. Particularly in those places where traditional owners have received up-front rent for a township lease, that rent has been used to acquire and develop new enterprises. There are positive and negative aspects to this development, but more importantly it is a very limited mechanism for encouraging economic development in Indigenous communities when far more is required.

In a similar way, the reforms are flawed because of the model of governance that they implement. Most concerning is the way in which community residents in the Northern Territory are sidelined from decision-making under the new structures, particularly under township leases. Combined with the amalgamation of local shires, this has had a significant disenfranchising effect on community residents.

294   *Conclusion*

Conclusion three: an alternative framework

The third major conclusion is that there are better ways of approaching the task of developing a land reform model for communities on Indigenous land; however, in order to do so it is first necessary to clarify the preferred approach to certain 'cardinal issues'. The book sets out a two-step framework for developing an alternative model. The first step is to clarify the main variables, or the things that need to be decided upon. Those variables coalesce around: the identity of the 'underlying land-use authority'; the approach taken to the allocation of land and infrastructure; and the form of tenure provided to occupiers. The second step is to clarify the issues that determine how these matters should be decided upon. This is where the three cardinal issues fit in. The book argues that these issues should be clarified before decisions are made with respect to these variables. The first cardinal issue is an assessment of the market conditions in which the reforms will operate. This is particularly important for understanding the likely consequences of introducing transferable or marketable forms of tenure. The second is understandings of benefit provision, in particular the best available understandings as to what it is about the provision of government benefits that can be harmful and how that harm can be avoided or minimised. And the third cardinal issue is governance. Any land reform programme will institutionalise a particular approach to community governance, in a manner that may be long-term.

It is argued in Chapter 8 that there is no single best-practice model of land reform because market conditions vary, as do understandings of what constitutes best practice with respect to governance and benefit provision. It is, however, possible to draw some conclusions as to the parameters of an ideal model. With respect to the underlying land-use authority, it is argued here that there are advantages to an organisation that represents the interest of all community residents playing that role. With respect to forms of tenure, it is argued that there are advantages to taking a flexible rather than rigid approach, provided that the conditions allow for a sufficient level of latent or underlying tenure security.

It is finally argued that any land reform programme is best implemented as part of an integrated strategy. The economic development needs of communities cannot be met by land reform alone, no matter how well it is implemented. Development goals should be consistent between land reform and other areas of government policy – for example, planning practices and approaches to cost recovery should reflect (and not counteract) policies with respect to economic development. Having an integrated strategy also means recognising the ongoing need for government support in community life, rather than hoping that land reform will solve the problem of having remote and economically dependent communities. Finally, having an integrated strategy means incorporating the processes by which Indigenous community residents are given the means to exercise control over their own circumstances. While governments and commentators frequently refer to the need for Indigenous people to be given, and to take, responsibility for their own lives, existing approaches to land reform have made this more difficult.

9.3 The need for better policy

This book makes much of the international literature on land reform and its relevance to Indigenous land reform in Australia. That literature has been developed over the course of several decades. During that time, concepts, terminology and theories have become more refined. A great deal of careful thought has gone into the question of why previous reform efforts have failed and what can go right and wrong. It was a mistake for Australian governments to ignore this and to instead rely on intuitive or politicised understandings.

However, the international literature does not provide a single best-practice alternative to the existing reforms. To the contrary, when read carefully that literature helps clarify the way in which certain elements of the Australian reform context are unique. The complex and highly particular relationship between residence and land ownership; the extent to which the economies of remote communities are dominated by governments; the experience of Indigenous people as subjects of colonisation; the shallow history of Indigenous land rights; the influence of concerns about welfare dependence; the geography and demography of communities on Indigenous land – all of these make impossible a simple comparison between land reform in Indigenous communities in Australia and that in other countries.

This makes it even more important that reforms to Indigenous land in Australian are considered carefully and methodically. It is remarkable that the Australian Government spent so much time and effort preparing a 500-page report on customary land reform in the Pacific – so that it might be used as 'an information resource' for other countries – while never even publishing a land reform policy with respect to the reforms for which it is directly responsible. It is too late to undo all that has been done. There is, however, a clear need to base future attempts at land reform – both within Indigenous communities and on other areas of Indigenous land – upon more fully articulated understandings and more carefully developed policy. Such a policy is likely to be less exciting in content and tone than was the debate about communal and individual ownership, and less clear-cut than statements about 'secure tenure' would suggest. It is, however, likely to yield better results for the Indigenous people whose land and communities are affected.

296 *Conclusion*

Notes

1 Australian Agency for International Development (AusAID), 'Making Land Work, Volume One: Reconciling Customary Land and Development in the Pacific' (Commonwealth of Australia, 2008) vii.
2 Ibid.
3 See especially the glossary at ibid, 127–9.
4 Ibid, 10.
5 Ibid, vii.
6 Ibid, xv.
7 Australian Agency for International Development, 'Making Land Work, Volume Two: Case Studies on Customary Land and Development in the Pacific' (Commonwealth of Australia, 2008) vii.
8 Ibid, 107–28.
9 Editorial, 'Land Rights Should Apply to Individuals', *The Australian*, 19 February 2005, 13.
10 The parallels between this and Martin's 'strategic engagement' are described in Chapter 4.
11 Central Land Council, Submission No 347 to Senate Standing Committees on Community Affairs, Parliament of Australia, *Inquiry into Stronger Futures in the Northern Territory Bill 2011 and Two Related Bills*, 1 February 2012, 9.

Bibliography

Books/articles/reports/web pages

Australian Agency for International Development, 'Making Land Work, Volume One, Reconciling Customary Land and Development in the Pacific' (Commonwealth of Australia, 2008).

Australian Agency for International Development, 'Making Land Work, Volume Two, Case Studies on Customary Land and Development in the Pacific' (Commonwealth of Australia, 2008).

Australian Government, *Reforming Land Tenure Arrangements on Indigenous Held Land* (2012) www.otl.gov.au/docs/factsheet_1.PDF.

Central Land Council, Submission No 347 to Senate Standing Committees on Community Affairs, Parliament of Australia, *Inquiry into Stronger Futures in the Northern Territory Bill 2011 and Two Related Bills*, 1 February 2012.

Editorial, 'Land Rights Should Apply to Individuals', *The Australian*, 19 February 2005, 13.

Index

Page numbers in **bold** denote figures.

'73 emergency response communities'
194–5

Abbott, Tony 151–2
Aboriginal Benefits Account (ABA) 186,
240
Aboriginal communities 19, 24, 44;
background information about 95–7;
composition and identity of 96–7;
enterprise in 109; housing in 107; as
hunter-gatherer societies 67, 70;
informal tenure arrangements in
97–9; leadership in 99–100, 104;
local councils and 100–1; in
Northern Territory **11**, 32, 95–9;
organisations and governance
arrangements 99–100; overcrowding,
mobility and demographic shifts
105–6; problem with defining
household 106
Aboriginal land: as communal property
112–13; housing in communities on
107; informal settlements on 99; in
Northern Territory 9, 66–7, 72–81;
ownership of *see* Aboriginal land
ownership; three sets of reforms to
12–13
Aboriginal Land Act 1979 (NT) 78
Aboriginal Land Councils 75–8, 101–2,
130, 198, 270
Aboriginal land ownership 66–7; under
Aboriginal law 67–72; ALRA land
72–8; CLA land 78–80; communal
ownership of 112–3; formal 72–81;
history of 66; Pintubi ownership 69;
town camp land 80–1
Aboriginal land rights: in Northern

Territory 68; recognition of 1–2;
recontesting 143
Aboriginal Land Rights (Northern
Territory) Act (1976) 1–2, 8, 128,
174, 226, 259; aim of ownership
structure under 74–5; checks and
balances on decision-making under
77; ground for passing of 128;
history of 73–4; land access and
permit system under 77–8; land
ownership under 74–8; needs-based
claims under 75; reviews of 71,
129–31; tripartite ownership
structure under 75–7
Aboriginal Land Rights (Northern
Territory) Amendment Act (2006) 174
Aboriginal land tenure 12, 16, 66,
67–72; allocation of rights under
137; clans 69–70; estates 68; family
groups and bands 70; five key
elements of 68–72; levels of
connection and rights 69; ownership
under 72; religious and economic
institution 70; residential
communities 70–2
Aboriginal Land Trusts 75–6, 193
Aboriginal owners *see* traditional
Aboriginal owners
Aboriginal people 7–8; needs-related
entitlements 131; as non-traditional
owner residents 14–15, 95, 147, 178,
241, 243, 248, 279
Aboriginal residents, housing for
105–7, 223–35, 270–1
Aboriginal Tent Embassy 73
Aboriginal Torres Strait Islander
Commission (ATSIC) 133

298   Index

Alice Springs 9, 67, 80–1, 134, 191–2, 194, 196
alienability for occupiers: economic consequences of 41–4; 276–7; right of 276
allocation of property: criteria-based 271; decisions made with respect to 270–3; economic benefits of alienability for occupiers 276–7; enterprise ownership and 271–2; impact of alienability on 277–8; residential housing 270–1; service providers 273; *see also* allotment of Indigenous land
allotment of Indigenous land 15–16, 49–50; freehold instrument 201–2; granting freehold 202–3; impact on native title 203–4; steps for 201–3
ALRA *see* Aboriginal Land Rights (Northern Territory) Act (1976)
ALRA land 12, 16, 67–8, 72–3, 101, 113, 187, 206, 261, 268; history of 73–4; mechanism for leasing 97–9; ownership of 74–8; rent on 279
Altman, Jon 5–6, 102, 132
Anangu Pitjantjatjara Yankunytjatjara Land Rights Act (1981) 259
Anindilyakwa lease 177–8, 180
anticommons: creation of 268–9; tragedy of 31, 269
Areyonga 97
Arnhem Land 73, 177
art studios 109
AusAID (Australian aid agency) 32, 290–1
Australian Anthropological Society 71
Australian National Audit Office (ANAO) 224, 231
Australian, The 1, 134, 139–40, 143, 265
authority in Aboriginal communities 111; as dispersed governance 103; relationship with traditional status 102–3

Banks, Gary 132
Benefit provision, understandings of 263–5
Bennelong Society 132
Blackburn, Justice 71, 73
Brough, Mal 2, 142, 134, 139, 148, 187, 190, 242–3, 271

Caging the Rainbow (1998) 111
Calma, Tom 141

Cape York Institute (CYI) 229–31
Central Land Council (CLC) 4, 79, 98, 139, 237, 260, 267–8, 275, 293
CLA land 9, 12, 67, 96, 98, 103, 113, 187, 192–3, 270, 293; history of 78–9; ownership structure of 79–80
collateralisation: consequences of 42–3, 276; *see also* de Soto, Hernando
collective ownership of property 4, 24–5, 28, 39, 44, 136, 269, 272
colonisation of Australia 5, 7
Commercial Sublease Application Form 181
commons, tragedy of 24, 31
Commonwealth Bank 238
communal–individual ownership dualism 3, 17, 147, 186, 272, 291–2
communal ownership of businesses 138, 241
communal ownership of land 14, 24, 35, 94, 104, 112–13, 129, 133–4, 136, 138, 140, 145, 272, 291; connection to debate about welfare 142–3; debate on 129–48; emergence of concerns about 131–2; home ownership and 140–1; impact on economic development 139–40; level of generality during debate about 136–8; policy and culture 142; political context for debate about 132–3; subject matter of debate on 135–8; tension and compromise 143–4
communal property: meaning of 27–8, 33, 34; relationship to sharing norms 104
community-based businesses: non-profit 133, 272; profit making 272
community employment 277
community governance 99–103, 275; impact of reforms on 14, 242–5
community housing 107, 110, 227–9; concerns with 227–33; type of tenure system for 110
community interest, concept of 267–8
Community Land Trusts (CLTs) 260, 270
community living area land see CLA land
Community Management Groups 269
community residents 267–8
Consultative Forum 180, 243; role of 180–1
Council of Australian Governments (COAG) 152; Select Council on Housing and Homelessness 224–5

Index 299

countries, meaning of 68
Crown land, lease of 29, 74, 187, 191
customary ownership of land:
    characteristics of 31, 67, 137;
    concept of 30–1; norm-based 30;
    relationship with informal
    settlements 34; in sub-Saharan Africa
    34
customary tenure system 30–1, 34, 36,
    38, 40, 45, 99

Darwin 9, 67, 72, 80–1, 177, 186, 196
Dawes Act, United States 49
dead capital (poverty) trap 131, 231
Deed of Grant in Trust (DOGIT)
    200–1, 261
demand sharing 104
De Soto, Hernando 42, 51, 94, 131,
    138, 232; on benefits of capitalisation
    232; *Mystery of Capital, The* (2001)
    38–9, 131; on social contract 138;
    theory of capital 16, 38–9; on
    'Western-style' property rights 48
dispersed governance 100, 103
Duncan, Ron 132

enterprise: in Aboriginal communities
    12, 109, 182–3, 204, 235–7;
    ownership 44, 100, 241, 264, 271–2
estates 68
Executive Director of Township
    Leasing (EDTL) 179–80, 205, 226,
    235, 241, 261, 266, 273–4;
    allocation of subleases 181–2;
    policies and practices of 181–6;
    process for grant of subleases 181–2;
    rent on subleases 184; terms of
    subleases 182–4

formal tenure systems 32–3
formalisation: alienability and 49; and
    allocation of legal rights 47–8;
    allotment and 49–50; endogenous
    and exogenous 46–7; of informal
    settlement 46–7; of informal tenure
    system 46; mandatory formalisation
    235–6; property rights and 48–9;
    tenure security and 48; types of 45–6
formality, concept of 33
Forrest Review, The 152
Fraser, Malcolm 74, 77–8, 80
fringe camps 80

Gordon, Sue 139

Gove land rights case 68, 71, 73
growth towns 97, 195

Hardin, Garrett 24, 31
Heller, Michael 269
Hicks, John 243
home ownership 13, 133, 182, 278;
    debate about communal ownership
    preventing 140–1; form of tenure
    required for 225–7; Home
    Ownership on Indigenous Land
    (HOIL) Program 223–4, 226, 231,
    246; implementation of 223–5;
    Katter leases 140–1, 201, 229–30;
    open, closed and regulated markets
    225–6; 'pride of place' programmes
    229; in Queensland 201, 227; sense
    of 229; as solution 228–30; and
    township subleases 185, 226–7
homelands 9, 95–6, 188; *see also*
    outstations
Housing Act (1982) 196
housing, for Aboriginal residents
    105–7, 223–35, 270–1; allocation of
    107; informal and community
    housing 107, 110; overcrowding and
    106; shortage of 106; as source of
    cultural and social security 106; type
    of tenure system for 110
housing management 13–14, 192,
    196–7, 227, 234
housing precinct leases 13, 195, 199;
    and shift to public housing 234, 227,
    230
housing problems: houses not
    sufficiently well cared 228–30; nature
    of 228; role of government 233–5;
    social housing as harmful welfare
    232–3; tenure arrangements
    restricting supply 230–1; use of
    houses as collateral 231–2
housing reforms: and change in housing
    policy 194; government 'ownership'
    of housing 195–6; priority
    communities 194–5; public housing
    model 196–7; rents and 199–200; to
    residential housing 194–7; and 'secure
    tenure' policies 193–200; '73
    emergency response communities' 194
housing, types of 107
Howard, John 2, 132, 142–4, 147, 194
Howson, Peter 132, 143

Ilpeye Ilpeye town camp 192

300 Index

income management 186, 263
Indigenous Community Housing
 Organisations (ICHOs) 107, 174,
 194, 196, 227–8, 230, 234
indigenous land: allotment of 15–16,
 200–4; debate about economic
 development on 138–9; historical
 debate about 129–31; debate about
 private ownership of 134; rent
 14–15, 199–200; return of 5–6, 7
indigenous land ownership, in Australia
 5–7, 24, 136, 146; emergence of
 debate on 133–4
indigenous land rights: in Australia 1–2,
 26; in Queensland 200
Indigenous Land Use Agreement (ILUA)
 200, 203, 244
indigenous social land ethic 34
individual occupiers, rights and duties
 of 34
individual ownership of land 5, 14, 32,
 44, 105, 129, 140, 145, 148, 150–1,
 271, 291; creation of 204–5
inequitable ownership 43
informal housing 110
informal settlements 32, 46;
 formalisation of 46–7; informal
 tenure systems and 33–4; relationship
 between landowners and occupiers in
 34–5
informal tenure arrangements 32–3;
 characteristics of in Aboriginal
 communities 99–110; and dispersed
 governance 103; formalisation of 46;
 and housing for Aboriginal residents
 105–7; informal community housing
 and 107; informal tenure systems and
 informal settlements 33–4; land
 ownership and 137; property and
 sharing norms and 104–5; security of
 tenure and 106
infrastructure, housing: advantages of
 formalised tenure 244–5
insecure tenure *see* tenure insecurity,
 risk of
Intervention *see* Northern Territory
 Emergency Response (NTER)

jangkayi (men's camp) 106
jilimi (women's camp) 106
Johns, Gary 132

Katter leases 140–1, 201, 207, 229–30
kinship networks 103–4, 111

Labor Party 1–3, 73, 135, 149, 152
laissez-faire collectivism 16
Land Act (1998), Uganda 45
Land Councils: Aboriginal Land
 Councils 4, 75–6, 78, 81, 130, 174;
 bicameral system of 130; Central
 Land Council (CLC) 4, 98, 139, 237,
 260, 267, 275, 293; Northern Land
 Council (NLC) 79, 98, 132, 178,
 236, 260; Regional Land Councils
 (RLCs) 130; Tiwi Land Council 97,
 239, 243
land markets 49; alienability and 41–4;
 allocation of 43–4; consequences of
 262, 278; collateralisation and 42–3;
 creation of 222, 238–9, 246, 259,
 281; informal 41; realisability effect
 41–2
land-owning clan 69–70
land redistribution 26
land reform: and allocation of land
 and infrastructure 261; alternative
 approaches to 258, 260; concept of
 26–7; and creation of land markets
 238–9; culture, impact of 266–7;
 evolutionary theory of 35–8, 51;
 factors determining the approach
 taken to 262–7; in form of tenure
 granted to occupiers 262;
 framework for development of
 model for 259–67; governance, issue
 of 265–6; impact on relationships
 242–4; increased formalisation and
 the role of governments 37–8;
 influential ideas in relation to 35–9;
 main variables in model of 260–2;
 market conditions, issue of 263;
 Mystery of Capital, The (2001)
 38–9, 131; need for policy on
 280–2; parameters of an ideal model
 of 267–80; principles for 144;
 renewed focus on 151–3; shift in
 language for 150–1; shift towards
 certain types of property rights
 35–7; starting point for 94–5; two-
 step approach for developing model
 for 259–60; underlying land-use
 authority 260–1; and understandings
 of benefit provision 263–5
land reform policy, need for 295
land rights: legislation 2; schemes 1, 6,
 66–7, 172, 200
land tenure 31–2; Aboriginal *see*
 Aboriginal land tenure; reforms in *see*

land tenure reform; Western Desert 68

land tenure reform: types of 45–50

land-use decision-making 76, 102, 261

landlords 228, 230, 275

landowners: empowerment of 15; relation with occupiers 34–5

leases: absense of in Aboriginal communities 97–9; Katter leases 140–1, 201, 207, 229–30

leasing of land: in Aboriginal communities 98; ALRA land 97

loans, home 224

local councils 98, 100–1, 102, 103, 107–9, 111–12, 202–3, 234, 243–4, 260–1, 265, 268–9

Macklin, Jenny 149–50, 196, 245

McMahon, William 1, 73–4

Making Land Work (AusAID report) 290

Maralinga Tjarutja Land Rights Act (1984) 259

market allocation 43–4, 276–7

market-based tenures 38

Merlan, Francesca 70–1, 111

Milikapiti lease 177–80

mortgage 30, 43, 49, 153, 176, 223–4, 231–2, 238, 276

Mundine, Warren 133–4, 272

Mystery of Capital, The (2001) 38–9, 131

National Indigenous Council (NIC) 133–4, 142, 144

Native title 6, 132–3, 143, 192, 200, 259; impact of reforms on 8, 203–4

Native Title Act (1993) 6, 200; amendment of 133

Newman, Campbell 265

Nguiu (Wurrumiyanga) 97, 98, 107, 243; *see also* Wurrumiyanga lease

non-government organisations (NGOs) 101, 104, 108, 137, 146–7, 182, 184, 225, 235, 273, 276

Non-Tiwi Permanents Residents 180

Northern Land Council (NLC) 79, 98, 132, 178, 236, 260

Northern Territory 6; Aboriginal communities in **11**, 66; Aboriginal land rights in 68; case study on land reform 8–12; communities on Aboriginal land in 95–9; land rights 74; map of town camps in **10**; three sets of reforms 12–13

Northern Territory Emergency Response (NTER) 12, 135, 173, 186–93; announcement of 186–7; expiry of the five-year leases 189; five-year leases 187–8; future of 192–3; lease terms 188; occupiers 189; permit reforms 189–91; power to acquire town camp land 191–2; rent 188–9; statutory rights 191

office space 108, 281

outstations 9, 12, 19, 95–6, 100, 111, 188, 194, 224

ownership of land: Aboriginal *see* Aboriginal land ownership; division of under allotment 49; fractionated 50; indigenous land ownership 5–7; individual *versus* collective 44; individual *versus* communal debate 4–5; and informal tenure arrangements 99, 137; traditional 15, 17, 67–72

pastoral lease 6, 9, 29, 79, 95–6

Pearson, Christopher 142

Pearson, Noel 131, 143, 151, 232–3

Peterson, Nicolas 70, 104, 234, 280

Pintubi-Luritja language 97

Pintubi ownership 69

PricewaterhouseCoopers (PWC) 194

'pride of place' programmes 229

private property: calls for 5, 136, 138, 142–3; collective ownership of 28, 44; and evolutionary theory 35; meaning of 27–30; and sharing norms 104

profit-making businesses 133, 261, 272

property regimes: categories of 29; and commons and anticommons 31; communal property 27–8; concept of 27; for customary and traditional ownership 30–1; open access to 27–8; overlaping of 29; private property 27–8; private property rights 29–30; state property 27–8

property rights 26; alienability and land markets 41–4; allocation of 40; consistency and flexibility 44–5; demand for 37; evolution of 35–6; formalisation of 48–9; individual and collective ownership 44; tenure security 40–1; types of 39–45; Western-style 39, 48

public housing 13, 107, 196–7; housing precinct leases and 227

Index

Queensland, Australia: allotment of indigenous land in 201–4; home ownership in 227; indigenous land rights in 200; Katter leases 140–1, 201, 229–30; leasing indigenous land in 201

reallocation of land 16, 47–8, 108, 184, 275, 278
Reeves, John 71, 130, 260, 269
Reeves Report 71, 101, 130–1
Regional Land Councils (RLCs) 130
remote settlements 9, 19; *versus* town camps 12
rent 14–15, 109, 199–200; on ALRA land 67, 98, 279; calculation of 199; consequences of 131, 206, 235, 237–8, 242, 264, 258, 278–9; for the five-year leases 188–9, 236; for housing 107, 114, 233; increase in 236–7, 244; as increase in costs of doing business 237; as land owner income 237–8, 240–1; on township subleases 184; under township leases 176, 178, 186
residence: relationship to traditional ownership 67, 70–2
residential communities 70–2; emergence of 95–6
residential housing 19, 105, 174, 181, 222; decisions made with respect to allocation 270–1; home ownership 223–7; housing precinct leases and shift to public housing 227; reforms to 194–7, 246
Residential Sublease Application Form 181
Residential Tenancies Act (1999) 196
Rogers, Nanette 134
Rowland, Barry 130
Rudd, Kevin 140, 176

secure tenure policies 13, 19, 82, 112, 189, 193–7, 235, 243, 274, 293; housing reforms and 193–200; beyond housing 197–9, 247; outcome under **198**; in Queensland 201
secure tenure terminology 17, 19, 32, 149–51, 152, 186, 205–6, 292
self-determination, right to 71, 113, 142
Serviced Land Availability Program (SLAP) maps 109
service hubs 195

service providers 12, 14, 108–9, 182, 199, 206, 222, 235–6, 239, 261, 270, 276–8; allocation decisions 273; anecdotal evidence of 293
Shillito, Lewis 260, 269
'sit down money' 2
sites, meaning of 68
social burden 104
social capital 104
social contract 39, 94–5, 138
social engineering 142
social housing 182, 203, 264; availability of 271; expenditure 230; as harmful welfare 232–3; welfare impact of 271
social investment 237
squatter settlement 30, 34–5, 38, 47, 99
staff housing 19, 105, 108–9, 182, 222, 273
state property system 27–8, 34, 99; tenure system 33
Stolen Generation 133
store buildings 109, 261, 272
strata title 29, 269
Stronger Futures 12, 186, 192–3
Sutton, Peter 67–9, 71–2, 130, 146, 260

tenancy: agreements 196–7, 202, 227, 233; management of 107, 195, 227, 233
Tennant Creek 9, 67, 80–1, 191, 194
tenure: of Aboriginal land *see* Aboriginal land tenure; and culture 145–6; customary 34; economy and relationships 146–7; formal 32–3, 275–9; formalisation of 32–3, 48, 235, 244–5, 247; form of, granted to occupiers 273–5; freehold-like 262, 273; informal *see* informal tenure systems; informal settlements 33–4; insecure 31–2; land 31–2; market-based 38; and policy 147–8; reforms in *see* land reform; security 31–2, 40–1, 48, 106, 228–9, 234; *see also* land tenure
tenure insecurity, risk of 31–2, 108
three cardinal issues 18, 257, 262–7, 294
Tiwi Land Council 97, 239, 243
Tiwi Islands Regional Council 183, 237
Toohey, John 77, 130, 242
Torres Strait Islander 7–8, 24, 200–1

town camps 9, 19; difference with remote communities 12; history of 80–1; housing associations 81, 194; map of 10; ownership structure of 81; reforms to 187, 191–2

town corporation 260, 269

township lease communities, new enterprises in 239–42

township leasing 12, 97, 135, 142, 152, 261, 293; community benefits under 178–9; cost of 186; development of model for 174; elements of 174–5; exemption from certain laws 176–7; home ownership under 226–7; identity of the leaseholder for 176; mortgage of 176; outcome under 175; overview of 173; policies and practices of the EDTL for 181–6; pre-existing tenure arrangements 175; preserved rights and interests 177; rent and other benefits 178–9; restrictions on the terms of a section 19A lease 176; restrictions on transfer of subleases 179–80; under section 19A of ALRA 174–5; subleases and licences 179–80; three existing 177

traditional Aboriginal owners 17, 75–8, 80, 102–3, 107, 111, 203, 238, 241; definition of 75, 130; relationship with residents 15, 69–71, 97, 113, 147, 178, 200, 242–4, 267–8

traditional ownership of land *see* customary ownership of land; *see also* Aboriginal land tenure

'tragedy of open access' 31

'tragedy of the anticommons' 269

'tragedy of the commons' 24, 31

underlying land-use authority 294; allocation of control with occupiers 275–6; meaning of 260; parameters with respect to *see* underlying land-use authority, parameters with respect to

underlying land-use authority, parameters with respect to: acting in the interest of community residents 267–8; alternative models for 269–70; avoiding an anti-commons 268–9; distinction between constituency and membership 269

urban settlements in South Africa 34

vacant land 105, 109–10, 188, 203, 239; development of 273

Vanstone, Amanda 2, 134, 139, 143, 243, 265

Viner, Ian 74

'virtuous cycle' of economic growth 38

welfare dependency 232, 263

welfare reform 3, 26, 152, 263; relationship to land reform 264–5

'Western Desert' area 68–9, 71

White Paper on Developing Northern Australia 152

Whitlam, Gough 1–2, 73–4, 77, 80

Woodward, Edward 2, 68–71, 73–7, 79–80, 98, 104

Wurrumiyanga lease 177–81, 240, Wurrumiyanga subleases, table of 183

Yolngu people 73

Yulara native title case 68

Yunupingu, Galarrwuy 142, 260, 270

yupukarra (married people's camp) 106

eBooks
from Taylor & Francis

Helping you to choose the right eBooks for your Library

Add to your library's digital collection today with Taylor & Francis eBooks. We have over 50,000 eBooks in the Humanities, Social Sciences, Behavioural Sciences, Built Environment and Law, from leading imprints, including Routledge, Focal Press and Psychology Press.

Choose from a range of subject packages or create your own!

Benefits for you
- Free MARC records
- COUNTER-compliant usage statistics
- Flexible purchase and pricing options
- All titles DRM-free.

Benefits for your user
- Off-site, anytime access via Athens or referring URL
- Print or copy pages or chapters
- Full content search
- Bookmark, highlight and annotate text
- Access to thousands of pages of quality research at the click of a button.

Free Trials Available
We offer free trials to qualifying academic, corporate and government customers.

eCollections

Choose from over 30 subject eCollections, including:

Archaeology	Language Learning
Architecture	Law
Asian Studies	Literature
Business & Management	Media & Communication
Classical Studies	Middle East Studies
Construction	Music
Creative & Media Arts	Philosophy
Criminology & Criminal Justice	Planning
Economics	Politics
Education	Psychology & Mental Health
Energy	Religion
Engineering	Security
English Language & Linguistics	Social Work
Environment & Sustainability	Sociology
Geography	Sport
Health Studies	Theatre & Performance
History	Tourism, Hospitality & Events

For more information, pricing enquiries or to order a free trial, please contact your local sales team: www.tandfebooks.com/page/sales

www.tandfebooks.com